SURVEY
OF
WORLD
CULTURES

SURVEY OF WORLD CULTURES

Donald N. Wilber

United Arab Republic
EGYPT

its people   its society   its culture

with the assistance of

FAHIM I. QUBAIN and HELENE L. BOATNER

HRAF PRESS

NEW HAVEN

Already Published in This Series

LIBRARY OF CONGRESS CATALOG CARD NUMBER: 68-22208
© COPYRIGHT 1969
HUMAN RELATIONS AREA FILES, INC.
NEW HAVEN, CONNECTICUT
ALL RIGHTS RESERVED
MANUFACTURED IN THE UNITED STATES OF AMERICA BY
UNITED PRINTING SERVICES, INC.

PUBLISHER'S NOTE

A NONPROFIT CORPORATION founded in 1949 to collect, organize, and distribute information of significance to the natural and social sciences and humanities, the Human Relations Area Files is today supported by twenty-four member universities and research organizations here and abroad. The research program is centered on the continuing development and expansion of a unique system for codification of basic source materials to facilitate cross-cultural research. Corollary programs have included the compilation of bibliographies, the translation of foreign sources, and the preparation of comprehensive country handbooks. To implement the policy of making important research materials more readily available, a publication program was initiated. As the demand for the first small editions of translations, monographs, and bibliographies grew, publishing activities were extended and given a separate identity as the Human Relations Area Files Press.

HRAF Press publishes several different series of books at present, including this series of new country studies. The purpose of the *Survey of World Cultures,* of which *UAR-Egypt* is the fourteenth in the series, is to bring together in one comprehensive volume all those aspects of a country and culture—geography, history, government, politics, economics, sociology, art—usually scattered among a variety of sources. Each book represents a collation and synthesis of the best and most authoritative materials available on the country, including foreign and unpublished information. It is hoped that this series will in some measure help to meet the need for better understanding of other peoples in an increasingly interdependent world community.

This volume represents a very extensive revision of *Egypt*, published by the Human Relations Area Files in 1957 as part of its Country Survey Series. At that time the country, under a self-proclaimed revolutionary regime, had embarked on a course whose goals were still undefined. A decade after the revolution of July 1952, President Nasser stated: "We had the courage, at the beginning of the revolution, to declare that we had no theory, though we did have clearly defined principles. We declared that we would proceed by trial and error to construct a theory."

This theory went through several stages before it arrived at the concept and application of the Arab Socialist Union, which assumed a doctrinal form in 1961 and 1962. Because of the far-reaching changes that have taken place in Egypt since 1952, and because of the impact of Arab socialism on the political, social, and economic life of the country, emphasis has been placed in the present volume on the developments of these years. President Nasser, who usually speaks as "I," has declared that these changes will go forward whether or not he is at the head of the state, and there is no reason to question the sincerity of his statement. What we are witnessing, therefore, is the decision of Egypt to take the path of socialism—the path that leads to Communism if it is followed with proper devotion and without deviation.

As related to the earlier *Egypt*, many of the chapters of this volume have been entirely rewritten. For his share in this task, I express my deep appreciation to Dr. Fahim I. Qubain, who wrote Chapters 11 and 12, probably the most vital and informative in the book. Also, to Helene L. Boatner, who reviewed, amended, and improved drafts of Chapters 17 through 21.

In 1958 Egypt joined with Syria to form the United Arab Republic. After Syria withdrew from the union in 1961, the surviving partner continued to call itself the United Arab Republic. Since this partner refers to itself both as Egypt and as the United Arab Republic, the decision was made to use Egypt throughout this work, as Egypt (Misr) will certainly survive the use of other designations for the country.

The present text was largely completed at the time of the Arab-Israeli war of June 1967. While a determined effort has been made to deal with the causes and results of this outbreak, conclusions as to its long-term impact on Egypt should be accepted as tentative.

DONALD N. WILBER

September 1967
Princeton, New Jersey

The transliteration of place names, personal names, and descriptive terms from the Arabic script always offers problems. In the transliteration of personal names, an effort was made to approach uniformity within a system based on that employed by the Library of Congress. In some cases, however, such names have been Anglicized to conform to common usage.

Arabic words are italicized and defined the first time they are used in the text.

Weights and Measures:

The metric system is used in Egypt. Tonnages are expressed in the text as metric tons, and most figures follow the metric system. In a few cases the term "mile," etc., may be used, in order to clarify relationships for the reader not too familiar with the metric system—as, for example, the "number of persons per square mile."

Equivalents:

> 1 Egyptian pound (£E) = $2.30 U.S.
> 1 feddan   = 1.038 acres

Fiscal Year:

The Egyptian fiscal year begins on July 1.

CONTENTS

Contents (*continued*)

LIST OF ILLUSTRATIONS

LIST OF TABLES

List of Tables (*continued*)

United Arab Republic — Egypt

CHAPTER *1*

The Culture and the Society

EGYPT HAS BEEN APTLY DESCRIBED as an age-old hydraulic society, always with a highly centralized government and an army ready to resolve conflicts among political, economic, and ideological forces. While this description remains generally valid, the atmosphere of this ancient land is now charged with new currents—those of national pride, Arab nationalism, and Arab socialism.

Egypt was one of the first countries to be incorporated into the expanding Arab empire 1,300 years ago. An Islamic nation ever since, Egypt is commonly identified by its own people and others as an "Arab" country. There is justification for this claim in Egypt's centuries under Arab rule, in its Arabic speech and Moslem faith, and in its current effort to place itself at the head of a revived and united Arab world. There is, however, a specific quality about Egyptian life, a distinctiveness which has its roots in a pattern of existence in the Nile Valley long antedating the rise of Arab Islam. While Egypt shares much with its Middle Eastern neighbors, it remains uniquely Egyptian.

Territorially, the early history of the Middle East was a record of the development of two centers: the Nile River and the Fertile Crescent, a strip of arable land curving northeast from Palestine and south to the Persian Gulf. These two centers have by no means been isolated from each other, but they have developed differently. The Fertile Crescent has always been open to large-scale population movements, and a succession of peoples and civilizations have passed through it. The Nile Valley and Delta, on the other hand, provide a constricted arena in which a single people, under their own or alien rulers, have preserved themselves and their way of life for thousands of years without any real break in continuity. Egypt has taken part in and often been deeply af-

1

fected by events elsewhere in the Middle East, but it has never lost its essential Egyptian identity.

Like other Middle Eastern countries, Egypt today is caught in a headlong process of change. Set into motion in the last century by the impact of the West, that process has developed an impetus and a dynamic of its own, and during the past decade it has been rapidly gaining momentum. Egypt today is in the center of an upsurge of Arab (Islamic) nationalism in North Africa and the Middle East, an upsurge which cuts across political boundaries and reflects the national aspirations of the individual countries in the area. Contemporary development of Arab self-consciousness emerges as a two-edged sword that works toward both regional unity and divisive local nationalisms. The ultimate outcome of these tendencies may be a strong Arab Middle Eastern political power, but it is also likely that for the indefinite future, local nationalism will continue to flourish and to endanger international arrangements in the region.

An emotion-charged awareness of the Islamic and pre-Islamic past is stimulating and shaping national aspirations in a Moslem world which derives a measure of unity from language, history, religion, and a common pattern of thought, as well as from factors associated with the introduction of modern technology. All of these elements are present in the nationalist ferment in Egypt today, and they are given added force by education, the press, and the radio. Egypt's 4,500 years of recorded history, antedating the Islamic period, provide a tremendous store of materials from which a sense of national worth and mission can be constructed. Egyptian leaders are calling upon the people to take pride in their "Pharaonic heritage" and are striving to make of the ancient glories a backdrop for Egypt's present world position.

Land and Cultivation

Geography is perhaps more obtrusive in Egypt as a factor in the life of the people than it is in most countries. Pressed by the desert onto the banks of a single river, Egypt's population has found that river both bountiful and demanding: bountiful, in that the waters of the Nile have been a reliable source of food and wealth since the earliest cultivators moved into the Valley in prehistoric times; demanding, because for the mass of the people the price of extracting a livelihood from the river has been a lifetime of unremitting and scantily rewarded toil. The Nile has left its imprint on all the people of Egypt, from the officials and businessmen who must concern themselves with the problems of a one-crop economy to the fellah (peasant) who spends every daylight hour in the fields.

During the course of Egypt's development, the major problems presented to its inhabitants have centered on the use and management of the Nile. The solutions to these problems have given to Egyptian society and culture its characteristic form. The need for unified water control, for example, has been reflected in Egypt's historic political unity under a highly centralized and autocratic government. A crude agricultural technology applied to the fertile silt of the river could be made to yield heavy food surpluses only by the prodigal use of human labor. Land was wealth, and a man's relationship to the land became a basic factor in defining his place in the social scheme. Even today, when urban and industrial forms are supplementing the basic agricultural pattern, the ambition to hold land is hardly less strong in the city dweller than in the peasant. Early Egyptian science and religion both show their connections with the all-encompassing preoccupation with the Nile. Ancient Egyptian mathematical knowledge stemmed from the effort to maintain accurately the boundaries of the fields that would be flooded every year and to predict with certainty the annual rise and fall of the river itself. The cult of the Nile was a major element in the Pharaonic religion, and remnants of it still exist in the countryside beneath the overlay of Islam and Coptic Christianity.

The Nile remains the ultimate term of Egypt's existence, just as it has been since the earliest times. Of the country's 386,200 square miles, only some 13,600 are accessible to irrigation from the Nile. This area of the Nile Valley and Delta is historic Egypt, and there the life and work of the country still are concentrated. For the peasant majority, the desert that rims both sides of the Valley is less a territory than a threatening, thrusting barrier; one does not enter that wasteland, but seeks only to hold it back from the irrigated fields. The traditional focus, then, has been not outward, but inward, on the river. Modern involvement in international politics and trade is widening Egyptian horizons, but the dominant motif of national existence from day to day continues to be the Nile and the problems of its utilization.

3

Village and City

The cultivated land of the Nile Valley and Delta is very densely settled, with the many, many villages situated on the least productive plots of grounds, such as on rocky outcroppings or along the edge between the desert and the sown. The villages are basically self-contained and self-reliant units, inhabited for centuries by the same kin groups, made up of people who are somewhat suspicious of outsiders. The dreary round of drudgery, lived out in hovels at a subsistence level, has been relieved primarily by group participation in marriages and funerals and in religious ceremonies. Long subservient to landowners, the peasants knew they were inferior beings—inferior to the man with land and inferior to the educated folk. Now the government brings to the villages better means of sanitation, better ways of raising crops, and facilities for both health and entertainment, and at the same time tells the peasants that they are the respected backbone of the country.

The overcrowded conditions of village life result in an unending stream of people, usually the younger males, toward the cities. The urban population now numbers 40 per cent of the total population. Half of these migrants have settled either in Cairo, with its over 4 million people, or in Alexandria, with almost 2 million. Other centers, including such new industrial and manufacturing sites as Mahalla al-Kubra and Hilwân, also attract swarms of workers. The newer recruits to the factory labor force live much as they did in the villages—among their own kind and in housing that is just about as inadequate. It is the other classes of Egyptian society who enjoy what the cities have to offer.

The Elite and the Masses

In Egypt and throughout the Middle East the social order is riven by a great gap which separates a small elite from the mass of the people. The elite comprises the educated, the government officials and military officers, the Western-style businessmen, and—until recently—the big rural landowners. The masses include the great peasant majority of the villages and a growing body of urban workers.

Wealth, occupation, and education have traditionally defined the boundaries of this gap, which has been widened in modern times by Western impact. Economically, the demands and oppor-

4

tunities of the world market have converted Egypt's old diversified subsistence agriculture into a single-crop system of cotton production for export. This shift brought more wealth into the country, but the distance between rich and poor widened as the minority grew richer and a spectacularly increasing majority grew poorer. Modern trade and industrial development also stimulated an urban growth, which sharpened the traditional contrast between town and country. Socially, the new occupations and the new knowledge from the West drove still deeper the rift between the urban-centered elite and the rural mass. Where once a common set of traditional values had provided points of contact between the two, the Westernization of the elite rendered it less able than it had ever been to communicate with—or to lead—those below.

In the family- and village-bound social setting of Egypt, almost the only source of natural leadership above the village level is the elite. To the extent that the elite is not merely separated but actually isolated from the people, it is capable neither of grasping the increasingly large-scale problems with which it is confronted nor of commanding popular support. And yet the need for such capability is mounting. Although the peasant is still preoccupied with his traditionally local concerns, social and economic pressures are beginning to force him to look outward. He and his former fellows who have moved to the cities have not been immune to Western influences nor to the promises of a fervidly nationalistic government. As their expectations have increased, so have their potential dissatisfactions.

There are many indications that new lines of communication are being thrown across the social gap. The government is employing all the media of public information and education to persuade the people to give it their active support in the service of an ideal of national unity and strength. President Nasser has emphasized his own origins in a family of moderate means, and the fellah and the workman are being idealized as the embodiments of the "new Egypt." Professional people as a group still cling to the comforts and emoluments of the cities, but some, moved by recognition of need, are taking their skills to the squalor of the villages.

It is also possible to speculate on the composition of a new elite which is being formed by the policies of the government. This elite would include the members of the National Assembly—half of whom must be peasants and industrial workers—those holding Superior, Higher, and Grade One posts (the top managers of the

5

government factories, establishments, and enterprises), the leading administrators of the Arab Socialist Union, the ministers and deputy ministers of the cabinet, and the best-known writers and professional people. Such an elite would be, in fact, a proper mixture of the proletariat and the intelligentsia in a socialist society.

Role of the Government

The Egyptians were among the first peoples to develop an elaborate structure of public administration. Two notable characteristics of the government pattern were already clear 5,000 years ago. One was centralized authoritarianism. The ruler—Pharaoh—was not merely divinely ordained; he was God. Under his absolute authority, a large and complex hierarchy of civil and religious officials carried forward the daily business of government. There were times during Egypt's long dynastic period when this absolutist principle was challenged from below, and for relatively brief periods local or regional forces succeeded in asserting themselves against the central power. The authoritarian principle, however, always reasserted itself, and it was preserved by the succession of foreign rulers who governed in Egypt from 525 B.C. to the present century.

The second characteristic feature of Egyptian government tradition has been the limited scope of official activity. From the time when the pyramids were built until very recently, Egypt's rulers have limited their concerns largely to fiscal and judicial matters, the control of the waters of the Nile, and, in prosperous periods, to large-scale public works. It did not occur to them to go much beyond these functions, for in other spheres of life essential social services and controls were traditionally maintained by such units as the family and the village. So long as agricultural production was maintained and taxes were collected, there was no occasion for the government to interfere with the autonomy of these units. The authority of the government was absolute, but its direct impact was cushioned by a web of kin and local groups.

The tradition of highly centralized and authoritarian government maintained by the Pharaohs was continued by Egypt's successive alien rulers. The Egyptian people themselves rarely challenged their overlords, for they had never been in a position to participate significantly in the political process. After the close of the dynastic period, no native aristocracy existed to lead them in a struggle for local autonomy, and no tradition of popular or individual initiative in public affairs developed. Centuries of experience with political rapacity and almost no experience with official concern for the general welfare led most of the people to consider the government an adverse interest, profoundly to be distrusted.

Egyptian rulers in the past were content to govern in terms of this mosaic of local self-sufficiency and autonomy. The rulers themselves, during the hundreds of years Egypt was under foreign domination, were not Egyptian. They were further isolated by the fact of their residence in Cairo, one of the country's few cities, where they were surrounded by a small urban elite almost as far removed from the life of the people as they were. Their chief concerns were the collection of taxes and the control of the Nile as the source of the country's wealth.

The current effort to transform Egypt into a modern national state is the outcome of a century and a half of Western influence and domination. Not only have Egypt's leaders adopted nationalist ideals and ambitions learned in contact with the West but they are also impelled by the pressure of Western-induced social and economic change. When in 1952 the new military regime expelled King Farouk from the country, it signalized the fact that it was committed to broadening the base of its political support beyond the traditional urban and rural elite. The present government sees the Egyptian people no longer as a merely passive economic asset, but as a potentially active force to be channeled into the building of Egyptian industrial and military power and into the assertion of Egyptian leadership in the Arab world. What is involved is nothing less than breaking down the ancient barriers of family and village exclusiveness and constructing a new and more unified pattern of Egyptian loyalty.

In Egypt it is constantly alleged that the revolution of July 1952 is still going on. That bloodless revolution was not in any way a reflection of a class struggle—feudalism and capitalism were stamped out by decree and without any resistance. Since the mass of the people were never caught up in a violent revolution, the word itself may have little real meaning for them.

Egypt's leaders are today calling on the Egyptian people for loyalty to the Egyptian state and to a set of unifying national ideals. The government may in the course of time succeed in constructing this essentially Western pattern of allegiance, but the task will not be an easy one; the basic Egyptian loyalties have been and are

7

set in a much narrower framework than the national state, and they attach to smaller units. Family, village, ethnic community—these, and not the nation, continue to bound the horizon of the great majority of Egyptians. For the rural population in particular, these units, and not an abstract "Egypt," are the present reality.

The broad powers wielded by the government of President Nasser are in the authoritarian Egyptian political tradition. The scope of the exercise of those powers, however, represents a new trend. In the pursuit of its nationalist goals, the government seeks to inject itself into areas of Egyptian life which have in the past been managed by other institutions and in other ways.

The aims of the government were defined and explained at great length in the National Charter of 1962. President Nasser had previously boiled down these objectives to a single phrase, "a democratic, socialistic, cooperative society." To build this society, he said, "imperialism, monarchy, feudalism, and capitalism were thus all stamped out." The role, then, of the present government is to try to build this society, largely through decrees and the operations of a complex, expanding bureaucracy.

It is also the role of the government to enmesh the people in the Arab Socialist Union and in cooperatives. Failure to make satisfactory headway may lead to repressive actions against laggards, with fear replacing enthusiasm as the motive for participation. Indeed, the creation of the Committee against Feudalism suggests that coercion is in the offing. The industrialization of the country will demand a long-continuing effort from all Egyptians, and the government must provide jobs for all who are able to work and also convince them that hard work is in both the nation's interest and their own.

Ideologies that compete with socialism are not welcome. Thus, Islam has been subordinated to socialism, and even to some extent identified with socialism. The decline of the pervasive influence of the faith in public and private life seems to be encouraged by the government in such actions as the displacement of religious canon law and in the apparent subservience of the religious leaders to the policies of the state.

National Attitudes

The color green has long been associated with Islam, and appears in the flags of most Moslem countries. After the revolution of 1952, the Egyptian flag was not altered: it remained a white crescent enclosing three stars on a green background. A stylized eagle also came into prominence on posters and the covers of official publications. With the union with Syria, a new flag was designed for the United Arab Republic: a tricolor of horizontal red, white, and black stripes, with two green stars on the central white stripe. The eagle also became a national symbol: on its chest a shield displays the stripes and stars of the flag, and in its claws is a scroll with the words "Al-Jumhuriya al-Arabiya al-Muttihada [United Arab Republic]."

In addition to marshaling Islam into the service of nationalism and socialism, the secular trend is apparent in the institution of new national holidays. These include National Day (July 23), which commemorates the coup d'etat of 1952; Liberation Day (June 18), the day chosen to celebrate the departure of the last British troops in 1956; and Victory Day (December 23), the date of the evacuation in 1956 of the Suez Canal area by British, French, and Israeli troops.

Certain themes have been so persistently promoted since 1952 that they can be assumed to have become a part of the national attitudes. These include: glorification of national unity, faith in a strong national army, hope in the future of Arab unity, and hatred for imperialism.

The speeches of President Nasser are always long—they usually last about two hours. Each contains the same review of the crises endured since 1952 and of the way that victory came out of defeat. A description of Egypt's economic progress is followed by an attack on the country's enemies. The audiences are taken behind the scenes of international diplomacy, they are given dire accounts of the intentions and actions of enemy powers, and they hear violent language directed against the imperialists, while the fabric of the speech is interspersed with jokes.

The characteristics of Nasser's speeches are in harmony with national attitudes. A local observer of the scene has described the temperament and character of the Egyptian people in appropriately related terms. The Egyptian is very sensitive to criticism, she points out, but very ready to criticize others, and he has a deep sense of personal pride. Aggression, an attitude that is much admired by most Egyptians, may be expressed in impulsive and flamboyant speech. Emotionalism and boasting are also favored elements of conversation. Shame is to be avoided: it is shameful

9

to acknowledge failure, but almost as much so to rejoice over success. In addition, she says, the Egyptian does not hesitate to depart from the truth in an attempt to attain a chosen goal.

The Arab-Israeli war of June 1967 led the Egyptians to review their national and emotional attitudes. Muhammad Heykal, editor of *al-Ahram* and spokesman for President Nasser, wrote:

> We, however, also commit numerous mistakes. Our first mistake is that many times our statements include expressions that are more than we actually mean and beyond our capabilities, such as the calls for killing, crushing and so forth, which went out over our radio stations. . . . Our second mistake is that we do not present our cause well to others. We think that because right is clearly on our side this should in itself be enough to convince others, and that when others fail to be immediately convinced this is due to their ill will and thus we become upset. This is a state of affairs which can easily be depicted as fanaticism.

The editor of *al-Musawwar* wrote:

> The mistakes were grave and numerous. In our rapid progress in the last few years on the political, social, industrial, and military fronts, we neglected serious gaps and imbalances. We came out of the limited, stagnant agricultural society into a big, dynamic, growing nation with international influence. But we carried with us into the new stage many of our old shortcomings: individualism, sensitivity, social ambitions, and the preoccupation with giving the impression that we were doing our duty instead of actually doing it. We carried with us from the old world the faults of disorganization and scientific inaccuracy.

These and other current commentaries reflect the official interest in a dispassionate examination of prevailing public and private attitudes and the conviction that Egypt cannot afford to cling to attitudes which have proved to be detrimental to the political and economic development of the country.

CHAPTER 2

Historical Setting

THROUGHOUT ITS LONG DEVELOPMENT, from prehistoric times to the present, the Nile Valley has received numerous accretions of people, each bearing variant cultural contributions and patterns of life. The skeletal remains of the prehistoric peoples, who were in the area when North Africa was beginning to dry up with the retreat of the last ice sheet in Europe, show striking similarities to those of modern Egyptians. The progressive desiccation of the grasslands of the region drew these seminomadic food gatherers and hunters to the still swampy valley of the Nile, where they began to practice simple agriculture and animal husbandry. Whether these skills had an independent origin in Africa or were diffused from southwestern Asia is not clear, but the Sinai Peninsula then, as now, provided a corridor for the passage of peoples and cultural influence between Asia and Africa. By 6000 B.C., the Nile Valley was the scene of a neolithic ("New Stone Age") culture, marked by the characteristic elements of settled village life: pottery, agriculture, and domestic animals. The archaeological sites of this period reveal the beginnings of the burial customs that were so highly elaborated at a later date by the dynastic Egyptians. Physically, these prehistoric inhabitants of the Nile appear to have been members of the same brunet, long-headed, Mediterranean stock that dominates the area today.

Historically, the constricted valley of Upper Egypt in the south and the swampy fan of Lower Egypt in the north form a geographical division of the country which has been reflected in certain cultural differences and a tendency toward political disunion. The first Egyptian dynasty was the outcome of a struggle for supremacy in which Upper Egypt prevailed. Thereafter, with the growth of urban power in the Nile Delta, Lower Egypt more often dominated the south, as it does today.

11

The penetration into Egypt of peoples and influences from outside by no means ended with the close of the prehistoric period. The cavalry of the Asian Hyksos pushed through the Sinai Peninsula and briefly conquered the country in the middle of the second millennium. Ethiopians were followed by Assyrians, and the influence of a civilization fully as complex as the one already established in Egypt was brought in with the Persian conquest. Later came Alexandrine Greeks, Romans, Byzantines, Arabs, Syrians, Turks, Albanians, and Circassians.

All have left their impress on Egypt and its people, without fundamentally altering the deeply-rooted and peculiarly Egyptian culture. All of these historic arrivals came as conquerors or as members of privileged groups. As such, they tended not to be assimilated but instead to preserve their ethnic identities apart from the Egyptians whom they ruled or manipulated. A major theme of the modern Egyptian nationalist upheaval has been denunciation of the remnants of these groups as alien and the demand that they be displaced in power and social prominence by native Egyptians.

Ancient Egypt

The Old Kingdom. The first two dynasties are obscured by lack of information, but the IIIrd dynasty (ca. 2980) was the beginning of a brilliant period, known as the Old Kingdom, which lasted through the VIth dynasty to 2475 B.C. Autocratic power became highly centralized in the hands of the Pharaoh. The great pyramids were built in the IVth dynasty. The force of the Pharaonic religion and the correlative power of the state are symbolized by the Great Pyramid, the tomb of King Khufu (Cheops), which rises 481 feet and contains 2,300,000 blocks of limestone.

Beginning with the Vth dynasty (2750 B.C. to 2625 B.C.), royal prestige and power declined with the growth of the power of the priests and the nomarchs (governors of the nomes, or provinces). The VIIth and VIIIth dynasties (2475 B.C. to 2445 B.C.) represented a period of social revolution, in which the common people successfully challenged the extreme authoritarianism of the royal power. The IXth and Xth dynasties (2445 B.C. to 2160 B.C.) seem to have been a time of transition to a feudal or quasi-feudal regime, in which royal authority extended little beyond the capital at Heracleopolis (in the vicinity of modern Al-Faiyûm).

12

The Middle Kingdom. The XIth and XIIth dynasties (2160 B.C. to 1788 B.C.) comprise a great period, known as the Middle Kingdom, which saw the revival of royal authority in a modified and less absolute form. A kind of state socialism had developed, and the power of the Pharaohs was now exercised through an elaborate bureaucracy, which assigned lands and trades and administered the proceeds. Commoners had access to official appointments and could rise in the state service.

An interim period, from the XIIIth through the XVIIth dynasties (1788 B.C. to 1580 B.C.), witnessed both a renewal of internal troubles and an invasion by the Hyksos—the first of the large-scale foreign invasions which finally were to bring to a close the dynastic period. It was probably just prior to this time that Semites in the Sinai Peninsula developed an alphabetic writing system based on symbols taken from the Egyptian hieroglyphics. This invention was one of the greatest in human history, providing the foundation for all subsequent alphabets.

The New Empire. The period of the XVIIIth through the XXth dynasties (1580 B.C. to 1090 B.C.) is known as the New Empire. These years marked the peak of the power of ancient Egypt. Egyptian thought took a secular turn, and the art of the time is characterized by a preoccupation with the details of daily life and a technical brilliance which some critics find rather sterile compared with earlier phases. Egyptian wealth and power were at their height, and the military campaigns of Thutmose III brought Palestine, Syria, and the area of the northern Euphrates within the boundaries of the Empire. Military expansion involved Egypt in a complicated system of international relations, in which such modern diplomatic devices as embassies, alliances, and treaties were employed.

The end of the New Empire at the close of the XXth dynasty (1090 B.C.) saw the decline of Egyptian power, which thereafter was only temporarily restored by particularly able kings, as in the XXVIth (Saite) dynasty. In 525 B.C., with the entry of the Persians, the period of Egypt's ancient greatness came to a close.

Post-dynastic Egypt

A natural division of Egyptian history might be made at 525 B.C., when the period of dynastic Egypt ends and the country emerges

as a province of the Persian Empire. That year marks the change
from an independent Egypt to Egypt under foreign rule, as it was
destined to remain for many centuries. The conquest of Egypt by
Alexander the Great in 332 B.C. has instead been chosen as a turning point, however, for the arrival of Alexander heralded the introduction into Egypt of an entirely new Indo-European influence.
Both Alexander and the Persians employed in Egypt the concepts
of absolute monarchy that had been part of the experience of the
Nile Valley since the days of the earliest Pharaohs. But whereas
under the Persians, Egypt's political relations had continued to be
oriented to the Fertile Crescent, northeast and south beyond the
Sinai Peninsula, for the first time under the Greeks, the country
found itself looking across the Mediterranean. The coming of
Alexander moved the center of gravity of Egypt's political and
cultural relationships and involved Egypt in the dynamics of the
Mediterranean—where it has been involved for the most part ever
since.

With the defeat of Darius, the Persian, in November 333 B.C.,
Alexander turned to the consolidation of his forces in Egypt and
the eastern Mediterranean. After the Persian satrap in Egypt had
submitted, Alexander entered Memphis, where, in contrast to the
Persians, he paid homage to the native gods and consulted their
oracles. The Egyptians had not been tractable subjects of the
Persians, but they seem to have accepted the more flexible Alexander without difficulty. The priests of Amon could receive him as
the son of the god, employing the conventional Egyptian salutation
to new kings. With characteristic energy, Alexander at once began
the construction of the Greek city of Alexandria, which was to
become one of the great centers of the Mediterranean world. Greek
settlers, moving into their new domain, brought their Egyptian
subjects into cultural and political collaboration with themselves,
thereby setting in motion a process of cultural synthesis which was
to affect Europe no less than Asia. Alexander's brief rule on the
Nile was the prologue for the Egypt of the Ptolemaic period, during which the great Macedonian's successors continued on a less
grandiose scale the work he had begun.

Alexander, and perhaps to a lesser extent the Ptolemies, applied
the social policies of the melting pot in Egypt. Although the Greeks
tended to settle in separate, privileged communities and were not
subject to certain legal disabilities and obligations imposed upon
Egyptians, such as corvée labor on the canals and embankments,

14

there was no severe racial discrimination. The Ptolemies were intensely practical administrators, intent upon developing as tangible a base of power and prestige as possible. Where Egyptians could not conveniently be used, as in the military forces, outside groups were brought in, and although these groups tended to live in their separate communities, still there was little of the "master race" concept as such. For the imported ethnic groups to maintain their separate cultural identities and places of abode was consistent with the traditional Egyptian pattern, and this continues to be true in Egypt and the Middle East today, where villages of diverse peoples are to be found living side by side but with little communication between them. Under the Ptolemies, only a few Egyptians rose to high official position, for government was the monopoly of the rulers. Most Egyptians were confined to the classes of cultivators and artisans; then, as throughout the long period that followed, Egypt was not a cohesive national state, but an entity in which a native population was ruled by a foreign group, employing the techniques of bureaucratic absolutism.

As the Ptolemaic period drew to a close, the increasing weakness of the royal government enabled various contestants for the throne to appeal to the Egyptian population for support. The result was to give to the Egyptians a position of greater equality with the Greeks. In this there is, perhaps, an analogy with President Nasser's current appeal to the masses in his search for political support outside the circle of the old ruling group.

The Roman and Byzantine Period: 30 B.C.—642 A.D.

With the establishment of Roman rule by Augustus in 30 B.C., Egypt again became a province of an empire, as it had been under the Assyrians and Persians and, briefly, under Alexander. Egypt had a widespread reputation for disorder, and as the principal source of the grain supply of Rome, it was brought under the direct control of the Emperor, in his capacity as supreme military chief, and garrisoned with a powerful force. The Emperor ruled as successor to the Ptolemies—"Pharaoh, Lord of the Two Lands"—and to him were attributed the conventional divine qualities assigned to Egyptian kings. All the land was royal domain. Once again Egypt and its conquerors adapted to each other, although Roman practice and institutions of government and religion were formally established. Rome was particularly careful to bring the priesthood,

15

the invariable source of Egyptian nationalism, under its control, while guaranteeing its traditional rights and privileges.

The advent of the Romans further intensified the social problems that had been created by the injection into Egypt of a privileged Greek minority under the Ptolemies. Those of Hellenic culture undoubtedly continued to enjoy special advantages, such as the privilege of paying a reduced poll tax, but Roman rule brought a new elite and complicated the alignments of the old ones. As practical administrators who were interested in knowing just what they had in their Egyptian province, the Romans reached far down into the society in their management of affairs, employing such measures as a regular, house-to-house census of property and persons. Dynamic, secular, and utilitarian, they exposed post-Ptolemaic Egyptians to a new variant of European culture.

Christianity was received early in Egypt, and the new religion quickly spread from Alexandria into the hinterland of the country, reaching Middle and Upper Egypt by the second century. According to one account, the mission that carried Christianity into Egypt was that of St. Mark, in 37 A.D., and the founding of the Christian Church in Alexandria is fixed at around 40 A.D. From the start, Egyptian Christianity had a tendency toward heretical movements, in particular Christian Gnosticism—placing great stress on the redeeming function of knowledge—which may also account for the popularity of the Gospel of St. John, with its doctrine of the Logos. Egypt was also the early center of the development of Christian monasticism. Prior to the onslaught of Islam, Christianity was almost completely extinguished in the disorders that accompanied the collapse of the Roman Empire in the West, but the Coptic Christian Church has survived down to the present time.

Gradually, as the third century advanced, the decay that beset the Roman Empire was more and more manifest in Egypt. It became increasingly difficult to fill the urban civil magistracies. Civil war, pestilence, and conflict among claimants to the imperial power beset the Empire. A renaissance of imperial authority and effectiveness took place with the Emperor Diocletian, during whose reign, beginning in 284, the division between the eastern and western Roman Empires took place. Egypt continued as a province of the eastern Empire, which had its capital at Byzantium (later, Constantinople; today, Istanbul). Diocletian inaugurated drastic political and fiscal reforms and greatly simplified imperial administration. Because he saw in Christianity a threat to the

Roman state religion, he also launched a violent persecution of the Christians, which fell on the Coptic Church in Egypt with greater severity than any persecution it was to know under the Moslems. The sectarian doctrinal divisions of the Egyptian Church came to the fore as a central factor in Egyptian history during the Byzantine period, for Egyptian opposition to the imperial rule was often expressed in religious terms. When Constantinople, the eastern capital, was heretical, Egypt rallied to Roman Catholicism; when the capital was Catholic, Egypt fell into heresy.

During the latter part of the Byzantine period, signs of decay multiplied again in Egypt. By the seventh century, evidence of the retreat of Hellenism could be seen in the declining use of the Greek language. Coptic was again coming to the fore, and even the dignitaries of the Church were losing their ability to communicate in Greek. At the same time, the eastern Empire came under heavy assault from the north and east. In 616 A.D., the Persians again conquered Egypt, but their triumph there was short-lived. In 639, the Arabian General Amr ibn al-As won from the Second Caliph of Islam consent to invade Egypt. The invasion was overwhelmingly successful. In September 642, the army of the Byzantine Empire sailed out of the harbor of Alexandria. The wave from the other side of the Mediterranean had subsided. Absorption of the country by the Arabs proceeded with breathtaking speed. After nearly a thousand years, Egypt again looked northeast to Asia.

The Arab Period, 642-1517

The Arab conquest of Egypt under the banner of Islam was a Semitic engulfment of the country. It was only a part of a larger movement creating an Islamic Empire, which once reached from the Atlantic Ocean to the frontiers of China. The invaders from the Arabian Peninsula carried swords and a will to rule, but they also brought a simple, compelling religion and a workable code of law, both of which they implanted among the peoples they found in their path. Their impact in Egypt was not the limited one of the Greeks. The Islamic faith spread through the land more quickly and more widely than Christianity had done. More slowly, but inexorably, the Arabic language supplanted the old Coptic Egyptian. The institutions of marriage and of property ownership were transformed. Basic Egyptian patterns as expressed in the life of the fellah cultivating the banks of the Nile remained, and not all that had been learned under the Greeks and the Romans was forgotten. But the transformation that took place was so profound that it must be reckoned one of the great revolutionary developments of history.

Politically, the Egyptian Arabian era may be divided into a number of dynastic periods: first, the Umayyad caliphate; and then the Abbasid, the Tulunid, the Ikhshidid, the Fatimid, the Ayyubid, and the Mamluk (Slave) dynasties. During some of these periods, Egypt was ruled as a province from afar. In others, during periods of disunity in the Arab empire, Egypt's local (but always foreign) rulers could assert their authority and transform Egypt into an independent, sovereign state. At still other times, Egypt itself became the headquarters of an Arab caliphate and empire.

The vigor of the Mamluk dynasties (1252-1517) gradually declined with the growth of the power of the Mamluk governors of the various provinces to assert independent authority. Decay at the center of the imperial apparatus was accompanied by the rise of obtrusive and obstructive power at the extremities. Under these conditions, Egypt was ripe for the assault of the Ottoman Turkish Selim I, who incorporated the country into the Ottoman caliphate in 1517.

The Ottoman Caliphate, 1517-1914

The Turks introduced very little political change or reform into Egypt. As a pashalic of the Empire under a Turkish pasha (viceroy), the country was divided into 12 *sanjaks* (provinces—the word is Turkish for flag), which were the equivalent of the 12 *liwa* (the Arab provinces—Arabic for banner). Each of the 12 was placed under one of the Mamluks, who surrounded themselves with the usual following of slave warriors. In the roughly 280 years of direct Turkish rule, at least a hundred pashas succeeded each other. As time went on, the control of the pashas became ever more shadowy and the army more undisciplined and violent. Gradually, the Mamluk beys emerged as the real authorities in the land. Mamluk power reached its peak in 1769, when Ali Bey became powerful enough to expel the pasha and declare Egypt's independence. Ali Bey went on to conquer Syria and Arabia, but he was soon betrayed to the Sublime Porte (the Turkish caliphate) by a slave, Abu al-Dhahab, who became his successor under a reaffirmed Turkish suzerainty. Turkish vulnerability had nevertheless been revealed by Ali Bey's brief career. The struggles among the Mamluk beys for control of Egypt continued until 1798, when a new conqueror, Napoleon Bonaparte, appeared in the Delta and set the country upon a new course of history.

The brief but dramatic sojourn in Egypt of Napoleon's army, accompanied by a retinue of French scientists, initiated the Egyptian tradition of strong attachment to French culture. More significant, the Napoleonic adventure dramatically accented the importance of Egypt as the last base of enfeebled Turkish control over Syria and Arabia and as a vital communications link with India and the Far East. Suddenly the whole Middle Eastern area, with Egypt as an important focus, was precipitated into the vortex of European power politics and diplomacy, where it has been ever since. Europe had once again moved onto the Egyptian horizon, although not to the exclusion of that large part of the Asian world to which Egypt was bound by the ties of Islam.

Muhammad Ali. At the turn of the nineteenth century, Egypt was pushed into the modern era by the developing power of industrial Europe. But in Egypt itself, the principal agent of the changes that followed was an Albanian Moslem officer in the Turkish forces, Muhammad Ali, who had assisted in driving out the French forces. In 1805, the Sublime Porte designated him pasha, or governor, of Egypt, and from that time until just before his death in 1849 his story is essentially that of Egypt. As an enthusiastic importer of European culture and techniques, he was a modernizer whose political methods were nevertheless those of the authoritarian past. A dynamic economic innovator, he cast European techniques into a framework of nationalization and state socialism which was unfamiliar to the Europe of his time and completely novel in the Arab world. By a policy of confiscation, he became the sole proprietor of land; through a system of monopolies, he became Egypt's exclusive manufacturer and contractor. Armed with such power he worked an economic revolution, particularly in the building of canals for irrigation and transportation, in the promotion of scientific agriculture, and in the introduction of cotton cultivation in the Delta. No less energetic in the sphere of education, he fostered training in engineering and medicine, imported academicians and physicians from Europe, sent students abroad to be trained in needed skills, and imported training missions, educational and military, for the education of Egyptians at home.

19

Muhammad Ali was well aware that in Egypt political and military power must coincide, and he devoted much attention to the construction of an Egyptian army and navy. One of his early steps in this connection was to crush the Mamluks, who under the Ottoman caliphate had been confirmed in the power they had usurped during the Arabian period. The means chosen by Muhammad Ali are characteristic of a tradition in which the alternatives to ignominious surrender have been guile and violence. On the eve of the departure of an Egyptian force for Arabia, the Mamluk beys were invited to a reception, the main feature of which was an ambush prepared by their host. The departing guests were cut down in the streets, and of those who were taken alive most were tortured and executed.

For his new forces, Muhammad Ali found employment which had a bearing upon international affairs. Between 1811 and 1818 he pursued a war against Arabia. In 1820 his armies began an invasion of the eastern Sudan. This was the beginning of a movement that was to occupy his successors and constitute a problem for Anglo-Egyptian relations down to the present time. Another military venture in the late 1820s found the Egyptian pasha assisting the Turkish sultan in the repression of Greek independence —as a result of which, Turkey and Egypt were forced off the eastern Mediterranean by the destruction at Navarino of their combined naval strength. Muhammad Ali's fourth and most important foreign venture was a war against the Sublime Porte itself, the occasion for which was the sultan's refusal to honor his commitment to give Syria and Morea to Muhammad Ali in return for assistance in repressing the Greek rebellion. The Egyptian forces came within sight of Constantinople, but the Great Powers, committed to the preservation of Turkey and fearing a threat to their lines of communication to the East, forced Muhammad Ali to withdraw his troops to Egypt. The one tangible benefit by Muhammad Ali from the adventure was a decree of the Porte making the pashalic of Egypt hereditary in his family and another granting him the government of the Sudan.

The great pasha's immediate successors, Abbas I (1849-54), Said (1854-63), and Ismail (1863-79), were uniformly less capable than he. Abbas I has been described as a reactionary, and Said as a jovial, gargantuan sybarite. The latter, although he initiated the building of the Suez Canal, also began those colossal expenditures and personal extravagances which, enlarged under Ismail, finally brought a bankrupt Egypt under British control in the latter part of the century.

Ismail's financial irresponsibility invited the subordination of the country to great power interests, and this fact was not offset by his being granted in 1867 the title "Khedive of Egypt." In 1875, England under the ministry of Disraeli was able to purchase Egypt's shares in the Suez Canal. A year later, Ismail was forced to accept the establishment of a French-British Debt Commission to manage a receivership for Egypt's fiscal affairs. Ismail tried hard to place responsibility for the financial impasse on others and to placate local and foreign opinion by accepting constitutional limitations upon his khedivial authority, but finally his policy became too sinuous for the Dual Control (Great Britain and France), and in 1879 he was forced to abdicate in favor of his son Tewfik and to go into exile at Constantinople, where he died in 1895.

Tewfik was confronted with financial and political chaos, and his situation was complicated by the outbreak of a nationalist and military revolt under Arabi Pasha, the first Egyptian leader in modern times to come from a fellahin background. The British reacted to the disorders with a naval bombardment of Alexandria in July 1882, and by landing a British army, which defeated Arabi Pasha at the battle of Tell al-Kebir and went on to occupy Cairo. The British occupation of Egypt and the virtual inclusion of the country within the British Empire began at this time.

British occupation and the rise of Egyptian nationalism, 1882-1914. The record of the British occupation of Egypt is in effect the story of three outstanding proconsuls of empire. These three men, bearing the official titles of British Agents and Consuls-General, were the Earl of Cromer (formerly Sir Evelyn Baring), Sir Eldon Gorst, and Lord Kitchener. During this period, it was the British Agency and not the Khedivial Palace which was the real locus of authority. An Egyptian ministry continued to function under the khedive, whose decrees were ostensibly the main form of government decisions, but the basic policy was British. The khedive became a major symbol of growing Egyptian nationalism, which manifested itself in the appearance of political parties. Most important among these parties was the Egyptian Nationalist Party (al-Hizb al-Watani) led by Mustafa Kamil, a young lawyer. The British representatives saw their task as twofold: to bring fiscal and government reform to Egypt, and to accommodate as much as possible

21

Egyptian desires for political self-expression and—despite the opposition of Egyptian conservative groups—constitutional representative government.

The British success in bringing about fiscal reform was outstanding. Early in the occupation, budgets were balanced and began to show a surplus; within 20 years, the government could plan an expenditure almost two and a half times what had been possible in the 1880s. British control also brought administrative reform and expanding economic and agricultural services. The scant attention paid to education during this period represents an omission for which the British continue to be criticized in Egypt.

Under the leadership of Lord Dufferin, who had been Ambassador in Constantinople, the British effected the establishment of an Egyptian constitution designed to set forth the limits of government authority. Under this constitution (embodied in the Organic Law of May 1, 1883), provision was made for an elective structure of government under the khedive in an effort to stimulate the development of democratic political processes, even though the British sponsors were not optimistic about the possibilities. These proposals were adopted under pressure from a liberal government at home in England, but they also reflected Lord Dufferin's realization of the central importance of coming to terms with rising Egyptian nationalism. A major problem in Anglo-Egyptian relations during this period was the question of the special court system and laws for the protection of the rights of foreigners: the special privileges accorded foreigners under the terms of the Capitulations imposed on the Sublime Porte were a constant source of Egyptian resentment and a stimulus to nationalist sentiment.

The British Protectorate, 1914-22

The outbreak of the war in 1914 focused attention on the strategic importance of Egypt and the Suez Canal to the British lifeline to the East. Upon Turkey's alignment with the Central Powers and the adherence of the khedive, Abbas Hilmi II (1893-1914), to the Turkish cause, Britain declared a protectorate over Egypt, and the nominal rule of the Ottoman caliphate came to an end. The title "Khedive" was abolished, and Abbas' uncle, Hussein Kamil, succeeded to the throne with the title "Sultan." Upon his death in 1917, he was succeeded by his brother, Prince Ahmad Fuad.

The failure of British and Allied attempts to force the Dardanelles and secure the passage of the Straits heightened Egypt's importance in the prosecution of the war, not least of all as a base of operations against Arabia, Syria, Palestine, and other Turkish possessions in the Middle East.

Egyptian nationalism was relatively quiescent in the early phases of the war, but by 1917, when the Allied victory began to be visible and following President Wilson's pronouncement of the principle of national self-determination, demands for Egyptian independence and for representation at the peace conferences multiplied. By late 1918, a new, broadly-based, nationalist political organization, the Wafd al-Misri (the Egyptian Delegation), emerged under the leadership of Sa'd Zaghlul Pasha as the most important Egyptian political party—a position which it held for the next generation and a half. The initial purpose of the Wafd was to prepare the Egyptian case in London. Agitation and unrest continued and heightened after failure to get a hearing at Paris. Finally, when police measures proved abortive, the British government responded by sending a special mission to Egypt under the leadership of Lord Milner. Following an investigation, the mission proposed the renunciation of the protectorate, a declaration of Egyptian independence, and a treaty of alliance—all subject to certain guarantees respecting British and foreign interests. Negotiations failed, and in February 1922 the British unilaterally declared their acceptance of the principal Milner recommendations (except for the treaty of alliance) and set forth conditions for the formation of an Egyptian ministry. Pending an agreement between the two countries, the following were reserved to absolute British control: imperial communication in Egypt, Egyptian defense, the interests of foreigners, and the Sudan. In tacit recognition of the declaration, Fuad assumed the title "King" on March 15, 1922. Egypt was thus independent, at least by formal pronouncement, of the British government, although it continued to bear certain disabilities.

Independence

A new constitution was promulgated in April 1923. It made no claim to Egyptian sovereignty over the Sudan, and this issue was held over for subsequent adjustment between the British and Egyptian governments. In September 1923, the nationalist leader Zaghlul Pasha returned from exile. His party, the Wafd, won a sweeping success in the elections of January 1924. Zaghlul went to London to negotiate with the British, but negotiations with the Labor Government of the time foundered over the issue of the Sudan, and Zaghlul returned to Egypt, having failed in his mission.

Rioting broke out, in the course of which the British Governor General and Sirdar of the Egyptian Army, Sir Lee Stack, was assassinated in Cairo. The crime climaxed a series of murders of British subjects which had begun in 1920. The British demanded the removal of all Egyptian personnel from the Sudan, and Zaghlul, who was under the pressure of bad relations with the Palace, took the occasion to resign. He had succeeded in initiating a modicum of parliamentary government in Egypt and in transforming the Wafd into the dominating political force in the country. Al-Hizb al-Watani went into relative eclipse. Upon his death in 1927, Zaghlul was succeeded by Mustafa Rasha Nahas Pasha, who remained a dominant figure in Egyptian politics until recent times.

Other parties also rose during this period, especially the Liberal Constitutional Party and the Saadist Party, which were used by King Fuad as counters to the Wafd. There were also a number of minor groups, which amounted to little more than the personal followings of particular political leaders. The other important political force to emerge in the country after the war was the al-Ikhwan al-Muslimin (Moslem Brethren), which by 1946 had reached a membership of two million. Demanding stricter and purer observance of the tenets of Islam, it represented the anti-Western, anti-British forces of fanatical Pan-Islamic nationalism in the country. The Wafd and the Ikhwan remained in conflict and competition down to the post-World War II period, with the Wafd increasingly showing the signs of corruption that made it and other Egyptian political parties easy targets of the puritanical Moslem Brethren. During this period the Communist Party of Egypt was banned, and this ban has never been lifted.

The Treaty of 1936. In the political situation that prevailed from 1924 to 1936—the year of the death of King Fuad—three forces competed with each other: the Wafd, the royal prerogative (the Palace), and British power. The first two were agreed upon one thing, the desire for real independence from Britain. On other grounds they were at odds, with the Wafd working to curtail the royal prerogative, and King Fuad striving to prevent the Wafd from forming governments which might carry out the popular Wafd program. In the course of the struggle, the constitution was suspended in 1928, restored in 1929, replaced in 1930 by a modification favoring royal authority, and restored again in 1935. During part of this period, Mustafa Rasha Nahas Pasha led the Wafd in violent, extraparliamentary opposition to the government of Ismail Sidqi Pasha.

One constructive development of this period was the successful negotiation of an agreement with Britain. The Italian invasion of Ethiopia had underscored the vulnerability of an Egypt unsupported by Britain. King Fuad worked for and produced a united front, and restored the constitution as a bid to the Wafd. In May 1936, the Wafd won in the elections, and Nahas Pasha led a delegation, representing several parties, in negotiations with Britain. Agreement was reached in August 1936.

By the terms of this milestone treaty, the occupation of Egypt was terminated. Britain retained the right to maintain troops for 20 years along the Suez Canal and the right to have the Royal Air Force fly over Egyptian soil for training purposes. In the event of war, the treaty provided for large-scale mutual assistance. Moreover, it was agreed that the alliance would be extended after 1956. It was stipulated that the Sudan could continue to be ruled under the Agreement for Condominium of 1899, with the proviso that Egyptian troops would be readmitted into the Sudanese military forces. Britain undertook to sponsor Egyptian membership in the League of Nations, and Egypt gained admission in 1937. In the same year, by agreement of the Capitulatory powers at Montreux, the Capitulations were abolished, and the progressive abolition of consular courts and mixed courts began. This abolition was brought to completion in 1949, when Egyptian courts took over all judicial functions in the country. The advances of the years 1936 and 1937 were modified and restricted by King Fuad's death in 1936 and the subsequent outbreak of World War II, but a great step forward had been taken.

Egypt in World War II. With the outbreak of World War II, the war clauses of the 1936 treaty were applied, rather than those relating to Egypt's independence. It was not until 1947 that British troops finally left Upper and Lower Egypt. During half of that time they were present on a war footing, with Egypt functioning as a base of Allied operations. On British advice, Egypt declared her neutrality but provided more assistance to the Allied cause than was stipulated by the treaty.

25

The war deepened the cleavages of Egyptian politics. The young King Farouk early showed his independence by refusing to accede to Wafd demands for dismissal of the Saadist chief, Ali Maher Pasha, as head of the Royal Cabinet. Farouk's temperament came into conflict with the dictatorial nature of Nahas Pasha, with the critical issue between them being the attitude toward the war. In this conflict, King Farouk came to symbolize what was suspected of being a pro-Nazi attitude, while Nahas Pasha and the Wafd represented a strongly pro-Allied position. Farouk was forced by an ultimatum from Lord Killearn (the British Ambassador) and by a show of British military strength before the palace in February 1942 to appoint Nahas Pasha as Prime Minister. Throughout the critical phases of the war, especially in North Africa, Egypt under Wafdist leadership wholeheartedly supported the Allied cause. As the war progressed toward victory, the Wafdist tendency toward corruption, second thoughts on its involvement in the British humiliation of King Farouk, and a disastrous malarial epidemic in Upper Egypt created a situation in which it was possible for Farouk to dismiss Nahas Pasha. This he did in October 1944, at the very moment Nahas Pasha had brought to completion the agreement creating the League of Arab States.

Nationalist feeling became more and more inflamed during this period. The Wafd, once again in opposition, began to exploit this feeling, which had been intensified by inflation and the Wafd's own record of misgovernment. Nevertheless, the Egyptian government under Ahmad Maher Pasha declared war against the Axis in February 1945, with British acquiescence, in order to be able to participate in the peace settlements. Paradoxically, this act, which made Egypt an outright ally of Britain—the great opponent of Egyptian nationalist demands—was necessary in order to serve Egyptian nationalist interest in the international arena.

Egypt since 1945. In July 1952, a group of army officers with General Naguib as their nominal leader precipitated a coup d'état, marking the beginning of an Egyptian political and social revolution. King Farouk was forced to abdicate and to leave the country. Soon the monarchy itself was abolished and a republic proclaimed. Gamal Abdel Nasser, then a military officer, emerged as the strong man of the government. In 1956, he became President of the new republic under a constitution adopted and proclaimed the same year.

CHAPTER 3

Geography and Transportation

Geography

EGYPT, IN THE NORTHEASTERN EXTREMITY OF AFRICA, lies in the desert belt that stretches across the Northern Hemisphere from the Atlantic Ocean through Arabia and Iran to China, the main habitat of the Islamic peoples. Covering about 386,200 square miles and rectangular in shape, Egypt (from the Greek Aegyptus, called Misr by its inhabitants) is about the size of Texas and New Mexico together, and its desert areas bear many physical and climatic resemblances to the desert regions of those states.

Of the boundaries of Egypt only the coastal ones are natural, and one of these, the eastern (Red Sea), extends into a non-natural boundary across Sinai. The western frontier as it exists today was defined by an agreement with Italy in 1925. The southern limits were fixed under the Sudan Condominium Treaty of 1899. Thus the two land boundaries are the results of modern agreements and, because of the nature of the terrain through which they pass, are little more than political abstractions: they have no relation to ethnic divisions, and they are only vaguely understood and rarely observed by the nomadic herdsmen of the desert (the Bedouin), who cross and recross them in search of forage and water for their flocks. Much the same situation applies even to the eastern coastal boundary: the desert east of the Nile is inhabited by Bedouin and the coast by fishermen, all of whom have close kinsmen in Saudi Arabia, a hundred miles or more away across the Red Sea. Only at the northwestern frontier posts and at the river station and Sudan railhead at Wadi Halfa would a traveler be conscious of entering a different political entity.

The trans-Sinai boundary, demarcated in 1906, runs from the northern extremity of the Gulf of 'Aqaba to the Mediterranean near Rafa. The Gaza Strip, a 258-square-mile tongue of desert running along the Mediterranean northeastward from Rafa, was under Egyptian administration from the end of the Arab-Israeli war in 1948 until it was overrun by the Israelis in November 1956 and again in 1967. At the end of 1956, the status of this area was disputed. Formerly part of Britain's Palestine Mandate, and primarily Arab in settlement, the Gaza Strip is a political tinderbox, crowded as it is with many thousands of Arabs who fled their homes in Palestine when the war turned in Israel's favor in 1948.

The location of Egypt is such that the country would, under normal political conditions, be easily accessible by land from the northwest and northeast. To the northeast, the passage by road and rail across Sinai will remain blocked as long as the Arab-Israeli tension persists in its present overt and often violent form. A good graveled and black-top road enters Egypt from Israel near Gaza and swings south at Al-'Arîsh to join another all-weather highway which runs from Jerusalem through Beersheba to the Suez Canal at Ismailia and thence to Cairo. The railroad also carried heavy passenger and freight traffic from Egypt to Haifa, which is an important distribution center for points to the north and east.

Communication between Egypt and Libya is maintained to the northwest by a first-class coastal road, which can be followed as far west as Casablanca. Inland from this North African highway, however, there is no modern means of overland ingress to Egypt, and vast sand dunes, impassable even to desert-wise Bedouin, restrict entry in this direction to the tracks linking the western oases with the Nile Delta and Valley. The strategic Western Desert Railroad, which was put to good use by the Allies in World War II, has now been extended from its former railhead at Mersa Matrûh to Tobruk, where it meets the coastal highway.

The excellent harbors of Alexandria and Port Said give easy access to the country from the Mediterranean, while Cairo and the Delta may be reached from the east through Suez and Port Taufiq at the southern extremity of the Suez Canal, the vitally strategic waterway that opened in 1869 and converted Egypt's isthmus of Sinai from a barrier to a corridor through which maritime traffic could pass to India and the Far East. The Red Sea coast of Egypt offers very limited entry facilities, although the ports at Tor, Abu Zenima, Port Safaga, Hurghada, and Al-Quseir are used to take on cargoes of locally-mined manganese and phosphates. To the south, a desert road now connects Aswân with Wadi Halfa, bridging the gap which separates the Egyptian and Sudan railways.

Preliminary surveys have also been made for a railroad link. Access to Egypt by water from the south is hampered by the cataracts of the Nile, but the journey from Cairo to Khartoum can be accomplished by means of a river-railroad combination. With these exceptions, conditions similar to those of the western desert are found in the south.

In recent years, Cairo has developed into an important air crossroads. As was proven in World War II, the nature of the terrain favors the rapid construction of serviceable airfields. A great deal of passenger and freight traffic from Egypt to central and southern Africa now moves by air, while from the Cairo airport, served by the main Egyptian airline and most of the major international companies, it is easily possible to make direct connections with any part of the world.

Of primary strategic importance since the beginning of recorded history, Egypt has many times been able to develop and expand its boundaries by conquest. On the other hand, internal dissensions have more often weakened the political and military organization of the country to the point where it became the prey of ambitious and more powerful peoples who not only coveted Egypt's riches but sought also to place themselves in a dominant position in the Middle East by controlling the isthmus of Sinai.

Thus, during periods of political and military ascendancy, Egypt —which at various times ruled empires embracing what are now the Sudan, Israel, Jordan, Saudi Arabia, Syria, Lebanon, and part of Iraq—was from time to time in a position to introduce its culture into countries many hundreds of miles from the Nile Valley. Conversely, the recurrent invasions to which the country was subjected permitted the absorption of cultures other than Egyptian. Since the beginning of the Islamic era, however, the boundaries of Egypt have undergone little change. Although Egypt's troops occupied Syria and parts of Saudi Arabia and the Sudan in the nineteenth century, they did not remain long enough in these countries to consolidate any new boundaries, even had it been Egypt's intention to do so. The treaties of 1899 and 1925, delineating the Sudan and western boundaries, merely confirmed formally what had been tacitly assumed for many years.

Lack of education has limited the concepts of the fellah concerning the outer world. The Nile Delta is his universe; the physical limit of his interests coincides not only with the dividing line between desert and civilization but, in most cases, with his own

29

landmarks. To the fellah, the desert is an unknown and therefore hostile world, which must be given a wide berth. The true Bedouin, in turn, despises the fellah and all that the fellah stands for; the cultivated fringes of the desert are still subject to Bedouin depredations. Nevertheless, the Bedouin, like nomads everywhere, are coming by degrees to recognize the inevitability of sedentarization, and their assimilation by the cultivators has been a continuing process for many years.

The Egyptian intellectuals, the bourgeoisie, and to a lesser extent the city proletariat are more likely than the fellahin to have an appreciation of the size, boundaries, and strategic importance of their country. A potential source of trouble is the dissatisfaction, in recent years, of these articulate groups with the southern boundary and their deeply-felt conviction that the Sudan boundary, beyond which lie the sources of the water upon which Egypt is dependent for life, is arbitrary and that the Nile Valley is a natural unit. The basis for such feelings with regard to the western frontier is lacking, since the water factor, common to most boundary disputes in the arid Middle East, is not involved in that region. To the northeast, however, the Egyptians see not water but vital military and strategic interests at stake: should the boundaries of Israel at any future time be advanced—and remain—across Sinai, the Suez Canal would be endangered and a large proportion of Egypt's mineral and petroleum resources would be cut off.

Physical Characteristics

The Nile. Seen from the air, Egypt presents a striking resemblance to the standard colored map. A flight along the Nile Valley from Wadi Halfa to Cairo reveals one wide river flanked by narrow strips of green cultivation that end abruptly at the limit of irrigation and give way to drab brown desert, dotted with outcroppings of darker rock and patches of paler sand. The Nile is, in effect, Egypt, fertilizing and irrigating its soil, serving as an important means of internal communication, and opening a gate to Central Africa. From prehistoric times, the enduring efforts of Egyptians have been directed toward the fullest possible utilization of the waters of their rivers.

By the time the Nile reaches Egypt, its waters have been swollen from three main sources: the Atbara and the Blue Nile, originating in Ethiopia, and the White Nile, whose springs lie in the equatorial regions of British East Africa. The characteristic feature of the Nile is the seasonal flood between July and December, when an average rise of 24.6 feet is registered at Aswân and 14.8 feet at Cairo. The flood water is carried by the Blue Nile and the Atbara from the Ethiopian highlands; the waters of the White Nile, regulated by their passage through the Central African lakes and diminished by the enormous amount of evaporation over the Sudd (swamplands of the southern Sudan), flow much more evenly and in winter supply the bulk of the discharge.

One of the great natural features of the world, the Nile has played a prominent part in the early development of the human race. It affects all of Egypt, the Sudan, Uganda, much of Ethiopia, and parts of Ruanda-Urundi and the Congo republic. Flowing for 4,160 miles from its most remote source near Lake Tanganyika and watering a basin of more than a million square miles, the Nile influences in varying degrees the lives of the millions of people along its course. To it, Egypt owes its physical existence, for without the river the fertile valley would return to the desert which presses on either side. The entire area of Egypt is dependent on irrigation, and with the present irrigation system, Egypt's cultivable land provides two and sometimes three crops a year.

The Nile Valley. The Nile enters Egypt near Wadi Halfa, in the cataract region that stretches from Khartoum to Aswân. From Wadi Halfa to Aswân, a distance by river of just under 200 miles, the channel is a narrow groove through cliffs of sandstone and granite. Below Aswân, the cultivated strip widens to an average of 12 miles, and over the 200 miles south of Cairo the river tends to cling to the eastern bluffs, so that cultivation and the chief towns are confined mainly to the western bank, where there is a very gradual slope of several miles before the foot of the escarpment is reached.

The Delta. At Cairo, the Nile Valley spreads out to form a fertile delta, 155 miles wide at the base and about 100 miles from north to south. Once a broad estuary, the Nile Delta is now among the most intensively cultivated areas of the world, thanks to the rich deposits of silt brought down from Ethiopia in the past. Seven branches of the Nile used to run through the Delta; in the course of the centuries these have been controlled, and the river has now been diverted into two main streams—the Damietta and Rosetta branches—and a network of drainage and irrigation canals. In the north, near the coast, the Delta embraces a series of salt marshes and lakes, the high rate of evaporation from which produces periods of uncomfortably humid weather.

The deserts. The desert area of Egypt—over 96 per cent of the country's total land area—may be divided into three regions: the Libyan, or Western Desert, which extends from the west side of the Delta and the Nile Valley to the Libyan border; the Eastern, or Arabian Desert, from the Nile Valley and the Suez Canal to the Red Sea; and the Sinai Desert, which has a common frontier with Israel on the east and is separated from Egypt's Eastern Desert by the Red Sea and the Suez Canal.

South of the Delta, the deserts on either side of the river are very different in character. The Eastern Desert is rugged and mountainous and is much cut up by deep valleys (wadis), down which occasional heavy rains bring brief but deep torrents. Such rains are rare, however, and a wadi may remain dry for several years at a time. The desert cliffs, particularly those to the east, are in many places close to the river, and it is only between Asyût and Luxor that cultivation on the eastern bank covers any considerable area.

The Western Desert is not cut by wadis, and the occasional drainage lines do not bring down torrents like those that pour down the watercourses of the east. Lower and much more undulating than the Eastern Desert, the Western Desert is nevertheless sharply divided from the Valley at the limit of irrigation. It stretches away west of the Nile across Africa to the Atlantic Coast and is one of the most desolate regions in the world. Wells are few and far between, although a hundred miles or so to the west of the Nile Valley there is a chain of large depressions, the oases (Faiyûm, Baharîya, Farafra, Dakhla, Khârga, and Siwa)—now called the New Valley—in which water is near the surface and where there are villages and cultivation. Tracks, which hold their identity because of the gravelly nature of the desert, run from the Nile Valley to these oases.

The Sinai Desert, a triangular area with its base on the Mediterranean, is somewhat different in topography from the deserts bordering the Nile. Two-thirds plateau, with occasional peaks rising to 8,000 feet, Sinai has a heavier rainfall, and its desert character is relieved by numerous wells and oases which support centers of habitation and which formerly were focal points on trade routes.

32

Water draining toward the Mediterranean from the northern escarpment of the main plateau supplies sufficient moisture to permit a fair amount of agriculture in the coastal area, especially near Al-'Arìsh.

The cities. The chief cities of Egypt lie in the Nile Delta or in the main stream of the Nile above Cairo. Cairo, the largest city in Africa, not only is Egypt's administrative capital but also has the largest concentration of industrial and commercial enterprises. Alexandria, the second city, is the principal port, while the cities of Port Said and Suez, at the northern and southern extremities of the Suez Canal, have risen from small settlements to cities of over 100,000 population in 80 years. Egypt's concentrated water supply is responsible for the geographical location of its cities; away from water there is little or no settlement of any kind. With the industrial development of the Delta, new cities (Mahalla al-Kubra, Kafr al-Zaiyat) have sprung up; old ones (Tanta, Zagazig) have emerged from torpor. As in many other countries, the drift to the towns is quite marked.

Climate

The Egyptian climate is characterized by a two-season year, by long hours of blazing sunshine, and by a lack of rainfall. Climatically, the year falls into two parts: a cool winter from November to April and a hot summer from May to October. Spring and autumn, as experienced in more temperate lands, are unknown. There is almost no "bracing" period in the spring and fall, practically no trees shed their leaves in winter, and crops ripen in April and May as well as in July and August. Except for the variations in temperature, there is little difference between the seasons.

Extreme temperatures during both seasons are tempered by the prevailing northerly winds. In the coastal regions, temperatures range between a mean maximum of 99 degrees F. and a mean minimum of 57 degrees F. Wide daily variations of temperature occur in the inland desert areas—ranging from a mean annual maximum of 114 degrees F. during the hours of daylight to a mean minimum 42 degrees F. after sunset. During the winter season, the temperature in the open desert often drops to 32 degrees F., and even in the Delta and in the northern part of the Nile Valley, light frosts are not unknown. The mean annual temperature in

Egypt increases slightly from the Delta to the southern border and then remains steady as far south as Khartoum. Except, perhaps, for the summer humidity of the Delta, the only really unpleasant feature of Egypt's weather is the hot, sand-laden wind from the south (*khamsin*), which comes between March and May.

The third characteristic of Egypt's climate is lack of rainfall. As would be expected, most rain falls along the Mediterranean Coast, though even here the average annual precipitation is only eight inches. Inland, the amount falls off rapidly, until at Cairo it averages just over an inch a year. Beyond a line that could be drawn east-west through Cairo to Merowe in the northern Sudan, the precipitation is less than an inch. At Asyût, for example, the average annual rainfall is a fifth of an inch, and south of Asyût, years may pass without rain. At Merowe, however, which is on the northern fringe of the tropical rainbelt, rainfall rises to one inch. The rain in Egypt falls mostly in winter.

In the Delta, rain can create unpleasant conditions in the villages. Although paving is being increasingly introduced, the roads are still generally of packed earth. Excellent in dry weather, they become slippery after a little rain, making travel of all kinds difficult. As many roads lie along the banks of canals or drains, it is by no means uncommon for vehicles to skid into the water.

Transportation

Provided by nature with a flat terrain which offers few obstacles other than waterways to any form of transportation, Egypt possesses a network of railroads, roads, and waterways, comparable in extent in relation to area with those of many countries which in other respects have attained a higher level of economic development. The present road and rail networks have resulted from the enterprise of the British during their occupation of the country. In general, the British favored the construction of railways over roads.

Railroads. Most of the railway system is standard gage, and the bulk of it was state-owned prior to the nationalization of properties which began after 1952. Rail lines cover 7,300 kilometers, of which some 1,500 kilometers are narrow gage.

The country falls naturally into three transportation zones: Upper Egypt, the Delta, and Faiyûm. Upper Egypt is served by a double-track line which runs south to near Aswân, with an extension to the site of the High Dam. Normal traffic is increased by the shipment of chemical fertilizers and iron ores to the north. Lines run from Cairo to Suez, to Ismailia, and to Port Said on the Suez Canal, and to Damietta, Rosetta, and Alexandria on the Mediterranean Sea. Another line runs west from Alexandria to Mersa Matrûh, while the Faiyûm area is served by a main line and a network of narrow-gage lines. The weakness in the railway system is that not enough lines run from east to west across the Delta, due to the obstacles presented by countless canals and streams.

River navigation. Egypt's navigable waterways total about 3,340 kilometers and are divided almost equally between the Nile and its branches and an extensive series of canals, as well as about equally between Upper Egypt and Lower Egypt. The Nile is navigable from below Aswân to Cairo and thence to the sea along its Rosetta branch. Most of the canals are navigable throughout the year, although boats with heavy drafts may have difficulties in winter. Egyptian geography is such that railroads and waterways run parallel to each other, thus being brought into competition. In recent years, the river fleet of over 12,000 sailing craft and motorized barges has measurably increased its share of traffic. Winds favor sailing craft headed south on the Nile, while the current aids them going north. Major items of the Nile traffic include fuels, construction materials, agricultural products, and iron ore from Aswân.

Ports. Most of Egypt's external traffic is by sea. Alexandria is the country's busiest port, handling well over half the total volume of imports and exports, and the size of its two harbors makes it the largest port on the Mediterranean. In 1963, a vast maritime passenger terminal was opened there.

Port Said on the Suez Canal handles both foreign trade and transit trade. It is equipped with a shipyard and a very large floating drydock. Suez with its oil refineries is the point of departure for oil pipelines leading to Cairo, and is a transshipment port for ores mined in Sinai and along the Egyptian coast of the Red Sea.

The Suez Canal. The Suez Canal, a narrow valve about 100 miles in length through which passes most of the trade between Europe and Asia, gives Egypt a strategic importance in international economic relations that far exceeds any direct Egyptian contribution to the process of trade itself. No foreseeable shift of global trade routes or change in the pattern of world industry is likely to diminish greatly the ultimate economic, political, and military significance of the Egyptian land bridge between Africa and Asia and the water artery which cuts through it. The Suez Crisis, beginning in mid-1956, bore witness to this fact. Geographically a focal point of great power interests, Egypt has acquired a prestige which is related not to its own strength but to its capacity to jolt the balance of world power in serving as a kind of strategic fulcrum of forces outside itself.

When Egypt under the Pharaohs was the dominant power in the Mediterranean world, Egyptian canal builders connected the Nile cities with the Red Sea for trade in gold, ivory, spices, and other commodities from the eastern coast of Africa and the areas bordering the Persian Gulf. The first canals were cut from the port of Clysma (Suez) on the Red Sea to the Bitter Lakes and through the Land of Goshen to connect with the then easternmost branch of the Nile north of Bubastis (near present-day Zagazig). Later, a more direct canal was cut to the main body of the Nile at Babylon (Cairo). For many centuries, these waterways alternately filled up and were cleared for use. Their neglect was often deliberate, resulting from the fear that they would facilitate the approach of foreign invaders from the east.

With the rise of modern Europe and the growth of industry and seaborne commerce, men began to think again of canal building in Egypt, this time from the Mediterranean itself to the Red Sea. France took the initiative, and the Suez Canal was brought to completion in 1869 under the leadership of the French promoter Ferdinand de Lesseps. Numerous obstacles had to be overcome, only one of which was the widely-held conviction that the level of the Red Sea was more than 30 feet higher than that of the Mediterranean. More serious was the opposition of Britain, which, throughout the nineteenth century and into the twentieth, was in competition and frequently in conflict with France in the eastern Mediterranean. The British feared the alterations in the status quo that might be brought about by the Canal. They preferred the existing communications across Egypt and the Sinai Peninsula or a railroad transshipping line to a canal that would be subject to French or international influence. Only upon its completion did the British begin to recognize its vast strategic and economic importance to the growing Empire, an importance that has increased through the years, particularly from the strategic standpoint, to the point where the control of the Canal can literally affect the very survival of Britain and other great powers as they are presently organized. From the beginning, Britain has maintained its position as the largest user of the Suez Canal, for as the British Empire shrank, the activity of the Commonwealth, in which international commerce and trade are of vital importance, expanded.

In August 1949, the Compagnie Universelle du Canal Maritime de Suez concluded an agreement with the Egyptian government, setting forth new conditions of administration more favorable to Egypt, including a provision to enlarge the country's representation on the board of directors to 5 of its 27 members. However, the company continued to dominate the board of directors. Presumably, this agreement met Egyptian demands, but the regime that came to power in 1952 regarded anything less than complete control as a limitation of the country's sovereignty and independence.

On July 26, 1956, the government nationalized the Canal. The resulting crisis highlighted the magnitude of the international stake in the Canal, and the implications of the transfer of its control to a single nation. Any shutdown, for whatever reason, can immediately cause shortages and higher prices throughout the world.

In 1955, the Canal carried 14,666 vessels, with total cargoes of 115.8 million tons, and collected $93 million in transit dues. With a draft of 35 feet, it took oil tankers up to 30,000 tons. Following nationalization, the Suez Canal Authority was established to operate the Canal and the nine separate companies concerned with maritime supplies, communications, and shipyards. In the year ending June 30, 1966, the Canal handled 20,285 vessels, with a total cargo of 250 million tons for revenues of $197.3 million. Seventy-two per cent of these revenues came from petroleum in transit. Since 1956, about $230 million has been reinvested in improvements to the route and its services. The draft has been increased to 38 feet, so that the Canal can handle oil tankers of 60,000 tons.

Revenues may fail to increase should shippers decide to send supertankers—those of 200,000 tons and more in capacity—around Africa as being more economical than paying to continue sending smaller vessels through the Canal. To meet this challenge, the Suez Canal Authority has considered increasing the draft to 48 feet, as well as running a pipeline along the Canal so that oil can be transferred from tankers in the Red Sea to those in the Mediterranean. The financing of any such plan is a problem, however, since the Suez Canal Authority must turn over its hard currency earnings to the central treasury, and to obtain funds for improvements it must compete with other agencies of the government which are engaged in development programs.

In July 1958, the Egyptian government agreed to pay $81,221,000 to the former owners of the Canal. Egypt has recognized the validity of the Convention of Constantinople of 1888, which guarantees that ships of all nationalities may pass freely through the Canal, in peace and in war. However, Egypt bars Israeli ships, on the grounds that it is technically in a state of war with Israel.

Roads. About a fourth of the country's total road mileage of some 30,000 kilometers is paved. A program of road building has been given priority in recent years: among its results are the fine new highways joining Cairo and Alexandria and Cairo and Port Said. Egypt has manufactured passenger cars, trucks, and buses for several years, but production is low. In recent years between 2,000 and 5,500 passenger cars and about 1,000 trucks have been built annually. There may be as many as 100,000 motor vehicles in the country. The quantity of goods carried via road has risen rapidly during recent years. The motor bus has become an important institution in the countryside, particularly in the Delta. The fellahin are now avid bus riders, and on market days the buses are crammed with people, garden produce, eggs, and live (often uncrated) poultry.

Air. Misr Airworks began its operations in 1933 and had since then extended its services to the Middle East, Africa, and Europe. In 1960, the company was nationalized, and at the end of the year was merged with the Syrian airlines to form the United Arab Republic Airlines. Still later, the Egyptian Public Foundation for Air Transportation was established, with the U.A.R. Airlines Company and the Misr Airlines Company as its component parts. In March 1967, however, a new parent organization came into being —the United Arab Aviation—which included the United Arab Aviation Company, the Karnak Transportation and Traveler's Company, the Public Service Aviation Company, and the Egyptian Aviation Company.

The Cairo International Airport serves some 30 foreign airlines.

Its excellent facilities have enabled it to surpass Beirut as the major airport on the routes between Europe and the Middle and Far East. Airports for internal services are situated at Cairo, Alexandria, Port Said, Luxor, Mersa Matrûh, Aswân, Asyût, Minya, Embaba, and Tor. All the planes are run by Egyptian crews, who receive training at the Civil Aviation Training Center, adjacent to Cairo. The Cairo International Airport is operated by the Ministry of Military Production.

Animal transport. Egypt's few Bedouin continue to breed and deal in camels, but their living becomes more precarious as automobile transport replaces the traditional camel caravan. The old caravan routes, from the west and southwest through the oases to the Delta, bear less traffic each year as more desert trails are improved sufficiently to take motor traffic. The road and rail system that leads through Sinai to the countries of the northeast is well developed.

Of the few ways left to the camel caravan operator to be assured of a cargo, the most important is to take the risk of running contraband, usually in the form of narcotics or guns. In general, running contraband has harmed the traffic, since desert patrols have imprisoned for smuggling a good proportion of the decreasing number of people capable of training camels and organizing caravans.

The donkey is still used widely as a beast of burden in the Nile Delta and the Valley. Nearly every fellah possesses a donkey, which is used for carrying both produce and members of the family, though its employment as a carrier on market days is lessening as more and more buses link up the villages.

39

CHAPTER 4

Population and Ethnic Groups

Population

Size, density, and distribution. The census of 1965 gave the country's population as 30,083,419. In 1947, Egypt had 19,022,000 people, and in 1960, some 26,085,366. Official statements record an average annual increase in population of 2.7 per cent, up from the 2.4 per cent of recent years. This figure may be low, since births totaled 1,367,972 in 1964 and 1,334,260 in 1965.

A breakdown for the ethnic and religious communities as reflected in the 1965 census indicates that there were 2,807,500 Christians, 91,660 of the non-Egyptian minorities—Greeks, Syrians, Lebanese, Italians, Armenians, French, British—and 2,484 Jews.

The population, with the exception of some 78,000 nomads and a sedentary population of 350,000 in the frontier governorates, is concentrated within the 13,600 square miles of the Nile Valley and its delta. The population density of this settled area therefore averages about 2,200 persons to the square mile.

Egypt is divided into 21 governorates and 4 frontier governorates (as listed below with 1965 population figures).

Upper Egypt

Governorate	Capital	Population
Cairo	Cairo	4,196,998
Giza	Giza	1,645,224
Beni Suef	Beni Suef	924,008
Faiyûm	Faiyûm	930,961
Minya	Minya	1,702,969
Asyût	Asyût	1,416,955
Sohâg	Sohâg	1,684,576
Qena	Qena	1,469,769
Aswân	Aswân	521,777

Lower Egypt

Governorate	Capital	Population
Alexandria	Alexandria	1,800,951
Port Said	Port Said	282,826
Suez	Suez	264,025
Damietta	Damietta	432,401
Beheira	Damanhûr	1,976,891
Gharbîya	Tanta	1,892,874
Sharqîya	Zagazig	2,125,376
Daqahlîya	Mansûra	2,279,139
Minûfîya	Shibîn al-Kôm	1,467,600
Qalyubîya	Benha	1,210,703
Kafr al-Sheikh	Kafr al-Sheikh	1,121,677
Ismailia	Ismailia	344,449

Frontier Governorates

Al-Bahr al-Ahmar (Red Sea)	34,736
Mersa Matrûh	123,758
Al-Wadi al-Jadid (New Valley)	60,306
Sinai	132,782

The governorates of Cairo, Alexandria, and Giza are basically very large urban complexes. Some 15 other cities range in size from above 50,000 people to nearly 300,000.

Population projections based on the current estimated rate of increase of 2.7 per cent annually indicate that Egypt will have 35 million people in 1970, 45 million in 1980, and 52.5 million by 1985.

Birth and death rates. In the period 1917-46, the average crude birth rate was 42.4 per cent per thousand and the average crude death rate 27 per cent. By 1963, the crude death rate was down to 15.4 per cent, reflecting a longer life expectancy of approximately 16 years for males and 11.7 for females. At birth, the life expectancy of males was 51.6 years and of females 53.8 years. The mortality of infants under one year of age remains very high, but this figure is decreasing.

The high birth rate can be attributed to a variety of causes, outstanding among which are the poverty and ignorance of the Egyptian fellah, coupled with the value he places on a large number of offspring. The large-scale cotton cultivation, which for a century has dominated Egyptian agriculture, must also be reckoned as a

41

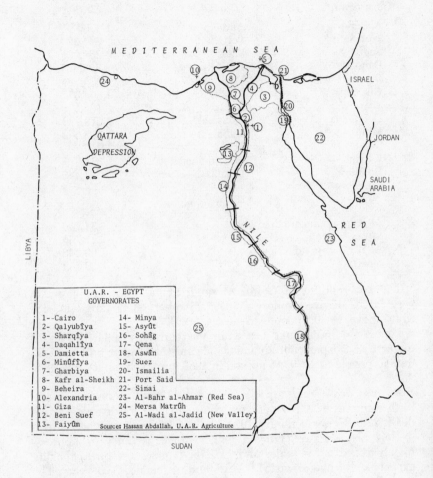

MEDITERRANEAN SEA

ISRAEL

JORDAN

SAUDI ARABIA

QATTARA DEPRESSION

LIBYA

NILE

RED SEA

SUDAN

U.A.R. - EGYPT	
GOVERNORATES	
1--Cairo	14- Minya
2- Qalyubîya	15- Asyût
3- Sharqîya	16- Sohâg
4- Daqahlîya	17- Qena
5- Damietta	18- Aswân
6- Minûfîya	19- Suez
7- Gharbiya	20- Ismailia
8- Kafr al-Sheikh	21- Port Said
9- Beheira	22- Sinai
10- Alexandria	23- Al-Bahr al-Ahmar (Red Sea)
11- Giza	24- Mersa Matrûh
12- Beni Suef	25- Al-Wadi al-Jadid (New Valley)
13- Faiyûm	

Source: Hassan Abdallah, U.A.R. Agriculture

primary contributing factor, since children are employed and are thus at an early age turned into sorely-needed contributors to the family income. Among the fellahin, the birth of a child each year during the wife's childbearing period is a normal event. One child in seven dies at birth, and disease, in spite of improved conditions, still takes a heavy toll of children under ten years of age.

Underlying these more obvious factors are the traditional disapproval of celibacy, the prestige of married women, and the security against divorce which children provide for their mothers. Nearly all women marry at least once, and the divorce rate is very high. The average family has 5.2 persons, with the rural figures 48 per cent higher, and the average age of the population is now 24.4 years, a figure which is becoming lower each year. The notion that polygamy is responsible for the elevated birth rate is suspect, since estimates suggest that polygamous households represent only 3 per cent of the total.

The population of the country is fairly evenly divided between the sexes; in 1965 males outnumbered females by 2 per cent.

Migration. There is practically no emigration from Egypt and very little immigration. After the departure from the U.A.R. of Syria, a Syrian official stated that the central government had made plans to settle 4 million Egyptian peasants in the sparsely settled Ghab and Al-Jazira regions of Syria.

Within the country, two main streams of migration are evident: from Upper Egypt to Lower Egypt, and from the agricultural areas to the towns. The facts that Upper Egypt has a greater population density than Lower Egypt and that the crop area per person is smaller provide an important economic inducement for migration from the south. In addition, statistics reveal that the average family income is considerably higher in Lower Egypt.

The men of Upper Egypt, who suffer much less than those of the north from debilitating endemic diseases, can often find work in enterprises for which the northerner is unfitted. Furthermore, the people of Lower Egypt seem to be more attached to the soil than those of the Nile Valley. Even so, migration to the Delta from the south has not yet equated density of population and resources. Although some provinces may be oversaturated—Giza, in the immediate vicinity of Cairo, for example—there is an actual shortage of labor in other Delta areas.

Of greater social significance is the migration to the cities of the

Delta, where industry is concentrated. Since 1937, the population of Cairo has risen from 1,312,000 to over 4 million in 1965, and that of Alexandria from 686,000 to about 1,800,000. The population of some of the other large cities also has increased at a rate greatly exceeding the average for the country as a whole, and Egypt's urban population is some 40 per cent of the total, with over half in Cairo and Alexandria. During World War II, the movement into the towns was given great impetus by the opportunities for employment provided by the Allied armies and was given another impetus in the recent decade by the construction of large industrial complexes.

Population trends. Egypt's population, which increases at a frightening rate each year, must be supported by a crop area which can be expanded only to a modest extent. Better farming, in particular the greatly increased yields through use of fertilizers and year-round irrigation, can produce more food for more mouths, but measures of birth control can radically lower the birth rate only after many years. In the meantime, the increasingly large proportion of children in the population places an added strain on the working segment. Egypt's present answer to the population pressure is, as will be demonstrated, forced industrialization of the country.

Ethnic Groups

Egypt lies at one of the great crossroads of human migration, and its history is part of the larger history of the peopling of the Near East and the Mediterranean basin. Out of Asia came populations whose passage through the Sinai Peninsula or across the Red Sea led them into the Nile Delta or into the valley trough farther south. From the desert on either side of the Nile, nomads were drawn to the water and the wealth of the great river. Ships from the northern shore of the Mediterranean brought still other peoples, whose objectives were sometimes to reach Egypt itself, sometimes to follow the trade routes to the east and south. Southward, Negro Africa pressed on Upper Egypt, and slaves and occasional invaders from this region introduced a Negroid element into the Valley.

These movements have affected the physical and cultural inheritance of the Egyptian people, but they have never submerged the basic Mediterranean white population and its way of life, which has been distinctively Egyptian since prehistoric times. The outcome of racial mixture and culture contact in Egypt has been not heterogeneity, but a remarkable uniformity, and the vast majority of Egyptians remain as Egyptians were when the pyramids were built, essentially a single people sharing a common ancestry and culture.

Differences do exist. Physically, skin color is lighter in the Delta than in the upper Nile Valley. Negroid characteristics are common in the region south of Aswân. The European and other foreign minorities are concentrated in the towns. Culturally, the settled existence of the fellah in his villages and fields along the Nile contrasts sharply with the nomadic pattern of the Bedouin of the Egyptian deserts. Both Moslems and Copts share a common Egyptian culture, but they are set apart by different religious faiths. Throughout Egypt, the life of the towns, with their complex social structure, foreign minorities, and Western influences, differs greatly from the traditional order of the countryside, where about 62 per cent of the population lives much as it did in Pharaonic times. None of these differences, however, overrides the larger identity which marks the inhabitants of the Nile Valley.

Geographically, Egypt's position as a crossroads between Asia and the Mediterranean basin has not meant that the country itself has been a thoroughfare. The Nile Delta, connecting with the Sinai Peninsula, forms an easy passageway between Asia and North Africa and is readily accessible by sea, but the cliff-rimmed Nile Valley to the south is a narrow pocket in a territory which in historic times has always been desert. Large-scale foreign population movements could take place along the coast without greatly affecting the Valley or even the southern part of the Delta. Culturally, the Egyptians early developed a self-contained society which was highly resistant to the effects of alien intrusions, even though the country was almost continuously under alien rule from the Persian conquest in 525 B.C. to the present century. Egypt's conquerors came not to settle the country but to control and exploit it, and they concentrated in the cities, where they governed without mingling with the mass of the population or much altering its basic way of life.

The significant distinctions among the Egyptian people, then, are not ethnic in the sense of any marked divisions along racial lines. The bulk of the population, with some Negroid admixture in the southern part of the Nile Valley, are of the same brunet-white physical type that is found from northern India to Gibraltar and on both sides of the Mediterranean. Culturally, the members of the great peasant majority—Moslem or Copt—share a single way of life, rooted in their common Egyptian heritage. There is no clear-cut color bias in Egypt, and Egyptians generally are quick to resent any evidence of it in Western countries. Various observers have remarked, nevertheless, that wealth and position being equal, the person without Negroid characteristics enjoys social advantages in Egypt over one who has such traits.

Physical Types

The portraits painted in the time of the early Pharaohs might well be those of modern Egyptians, and the type is best preserved in the peasantry. Rather heavily built, the fellah is of moderate stature —usually not more than five-feet-five. His head is characteristically long and narrow, his face broad, with strong jaws, prominent chin, full lips, and straight or concave nose of medium height and breadth. Skin color is basically brunet-white, but may shade to medium or dark brown in southern Egypt. His hair, which may be straight or wavy but not often curly, is almost always black.

There are, of course, variations in this rural population. The Moslem fellahin are generally somewhat darker skinned than the Copts, who, having tended to marry only within their own group, remain closer to the physical type of Pharaonic and early Christian Egypt. In general, the inhabitants of the Delta are somewhat shorter in stature than those of the Nile Valley to the south, and the latter, being less debilitated by disease and inadequate diet than the Delta dwellers, seem to be more robust.

Much wider variations may be seen in the cities. Successive waves of foreigners have entered Egypt—from the Persians in the sixth century B.C. to the Europeans of modern times. The Arabs converted Egypt to Islam; various groups of Turks ruled the country; and Circassians and Negro Africans were introduced at various times. All these immigrants have gradually mingled in the towns, producing a wide range of physical types.

Egypt's few remaining Bedouin, who move their flocks in search of pasture in the deserts on either side of the Nile Valley, contrast with the fellahin in their taller stature and more slender physique. Now reduced in number to around 78,000, they are gradually being absorbed by the sedentary population of the cultivated area. Evidences of Arab and Negro admixtures are to be found in the oases, particularly at Khârga, where for hundreds of years Arab slave traders paused with their caravans of Negro slaves on the way to Egypt and the countries of the Arab world. The aboriginal population of the Egyptian oases resembled closely the fellahin type, but today a fair proportion of the population shows Negro traits.

The Nubians of Upper Egypt, who are concentrated for the most part in the area to the south of Aswân and who supply much of the domestic labor for the cities of the Delta, are generally darker and taller than either the fellahin or the townsmen. Taking their name from the Nobatae, a Negro group which entered the region in Roman times, the present-day Nubians are a mixture of this stock with the indigenous fellahin.

The remaining ethnic groups—all newcomers except for the Jews —have remained self-contained, and intermarriage with indigenous Egyptians is extremely rare.

The Moslem Majority

The fellahin. Over 20 million Egyptians are fellahin, or field workers, whose unremitting toil—and that of their ancestors over thousands of years—has brought scant material reward. The townsman regards the fellah as a dull, cloddish yokel, and the term "fellah" has long been employed as an uncomplimentary epithet. Today, the efforts of Egypt's military regime to construct the foundations of mass support are giving at least a nominal prestige to the fellah's estate. In the fields, the fellah usually wears a high-domed skull cap of a feltlike material and a long *galabia* (tunic), unbleached or dark blue, which is never replaced until it literally falls to pieces. The only variety introduced into the drab, hard-working life of the fellah is an occasional visit to the nearest market or the celebration of a family wedding or circumcision, which are occasions for the wearing of holiday finery. When dressed in his best clothes, the fellah wears a loose undershirt and voluminous cotton drawers, held around his waist with a cord. Over the shirt he puts on a gay striped waistcoat that has numerous small buttons, and he adds a galabia with an open front to show off the waistcoat. This galabia is of much finer material than the one for everyday wear, and it must usually last a lifetime. Bright yellow, heelless slippers are often worn.

Peasant women wear long wide drawers, a long chemise, and a

47

shapeless black cotton dress (which among the more prosperous may be of finer material) with long sleeves and a flounce that trails behind on the ground. Outdoors it is customary to wear a black headdress, similar to a nun's veil, which can be pulled over the face. Fellahin women are not habitually veiled, although they sometimes wear a coarse lace veil, to which a metal bobbin is attached to hide the shape of the nose. Common ornaments are coin and bead necklaces and earrings, silver, gold, or glass bracelets, and anklets of copper or silver. Kohl (antimony powder) is applied to the eyelids, and henna to hands, fingernails, feet, and hair.

The Moslem townsman. Ethnically, the Moslem townsman can be an indigenous Egyptian, a Moslem immigrant from one of the other Islamic countries, or a blend of these two. It is in the towns that the Egyptian population shows its greatest physical and cultural diversity. Most of the townsmen are conscientious Moslems, but a growing number are drifting away from religious belief and practice.

Today the great majority of middle- and upper-class males wear European-style clothing. The galabia is almost never worn by members of these groups, and the tall tarboosh, or fez, which used to be the distinguishing mark of the Egyptian, is fast disappearing. The wives and daughters of upper- and middle-class Egyptians also have adopted Western clothes and frequently go out in public unveiled.

The galabia, when seen in the town, indicates either that its wearer is either from the lower or lower-middle class or else that he is a traditionalist; in the latter case he is quite probably a Moslem dignitary, for whom a galabia of rich material, a silk sash, and a turbaned tarboosh are standard garb. Even among religious leaders, however, Western dress is becoming more common.

Indigenous Minorities

Egypt's principal indigenous minorities are the Copts, Bedouin, and Nubians. Syrians, Lebanese, and other Moslem inhabitants of Egypt, although technically alien, are thought of as indigenous because of their religion, as are Arabic-speaking Christians.

The Copts. Egypt's population is comprised of two major religious groups, Copts (Egyptian Christians) and Moslems. One of the first countries to adopt Christianity, Egypt prior to the Arab invasion of the seventh century was almost entirely Christian. The Arabs brought Islam in a swift conquest; Christianity, however, was not obliterated, and the Egyptian Christian Church today has about 2,500,000 adherents.

One result of this religious division was that the thoroughly indigenous Copts were put in the position of an ethnic minority. The Copts assert that they are the only "true" Egyptians, basing their claim on their traditional reluctance to marry out of their own group and contrasting this reluctance with the relative readiness with which Moslems of the various peoples represented in Egypt have intermarried.

Physically, there is little to distinguish between the Copts and their Moslem countrymen. Differences in dress or way of life are not noticeable. In the cities, the Copts have traditionally been white-collar workers in business and government; few of them are found engaged in manual labor. Although Moslem and Coptic villagers seem to have no antipathy to one another, in the cities there is a certain degree of tension, which has at times flared into overt hostility.

The Bedouin. The Bedouin of Egypt, now numbering only about 78,000, are closely related to the tribes of the Arabian Peninsula through more or less remote Arab ancestors who wandered into Egypt at various times over the centuries. Economic necessity is gradually forcing the Bedouin out of the desert and into the Valley and the Delta, and there is no doubt that their assimilation is only a matter of time.

Today the Bedouin in Egypt can be divided into four categories: pure nomads, partial nomads, partially assimilated, and completely assimilated. The pure nomads wander in Sinai and in the lands immediately west of the Suez Canal, as well as in the Western Desert. Many of them have relatives in the cultivated areas, whom they visit from time to time, and a certain number prolong their visits until they become sedentarized. The partial nomads occupy parts of Sinai and the coastal strip west of the Nile, where they engage in sporadic agriculture. The partially assimilated Bedouin occupy the agricultural zone immediately adjoining the desert, where they live a settled existence but still engage in some herding. They trade with, and occasionally steal from, the purely agricultural fellahin, and in the course of time they begin to intermarry

with them. The completely assimilated Bedouin have usually penetrated farther into the settled area, where they have become farmers
almost as dedicated as the fellahin. Under these conditions of life,
it is increasingly difficult to distinguish the former nomads from
their fellahin neighbors. Assimilation was for a time slowed by a
law which, in exempting all Bedouin, settled or nomadic, from
military service, encouraged members of this group to preserve
their minority identity. With the modification of the law to apply
only to pure nomads, it has become unusual to find any group in
the central Delta region claiming Bedouin descent.

The Nubians. South of the dam and railhead at Aswân and beyond
into the northern Sudan live the dark-skinned Nubians. Before the
Aswân Dam was started, many of these people farmed in the narrow upper reaches of the Nile Valley, but when construction was
begun, much of this farming area was inundated and large numbers of Nubians were obliged to seek their livelihood by other
means. Many have gone into domestic service in the Egyptian cities,
and in that capacity they are likely to impress the newcomer to
Egypt as being more numerous than they actually are. Their reputation for intelligence, cleanliness, and honesty makes them much
sought after as cooks, waiters, doorkeepers, and household servants.

Few Nubians come to Lower Egypt as permanent residents. They
usually leave their families at home, where they return for vacations and where they settle down when they have saved enough
to retire. They do not mingle with the Egyptians, and they live
either on the premises of their employers or in small colonies in the
working-class districts. Regarding themselves as superior to Egyptians, they tend to be highly critical of things "Egyptian" and particularly of Egyptian politics. The Egyptians, on their part, affect
a superiority to the Nubians.

Foreign Minorities

Egypt's small foreign minorities have until recently had an importance out of proportion to their size. Some of them, such as the
British and French, had behind them the prestige and authority of
great Western powers, and as a group they dominated the economic and cultural life of the country.

Meaningful statistics on minority groups are difficult to obtain,
since some members of such groups are stateless, while others hold
Egyptian nationality and are not listed in the census as members

of minorities. The last official statistics on minority groups were issued after the census of 1965 and showed a great decline from the numbers recorded in 1937. Approximately 55,000 Jews (of a former 63,000) had left the country, as had large numbers of French and British nationals and of Maltese and Cypriots holding British nationality.

Muhammad Ali was the first Egyptian ruler to encourage minorities to come to Egypt. His policy was followed by his successors, and the British, when they assumed control in 1882, continued to make it easy for foreigners to enter the country. Important factors in bringing foreigners to Egypt in those years were the privileges they enjoyed under the Capitulations. These bound the Egyptian government to exempt foreign nationals from the jurisdiction of its criminal courts and from all but very limited taxation and guaranteed them broad rights to conduct commerce freely in Egypt. The minority groups, who as merchants or industrialists usually brought money with them, moved automatically into middle- and upper-class positions in the cities. Except for certain Coptic elements, they effectively monopolized the most desirable positions in business and government until quite recently. Virtually no members of the foreign minorities were peasant farmers.

The Greeks, the largest of the foreign minorities, were heavily concentrated in Alexandria, where they played a prominent part in the import-export business and the cotton trade. Many of the Greeks in Alexandria and Cairo were extremely wealthy, and a great number of less prosperous Greeks were to be found scattered throughout Egypt doing business as small grocers, moneylenders, restaurant operators, and merchants. The Italians, the second largest minority, were largely engaged in business; they dominated the building industry as contractors, architects, builders, and supervisors.

The Jews of Egypt ranged from the very rich to the moderately poor. The richer ones were primarily engaged in banking and higher finance, and a good proportion of present-day Egyptian industrial development has been financed by Jewish investment. Some Jewish families lived in Egypt for hundreds of years, and until the political crises of the past several years were considered almost an indigenous minority. Those who arrived in Egypt following World War I were less favorably regarded, not only by the authorities but by some of their coreligionists who had been longer established in the country.

51

Those Armenians who did not accept Soviet Armenia as a home-land were accepted as permanent residents by the Egyptians, probably more than any other minority group.

Present Trends

The future of most of Egypt's foreign minorities is anything but secure. Moslem Egyptians and members of the various minorities admit privately that the foreigner will eventually have no place in Egypt, despite government assurances to the contrary. The foreign minorities are not likely to become Egyptians, with so many of whom they have only geographical residence in common. Few, if any, feel a strong loyalty to Egypt, and culturally and politically they look elsewhere. Many members of these groups have been educated in European schools in Egypt or abroad; French is their common language, and only a very few of them have bothered to learn to read and write Arabic—until recent legislation made it necessary to do so.

The Egyptians are well aware of the special position long enjoyed by the foreign minorities, and the growing Egyptian middle class is finding a response to its demands that the government make the jobs once monopolized by the minority peoples available to native-born Egyptians. Not yet able to compete with the minorities in terms of qualifications, the Egyptian majority is gradually replacing them in favored occupations through direct and indirect discrimination. The Jewish community, in spite of its size and former prestige, has practically disappeared. The British and French, unpopular with the Egyptians for many years, were largely ousted after the Suez Canal hostilities in late 1956.

The growth of Egyptian and Arab nationalism is slowly altering the complex pattern of kin and local loyalties which traditionally have fragmented the area. Within this pattern there could hardly be said to be a national "majority" group; rather there is a mosaic of villages and kin groups that have had to learn to live side by side despite differences of religion or ethnic origin. As nationalism and national patriotism take root, however, a national majority has begun to come into being, and there is steadily mounting pressure on the minorities either to conform or to disappear.

CHAPTER 5

Languages

The National Language

ARABIC, INTRODUCED BY THE ARAB CONQUEST IN 640 A.D., is the official language of Egypt and the native tongue of 98 per cent of the population. Spoken in various dialects from Morocco in the west to Iraq and Saudi Arabia in the east, as well as by most of the population of the Sudan and by scattered minorities elsewhere, Arabic is a Semitic language related to Hebrew, Phoenician, Syriac, Aramaic, various Ethiopian languages, and the Akkadian of ancient Babylonia and Assyria. More distantly, this Semitic group of languages is related to Berber and ancient Egyptian. Coptic, the descendant of ancient Egyptian, probably ceased to be a spoken language as early as the sixteenth century; it survives only in books and in the liturgy of the Coptic Church.

Indigenous Minority Languages

Besides Arabic, three indigenous languages are spoken in Egypt—Berber, Beja, and Nubian. Siwa Oasis, near the Libyan border in the Western Desert, has a population of about 5,000, most of whom speak Berber. The men of Siwa are bilingual in their native Berber and in the official Arabic, but most of the women, traditionally excluded from public activity, speak only Berber. Culturally and economically of minor importance in Egypt, the Berber of Siwa is of interest in that it represents the extreme eastern outpost of the Berber branch of the family of Hamito-Semitic languages. Berber is historically related to ancient Egyptian.

Along the Sudanese border from the Red Sea to the Nile lives a nomadic Beja minority of around 10,000 people. (The total population of the Beja tribes is around 100,000, but most of them live in Sudan.) The Beja do not write their own language, and the

53

knowledge of Arabic as a second language among them is not widespread. None of the women know Arabic, and the men seldom speak it fluently.

The Nubian dialect area extends from Aswân in Egypt to just north of Khartoum in the Sudan, but Nubians are found in every Egyptian town of any size. All of these Nubian emigrants also speak Arabic and are Arabized culturally. The use of Nubian as a written language is forbidden by Egyptian law, and all schooling is done in Arabic. As in Siwa, the men learn Arabic, but most of the women speak only Nubian. The total number of Nubian speakers, both Egyptian and Sudanese, is about a million, and the number in Egypt is between 150,000 and 200,000.

Historically, Nubian holds something of an endurance record for minority languages. As early as 1500 B.C., lower Nubia was brought under control by the Pharaohs and Egyptianized. Today, 3,500 years later, Nubian shows no more signs of being displaced by Arabic than it was by ancient Egyptian.

Arabic

Arabic exists everywhere in two different forms—classical and colloquial. Classical Arabic is relatively uniform throughout the Arab world, while the colloquial form differs from area to area, and many of its dialects—Egyptian and Moroccan, for example—are mutually unintelligible. All dialects of colloquial Arabic are as different from classical Arabic as Italian is from Latin. Colloquial Arabic is commonly looked upon as "very difficult" for foreigners, and classical Arabic as "very difficult" for foreigners and native speakers alike.

Phonetically, Arabic is rich in consonants, including a number that are formed in the larynx and at the back of the mouth. Structurally, Arabic is characterized by a grammar which to speakers of Indo-European languages seems highly complicated and by a vocabulary in which the majority of words represent variations on roots composed of three consonants. Thus KTB is a root having to do with "writing"; *KaTaB* is "he wrote"; *KaTTaB*, "he dictated"; *KāTaB*, "he corresponded with"; "*KāTiB*, "a writer"; *KiTāBa*, "writing"; and *KiTāB*, "a book." The colloquial differs from the classical language in various ways, notably in vocabulary and in the elimination of such classical features as the use of inflectional endings on nouns and verbs.

Spoken and written usage. Certain social circumstances call for the use of classical Arabic, and others call for the colloquial form. In general, however, colloquial Arabic is spoken and rarely written, while classical is usually written and rarely spoken. The chief use of classical Arabic is for writing of all sorts. Books, pedagogical materials, periodicals, street signs, personal letters (to a certain extent), train tickets, movie subtitles, and official records, etc. are written in classical. Arabic has its own alphabet of 28 characters. The writing runs from right to left. Usually only the consonants are written; there are special diacritical signs to represent the vowels, but they are used only in editions of the Qur'an, poetry, and books for children.

The difference between classical and colloquial Arabic adds to the difficulties of education. In learning to read and write classical Arabic, an Egyptian schoolchild must learn not only a complex set of visual and motor skills but what is in many respects a foreign language. Few students ever learn written classical Arabic thoroughly or achieve accuracy or fluency in it.

The circumstances in which classical Arabic is spoken are limited. Its widest use is in radio broadcasts, where all programs—with certain exceptions such as comedies, soap operas, and impromptu interviews—are in classical Arabic. Public speeches, some university lectures, and other formal occasions call for the classical form. The Egyptian parliament has also been conducted in classical Arabic. Mosque sermons are usually delivered in classical Arabic, but the colloquial is heard in the smaller mosques, where the imam (prayer leader) often has little classical learning. At the universities, lectures are increasingly given in colloquial, especially in the sciences, while classical Arabic is more and more confined to *belles lettres.* President Abdel Nasser, in announcing the nationalization of the Suez Canal in July 1956, delivered a precedent-shattering, three-hour speech in almost pure colloquial. Even where classical is exclusively used, as in news broadcasts, it is of variable quality and usually shows much colloquial influence. Probably the only people in the world capable of speaking grammatically correct classical Arabic are a handful of Moslem Qur'anic scholars and literary men and a few foreign Arabists.

The classical ideal. Popular opinions about classical Arabic are contradicted by actual behavior and trends in the Arabic-speaking world. Most Egyptians (and other Arabs as well) declare that it would be good if the colloquial should cease to exist and all Arabs everywhere should use only classical for both speaking and writing. But no serious effort is being made anywhere to realize this ideal, and parents continue to speak colloquial to their children. An often-expressed hope is that mass media of communication, such as radio and television, will help spread the knowledge and use of classical. That this will happen is doubtful, however, although such media may well lead to the introduction of more and more classical words and phrases into the colloquial vocabulary. Colloquial Arabic is looked upon not as a separate entity but as a corruption of classical Arabic. Classical Arabic is "correct," colloquial Arabic is "incorrect," and anyone who openly favors colloquial over classical is considered at best an eccentric and at worst a traitor who would destroy the unity of the Arab world.

The prestige accorded classical Arabic is in part due to its religious significance. Moslems believe that the Qur'an is God's word in form as well as substance. The words of the Qur'an are believed to be—with differences as to detail among the various sects—the very words that God spoke, recorded exactly as He spoke them. Since there are other languages God could have chosen if He had wished, there is obviously something special about the language God did choose. The Qur'an represents, therefore, an a priori standard of perfection, and deviation from it can only be for the worse. Revered for its association with the divine, classical Arabic is also admired as the pinnacle of linguistic beauty.

There is an indigenous tradition of philology among the Arabs, and there is an Arabic Academy in Cairo. Attention, however, is devoted exclusively to the classical language; the methods of study are traditional and do not reflect scientific linguistic technique. Grammar and composition are emphasized, and calligraphy is considered an important art form. Classical and colloquial proverbs, religious quotations of various sorts, and slogans are popular literary devices, and the ability to quote them appropriately on various occasions is a social asset.

Colloquial Arabic. Colloquial Egyptian Arabic is spoken in various mutually intelligible dialects. The chief dialectal division is between Upper and Lower Egypt, with the border line running just south of Cairo at the base of the Delta. There are local variations within these major dialect areas. There is also a difference between the urban and rural dialects. The most noticeable dialectal difference (and the one always cited by both Egyptian and foreign laymen) between the urban and rural dialects affects two sounds: the classical "j" (as in joy) of classical Arabic is pronounced "g" (as in go) in urban centers; the classical "q" becomes a glottal stop (as in the so-called "Brooklynese" pronunciation of "t" in bottle) in the urban dialect, but is pronounced "g" (as in go) in the rural areas.

Despite the blanket criticism of colloquial as "incorrect" vis-à-vis classical, the urban dialect of the Delta has more prestige than the dialects of Upper Egypt and the rural portion of the Delta. Speakers of the latter dialects give evidence of accepting the social superiority of the urban Delta dialect even while verbally denying it. To date, almost all studies of colloquial Egyptian Arabic have been confined to the urban dialect of Lower Egypt. Very little is known in a technical sense of the dialects of Upper Egypt and the rural Delta region.

Colloquial Arabic is the exclusive language of conversation. No matter how serious or formal the occasion, in any situation where people speak back and forth, actively communicating with one another, colloquial Arabic is used. Even court proceedings, unlike addresses in parliament, are in colloquial Arabic, although court records are of course written in classical Arabic. The circumstances where colloquial instead of classical is written are few, but increasing. One use of written colloquial is for humor: cartoon captions are in colloquial, and so are printed jokes. A fair amount of colloquial poetry appears in newspapers and periodicals, and from time to time an editorial appears in the colloquial. These examples of colloquial journalism, however, are probably too occasional to be interpreted as a general trend.

Colloquial Arabic is popularly disparaged. English-speaking Egyptians refer to it as "slang," and the term "Arabic," unless explicitly qualified otherwise, means classical Arabic. Such a question as "How do you say such-and-such in Arabic?" will usually elicit the classical form unless colloquial has been specified. This same use of the term "Arabic" is found among the foreign minorities. A cultured Italian-Egyptian or Greek-Egyptian is likely to say, "I don't know Arabic" or "I don't know Arabic very well." Such people usually speak fluent colloquial Arabic and are merely confessing their lack of competence in classical Arabic.

A common derogation of colloquial Arabic is that "it has no rules," and that "one may speak as one wishes." These statements represent misconceptions, for colloquial Arabic has as definite a grammatical pattern as any language. The misconception arises from several sources. There is the usual feeling of freedom and lack of restraint, born of familiarity, which one feels in speaking one's native language. The Egyptian never studies his native colloquial speech, and in studying classical Arabic, he observes that the colloquial contradicts many of the classical "rules." These deviations of colloquial from classical are stigmatized as errors by the teacher, not as a difference of structure in two different varieties of speech. Colloquial Arabic is considered unworthy of scholarly observation and study by all but foreign linguists and a few Westernized Egyptians.

Social uses of Arabic: names and naming. Arabic names are different in pattern from Western names in that almost all names have palpable linguistic meaning. In the West, only the scholar knows that Dorothy means "gift of God" and that Richard means "rich man," but Arabic speakers all know that the name Atiya means "gift of God" and Hamid means "praising God." An aspect of this meaning content of names is that some names are clearly Moslem, some early Christian, and some may be common to both. Many Christian names are similar to Western names and derive from a common Greek origin. A common pattern for Moslem names is Abdul- "slave of the-" followed by an epithet of God: thus, Abdul-Karim, "slave of the Generous One," Abdul-Latif, "slave of the Gracious One," and so on.

Formerly, family names in the Western sense were not used in Egypt, although given names did take account of genealogy. Today, family names are employed, but telephone directory listings in the cities are alphabetical by first instead of last names. Nicknames usually reduplicate some phonetic components of the actual name, although a totally unrelated name may be used (e.g. Wahid, nickname Wahwah; Mahmud, nickname Abu-Hanafi, etc.). Formerly, many members of the aristocracy had French-sounding nicknames (e.g. Fifi, Mimi). Much more so than in the West, the use of nicknames is restricted to intimate friends and family; they are never used publicly.

Politeness formulas. The politeness formulas, which strike the Westerner as unnecessarily tedious and time-consuming, are prominent features of both classical and colloquial Arabic usage. Many of these formulas are bound up with the Moslem religion and are, consequently, not used by Christians. A student learning a greeting or some other politeness formula would do well also to learn its social significance and to accept these formulas without becoming impatient with or irritated by them.

Foreign Minority Languages

Of the languages spoken by foreign minorities in Egypt, Greek is the most important numerically, followed by Italian and Armenian. There were formerly sizable British and French colonies in Egypt, but British actions in the Suez Canal Zone in the winter of 1951-52 led to the dismissal of British teachers of English throughout Egypt. The military activities in the Canal Zone in late 1956 led to a further expulsion of British and French nationals, and within a few months the number of native speakers of these two languages remaining in Egypt could hardly have been more than a few thousand.

The foreign minorities are (and were) concentrated in the cities, mostly in Cairo and Alexandria. Small groups of speakers of other languages are found in the urban centers. German (there is a German school in Cairo) and, more recently, Russian and Czech are heard, and numerous Middle Eastern and African languages are represented in the student body of the great Moslem university at Cairo, whose members come from an area reaching from Morocco to Indonesia.

Despite the restrictions it has placed on the indigenous minority languages, Egypt until recently has always respected the cultural and linguistic autonomy of its foreign minorities. The Armenian, Greek, Italian, and Jewish communities have long had their own schools, newspapers, and books. One of the best Armenian-English dictionaries is published, printed, and bound in Cairo. Radio Cairo's home service has broadcasts in the languages of these communities. However, outside of their own ethnic communities, these minority languages have had little cultural influence in Egypt.

French and English

The status of French and English has been different from that of the other minority languages. Widely learned as second languages both by Arabic-speaking native Egyptians and the foreign minorities, French and English stand high in the hierarchy of second-language learning. Native speakers of French and English rarely bother to learn any other language, even Arabic, and native speakers of Arabic scarcely ever learn any second language except French or English. The foreign minorities rarely learn each other's languages, but almost all of them know Arabic, and most learn either French or English, or both. Families, both native Egyptian and foreign, who send their children to French or English schools usually have the girls learn French and the boys English. Most speakers of minority languages in Egypt are literate, but a fair number of humble people—such as guides and servants—speak French and English without being able to read or write them. All British and French schools were nationalized in November 1956, but the status of the French and English languages will not soon be supplanted.

For many years, French was almost the exclusive language of business and society, and it was a medium of instruction at the universities. Even today, a person knowing only English is hampered in shopping in department stores, pharmacies, etc.; whereas a French speaker would have much less difficulty. Most of the non-Arabic home broadcasts on Radio Cairo are in French, and there are more newspapers in French than in any language other than Arabic. English-language films are provided with subtitles in both French and Arabic, but French films have only Arabic subtitles. Arabic films, if they have subtitles at all, have them in French, not English. Other foreign films have subtitles in Arabic and French and often in Greek, but not in English. The language of the Cairo and Alexandria stock exchanges was also French until the crisis of 1956, when it was abruptly replaced by Arabic.

The ascendancy of French as the chief foreign language had its beginnings with the French occupation of the country between 1798 and 1801. Muhammad Ali, the vigorous ruler of Egypt after the departure of Napoleon, was impressed with European power and resolved to remake the country in the image of Europe. Europe he knew through the medium of France, and it was to France that he turned for knowledge and inspiration. Large numbers of Egyptian students were sent to France, and French instructors were brought to Egypt. The Gallicizing of the Egyptian upper classes proceeded without competition from any other European source until the British occupation in 1882.

The pre-eminence of French as a bridge to European civilization was shaken by the British occupation. In government and in scientific and technical fields, English as a second language has no serious rival in Egypt today. French has prestige as a cultural heritage more than as an active force. The fact that there were slightly more speakers of French than English a few years ago was due to the popularity of French among the Greek and Italian minorities, but with the departure from Egypt of great numbers of the minorities, English is probably known by slightly more people today. Among native-born, Arabic-speaking Egyptians, English is more widely known than French. English is compulsory in Egyptian public schools, and the number of Egyptian students who are studying French is only a small fraction of those studying English. In the case of students holding government scholarships to study abroad, the proportion in favor of English has been overwhelming. The trend today, however, reflects Egyptian hostility to Britain, and students who would normally have been sent to Britain or France are now going to the United States, the Soviet bloc, and West Germany. Until recently, many teachers in Egyptian universities, especially in technical subjects, were British and lectured in English. They have now been largely replaced by Egyptians—usually British- or American-trained—who lecture in Arabic. Scientific textbooks of all sorts (medicine, engineering, agriculture, etc.) and research materials are still mostly in English, and the debate still goes on as to whether medicine and the sciences should be taught at the university level in English or in Arabic.

CHAPTER **6**

Religion

SOME 95 PER CENT OF THE PEOPLE OF EGYPT ARE MOSLEMS. The religious minorities comprise the Coptic Christians (2,500,000), comparatively small numbers of Latin Catholics and other Catholics in communion with Rome, members of various Orthodox bodies, a few Protestants, and a Jewish colony which once numbered over 60,000 but which has been greatly depleted as a result of recent political developments.

Islam and Its Tenets

Islam (the term means "submission" in Arabic) is the religion preached by the Prophet Muhammad, born in Mecca, Arabia, in 570 A.D. According to tradition, when Muhammad was about 40, he received a call from God, while engaged in solitary contemplation at the mountain of Hira. The calls continued, and Muhammad's preaching in Mecca against prevailing practices and beliefs earned the hostility of important personalities, who forced him to flee to Medina with his closest followers. This flight (*hijra*) in 622 marks the first year of the Moslem calendar. Having put down the civil strife he found in Medina, Muhammad was able to repel the attacks of the Meccans and ultimately to bring the entire Arabian subcontinent under his control. Mecca became the holy city, and its principal shrine, the Kaaba (a former pagan shrine with a black stone set in its east wall) became the central point of the annual Moslem pilgrimage to Mecca.

In the theocratic order established by Muhammad, he himself became judge, lawgiver, and social arbiter. He laid down the principles later incorporated in the Qur'an, the holy book of Islam, and the principles set forth in the Sunna, the supplementary body of tradition of Islam.

After the death of Muhammad in 632, the countries of the Near East succumbed in rapid succession to Islamic conquerors, and as early as 640 the Arab commander Amr ibn al-As began the invasion of Egypt, which had been a Christian country for several centuries. Six years later, the Arab conquest was complete; little more than a generation later, Christianity in Egypt had been practically submerged by Islam. The Coptic Orthodox Church survived, however. Since the Arab conquest, the dominance of Islam in Egypt has never been threatened. There is no doubting the attachment of the great majority of Egyptians to Islam—an attachment in faith and observance which is probably more marked than that seen in any country, with the possible exception of Saudi Arabia.

The fundamental article of faith of Islam is the testimony (*shahada*): "There is no God but Allah, and Muhammad is the Prophet of Allah." The recital of this phrase in full and unquestioning belief is all that is required for one to become Moslem. Other dogmas involve belief in a general resurrection, in the final judgment of all mankind, in the preordainment of every man's acts during life and of his ultimate fate. Four books of scriptural revelation are recognized: the Qur'an (disclosed to Muhammad by the angel Gabriel), the Pentateuch and the Psalms from the Old Testament, and the Christian Gospels.

The Qur'an, "the bountiful, the beneficial," sets forth all a man needs to attain salvation. The teachings of the four Gospels are accepted, but Moslems claim that the present texts are not as God revealed them. Other books interpreting the Qur'an but not regarded as divinely inspired are the Sunna and the Hadith—the traditions and sayings of Muhammad. There is a wide difference of opinion about the Sunna. Sunni Moslems—such as those of Egypt —accept the Sunna implicitly; the second largest Moslem group, the Shi'a, who live mainly in Iran and Iraq, reject the Sunna text as spurious and adhere to a tradition of their own.

Islam teaches that God has given to mankind a succession of revelations of divine truth through his prophets, and that each time the human race falls into error, God sends new prophets to lead it back into the ways of truth. Altogether there have been over 200,000 prophets since the creation of man, but of these the great ones are considered to be Adam, Noah, Abraham, Moses, Jesus, and—the last and greatest—Muhammad.

The basic teachings of Islam (the "Five Pillars") closely parallel those of the Bible. Insistence on the oneness of God, prayer, fasting, almsgiving, and the spiritual value of pilgrimage are also features of both Christianity and Judaism. Many of the things prohibited by Islam—the eating of carrion, blood, and swine flesh; the consumption of alcohol; and engaging in adultery, gambling, and usury —are also prohibited or condemned in the Old or New Testaments. Circumcision, a custom universal in the Islamic world, is not mentioned in the Qur'an. Males are circumcised in early childhood or, if converts to Islam, at any age.

Prayer. Every Moslem is required to pray, in a prescribed manner, five times a day. The formalized prayer consists of a series of obeisances made first from a standing and then from a kneeling position; in the latter position the forehead must touch the ground. These movements are accompanied by the intonement of set prayers, some of which are brief Qur'anic texts. Men should, whenever possible, make their prayers in a mosque, though they are free to pray by themselves; women usually pray in the seclusion of the home. The early morning prayer is made as the first streaks of light appear in the sky before dawn; then follow prayers at noon, in midafternoon, at sundown, and finally when all is dark and quiet. Ablutions are required before each prayer, and all prayers are offered facing the holy city of Mecca. On Fridays, all males are expected to attend the mosque at noon to take part in communal prayer (the form of prayer advocated by the Prophet as being most beneficial) and to hear the Friday sermon. Friday is in no sense to be considered the equivalent of the Sabbath, however, since the Qur'an enjoins the faithful to return to their business after hearing the sermon. (Nevertheless, Friday has become a business holiday in Egypt as a result of Western-derived social legislation. As a broken day, it was the obvious choice for a day of rest. Prior to 1952, Moslem-owned stores, if they closed at all, closed on Saturday or Sunday, the Jewish and Christian Sabbaths.)

Almsgiving. The Qur'an lays great insistence on the giving of alms (*zakat*). In early Islamic times, almsgiving was morally obligatory, and zakat—a fortieth of a person's annual income—was customarily given either in money or in kind to "the poor, the needy, those employed in [the zakat's] collection, those who are to be conciliated, slaves and prisoners, debtors, and to mosques for the 'Way of God.'" *Sadaqat,* or free-will offerings, are given principally to the poor, the needy, and to orphans. Until recently, social conditions in Egypt were such that the prosperous man had no opportunity to forget his obligation of almsgiving; he was everywhere accosted by hordes of suppliants, many of them professional beggars, whose persistence was not to be denied.

Nowadays few, if any, Moslems pay the zakat as prescribed in the Qur'an. There is, however, a poor rate levied in three degrees according to ability to pay, the amount being determined yearly by a *fatwa* (decree) of the mufti (religious leader and interpreter of the Qur'an) at the end of Ramadan. This charity, the Sadaqat al-Fitr (Charity of Breaking the Fast), is distributed by the heads of families to the poor. The names of the recipients are not divulged.

Ramadan—the Fasting. The severest test of a Moslem's ability to carry out the dictates of his faith is met during Ramadan, the ninth month of the Moslem calendar. During this period all are required to fast from daybreak (reckoned as the moment a black thread may be distinguished from a white one) until the last ray of light has disappeared from the sky. The fast involves abstention from all food, drink, and tobacco, as well as from all indulgence in worldly pleasure. Exceptions are made in the cases of the sick, the weak, soldiers on duty, and travelers. Ramadan is widely and vigorously observed in Egypt. Many sinners "cease to sin," drunkards and hashish smokers abstain, even many professional thieves curb their activities. Since the Moslem year consists of 12 lunar months and is shorter by 11 or 12 days than the astronomical year, Ramadan periodically falls during the midsummer heat, its observance then becoming a test of the utmost severity. The psychological effect of the fast is marked; as the month progresses the tempers of the people become shorter, personal violence and divorce statistics usually rise sharply, and riots are plentiful. The firing of a cannon at nightfall is the signal for all to repair home to break their fast, and, with hunger pangs increasing daily, it is not unusual for the evening meal to become a banquet which extends far into the night. Business in many instances comes almost to a standstill; household servants refuse to work. The tension is even harder to bear for the uneducated (who are likely to keep the fast more rigidly), and they tend to dramatize their sufferings to find favor before Allah. A somewhat more skeptical attitude toward full observance is to be found among the Westernized elements of the population.

Children begin to observe the Ramadan fast around the age of eight. For the next few years, they are obliged to fast until midday only; the later achievement of the first complete Ramadan fast makes an important milestone in a child's life.

Hajj—the pilgrimage. The pilgrimage to Mecca is regarded as the ideal culmination of every Moslem's religious experience. The Qur'an refers to Mecca as the "Station of Abraham"; according to tradition, the Kaaba was erected by him. Adam is said to be buried in Mecca, and the tomb of Muhammad is even claimed by some to be there. The Kaaba is not only the center of the earth, it is the center of the universe; it is the place where Heaven and earth join, where God is met face to face.

The uncompromising insistence of the Qur'an on the true holiness of Mecca has from the beginning made of the pilgrimage something which must be achieved at least once in a lifetime if humanly possible. Those who are too desperately poor to travel, however, are tacitly exempted.

Islam divides the world into the Dar al-Islam and the Dar al-Harb (Seat of War), with the latter consisting of all non-Moslem lands. The Dar al-Harb is confronted by the *jihad* (literally, exertion), the permanent struggle to make the word of Allah supreme. It is presented to Moslems as part of their collective duty to Allah —in a sense it is a sixth pillar of Islam. Muhammad himself recommended to the feuding Arab tribes that they compose their differences and divert their energies to the task of converting the world. The idea held by many non-Moslems that jihad is a "Holy War" is erroneous; the Qur'an makes it clear that Christians and Jews—"the people of the Book"—are not to be Islamized by force; the concept of jihad, however, has often been invoked by Moslem leaders forced for political reasons to wage war on non-Moslem states. Recent examples were the preaching of jihad by the Sheikh al-Azhar during the Suez Canal crisis of 1956 and in the war with Israel in June 1967.

The Moslem Community

The Moslem's relationship with his God is a personal and direct one; there is in Islam no communion of saints to intercede for sinners; there are no holy orders or sacramental institutions. Muhammad, the founder, was born an ordinary man; the divine revelations did not change his nature. As Bakr Abu, Muhammad's successor, said: "Muhammad is dead."

The radical monotheism of Islam and the puritanism of its mood, combined with the aesthetic limitations of the Moslem cultural heritage, has left the believer with an arid, if physically exacting, liturgy. Islam either lacks or has consciously rejected those elements that elsewhere make for the ceremonial sequences of the ecclesiastical year. In addition to being devoid of the high days and holy days that characterize Roman and Eastern Orthodox Christianity and are observed in varying degrees by Protestant sects, the religion of Muhammad has no institutionalized hierarchy. Theoretically, promotion from a lesser to a more important position lies on a demonstration of ability which attracts the favorable notice of the Ministry of Waqfs [Religious Affairs] and Social Affairs or the authorities of al-Azhar University. Actually, personal contacts, group pressure, and patronage play as important a role in religious promotions as they do in determining secular appointments.

Mosques are not in any sense hallowed or consecrated places. However ornate some mosques may be, they are all simply halls set aside for congregational prayer and for the delivery of the weekly sermon. The only appointed mosque officials are the imams, whose duty it is to lead in prayer and preach the sermon, and the mufti, the interpreter of Islamic law, who is attached to the secular court. The muezzin, who calls the people to prayer, is also appointed by the government, usually being chosen more for his fine voice than for his learning; he is frequently employed as a janitor of the mosque, sometimes living on the premises. In the smaller mosques the muezzin's duties may be performed by the imam. Since Islam provides for no formal ordination of imams, any reasonably well-qualified member of a group may act as prayer leader. In desert caravans, for example, it is still customary for any literate member—if there is one—to conduct prayer readings from the Qur'an.

The stipends for the imams and the muezzins are provided by the Ministry of Waqfs and Social Affairs and vary considerably according to the size, location, and type of congregation of the particular mosque. The imam of Cairo's huge Muhammad Ali Mosque, which is attended by large numbers of important people, would receive a much higher stipend than the imam of a mosque in a smaller city or in the countryside. He would, moreover, need to be a highly distinguished graduate of the University of al-

Azhar in Cairo—the oldest and most highly regarded of Moslem universities. The lesser imams, who live and work in unpretentious surroundings, are usually less well educated. Some, in fact, are only semiliterate and often receive such meager stipends that they are forced to make ends meet by doing part-time manual labor, either as independent workers or employees.

If it is the duty of the imam to preach the Qur'an, it is the responsibility of the mufti to interpret it. In the days before Western civil and criminal legal systems replaced Islamic law in Egypt, the muftis, who handed down legal interpretations as derived from the Qur'an and Sunna, were persons of great importance. Litigants sought a mufti who was known for his interpreting skill, and the controversies between certain learned muftis are famous. Many muftis became rich and influential. Today the adoption of secular law on the Western model has reduced the influence of the mufti considerably, although the title is retained and the Grand Mufti of Egypt is frequently called upon as an adapter of Western law to Islamic tradition. Muftis are now paid by the government.

In spite of the predominant position of secular law in Egypt today, the Moslem codes of jurisprudence (*madhab*) are taught at al-Azhar and elsewhere and have large numbers of adherents among the people. Most popular is the Shafi'i code. Less well supported are the Hanafi and Malaki codes, while the Hanbali code has only a small number of adherents.

The leading Islamic dignitary in Egypt today is the Grand Sheikh of al-Azhar University. In the absence of a hierarchy, this is an assumed rather than a defined pre-eminence, and would until comparatively recently have been challenged by the Grand Mufti. Theoretically, of course, no Moslem religious leader can be more than *primus inter pares,* and it is up to the individual to pursue his ambition independently, since there is no organization which could be used for this purpose.

In Egypt, as in Islam generally, birth is not an important factor in the success of a religious leader or the esteem in which he is held. The children of the wealthy classes rarely if ever seek their livelihood as imams or muftis. Either the candidates are drawn from families which have provided religious leaders for generations or they come from average middle-class families. Many begin as charity pupils in the religious schools.

Egyptians are Moslems of the Sunnite rite, the largest of the Islamic groups. Generally referred to as orthodox Moslems—though the question of religious orthodoxy hardly enters into the questions dividing Moslems—the Sunni, in addition to insisting on the Sunna as the "true" tradition, acknowledge the first four caliphs, Bakr Abu, Omar, Othman, and Ali (632-661), to be the rightful temporal successors of Muhammad. The Shi'a, next in numbers to the Sunni, claim Ali, the Prophet's son-in-law, as his legal successor and discount the first three caliphs as well as the dynastic caliphs who followed Ali. Other Islamic sects have varying attitudes toward the various traditions, but Moslems everywhere are united in their unquestioning acceptance of the Qur'an as the revealed word of God.

The visitor to Egypt is immediately struck with the profusion of mosques and the large numbers of persons visiting them at all hours of the day. The hours of prayer, announced by the muezzin from the minaret—or now more frequently relayed by loudspeaker—are remarkable for the throngs of men and women who converge on the mosques. The mosques are well attended throughout the week by men from all walks of life. Women of the poorer classes may also visit the mosques every day, except on Fridays, but those of the wealthy and Westernized groups are rarely seen there. Under the monarchy, Friday worship was an occasion for ostentatious professions of piety by the king and those surrounding him, and the tradition has been preserved by President Nasser. His presence at religious services in the course of his tours through the country has done much to rally the people behind the government. Realizing that the mass of the population has little understanding of Egyptian or Arab politics, Egypt's leaders are seeking support for government policy from the pulpit by appeals couched in the language of the Islamic faith.

One force working to strengthen the religious tradition is al-Azhar University. The Grand Sheikh of the university hands down rulings on interpretations of the faith and is now virtually a government appointee. He is, therefore, not likely to be a man who would embarrass the secular authorities, who, respecting the strength of the Islamic tradition, are not disposed to interfere as long as the Grand Sheikh and his colleagues at al-Azhar continue to support national policy.

The tradition of Islamic mysticism known as Sufism is common throughout the Moslem world. It first appeared in Iraq in the eighth century A.D., and as it spread it became essentially a popular movement, emphasizing love rather than fear of Allah and a

69

direct, personal devotion to Allah. While the *ulama* (teachers, learned men) claimed that truth could be found only through detailed knowledge of the arduously developed science of law, the Sufis sought truth through the living experience of Allah, culminating in a momentary union with Him. Sufism gave an emotional response to the people's religious instincts, which were all too often starved by the dry scholasticism of the ulama.

In the first four or five centuries of its existence, more and more non-Islamic popular elements, such as saint worship and celibacy, became a part of Sufism, and the ulama countered with increasing pedantry and repression. However, at the end of the eleventh century, the philosopher and mystic theologian, al-Ghazali, brought Sufism within the bounds of orthodox Moslem belief.

Sufi orders spread throughout the Moslem world: some developed beyond regional boundaries, some maintained large establishments, some had a popular and emotional appeal, while others attracted the better-educated members of the population.

Egypt has long been the home of many Sufi orders (singular, *tariqa,* plural, *turuq*), some of which were established as early as the thirteenth century. Until recent years, the majority of Egyptian males belonged to one or more of these orders, and 60 such orders still survive. Probably the most famous is the Badawiya, also known as the Ahmadiya, centered at Tanta in the Delta and named after Ahmad al-Badawi, who lived in the thirteenth century. The Sanusiya order also has many chapters in the western desert area.

Currently the head of all the Egyptian orders is Muhammad Mahmud Alwan, who presides over infrequent congresses of the orders. Each order is led by a Sheikh al-Sigada (Master of Devotions) who names the khalif of each *zawiya,* or local center. An order may have a few such centers or scores of them. The zawiya holds its *hadra,* or liturgical meeting, at a mosque, and the major activity is the *dhikr.* The dhikr features the incessant repetition of words or formulas in praise of Allah, often with music and dancing, and the purpose is to attain a state of ecstasy on the part of the participants. At a typical dhikr held in a small village, two lines of men face each other with musicians playing a drum and an oboe placed to one side. As the music and the chanting begin, the men sway forward and backward; as the tempo increases, movements become more pronounced, until their heads almost touch the ground; in time, the figures fall one by one in a trance state.

Today the prestige and appeal of the orders is on the wane. Not only is the chain of communication between the head of an order and the khalifs weak but the social functions formerly performed by the orders have been largely taken over by the state. Indeed, the government regards the orders with disfavor, since they do not fit into the socialist system. It should be noted that Hasan al-Banna, founder of the Moslem Brethren, belonged to a Sufi order, but left it to lead an active attack on the problems of Egyptian society. In contrast, the orders have no such programs and are both unwilling and unable to react to official hostility.

While the Sufi orders are a part of the orthodox life of Moslems, the worship of saints, prevalent throughout the Islamic world, has no such sanction. Nevertheless, the Egyptians have hundreds of saints, and Muhammad has become the first of them. His *maulid,* or birthday, is gaily celebrated by the illumination of Cairo and by ceremonies and performances, including a dhikr. The most re-nowned local saint (*wali*) is Ahmad al-Badawi, mentioned above, while Luxor has a shrine to Abu al-Haggag, built into the ancient temple of Amenophis III. Cairo even has its own two female saints —Sitta Nefisa and Sayyida Zainab, the granddaughter of the Proph-et. It is commonly believed that prayers and the presentation of oil at the tombs of these saints will bring the granting of wishes; while protection from evil is provided by amulets, consisting of little scrolls on which a verse or two of the Qur'an has been written.

In the towns, religious patterns are changing, like the patterns of other aspects of life. Although many members of the upper classes continue to be practicing Moslems, Western scientific and secular influences are presenting problems which are increasingly difficult for Moslem orthodoxy to meet. In the absence of a radical reinterpretation of traditional thinking, Islam has gradually given ground, and the adherence to the faith of large numbers of edu-cated city dwellers is little more than nominal. It is among the lower-middle class and the lower class of the cities that Islam maintains its strongest hold. Most of the superstition and folklore of the countryside, except for the use of amulets, have been dis-carded by these urban groups.

Both urban dwellers and village folk observe the religious festi-vals and holidays. Aid al-Kabir (the Great Feast) is the most prominent. Lasting four days, it commemorates Abraham's willing-ness to sacrifice his son, and it is marked by the yearly pilgrimage to Mecca. Aid al-Saghir (the Lesser Feast), lasting three days, is

71

also a time of high celebration and feasting marking the end of Ramadan; Maulid, the birthday of the Prophet, is a one-day commemoration, as is Ashura, the tenth day of Muharram, the first month, on which the death of Hussein, the son of Ali, is remembered.

The departure for the pilgrimage is a great occasion in Egypt. The ceremony of Mahmal, at which gifts of carpets and shrouds for the Kaaba at Mecca and for the tomb of Muhammad at Medina are presented and made ready for dispatch to Mecca, draws great crowds. This ritual must be completed in order to give time for the presentation of the gifts at their destinations on the eighth day of Dhu'l-Hijja, the last month of the Moslem year. Those who make the pilgrimage may assume the title of Hajji (pilgrim), which carries prestige in both religious and social circles.

The Impact of Secularism

In the traditional Moslem world, religion, law, commerce, and social policies are held to be inseparable. The precept for every action can be found in scripture or tradition; therefore every deed is a "religious" one. To deny this is to deny Islam in its totality, and herein lies the crux of one of the greatest problems facing Egypt and the Middle East generally, for Islam, like all religions claiming to be divinely inspired, is threatened by the relentless penetration of the secularism of the modern age.

Moslem thinkers have reacted to the secular impact in a variety of ways. The first currents of secularism were felt in Egypt with the introduction of Western innovations by Muhammad Ali, but it was not until the beginning of the twentieth century that ideas which had been maturing for years were coherently expressed. At that time, the reformer Sheikh Muhammad Abdu advocated educational reforms designed to expand the curriculum of higher studies in Moslem countries and issued interpretations of the law which radically changed traditional attitudes toward banking and the acceptance and payment of interest. The gradual industrialization of the country and the necessity of orienting trade patterns to those of the Western powers led to major changes in the economic life of the country. Secular civil law has now completely replaced the old religious code in Egypt with the exception of slight Islamic modifications in such matters as marriage, divorce, and inheritance.

The movement for the emancipation of Egyptian women is making much progress, particularly among the middle class. Members of the new generation of Egyptian women are beginning to take a larger place in public affairs as equals of the men, and their attitude toward Islam, like that of male intellectuals, is said to be tinged with skepticism. In addition, since Islamic custom had for centuries made second-class citizens of women and is still frequently invoked as a sanction for the preservation of the status quo, there is quite probably even hostility toward Islam among the leaders of Egyptian women's movements.

Another Egyptian reaction to the secularizing influence of the West has been the organization of the Moslem Brethren (al-Ikhwan al-Muslimin). Founded in 1928 by the government schoolteacher Hasan al-Banna, who urged a return to Islam as preached by Muhammad, the Brethren grew rapidly. There were precedents for the organization in the long history of Moslem secret sects, and the religious coloring, the arcane ritualism, and the glorification of the Moslem past appealed strongly to many who were ready to translate discontent with the modern world into action. Whatever may have been the original purpose of its founder, the Brethren, reactionary and xenophobic in character, plunged deeper and deeper into political intrigue. Its originally religious goals, if not lost sight of, were de-emphasized in an extremist program of political action. The Brethren was finally banned as a subversive organization in January 1954.

The ulama, most of them nowadays graduates of al-Azhar, represent an influential but unorganized group, which at first gave considerable support to the Moslem Brethren. With the outlawing of the latter and the firmer establishment of the military regime, the ulama acquiesced to the government program, and large numbers of them became active apologists for the government, not even opposing the secularization of education.

As for the imams, since their stipends are provided by the Ministry of Waqfs and Social Affairs (from the income from religious foundations), it is not surprising that many of them have allowed their pulpits to be used for political diatribes. The influence of the government may extend down as far as individual congregations—in that the mosques are maintained through grants by the Ministry of Waqfs and Social Affairs, and the withdrawal of this government support could have the effect of crippling a congregation.

Three main intellectual positions characterize modernist thought in Egypt. One leading writer, Ahmad Amin, has stated that the reform of Islam will come about by separating science from religion and by practicing *ijtihad*—free interpretation. According to this view, Egypt must not merely imitate the foreigner but must achieve a true understanding in terms of its own needs of the aims of Western civilization. Another modernist group advocates that free interpretation be applied to all matters of doctrine and not, as the trend has been, to jurisprudence alone. A third position, of which the leading apologists are Sheikh Ali Abdel Razek and Muhammad Khalik, calls for the separation of religion from the state. In addition, the younger intellectuals tend to regard Islam as a political force to be directed against foreigners, notably against the Western powers, which their leaders consistently label as imperialistic and colonialistic.

Islam and the State

The growing cleavage between traditionalists and modernists has weakened Islam in Egypt and probably elsewhere in the Middle East, in spite of appearances to the contrary. Egyptian government officials fulfill their religious observances, but for many the process appears to be more a matter of political convenience than religious conviction. Contradictions appear in the Friday sermons from week to week as the government line changes; government pressure on the ulamas and imams has lessened their prestige. The deterioration of Islam as a system of ideas capable of competing with the secular ideologies of the present day is likely to accelerate unless the traditional dogmas are vitalized by rethinking and recasting them in terms of current problems and needs.

At the present time, a concerted effort is being made to place Islam at the service of the state. This effort has resulted in the subservience of the religious authorities to the dictates of the government. In other forms, it appears in attacks against so-called reactionary Moslems and in attempts to relate and reconcile Islam with socialism—with Arab socialism and even with something called "Islamic socialism." The keynote of this campaign was sounded by President Nasser on March 12, 1965, when he stated: "The Moslem religion is a religion that is 100 per cent Socialist."

The month of Ramadan features so-called "Political Nights of Ramadan," lecture sessions organized by the Administration of Thought and Mission of the Arab Socialist Union. The declared purpose of these meetings is to discuss socialism, since religion is not isolated from politics and society. At a meeting held in December 1966, Ali Sabri, head of the Arab Socialist Union, discussed the revolutionary political work of the Arab Socialist Union.

Al-Tali'ah (The Vanguard), the theoretical monthly journal of the Arab Socialist Union, deals with Islam and with Islam and socialism. The issue of June 1965 had this to say, in part:

> Socialism is an integral part of the concept of humanity in Islam.
> . . . This link in Islam between socialism and humanity means that
> neither can exist without the other. . . . [The] Prophet Muhammad
> . . . established a precedent allowing the Moslem rulers to combat
> economic injustice by nationalization or redistribution of wealth . . .
> What a man possesses of money or property is not owned com-
> pletely by him. The state has some right in these possessions. . . .
> Beyond adequacy of the demands of life, the society has a right
> to what man possesses. Private ownership is just a nominal thing.
> In fact, the society is the owner.

This argument, very drastically abridged, to the effect that the socialist state is the owner of all property, is a seriously distorted version of the position of Islam on property rights.

In the issue of *Al-Tali'ah* of May 1965 the following material appeared:

> Furthermore, the misinterpretation of the preachings of the open-
> minded Islamic religion, as for example, the saying repeatedly
> quoted by many to the effect that it is Allah who makes some peo-
> ple rich and others poor, leads individuals in rural areas to adopt,
> unintentionally, nonsocialist conduct. . . . In my belief, among the
> means we should use to deepen the socialist concepts in the rural
> areas is to spread a sound understanding of the preachings of re-
> ligion among the villages in order to strengthen their conviction in
> the principles and concepts of socialism. There is no contradiction
> between Islamic principles and socialist principles. On the contrary,
> the sound socialist principles find their origin in the preachings of
> Islam. But in this effort we will meet great difficulties because there
> live in the rural areas some parasite pretenders and semischolars of
> religion who are inspired by reactionaries refusing development and
> evolution. In my opinion, they should be extended the same treat-
> ment given to the scientist or economist who does not gear his
> knowledge to the service of socialism. The government should dis-
> miss them from their positions because their intellectual stagnation
> greatly obstructs the application of Arab socialism.

75

Religious Minorities

Egypt's religious minorities number between 5 and 10 per cent of the total population. By far the largest of these groups are the indigenous Copts, who number around 2,500,000. Other groups include Catholic, Orthodox, and Protestant Christians, and Jews. Protestants are few in number, though recently a fair number of converts have been made among the Copts.

The Copts. The Copts claim to be the descendants of the ancient Egyptians. Egypt was Christianized in the early days of the Church, but in the fifth century the greater part of the Copts seceded from the main body of the Eastern Church, to which they had been attached, on a doctrinal question which acquired more force because of national resentment of Byzantine rule and sympathy for the Patriarch of Alexandria in his struggle for supremacy in the Church.

Moslem rule in Egypt brought the conversion to Islam of large numbers of native Christians, and even those whose loyalty to Christianity continued were influenced by the prevailing Moslem atmosphere and gradually adopted many of the externals of Islam. The Coptic language, too, died out among the people as both a literary and a spoken language, although it is still used side by side with Arabic in the Coptic liturgy.

About 95 per cent of the Copts are members of the Coptic Orthodox Church. Some 65,000 belong to the Coptic Catholic (Latin) Church. Numerically ascendant, the Coptic Orthodox Church is today in a serious state of decay. Its monastery-trained clergy show a general ineptitude in parish and evangelical work. The ignorance of a large proportion of its priests is despised by the better-educated—and therefore more influential—Copts.

The Coptic Church has little political influence in Egypt. Poorly supported by its followers and spiritually stagnant, its disintegration, according to many accounts, is becoming a headlong process. Defections are numerous, both to other Christian bodies and to Islam, and many of the educated youth are turning to agnosticism and atheism while nominally adhering to the Church. Egyptian Moslems, more overt in their dislike of Jews and Europeans, actually respect these same groups more than they do the Copts, and this attitude is not improved by Coptic insistence that the

Copts are the only true Egyptians. The Egyptian government, while it does nothing to arrest the deterioration of the Coptic Church, maintains an attitude of easy tolerance toward it.

Other Christian Minorities

The Catholic and Eastern Orthodox religious minorities, other than the Copts, draw considerable financial support from foreigners and persons of foreign origin living in Egypt. In 1947, these groups numbered about 275,000. The largest single group comprises Catholics of the Latin rite; members of the Greek Orthodox Church are only slightly fewer in number. Of the remaining groups, only the Greek Catholics, who employ the Syrian Melkite rite, number over 25,000.

The Christian minorities are almost exclusively urban groups, often very wealthy and extremely clannish. Irrespective of the Egyptian citizenship of some of their members, these groups as a whole are regarded as foreign, but despite the latent xenophobia of the area, most of the Christian minorities in Egypt have pursued their ways of life without suffering undue interference or persecution. In their turn, they have avoided involvement in Egyptian politics and any other conduct which might make them conspicuous.

The small success of Christian missions in winning converts among Moslems long ago dampened missionary enthusiasm in Egypt; if anything, the trend has been for Moslems to Islamize Christians. In the decadent Coptic Church, however, missionaries have had some success, particularly the Evangelical Protestants. The Coptic Catholic Church, established in the eighteenth century by European missionaries, is also drawing considerable numbers of converts from the Coptic Orthodox body.

The Jews

The Jews of Egypt lived mainly in Cairo, Alexandria, and Port Said and were divided into two communities—the Orthodox (Rabbinite) Jews and the Karaites. The latter accept the Scriptures but reject the Talmud (the body of Jewish civil and canonical law). The two communities never intermarried and rarely mixed socially in any way.

The Rabbinites included many old Egyptian Jewish families as well as the more recent arrivals from Europe. Among the latter were many eastern European Jews, in whom such traces of Zionism as exist in Egypt were to be found. Culturally, like some other foreign communities—notably the Armenian—the Rabbinites were largely Gallicized.

The Karaites were all members of long-established Egyptian families and were generally less prosperous than the Rabbinites. It was not unusual for the Karaites to be found as small merchants in the bazaars, wearing the customary galabia and tarboosh and fitting completely into the general domestic trade pattern.

The depth of the devotion of Egyptian Jews to the beliefs and precepts of Judaism is difficult to gauge. Certainly liberalism has made great inroads on orthodoxy, and the religious devotion of many of the country's Jewish intellectuals is limited to the nominal observance of such days as Passover, New Year, and the Day of Atonement.

The Jew in Egypt had known little persecution in the past, but there is no doubt that his relatively superior economic position made him the object of jealousy and envy. The mass of the population is bitterly poor, but destitute Jews have been rare. Cultural factors also enter in. Islam forbade usury; the Jew was frequently a moneylender. Islam forbade indulgence in alcohol; the Jew was a drinker of wine. Despite anti-Jewish sentiments and occasional anti-Jewish outbreaks, however, the Jewish experience in Egypt has until recently been an agreeable one.

The outbreak of the Arab-Israeli war in 1948 saw the departure from Egypt of the majority of overtly Zionist Egyptian Jews, with some 25,000 going to Israel or Europe. A new exodus, amid rumors of persecution, followed the Israeli invasion of the Sinai Peninsula in November 1956, and in 1965 a census listed 2,484 Jews still in Egypt. A third exodus, following the war of June 1967, is believed to have more than halved the above number.

CHAPTER 7

Social Structure

THE VAST MAJORITY OF EGYPT'S PEOPLE LIVE IN VILLAGES, each of which tends to be a self-contained unit. Largely self-sufficient in material things and left to their own political devices in local matters, Egypt's villages are like so many small societies, sharing in a common cultural tradition but largely isolated from each other in the concerns of daily life. The people of the towns and cities are dependent upon the agricultural base of the villages, but they live in a separate urban world that is socially and culturally very different in construction from village society, with which it has little direct intercourse.

Across this gap between town and country the points of contact are few and discontinuous. From the time of the Pharaohs, government inspectors and officials—the functionaries of a distant taxing and conscripting government—have operated in the countryside, as have the agents of absentee landlords, who have come periodically to give orders or to collect rents. What little the villager knows of urban life comes mainly through the bazaars and weekly markets, where he sells or exchanges his products for personal necessities; on such trips he may have occasion to frequent cinemas, coffeehouses, mosques, or the law court. Service in the army and exposure to the media of mass communication are making the fellah more familiar with the town, but the rural and the urban segments of Egyptian society are still remote from each other. The villager continues to feel inferior to the townsman, and he looks on the representatives of the landlord and the government with distrust; the educated townsman considers himself superior to the peasant, who is dismissed as ignorant, doltish, and constitutionally incapable of bettering himself.

Even the increasing migration from the countryside to the towns seems to have had little effect upon the urban-rural gap. In recent decades there has been a steady, large-scale movement from the villages and the nomad camps to the towns, but it has been mainly a one-way shift, with very little movement in the opposite direction. Whole families have moved from the villages, seeking to better themselves, and more than half of the men discharged from the army move to the cities. Some of these have made good, usually as small shopkeepers, while others have been absorbed into the ranks of unskilled servants and laborers. A few who have prospered return home to invest their savings in land and enjoy enhanced prestige among their fellows, and some of the failures return to their villages in disappointment; in general, however, peasant families who have moved to the towns—however harsh their experience there—are reluctant to return to their villages.

The separation of urban and rural Egyptian society has resulted in differences in the social stratification of the two groups. There is, however, an over-all pattern of social ranking which applies in both town and country, since the same basic criteria of status and prestige are recognized in both. Egyptian society, whether urban or rural, has until recently emphasized the ownership of land as the primary source of social status. It has been this factor rather than any principle of inherited class status that has constituted the basic criterion for the order of the rungs of the social ladder. Egyptian society has not been characterized by any system of fixed classes nor by an aristocracy based on inherited titles and associated lands. A family's status depended on the amount of land it inherited or acquired; the ability to accumulate more land was enhanced by favors granted in court and by appointments received in the government. By the same token, a family could lose status directly by loss of its lands—or by falling afoul of the government authorities, which usually resulted in loss of lands. Status could be acquired in other ways—by promotion in the government, by advancement in the professions or in the army, or by advantageous marriage—but rise in status had to be confirmed through the subsequent conversion of wealth to landholdings.

Since social status was based more on wealth than on occupation, it was common for landowning families to intermarry with families of either wealth or position that had been based on commercial interests or high government or army posts. This created in the upper levels of society a diversity of interests, combined with a consolidation of riches and power. On the lower levels of urban society, where occupations were more likely to be inherited, marriages were usually contracted within a particular craft group rather than between different groups. With the growth of middle-class interests in industry and the professions, however, marriages are now taking place among the various occupational groups, thereby contributing to the establishment of new areas of wealth and influence.

As a result of the mobility inherent in the system, Egyptians are less conscious of class distinctions, as such, than of the more extreme and obvious manifestations of status. In effect there have been two large class divisions: the rich of the cities and the predominantly rural poor. Since the wealthy landlords were also the possessors of political power, the cities became the domain of the "rulers" and the villages the territory of the "ruled." The social distance between the extremes was thrown into relief by the fact that the ruling class was largely of foreign origin. Between these two extremes existed an urban middle-class group—also largely of foreign origin—but this group was small and politically insignificant. The Westernization of Egyptian urban society, which began in 1820 and accelerated under British domination, served further to widen the gap between town and country, for it was the educated and well-to-do of the cities who acquired the veneer of Western culture, with its special symbols of wealth, power, and prestige.

Westernization nevertheless brought with it the first signs of a shift in the economic and political center of gravity in Egyptian society. Previously small and ineffectual, the middle class of the towns responded eagerly to new commercial and political techniques; its indigenous components began to expand relative to the foreign components, and it began to emerge as a threat to the old ruling groups. This threat became a reality in 1952, when the essentially middle-class elements of the army overthrew the monarchy and the government, expropriated the lands of the royal family, and drastically reduced those of the wealthier and more powerful landlords. It seems clear, however, that this upheaval was essentially a phenomenon of the cities, with little contribution from the rural areas.

Moslem Family Structure

The basic structure of the Moslem society of Egypt shows no trace of influences from alien cultures and religions. In this respect, Egypt is unlike India and Pakistan, where the caste system of the

Hindus led to the establishment of classes and castes among the Moslems. Nor is there any reflection of pre-Islamic practices. In Egypt, the family constitutes the basic framework within which the life of the individual is worked out, from birth to death. It not only provides its members with support and social orientation in childhood but remains for them throughout life the primary vehicle for economic cooperation, social control, and mutual protection. The first loyalty of the individual is to his family, on whose wealth, welfare, and reputation his own are dependent. This strong tradition of kin solidarity does not prevent the individual from making personal decisions, but it does serve to restrict any such decisions to the incidental ones of day-to-day living. The large principles on which the Egyptian family is founded exert too powerful a force for the individual readily to depart from them. These principles are reflected in the prescriptions relating to religious obligations, marriage, employment, the protection—and to some extent the management—of the family's property, and the defense of its honor.

Western influence and the general process of modern technological and social change are affecting the family as well as other aspects of Egyptian life, particularly in the cities. New economic forms are shaking the old self-sufficiency of the family; government institutions are pre-empting some of the welfare and control functions which in the past belonged solely to the family; and a rising Egyptian nationalism is articulating a political ideal of patriotism which may in time transcend the once-exclusive loyalty to the kin and local group.

The basic principle determining membership in the Egyptian family is kinship, reckoned in the male line. There are at least three kinds of groupings among kinsmen in the villages, in an ascending order of size but in a diminishing order in regard to relationship and closeness of association. These are the household, often an extended family consisting of several generations; then the lineage or clan, composed of a number of related extended families; and, in some villages, a further grouping of the lineages or clans into two larger groups, each of which is thought to be descended from a common male ancestor. Land and wealth—like family, lineage, or group—descend through the male line, and if the competition of relatives for these things is a divisive factor, still the shared interest and the need for cooperative effort serve to reinforce the unity of the household and, to a lesser degree, of the lineage. The preference for marriage between cousins contributes to the same end. In such a system, kinship and economic ties coincide with local residence, and the village tends to become the self-contained domain of a few large kin groups.

In all of these kin groups, authority is vested in the senior—or most influential or able elder—male. On the level of lineage or clan authority, however, the direct authority of the father of a household thins out to a more or less compelling advisory power. The lineage and even the extended family, if its members do not happen to reside in one household, are only informal units of economic cooperation, whose members may assist each other if they are on good terms. The basic unit of work and discipline is the household, and the larger kin entities tend to come to the fore mainly on public and formal occasions and in large matters of family discipline or mutual defense.

A typical household consists of husband and wife, unmarried children, married sons, and their wives and children. The pattern varies, however, and a household may include the father's sister or daughter, a paternal niece or nephew if orphaned, or a paternal cousin. The bond is blood relationship to the father, and it includes grandparents as well. The household may also take in married brothers and their wives and children, all living in the same compound, maintaining a communal guest house or room, and cooperating in group support. In one sizable Upper Egyptian village, the average household numbered four persons, but a household may—although this is rare—consist of several dozen persons residing in a compound or series of apartments.

Beyond the household, there is the group of related families, the lineage, whose members regard themselves as related through a more or less remote male ancestor. Frequently this forebear is believed to be a descendant of the Prophet Muhammad, in which case his male descendants assume the title of "Sayyid."

The sectional division of villages into two groups of clans or lineages, each section regarding itself as descended from a common progenitor, is less well documented for Egypt than for other parts of the Middle East. Where these two sections exist, the local population and village area is generally divided about equally between them. There are no restrictions on intermarriage or social exchange between the sections. The members of each group are supposed to possess certain characteristic physical and personal traits. Socially, the two divisions may sometimes mark the lines of partisanship in village disputes.

Authority in the family is vested in the men. Males are considered inherently superior to females, and the legal rights granted to women under Islamic law, while numerous, are inferior to those granted to men. Respect for masculine authority and seniority is carefully ingrained in the children. Much attention is paid to the formal deference owed by the young to their elders. Even a mature son may not sit next to his father in public. He should never sit while his father is standing, nor should he smoke in his father's presence. In any discussion with his parent he is expected to yield. Politeness to his father gives him standing in the community. Much hinges on his receiving his father's blessing, and nothing is more devastating than the paternal curse. The eldest son, if he is favored, becomes a kind of crown prince, acting in many cases for his father and receiving special privileges; younger brothers and sisters are expected to obey him on pain of being reported to the father.

In keeping with the aura of respect and awe in which, ideally, the father moves, he rarely becomes intimate with his children, and in their presence he maintains a formal demeanor with his wife. Affection between father and children may exist, but the tendency is to suppress its expression. A common saying is: "*Al-khof baraka* (Fear is a blessing)."

Children of both sexes are brought up by their mothers. Respect and regard are enjoined by the tradition of Islam, which says that "Paradise is at the feet of mothers." From an early age, the boys hear all the facts of daily life and its problems discussed by their parents, and they are aware that there is a time of anxious waiting until they are old enough to work in the fields. From close association with their mothers, the boys may acquire sentimental, romantic traits; while they are scolded by their fathers for frivolity and infantile play, and learn from them respect for age and scorn for women, even those of the family.

Punishment of children may be by cursing, deprivation of food (especially meat), slapping, or whipping. A display of anger by the parents is in itself a punishment, and the manifestation of parental wrath is often more effective than any other punitive action. Strong emphasis is placed on teaching the Egyptian child to conform to the patterns laid down by his elders and to avoid any action which might bring discredit on his family. Proverbs make learning easy, and almost every situation has a proverb to fit it. The advantages of cooperation and reciprocity, for example, are eloquently condensed in the aphorism "Hand washes hand." Originality is discouraged, and the popular acceptance of the immutability of man's fate is brought home to the child in his early religious teaching.

Both boys and girls are taught as soon as possible the duties they must assume as young adults, when ideally they will take over these activities and give their parents leisure in their old age. Compulsory—but not yet universal—primary school attendance occupies some children between the ages of 6 and 12. In the fields, boys under 13 are given the lighter tasks, such as directing the flow of water in the irrigation ditches. For boys over 13, there are the heavier tasks of carrying fertilizer and lifting water in the *shadoof* (bucket on a counter-balanced pole); when a boy's moustache begins to grow, he becomes a full-fledged man, taking his place as a working adult in the community. At puberty, the boy suddenly becomes a man. He is now expected to have aggressive masculine traits, but behind these remain the sensitivity acquired from contact with his mother. Indeed, most grown men are not above extreme displays of emotion.

The girls also follow a course of training in the tasks they must assume, from watching over smaller brothers and sisters to learning to bake. After a girl is 16, she is much more restricted in her movements than a boy of the same age, and from then on, if her family is conservative, she is largely secluded.

Familiarity among relatives shows a definite patterning. Fathers do not joke with their children, and there is no levity between husband and wife. Nor is there any public show of affection between parents; that would be considered shameful. From adolescence on, brothers do little joking with each other, and traditionally they were not supposed to go about together, lest they attract the "evil eye." Half brothers and half sisters are not expected to be on good terms, since they have not been nursed from the same breast and are rivals for the father's power and property. On the other hand, full brothers and sisters are expected to be cordial to each other. People generally feel more at ease with their mothers' families than with those of their fathers, since anything to do with fathers is associated with paternal sternness.

Jealousies arise in families, especially between half brothers and half sisters, each side watching carefully to see that the other receives no special favors from the father. Marriage arrangements are another source of intrafamily strife. When, in selecting a young man's wife, there is a choice between cousins on the father's and the mother's side, the losing branch may take its defeat badly. If an open quarrel breaks out, as not infrequently happens, a family council is called, which may or may not be able to end the enmity. Quarrels and splits within the family and violent feuds between lineages are common features of Egyptian village life. In one village, a feud has been going on for about 150 years. How it started is not known, but the rivalry has been bitter, with frequent bloodshed and killings. A family that loses a member in a feud of this kind feels in honor bound to take the life of one of the rival family. If the authorities arrest and execute one of the feuders as a murderer, this in turn automatically assures that some member of the other family will die. And so the feud continues.

Sexual Behavior

In the cities, general segregation of the sexes is no longer the rule, but in the countryside, the sexes are segregated from each other from the time of adolescence. Outside the family, men associate with men, women with women. In the more conservative villages, men and women even try to avoid looking at each other when passing in the street—the women either turn their faces away or draw their veils across their faces.

Children are separated as to sex about the age of 12, when boys and girls begin to perform distinctive chores and avoid playing together. Schools have so far been segregated, but consideration is now being given to making secondary schools coeducational; the universities have been coeducational for about 25 years.

Boys are circumcised between the ages of three and six: these occasions are marked by celebrations, including a meal to which the relatives of the child are invited. Female circumcision is widely practiced, both in villages and towns, but without publicity: the quiet celebration is attended only by women.

The traditional rules governing sexual behavior have always been rigid, and in the villages they remain so. From adolescence onward, sex is something of which to be ashamed. Unmarried girls must disguise the form of their bodies with extra garments. Reproof by parents for any sexual laxity inflicts acute embarrassment and shame on the offender, and there is violent disapproval of premarital sexual relations. Adultery is at the least an occasion for divorce, and often precipitates violent reprisals against the offenders.

Marriage is viewed by Islam as the only legitimate outlet for sexual activity. In the village, the absence of any romantic experiences during adolescence and the ever-present concept of women as the objects of male lust are factors which may be relieved by early marriages. In the towns, where marriages do not take place as early, boys may have premarital experiences. The present regime, which is somewhat puritanical, has made limited headway in reducing prostitution, so long established at Cairo and other cities. The Sharia (Avenue) Cot Bey, almost at the heart of modern Cairo, has brothels which cater to the less well-to-do, while a number of areas in the city are frequented by prostitutes, dressed in fairly extreme Western styles.

Marriage and Divorce

The strict religious regulation of marriage (varying in the several religious communities) is today supplemented by secular codes which apply to all, even though these are no doubt often violated (as with the prohibition against boys marrying before the age of 18 and girls before 16). Among Moslems, marriage is concluded as a secular contract between the families of the bride and the groom. Preferred marriage partners are cousins—an arrangement which keeps family property intact by uniting individuals who are already bound by collateral family ties.

The marriage contract stipulates certain conditions binding on each party, and in recent years there has been an increasing tendency for the bride's parents to add conditions pledging the husband to take only one wife, guarantee her a certain level of maintenance, etc. Each bride has a dowry, which the groom must match before the wedding. This bride price goes to the wife as indemnity in the event of divorce. The system puts a high premium on desirable young women from wealthy families, and many men, unable to match the dowry of an acceptable bride, marry late if at all.

The marriage contract, signed by the fathers of the bride and groom, is not valid until certified by a Moslem official and witnessed by one person for each party. When the contract is duly certified, the opening chapter of the Qur'an is recited, then a feast is held, at which the women of the bride's family sing and give the traditional cries of joy. The actual consummation of the marriage is variously practiced in the rural areas: a public display of the signs of the bride's virginity is always made. After the marriage, the groom maintains a formal reserve toward his wife's parents—whether or not he has known them previously.

In the villages, arranged marriages, usually between paternal cousins, continue to be the rule, but in the cities, the better-educated young men are increasingly likely to search for their own mates. They see the chic, socially experienced, European woman as the ideal, but they certainly do not want an Egyptian woman who is completely emancipated and who would not be submissive to her husband. Both in the villages and in the towns, the man hopes to acquire a wife who will take care of his wants and desires, while he maintains his freedom of action: in this unequal partnership he has all the rights and none of the duties beyond that of providing food and lodging.

Divorce is authorized by Moslem religious law at the will of the husband. In recent years, however, the right to divorce has been given to an increasing number of wives by writing it into their marriage contracts. To become valid, divorces must be formally registered with the government. The rate of divorce in Egypt is extremely high, scarcely surpassed by any other country. There are more divorces during the first two years of marriage than there are later on. Frequent divorces and rapid remarriages represent very upsetting experiences for the children who are involved. If they are age seven or younger, they go with the mother, but the father may claim them as they grow older. A divorced (or widowed) wife usually returns to her father's house unless she has mature children with whom she can live.

Female Moslems do not marry non-Moslems: in such a case, the woman would become an outcast and liable to death at the hands of her family. Very rarely, a Moslem male marries a non-Moslem, in which case the wife may retain her religion, but her children must be registered as Moslems. After a child reaches the age of seven, the mother may lose control of him if she has not become a Moslem or if she has been divorced.

Village Society

A village contains a varying number of extended families (*ahl*, or *dar*), each of which has a lineage or clan (*hamula*) relationship. In addition, there may be a secondary division of these families into groups who are presumed to be descended from a common male ancestor. Individuals may desert this closed system simply by seeking work in a nearby town, but it is closed to penetration. Families offering needed services—potters, carpenters, barbers, or millers—may move to the village, but they are never accepted into its society.

Shops are found in the larger villages, and the shopkeepers may or may not be members of the village society. The ownership of land and its use is valued above any other occupation; it is better to be a struggling farmer than a wealthy shopkeeper. Differences in apparent social status are wide; an extended kin group may include landowners, tenant farmers, and hired laborers. The traditional kin obligations tend to blur the differences in economic status.

Each village is headed by an *omdeh,* an unpaid official elected from among those in a village owning land. Nearly always an older man, he is held in great respect. One of his functions is to receive visitors and government officials in his guest house, and another is to select and hire the *ghaffirs,* the guards and messengers. Other specialized occupations in the village, dependent in part on its size, may include a religious leader, a postmaster, teachers, policemen, and government officials.

Disputes between village families are presented to an improvised council, sometimes called an "Arab council." Prolonged discussions, interrupted by efforts at mediation, serve almost literally to talk the dispute to death or, at least, to place it in a proper perspective.

The impact on the village of the external world, represented primarily by officialdom and the services it provides and secondarily by the radio and the press, have altered the traditional patterns of society. For example, the desire and ability of the individual to supply hospitality to casual visitors and to guests on the occasions of family celebrations are definitely on the decline. This expensive custom has given way either to spending money on newly available items or to saving money in response to exhortations by the government.

The individual in village society continues to feel inferior to all other elements in the country, in spite of the efforts by the government to convince the people that the future of the country is in the hands of the farmers and industrial workers. The villager would not dream of wearing European clothing, as government officials do. He is aware that his respected omdeh would have little or no standing in the nearest large town. Even the lowliest government clerk is above him on the social ladder, while the world of the great ones (*kibar*) and the important people (*'izam*) is acknowledged to be beyond his comprehension.

The tedium of everyday life is relieved for the men by visits to the coffeehouse and for the entire family by visits to that important social institution, the weekly market. The visits of animal circuses or mobile cinema units provide occasional excitement, while political campaigns produce an ephemeral group consciousness. The village may also, depending on its size, have other meeting places, such as the clinic, the cooperative, and the headquarters of the Arab Socialist Union.

An article in *Al-Tali'ah* in May 1965 underlined some of the problems encountered by the Arab Socialist Union in realizing socialism in the villages. According to its author, the village families protect their members, as always, even if some of them engage in nonsocialist conduct. Furthermore, solidarity among members of rural society against the ruling authorities still prevails, in spite of efforts carried on since 1952 to build a bridge of mutual confidence across the very deep abyss that separates the rural areas and the government. In the opinion of the author of the article, socialism must be preached to the rural masses, since only by a popular understanding of real socialism can diversionism be eradicated. As a commentary on this article, it may be said that preaching socialism to the Egyptian masses will not turn them into socialists: They will become "socialists" only when such conversion appears profitable or when they have seen that diversionists are purged.

Urban Society

The upper class. From early Ottoman times until the assumption of power by Muhammad Ali, Egypt had neither an hereditary aristocracy nor an hereditary royal family. Muhammad Ali's family, however, assumed a quasi-royal status, which became hereditary in fact with the accession after World War I of Muhammad's descendant, Fuad I. Throughout the latter part of the nineteenth century, the ruling family formed the center of a court, around which clustered a horde of wealthy landlords seeking to exchange their support for royal favor. Upon them such titles as "Pasha" and "Bey" were bestowed by the monarchy, but these titles were not hereditary—they expired with the death of the holders. Impermanent though they were, the titles were highly coveted, for they carried political power, influence, and certain privileges which usually led to the accumulation of still more wealth and consequently still greater influence.

With this mutually-reinforcing combination of affluence and political power, the great landlords were able to establish themselves firmly as an "elite" group at the top of the social scale. Collectively they controlled a disproportionate amount of the country's basic source of wealth, and consistently they provided the majority of the cabinet ministers, members of parliament, and high-ranking army officers. From such positions, further strengthened by intermarriage, they were able to control a top-heavy bureaucracy as well as the army and the police force, largely by the appointment of relatives and the use of patronage. They profited, furthermore, from the support of religious figures such as the ulama and the leading imams, all of whom viewed with alarm the growing secularization of the middle-class intellectual and professional groups.

Until 1952, this elite had little difficulty in maintaining its privileged position and effectively insulating itself from the rest of the population. Composed largely of persons of non-Egyptian extraction, notably Turks and Albanians, the ruling elite often scorned to speak Arabic, which it regarded as the language of the mob, and it affected so great an appreciation of European arts and letters that its members contributed little or nothing to the revival of indigenous culture that has developed as a reaction to Western influence. Conspicuous for its lavish spending and display of wealth, the group remained impervious to the growing unrest of the middle class and the misery of the peasants.

When on July 23, 1952, a group of junior army officers seized power, their principal target was the old elite. The royal family and those closest to it were divested of lands, and the holdings of lesser landlords were abolished. With the loss of their privileges, large numbers of wealthy people fled the country; those who remained sought cover by withdrawing from public life. The traditional privileged isolation of this group made its removal a matter of little consequence to other segments of Egyptian society. Wealth still remains the principal criterion for social status, but social acceptability seems now to be established on a broader basis than the mere possession of land.

The middle class. The forces which erupted in 1952 were the culmination of a steady process of secularization and Westernization that brought with it an increasing social, economic, and political awareness on the part of the Egyptian middle class. The long-standing political ineffectiveness of this group was due to several factors. In the first place, it had never been numerically large. Secondly, it lacked cultural or social homogeneity and showed little solidarity in terms of common goals; many of its members belonged to foreign minorities which were socially self-contained and politically less effective than their Egyptian counterparts. Thirdly, the upper levels of the Egyptian middle class were composed of professional men, newspaper editors, wealthy merchants, industrialists, some Western-educated intellectuals and technicians, and the higher clergy, all of whose traditional values and ambitions led them to emulate the upper class rather than to threaten its status.

On the other hand, it was precisely within the upper-middle class that Western influences produced the first visible signs of the stirring of social conscience and public spirit. Most of the welfare organizations and other projects for the public benefit were initiated by members of the upper-middle class. Such agitation as there was against the Egyptian agrarian system was also the work of some of the members of this group, who saw that the traditional preoccupation with land was tying up capital which might otherwise be used for the industrial and commercial development of the country.

Below the upper-middle class is a very large, heterogeneous element made up of civil servants, small merchants, shop attendants, journalists, skilled workers, and schoolteachers. These people live on fixed incomes that are scarcely adequate to provide nourishment and lodging in rented quarters. Since few of the women of this group work, the heads of the families look for extra, part-time jobs —a practice frowned on by the government—and are frequently heavily in debt. Joint family outings are few; the males join their friends at night to go to the cinema, sit in cafes, and walk along the bank of the Nile.

The lower-middle class is made up of the lower echelons of the occupations listed above, and also assorted employees in the service trades. In contrast to the higher levels of the middle class, this group shows its more or less recent rural antecedents in manners and dress. Little involved in the Western-inspired reformist movements of an earlier period, the urban lower-middle class today is responding fervidly to the nationalist and anti-Western slogans of the Egyptian government.

The lower class. The urban lower class, largely illiterate and desperately poor, includes nonskilled factory workers, porters, peddlers, street entertainers, and assorted drifters. Apart from their various occupational distinctions, the members of this group show considerable social differentiation among themselves. Some of this differentiation is based on the tendency in the Middle East for occupational groups to form social clusters almost like castes—particularly among families who have pursued particular occupations for centuries, passing a trade or skill from father to son and marrying within the occupational grouping. This tendency exists also among those members of the middle class who still follow traditional occupations, but is more pronounced among the lower classes. Other factors which contribute to social clustering are common ethnic or regional origin and religious affiliation. The most tightly integrated social clusterings are those in which occupation and other ties coincide to produce a special awareness of group affiliation. Domestic servants in Egypt constitute one of these groups. Most cooks, butlers, and houseboys come from Upper Egypt or below the Sudanese border; clannish in their largely hereditary calling, they are punctilious about gradations of status within their own group.

Social Mobility

Theoretically, the Islamic ideal of human equality leaves the way open for upward movement from the bottom to the top of Egyptian society. With the removal of the hereditary royal family and the present regime's reiteration of its concern for the "common man," this ideal has taken on somewhat more visible substance than it had prior to 1952. Formerly, a wealthy merchant would invest in land in the hopes of marrying his daughter to a member of an established landed family. A wealthy doctor, having accumulated sufficient money, would buy an estate on the Delta, hire a manager, and retire from practice. In this way, members of the middle class —or at least their descendants—managed to move into the ranks of the upper class. The converse was also true. Even before World War II, Egypt was witnessing the decline of certain elements, notably the smaller artisans, whose traditional trades had become less lucrative with the introduction of modern industrial techniques, and the heirs of landowners, whose estates had been made uneconomical by fragmentation.

Today, while ownership of land is still an accepted means of confirming one's status, other factors are assuming greater importance. Success in industry or international commerce is now a factor in social status and prestige, and government service is increasingly popular among young Moslems, who are moving into clerical positions formerly held by Copts. In keeping with this trend, education is also assuming greater importance as a means of rising on the social scale. Where once literature, the fine arts, and religious studies provided prestige for the individual, now training for commerce, industry, or government work may also open the way to wealth and position. Even the urban lower classes are becoming increasingly conscious of the advantages of education over the mere accumulation of small savings as a means to social position.

For the majority of the people, however, the new possibilities for social advancement are still overshadowed by practical limitations. For the villagers and the bulk of the urban workers, an economically and socially "useful" education is still largely unobtainable. Conscious of this, most of them pin any modest hopes they may have for self-betterment on the traditional devices. The ambitious fellah may be able to increase his landholdings and provide his sons with dowries for brides from wealthier and more influential families. Alternatively, he may marry his daughters to men from more socially secure families. The efficacy of these means is considerably reduced by the ease and frequency of divorce.

Thus the majority of the Egyptian population is still held by a kind of social inertia, and the direct impact of the modern forces making for social change has been felt most strongly by the middle and upper classes of the cities. Isolated by their poverty, most Egyptians have tended to see in the will of God a sufficient explanation for a harsh and narrow existence they could not mend. Today, however, a new factor has been introduced: The recent Egyptian aspirations to power are of a degree and kind that will require, if they are to be achieved, the transformation of the traditionally passive Egyptian masses into a source of active political, economic, and military strength. The success of the government in hastening this process will hinge by and large on the consistency with which it carries out its stated programs of social reform.

Minority Groups and Social Structure

The Coptic Christian indigenous minority in Egypt is represented on all levels of the social scale. The social organization of Coptic and Moslem villages is practically identical, and Coptic and Moslem elements in mixed villages have for the most part lived together amicably. The Copts, most of whom are literate, have always been prominent in civil service posts and in business administration and banking. On the whole, they have been loyal supporters of the nationalist movement, and their active participation in domestic politics has helped to protect their minority rights. In recent years, a growing number of educated Moslems have competed for posts traditionally held by Copts, and in the present period of intense Moslem Egyptian nationalism there appears to be some tension between Moslems and Copts, although the only overt evidence of this is the tendency for the government to favor Moslems when making official appointments.

Before 1956, the Jews—an urban group—were found mainly in the upper and middle classes. Occupationally, they were usually self-employed businessmen or employees in banks or commercial enterprises. In the period just after World War I, Jews were also increasingly to be found in the professions, particularly medicine and law, and in the entertainment business as cinema owners and night-club proprietors. The Egyptian Jews generally preferred to make their investments in banks or on the stock exchange; only rarely did they become landowners, though some families have been known to do so.

The monopolization of Egyptian banking, commerce, and industry by non-Egyptians led to the establishment in Egypt of foreign colonies, among which the Greek, Armenian, Syrian, Lebanese, Italian, French, and British (this last group including many Maltese) were the most prominent. Of these, the western European groups remained largely self-contained. The British and French were usually in a position to deal with the Egyptian upper and upper-middle classes on socially equal terms, but many Italians entered such businesses as catering and building and tended to be in contact with a wider selection of the Egyptian social spectrum.

Armenians, Syrians, and Lebanese were to be found in middle-class business circles throughout the country, and some of the Syrians and Lebanese, through wealth and long residence, found

95

acceptance in upper-class circles. The Armenians, who numbered many wealthy members in their community, also included a highly skilled artisan group—skilled, for example, in bookbinding and the restoration of works of art. Armenians were also prominent in artistic, literary, and musical circles. Among the Greeks, there was a range from the wealthiest elements to the lower-middle class, as well as many poor and virtually illiterate Greeks (often from the Aegean Islands), who worked in hotels and restaurants and as taxi drivers.

CHAPTER 8

Traditional Patterns of Living

MOSLEM SOCIETY IN EGYPT SHOWS NO TRACES of alien influences or of survivals from periods before Islam, but the traditional patterns of living of the villagers do reflect survivals from very ancient times. In the field of what may be called political nationalism, efforts have been made in intellectual circles to identify an Egyptian personality, sometimes described as the "Pharaonic personality." Such efforts are less conclusive, however, than the parallels between daily life now and that of early centuries. The wall paintings in the tombs of the Old and New Kingdoms depict men and women doing the same chores, engaged in the same activities, and in just the same manner that is still in vogue. The same implements raise water from the canals to the fields, mud bricks are made in an identical fashion, the carpenters saw boards and use bow drills in the same way, and women still wail at funerals with their hands bent over their heads.

In its patterns of living, Moslem society now reflects an increasing conflict between the *qadim*, the old, and the *gadid*, the new. Here new means not new ideas, but new objects. It represents a drift toward materialism; toward the desire to acquire possessions, rather than the fatalistic acceptance of a meager existence.

Devotion to Islam, in word and deed, and family solidarity and honor are the major features of the daily life of the villagers. One of the central values of Islam is the equality of all men before Allah, and, concomitantly, the brotherhood of all Moslems. This religious concept, reinforced by community-wide observance of the commemorative feasts and by the common discipline of Islamic prayers, fasts, and pilgrimages serves to level barriers of status and wealth.

The intensity of the allegiance given to the family and the lineage is achieved at the expense of society in general. The attitudes and views which concentrate on the advancement of one's own group lead to favoritism, nepotism, and corruption—patterns of behavior

97

that plague the administrative services of the government, yet are not really to be condemned. The hiatus between loyalty to the kin group and the need to build loyalty to the nation or government has proved to be the source of considerable difficulty in the building of modern Egypt, as in a number of other countries. In this context, we may cite the apparent disinclination of the trained Egyptian soldier to fight in a determined manner for the defense of his country.

In the daily life of a Moslem, the conscious orientation toward the supernatural, or Allah, is continually expressed in the conventions of ordinary speech, general behavior patterns, and attitudes toward natural events. Egyptians refer to themselves as being of the "nation of Moslems," *ummat al-muslimin,* and they seem to feel that they are Arabs first of all—Arabs rather than Egyptians, since the Prophet was an Arab, and the religion of Allah was revealed in Arabia.

Social Behavior

The distinctions in social behavior between men and women are greatly emphasized in Egypt, as in all Moslem countries. Men should be aggressive and assertive; women should be dependent and nonaggressive. Sex is considered as a primary function of the human being, and there are almost no bachelors nor spinsters in Egyptian society. The procreation of children for the continuation of the male family line is a major responsibility of marriage for both men and women. Woman's primary role is as a mother; her acceptance by her husband's family and her status within the family are determined largely by the bearing of children, especially sons. Her lack of male children will bring on either divorce or the introduction of another wife into the household. A great deal of concern is shown for the chastity and fidelity of women of the family, and, as a result, crimes of passion involving the abuse of women are comparatively rare.

Social bonds among men are based on behavior patterns of respect and deference. Older persons and those of higher social class are tendered ceremonial expressions of respect by their juniors and inferiors. Society is so arranged that nearly everyone is superior to someone: the poorest villager can still consider himself superior to a merchant who is in his village but not accepted as a lineage member. The symbols of prestige and social status include the own-

ership of many feddans of land, a good house with modern appur-
tenances, and good clothes. Status has its obligations, primarily
in the display of hospitality. Generous hospitality, in turn, serves
to attract followers and supporters, whether it is for elections to
the village council or to higher office.

The Egyptian lives in an authoritarian atmosphere, in which
questioning the judgment or decisions of a superior is not per-
missible behavior. In general, the fellah is passive and apathetic
to things that do not concern him personally or over which he
has no power. He may, however, be shaken by sudden impulses,
and may resort to suicide or murder to solve insoluble problems
of daily life.

The present conflict between the old, qadim, and the new, gadid,
takes a number of forms. The challenge of the new stems primarily
from actions taken by the government. More jobs of more different
kinds are available, travel is easier for the villager and is more
frequently undertaken—even the pilgrimage to Mecca—and the
blaring radio with its movie music is favored over local poetry
and singing. The villager is burdened with economic problems and
hopes that in some way the government, now projecting a benefi-
cent image, will resolve his monetary concerns. With good reason,
the young have begun to lose their respect for their elders. While
a village has a largely illiterate adult population, nearly all of its
children are literate. They know more about more subjects than
the adults do, and discord is inevitable.

The old values of society are challenged, while the new ones
are said to be contained within Arab socialism, which replaces the
society of families with a communal society.

Time and Leisure

Attitudes toward time are characterized by considerable leniency
in comparison with the stricter standards of Western countries.
The fellah is little inclined to worry about the future, and, as one
reflection of this attitude, he sees little need for haste and hurry.
A thing may just as well be done *bokra,* tomorrow, as today; while
any agreement about a future obligation concludes with *inshallah,*
Allah willing. Although attitudes toward time are relaxed, and
clocks and watches are not generally used in the villages, people
recognize the time of day and night quite accurately according to
the positions of the sun and the stars. When it is considered impor-

tant in ritual performance, time can be observed strictly, but time scheduling is far from being practiced in daily life.

The year is organized according to several different calendrical systems. In rural areas the Coptic calendar—a solar calendar with its New Year on September 10th—governs all phases of cultivation. Sowing, irrigation, and reaping are carried on throughout the year in strict accord with the weeks and months of this calendar. Moslem religious holidays are based on a lunar calendar, and occur at different times each year. Both Christian and Moslem dates are given on the mastheads of newspapers and magazines published in the country, and the government observes the Christian calendar. The weekly holiday runs from Thursday afternoon until Saturday morning, with Friday as the day for Moslem congregational prayer.

In addition to the great festivals of Islam and those honoring the most renowned saints, many celebrations are held at the tombs of local saints. These occur most frequently during the full-moon nights of summer. A crowd collects around a tall pole erected adjacent to the tomb. Women bring food, temporary booths spring up, and entertainment appears. The entertainment may include a dhikr, with its religious aspect so de-emphasized that it features female singers and the recitation of secular poetry, performers who thrust spikes through their cheeks, and snake-charmers. Secular holidays are of less importance to the villagers than they are to the people in the cities, who can witness the pomp and circumstance of the military parades that go with them. Then too, these holidays have a transitory nature, as they may commemorate events that are suddenly no longer commemorated as governments change.

Sports play a fairly important role in the leisure-time activities of the Egyptian people. The cult of the athlete has for many years been strong in Egypt's middle class, and Egyptian athletes, particularly weight-lifters, wrestlers, and long-distance swimmers, are objects of popular adulation. Soccer is the national game, and the Egyptian soccer league has some excellent clubs. Sports are increasingly emphasized in the schools, as are the physical aspects of the military training given to students of all ages.

But the favorite leisure-time activity for adults of all classes is conversation. Women receive female callers at home and pay visits to women in other households, although a woman may achieve an unflattering reputation if she pays too many calls. The great informal club of the men of the middle and lower classes of both town and country is the coffeehouse—still so called, in spite of the fact that tea has taken over from coffee as the preferred drink. The gregariousness of the Egyptian male is nowhere better demonstrated than in the coffee shop, where the *nargileh* (water pipe) is passed around as coffee, tea, and light refreshments are served to an endless stream of customers and card games and *trictrac* (backgammon) are played continuously.

It may seem strange to an observer that so many men in Egypt apparently have so much leisure time, but the coffeehouse, usually in the vicinity of a market place or shopping center, is more than a place of recreation; it is much used for the dissemination of news, for the arrangement of marriage contracts, and for commercial transactions. Occupying a key position in the formation of public opinion, the coffeehouse is often also a center of political intrigue. In the countryside, the coffeehouse remains one of the two places (the other is the mosque) where social affairs and the intricacies of village politics are discussed and where decisions are taken. The older customers informally assume the role of arbiters of the discussions that take place there. The oldest and most valued customer is in effect chairman, and he is surrounded by others whose seniority and personal force have given them the prestige to act as leaders and judges in the coffeehouse arena. These men regularly occupy the same seats—which according to custom are strictly reserved for them—and even should one of these seats be the only empty chair in the house, no stranger or comparative newcomer would be allowed to sit in it. The only rule for acceptance in the coffeehouse coterie is approval by the informal committee; once a man is accepted, the only admission fee is the price of a cup of coffee. To be shunned by the leaders is to be banished, and the rejected customer must seek a welcome in another—often a rival—institution.

Nominally merely a public place of refreshment, the coffeehouse sooner or later takes on many of the aspects of a private club. Customers do not go the rounds of the coffeehouses; they stick to one, or two at the most, where they are welcomed and where they can develop their social, commercial, and political relationships in congenial surroundings.

Residential Patterns

Villages are dotted everywhere across the fertile landscape. As the villages grow steadily in size, they tend to merge in many areas, with the open land around them diminishing. Formerly these villages were roughly circular, with a road running around each village; few roads penetrated the village, and these could be closed at night by gates. Now order and security reigns, and the villages stand open, their lanes straightened and widened. Among the numerous open spaces may be a cemetery, a threshing floor, a *birka*, or pond (created by the digging of mud or clay for construction purposes), or some other open area adjacent to a mosque or a shrine. All but the smallest villages have more than one mosque and several saints' tombs.

Each house has its own vestibule, complete with a *mastaba*, or bench made of mud brick. The homes of the poorest peasants have one or two rooms, which the family shares with their domestic animals and fowls; while the better houses display a number of rooms arranged around or along an interior court. As already noted, each house shelters an extended family. Ideally, newlyweds live in the bride's household during the first few months of marriage. Then after the birth of the first child, the bridegroom brings his wife home to live in the house of his father. Actually, such factors as landownership and the compatibility of family members may alter the pattern; a young couple may go on residing with the bride's family if the groom is poor in land or if his services are needed by his parents-in-law. Or brothers sharing the paternal household may quarrel and set up separate living arrangements; however, a separation is sometimes accomplished simply by closing the interior doors between the two parts of the house and converting each part into a detached apartment, with a separate outside entrance.

Within the houses, straw mats or coarse carpets cover the ground, and mirrors and pictures cut from magazines decorate the walls. The tiny oil-burning lamps, identical with those used in ancient times, are giving way to gas mantle, pressure lamps (Coleman), while gasoline pressure stoves (Primus) are taking over the cooking. Clothing and other household goods may be stored in chests. While a family may be no better off now than a few years ago, the shift to a complete monetary system from one that involved both cash and barter has spurred the acquisition of household items and objects.

Whereas all but the poorer houses have guest rooms, an affluent rural family may construct an entire building for its hospitality. This may be a *medyata*, or guest house, or, if constructed by the omdeh or the senior member of a clan, it is called the *duwwar*, the great house.

The fields, normally consisting of many small and irregular plots of land, surround the village and are reached by the footpaths and lanes that radiate from it. These plots are irrigated throughout the year. Irrigation mechanisms include both power-driven pumps and the traditional manual- or animal-driven devices for raising the water from canals and channels to the fields. A village is entitled to draw water from a feeder canal only at stated intervals, while powered pumps can draw from wells at any time.

Towns, distinguished as such if they have 5,000 or more residents, provide goods and services not ordinarily available in the villages, including a variety of local and imported items. The town may also be the administrative center of an area, with local courts, police station, tax office, and other government offices to which the villager must repair on occasion. In general, these towns are not related to trade routes or water resources, as is the case in other countries of the Middle East; rather, they are spaced just far enough apart so that each can serve as a major merchandising center for a large group of villages.

The residential areas of the towns and cities are predominantly urban slums. A very small percentage of the city folk live in comfortable houses, set within carefully tended grounds—the vast majority of the inhabitants are crammed into apartment buildings. Underemployment in the villages drives young people to the cities, where they congregate in quarters occupied by earlier arrivals from the same province, even from the same village. Thus, they lead village life in the midst of the city, most of them among the most economically depressed of the inhabitants.

On a higher level, the typical middle-class living quarters are an apartment of from three to five rooms. These rooms are grouped around a central hall, which has a corridor leading to the kitchen and the bathroom. The central hall serves as the dining room, while one of the other rooms is the seldom-used living room, and the others are bedrooms. The lady of the house, assisted by an adolescent female servant, does the housekeeping and the cooking. The meals are scanty, the apartment meagerly furnished, the rooms in need of repair and paint, and those facilities that are dependent on electricity or water are more than likely to be out of order.

103

Clothing

Throughout most of the year, warm clothing is not needed. During the winter months, it may be chilly at night, and it is usually so at dawn throughout the year, when the farmer arises. To a large extent, cotton fabrics have replaced the earlier use of wool.

The basic item of the male costume is the galabia, a long-sleeved, long and loose cotton gown, comparable in appearance to an ample nightgown. For everyday wear it is usually white, but on festive occasions an indigo or black one is worn. Beneath the galabia, a vest is frequently worn over a long white shirt and baggy white drawers. In the fields, the galabia may be tucked up around the waist, or, during the heat of the day, may be taken off, along with the vest and shirt. The head is covered with a round cotton cap or with a white turban, 'imma, wound around a felt cap. Formerly the majority of the men went barefoot; now most wear slippers. When circumstances call for immediate action, the fellah shucks off his slippers, tucks a corner of his galabia in his mouth, and takes off at a run.

It has been remarked that the basic costume of the Egyptian men and women is very similar, and this fact is alleged to have some significance—just what it is has not been clearly explained. Under a black galabia, the woman wears a more colorful shirt or chemise, white cotton drawers, and a band around the breasts. Her head may be covered with a kerchief, black or colored, or with black headgear which falls back over the shoulders without veiling the face. The village woman is not veiled. Formerly, the family wealth was worn by the women: pendants of silver and gold, diadems and pectorals, gold earrings, necklaces of coral and amber, and anklets. Nowadays fewer of these items are worn. Either they have been converted into cash to meet pressing economic demands, or into cash and then into savings. The women employ henna, obtained from the crushed leaves of the tree of the same name, to color their hair an orange-red, and, for festivals their hands and feet as well. Kohl, a mixture of antimony and carbon black, is used on the eyelids and eyelashes.

In the towns, male and female members of the lower classes continue to wear the costumes of the villagers, while the rest of the population wears European dress. The lower public servants wear trousers and white shirts without neckties, while the higher level personnel dresses quite inappropriately for the climate in woolen suits, including coats and ties. Formerly the mark of the townsman was the fez, or tarboosh, but now it is rarely seen. Instead, the head is left uncovered: Nasser never wears a hat of any kind, while King Farouk always wore a tarboosh. Women's wear follows the fashions of Europe, in keeping with the local climate. Dresses with rather full skirts, sweater-and-skirt combinations, and blouses and slacks are worn—the latter on holidays.

CHAPTER 9

Education

No COUNTRY OF THE MIDDLE EAST PLACES A HIGHER PRIORITY on education than does Egypt. Official statements on the value of education relate the subject both to the need of the state for well-educated persons and to the fact that education results in a higher income for the individual. In spite of many serious problems that must be overcome, progress in the expansion of educational facilities in recent years has been remarkable.

In 1960, about 70 per cent of the population ten years old and older was illiterate. Due to Egypt's high rate of birth, children under 15 make up over 40 per cent of the population—a proportion that is more than 50 per cent higher than that of most industrialized countries. The annual flood of six-year-olds is beyond the capacity of the primary schools to absorb, in spite of a very active program of school construction. Between 1953 and 1964, the number of primary-school pupils increased by 136.6 per cent, while the number of primary schools increased by only 14 per cent. At the preparatory level, the student increase was 46.6 per cent, while the number of schools increased by 178.8 per cent. Then, at the secondary level, student increase was 139.4 per cent and school increase 26.6 per cent. In this same period, the number of college graduates in the liberal arts increased by 204.5 per cent, and those in science by 270.6 per cent.

History of the Educational System

Education in Egypt represents an amalgam of the centuries-old, religiously-oriented Islamic tradition on the one hand and a Western-inspired, secular system on the other. Against this background of Moslem religious teaching and Westernized liberal education a new, more unified, and highly nationalistic educational system has emerged.

Al-Azhar University, in Cairo, has long been at the pinnacle of Egyptian traditional education, and is regarded as the world center of Islamic learning. Affiliated with it are a number of institutes in Cairo and provincial centers which offer preparatory religious training at the primary and secondary levels. Below these are the village religious schools (*kuttabs*), which are now dying out but which were almost the only schools in the country until the nineteenth century.

Kuttab is an Arabic word connected in origin with the root *ktb*, which has to do with writing. It means "the place where the Holy Book is learned." Situated in or near the mosque, the kuttab is still the only school in many villages, and there was some opposition to the new government schools on the ground that they do not provide a proper religious atmosphere.

Originally, kuttabs were financed largely by *waqfs* (charitable foundations). In 1906 they came under the supervision of the national government, which in return for financial aid insisted upon the inclusion of the three R's in the curriculum. The basis of learning in the kuttabs, however, is still the memorization of the Qur'an; reading and writing are of secondary importance. In addition to teaching village children (until recently almost exclusively boys), the kuttab teacher, who is addressed as "sheikh," may also function as imam of the mosque, and he usually exercises considerable influence over the beliefs and attitudes of the adult villagers.

A family may gain prestige by sending its children to the kuttab, but the time spent there is often regarded as an economic loss, since peasant children commonly help in the fields from a very early age. Usually, it is the younger brothers who attend the kuttab, while the older ones work on the land. In the tradition of the kuttab, practical training for economic tasks is left entirely within the province of the family. Pupils are expected to memorize the Qur'an by the fourth year at the kuttab, but the demands for child labor prevent many from finishing the course. The few who do complete it generally go to one of the institutes of al-Azhar to prepare for religious work or teaching.

The Arabic word for pupil or student, *talib*, literally means "seeker." In the Islamic tradition of teaching, oral communication and memorization are considered the best methods of transmitting knowledge. A good memory is highly valued, and memory training is started at the preschool age by the family. Traditionally, the pursuit of knowledge for Moslem scholars has been not so much

107

a question of probing the unknown as a process of learning the known, which is seen as eternal and unchangeable. The amassing of information and deduction from accepted premises constitute knowledge. A man is honored as learned on the basis of the amount of the Qur'an and the number of prophetic traditions he can quote or by the proverbs he can marshal in argument. (The Qur'an is frequently invoked to substantiate a point, even in discussions of nonreligious matters.) This emphasis on rote learning has left a deep imprint upon secular education in Egypt and frequently conflicts with Westernized teaching and experimental methods. Students are so conditioned to memorization as the major process of learning that even at the university level they are often embarrassed and resentful when called upon to exercise reason or initiative. Facility of verbal expression ranks high as an attainment of the educated man, and eloquence and diction tend to take precedence over substance.

Secular education in Egypt had its origin with the absorption of Egypt in the Ottoman Empire in 1517, but did not develop extensively until the period of French influence in the nineteenth century. Napoleon's invasion brought many French scholars to Egypt, and later Muhammad Ali (1805-48) set up schools on the French model with the help of French experts. He also sent many students to Europe. Upon their return to Egypt, these students exerted a considerable Westernizing influence by translating into Arabic European works on history, medicine, law, science, literature, and economics.

The foreign—largely mission—schools, which date from the rule of Muhammad Ali, have constituted another agency of Western intellectual penetration into the country. By 1878, 52 per cent of Egyptian boys in school were in European-administered institutions. Although American missionary activity in the Near East initially centered in Lebanon, its influence was beginning to be felt elsewhere in the Arab world by the late 1800s.

With the British occupation, the Ministry of Education came under British control, but neither the French language nor French influence was really displaced. Apart from insuring an adequate supply of trained clerical help in government, the British did little in the educational field other than to continue the practice of sending selected young men abroad to study. In fact, their failure to provide more schooling for the mass of the population has been the most criticized aspect of their rule, and is remembered with resentment and bitterness among Egyptians even today. By the turn of the century, dissatisfaction with the British response to insistent demands for the expansion of educational facilities produced a movement for the establishment of schools by municipalities. Many private schools were also founded about this time, including the establishment in 1908 of what is now Cairo University. In 1908, also, popular pressure caused English to be replaced by Arabic as the principal language of instruction in government schools. With the achievement of independence in 1923, Egypt embarked upon an ambitious program aimed at providing free public education.

The end of British rule by no means brought about the end of British influence in educational policy, however. English remained the language of instruction in many private and foreign schools, as well as a principal foreign language in state schools. The teaching of science, medicine, and engineering in the universities continued to be based on British patterns. Also dating from the period of the British occupation is the popular conception of education as a means to government position. Western influence as a whole has retained its hold on Egyptian education through the activity of the foreign schools and through the current prestige of secular-trained intellectuals, particularly those who have studied abroad. These, rather than the traditional religious leaders, are increasingly looked to for leadership.

The Present Educational System

The Ministry of Education exercises direct control over all schools up to the college level, prescribing the curriculum, appointing teachers, and setting general examinations. This control allows very little scope for initiative on the part of the teachers, especially with the recent emphasis placed on Arab nationalism and Arab socialism. The Ministry of Higher Education supervises the higher institutions of learning. State concern with education is reflected by the facts that in 1951 the national budget for education was £E 40.1 million and in 1964 £E 96.5 million, while in 1951 there were less than 2 million students and in 1964 nearly 6 million. All education is tuition free.

As early as 1925, compulsory education was introduced for children from ages 6 to 12. This proved unworkable, as did a second effort in 1930. In these and later years, the introduction of general elementary education was blocked by a number of problems. For one thing, there was general suspicion of government-provided education, a feeling among the villagers that the aims and methods of state schools were neither relevant to practical life nor suitable on religious grounds. An even more compelling factor in the evasion of school attendance was the paramount importance of children as a nonsalaried element of the agricultural labor force. And finally, there was the traditional belief that the education of girls was wasteful, if not useless.

The above attitudes have changed. Whereas in 1913 only 10 per cent of the primary and secondary school population was girls, it is now 37 per cent. Attendance in the primary schools now averages 85 per cent of enrollment, dropping to about 60 per cent in seasons when the children are badly needed in the fields. Also, the rural people now recognize the value of state education in leading to prestige in the local community and to civil service positions.

Primary, Preparatory, and Secondary School Curricula

Instruction is in Arabic, and the present-day curriculum embodies three stages: primary, preparatory, and secondary. This educational ladder is uniform for Egypt, Syria, and Jordan, according to an agreement signed in 1957 by the governments of these countries. The primary stage covers six years, from ages 6 to 12. Although compulsory by law, the capacity of the schools is less than the number of potential students. Courses include Arabic, religion, arithmetic, history, geography, civics, hygiene, physical education, and handicrafts. The relatively large proportion of time devoted to the study of the Arabic language and literature is necessitated by the substantial difference between the classical written language and the spoken language. The primary schools have as their aim the creation of good students who are proud of Arab nationalism and who are prepared to take their places in a democratic, socialistic society. About 1963, the Ministry ordered that Arab nationalism, socialism, the history of the Revolution, and the National Charter of 1962 were to be taught in the primary stage and at all higher levels. Tests at the end of each year lead up to a final, competitive examination. Success on this examination results in admission to the preparatory stage; whereas failure means the end of state education. About 70 per cent of the pupils do stop at this level.

110

The preparatory stage covers three years, and concludes with examinations for the secondary stage, also consisting of three years. The secondary schools are taught by university graduates. Mathematics, laboratory sciences, art, one or two foreign languages (English and French), and military training supplement the earlier curriculum. There are general secondary schools, with literary and science sections; industrial secondary schools; and agricultural secondary schools, each with an experimental farm. The industrial and agricultural schools represent the higher stage of the system of vocational schools, which begins at the preparatory level. Successful graduates of the general secondary schools may apply for admission to colleges; while those of the vocational schools may attend specialized institutes, but not colleges. Training centers for the fields of industry, commerce, agriculture, hotels, and tourism have a current enrollment of about 3,000 students; the centers appear to parallel the operations of the higher vocational schools.

Prior to 1952, nearly 300 private schools, some foreign-owned, attracted families of wealth and position. Arabic was not stressed in these schools, and, indeed, students and graduates proudly spoke other languages. These schools have now been either nationalized or brought under the control of the state.

Higher Education

Higher education is supervised by the Ministry of Higher Education and is represented by five state universities, some 40 state colleges and institutes, and one private university. About 120,000 students attend the universities, with girls making up from 20 to 25 per cent of this number, while some 26,000 students attend the higher institutes.

The Supreme Council of the Universities plans educational policy and research programs, coordinates working relations and courses of study between institutions, and advises the government on financial matters related to the universities. Each university is headed by a president or a rector (*mudir*), who is supported by a university senate, college councils, and department councils. Through numerous legal and administrative controls, the Ministry of Higher Education may influence university affairs, but in practice the several rectors enjoy a considerable measure of autonomy. Administrations and students are expected to promote the aims of the Arab Socialist Union, and students are encouraged to join the Socialist Youth Organization.

111

Al-Azhar was founded in 970 as a state center for prayer and the propagation of Islam. It became an institution of higher Moslem learning in 988—it is frequently referred to as the world's oldest university—and in all successive centuries, it has functioned both as a mosque and a school. Until academic reforms were begun in the third quarter of the nineteenth century, al-Azhar had no entrance requirements, no set courses of study, and no formal degrees. Students were housed in *riwaqs*, or residential quadrangles; they clustered around the teachers, who seated themselves at the bases of columns, and discoursed on the classics of the past. Study might stretch out over many years. When a student wished to leave, he would obtain a certificate from a teacher recording the subjects studied and the level of learning achieved.

In more recent times, a student was required to have nine years of preparation at an al-Azhar institute before he could enter the four-year courses of the Colleges of Islamic Law, Theology, or Arab Letters. He then had a choice of further specialization to prepare him to teach or to become a religious judge (*qadi*), and could take degrees roughly equivalent to a master's degree or doctorate. Al-Azhar was governed by a body of learned men (ulama), headed by the Sheikh al-Azhar, the government-appointed rector, who was recognized as the supreme religious leader in Egypt. In this post, the rector exerted considerable political as well as religious influence throughout the country.

After the revolution of 1952, a number of changes were made to bring the administration and curriculum of al-Azhar into line with the secular system of education, and the institution gained formal university status, under the name al-Jami'ah al-Azhariyah. The abolition of all religious courts in Egypt on January 1, 1956, made the future of graduates of al-Azhar appear bleak. In addition, the government named a series of military men to the post of Director of al-Azhar Affairs.

On June 23, 1961, the National Assembly passed a law which effectively "nationalized" al-Azhar. The institution was divided into several departments: the Supreme Council, al-Azhar University, the al-Azhar institutes, the Moslem Research Academy, and the department of Moslem Culture and Missions. The Sheikh al-Azhar presides over the Supreme Council and is recognized as the Grand Imam of Egypt, but his role is primarily honorary. To the three existing faculties, the law added those of Medicine, Agriculture, Business Administration, and Engineering and Industries, as well

112

as a faculty of Islamic Studies for girls. Al-Azhar has an enrollment of over 42,000 students in all its departments, including some 7,000 from foreign countries, with most of these Moslems from Asia and Africa. Nearly 10,000 students attend al-Azhar University itself.

Cairo University was originally established in 1908 as a private school. In 1925, it became the Egyptian University, in 1940 it was called Fuad I University, and in 1953 it received its present name. It comprises 12 colleges: Arts, Law, Commerce, Dar al-Ulum, Economics and Political Science, Medicine, Pharmacy, Dentistry, Veterinary Medicine, Agriculture, Science, and Engineering. Its libraries contain over half a million volumes, and the press affiliated with the University has published over 500 books. Specialized institutes include the Meteorological Institute, the Magnetic Station, the Institute of Oceanography, and the Marine Biological Station. Enrollment is over 41,000, of whom nearly 9,000 are girls.

In 1938, the Egyptian University established a branch at Alexandria, and in 1942 this branch became a separate institution called Farouk I University. After July 1952, it became Alexandria University. With nine colleges, this university has an enrollment of about 29,000 students.

Ain Shams (or "City of the Sun," from its situation at the suburb of Heliopolis) University was founded in 1950 as Ibrahim Pasha University, and in 1954 took its present name. With nine colleges, it has about 33,000 students. Asyût University was established in 1957: it has six colleges and nearly 8,000 students.

The American University of Cairo began operations in 1920 as a junior college. Essentially an American-type, liberal arts college, it is administered by a board of trustees in the United States. Some 1,000 students are enrolled in the Faculty of Arts and Sciences, School of Oriental Studies, Division of Public Services, Social Research Center, and English Language Institute. Instruction is primarily in English.

While it is unsound to try to characterize Egyptian university education in a few words, a brief comment seems appropriate here. In general, the system of instruction is closer to the French than to the Anglo-Saxon model: Professors may lecture to very large classes, there is limited contact between teachers and students, and heavy stress is placed on the examinations held at the end of each semester. Trends in education matching the trend of the times, the brightest students take up medicine, engineering, or the sciences.

113

Egypt continues to send both students and teachers abroad. Each year, there are about 6,000 Egyptians studying in foreign universities. Government permission, based on the applicant's qualifications and his field of study, is required before such a student may leave Egypt. The largest number of Egyptians are in West Germany, with somewhat smaller numbers in the United States, Austria, the United Kingdom, and the Soviet Bloc countries. At the same time, there are close to 20,000 foreign students in Egypt, largely from Arab-speaking countries (although 2,000 come from non-Arab African states). Also, Egypt exports teachers for all levels of instruction: in 1964 there were 4,500 teachers and several hundred professors abroad. Algeria had 2,000, Libya 825, the Sudan 740, and there were large numbers in Somalia, Kuwait, Yemen, and Saudi Arabia as well as in several other countries. Needless to say, these teachers and the Egyptian Cultural Centers in these countries serve to support the policies of the state and the goals of Arab socialism.

A major problem of Egyptian education has been aptly described as its "nonfunctional character." This lack of suitability to indigenous needs has begun to assume serious proportions in the shape of a yearly crop of several thousand young men and women unsuitably educated for the positions that exist. White-collar unemployment has now reached a sizable figure. Moreover, the dissatisfaction of many young people with any but government or other urban positions may well have serious economic repercussions. Higher education has often proved a means of luring the more able students permanently away from their home communities, where their training is badly needed. In the eyes of most young people, education is still primarily a path to the comforts of city life and to a career in politics, civil service, law, journalism, or teaching.

The government is alert to this problem and is actively taking steps to integrate education more closely with Egypt's vital needs. Stress is being placed on the value and dignity of manual and industrial labor, and the number of vocational training institutes has risen to 3,029 in 1964. The Teachers Colleges, which numbered 62 in 1953, rose to 71 in 1964, with a total of 41,259 students. Their graduates are encouraged to take posts at the lower level schools in villages, as well as to volunteer for posts abroad.

Students in Egypt, as elsewhere in the Middle East, are conscious of themselves as a distinct and powerful group. They are fully aware that in a largely illiterate population the educated wield authority disproportionate to their numbers. Until recently, particularly at the university level, they tended to engage in political activities and to make their influence felt through strikes and demonstrations which disrupted discipline and often caused the suspension of classes. Political parties and nationalist leaders often incited students to political action. The Wafd (traditional nationalist party), for example, made frequent use of student demonstrations against the British. More recently, many students participated in the riots of January 1952; it is reported that Communist student leadership played a prominent role. "Freedom battalions" were recruited from several universities, and normal educational work came to a standstill for several weeks.

But this situation has now changed. Government and school authorities exercise a careful control over such student activities. Demonstrations are permitted only when sponsored by the government itself, and, as indicated earlier, student activity is expected to conform to the aims of the Arab Socialist Union. Student unions were the subject of a lengthy Presidential Decree of December 1966. According to its articles, the students of every university shall form unions with the aims, among others, of participating in the consolidation of the Socialist Society and the Youth Organization of the ASU, and of informing these organizations about the nation's history of liberty, socialism, and unity.

CHAPTER *10*

Art and Literature

ARTISTIC AND INTELLECTUAL EXPRESSION HAS BEEN of central importance in the Egyptian tradition—not so much for its own sake as
in relation to the Islamic faith with which it was identified and
which supported it. Until the latter half of the nineteenth century,
Egyptian artistic and intellectual activity was almost exclusively
religious in its inspiration. The visual arts, restricted in their scope
by religious prohibitions, were conceived primarily as a means of
expressing the glory of Allah. Jalal al-Din al-Rumi, the thirteenth-
century Persian mystic, put it, "the external form [of the artist's
work] is for the sake of the unseen forms; and that took shape for
the sake of another unseen [form]." Similarly, intellectual expression was bound within the tight limits of the literal word of God
as set forth in the Qur'an. After a brief flowering of intellectual
activity in the early days of the Islamic conquest, Moslem thinkers
turned to the exegesis of God's word and away from any original
attempt to illuminate His nature. One student of the area writes
that "all their [the Arabs'] intellectual powers were directed into
the effort to build up the structure of the religious institutions of
Islam and to make it dominant in every relationship of social life
as it already dominated their mental life."

Out of these efforts emerged a remarkably unified pattern of
life and thought. Religion provided the code by which life was
to be governed; art, drawing upon religion, lent beauty to that life,
and the intellect served to interpret and maintain it.

Restricted as it was to a narrowly defined interpretation of
Islamic doctrine, creative activity in the Arab world for at least
the 300 years preceding the nineteenth century emphasized an
appeal to the emotions rather than to reason. The consequence for
art and literature was an emphasis on inspired detail at the expense of over-all balance, unity, and coherence. The outcome of
this emphasis has been described as a "series of separate moments,

each complete in itself and independent, connected by no principle of harmony or congruity beyond the unity of the imagining mind."

Into this static context in the early years of the nineteenth century was exploded a dynamic Western intellectual and artistic tradition, in which both the rational and the emotional were present and tension was achieved in the conflict between the two. This alien tradition had an identity apart from religion, and it tended to destroy the traditional union of religion with other aspects of Egyptian life. Hereafter, the monopoly of Islam over Egyptian artistic and intellectual efforts was to decline, and in many cases these efforts were to be turned against religion itself. Once the initial shock was dissipated, the reaction of the Egyptian elite to Western contact often took the form of slavish imitation. Years passed before any serious attempt was made to adapt Western culture to Egyptian realities, and only recently has there been an effort to evaluate the Western achievement in terms of its meaning to Egypt.

Today a number of points of view compete for favor and support, particularly among the elite. One (perhaps best exemplified by Sayed Koth's *Social Justice in Islam*) calls for complete rejection of all forms of Western innovation and a return to a pure Islamic faith and practice. Another proposes adoption of Western technique as a means of reviving the true values of Islamic culture. The relative success of these schools of thought often can be discerned in current artistic and intellectual productions and has some value as a barometer of the urban Egyptian reaction to Western influence.

Despite centuries of exposure to foreign influences, certain aspects of Egypt's art and thought continue to reveal their distinctively Egyptian origin. Among these, there is the emphasis on the fanciful. The versatility of the Egyptian imagination is one of the most striking features of Egypt's long literary tradition. The shipwrecked sailor who peoples a remote isle with beasts and gods (Middle Kingdom), the Coptic saint who converses with the dead from the underworld (Christian era), the Moslem hero who bends the ogress to his will (Islamic period), and the humble hawker of peanuts and melon seeds who becomes a wonder-working saint in the eyes of the Cairene doorkeepers (modern) are all typical of Egyptian fantasy. A love of the picaresque finds its outlet in tales of thieves and sharpers, humble men of the cities who, by a combination of audacity and craft, defy and outwit the rich and the mighty amid the acclaim of the dispossessed. Underlying many

117

of the most persistent literary themes appears to be a desire to escape harsh reality or to fix blame for the common plight.

An important and persistent characteristic of Egyptian intellectual activity is the lack of interest in theoretical, as contrasted with applied, effort. Historically, the Egyptians have not demonstrated any remarkable prowess in such speculative fields as theology or philosophy. The speculative literature of the last centuries of ancient Egypt was neither large in quantity nor profound in thought. Christian Egypt is remembered for its monasticism and mystical poetry rather than its theology. In the Moslem period, the theories upon which Islam as a religion and as a body politic are based were developed in Medina, Damascus, and Baghdad, and the Egyptian contributions to them were minimal. A similar neglect of the theoretical is apparent in other fields. The pyramids constructed early in Egyptian history evidence a practical knowledge of the basic principles of mathematics, but it remained for the Greeks to actually formulate and develop these principles into more complex and theoretical mathematics.

Traditionally, the Egyptian artist and thinker, as the bearer and illuminator of his society's sacred knowledge, has participated in the glory and prestige accorded that knowledge. He was honored, not as the possessor of a particular talent, but as an instrument of God's creativity. The drift of Egyptian artists and intellectuals away from religion in our time has not brought any appreciable diminution of their status. Indeed, many Egyptians, caught in the conflict between Western and traditional values, have ceased to look to the religious authorities and have turned instead to the Westernized intellectuals for guidance out of the impasse.

Aware of the importance of arts and letters in the development of material pride and international prestige, the Egyptian government has for some years been active in the support of artistic and intellectual talent. Students who show promise in their early schooling may be granted government scholarships for further study at home or abroad. The government also sponsors a number of permanent art exhibits, which permit young artists to become known to the public. In special circumstances, the government may itself finance artistic and literary projects or encourage certain types of work by holding competitions for which prizes are offered. The plethora of paintings giving the Egyptian version of the Port Said invasion in 1956 provides an example of the way in which Egypt's artists can rally—or be rallied—to a national cause.

118

Despite government financial and other assistance, however, it is difficult for artists or intellectuals to achieve prominence or financial security. Most of them are obliged to practice their skills only as week-end hobbies. Others more fortunate are able to find positions in schools, research institutions, museums—most of which are owned or controlled by the government—or on newspapers.

Very little has been recorded about the position—symbolic or social—of artists and intellectuals in Egypt. The importance of additional information on this point is indicated by the susceptibility of this group to international influence of all kinds and the strategic position they occupy in the communication of ideas within the country and in the construction of the national self-image.

Artistic and Intellectual Background

Egypt was one of the earliest centers of advanced intellectual and artistic activity. Archaeological discoveries indicate that by 3000 B.C., Egyptians were working in practically all the fields of art. Both the Greeks and the Hebrews were influenced by developments in Egypt, and their own legacies to the Western world incorporated more than a little of this borrowing. Later, Egypt played an important role in the cultural development of the Mediterranean and Middle Eastern worlds, and it influenced and was influenced by the major civilizations of that region.

Ancient Egypt. Ancient Egypt employed many of the literary forms that are in use today. Poetry, important throughout Egyptian history, reached a high degree of elaboration. Prose also developed early, and by the end of the Middle Kingdom almost all of the characteristic modes of Egyptian prose were present—the tales of voyage and adventure, stories of heroism and war, and above all the tales of fantasy, wonder, and witchcraft. Prominent among such tales of fantasy is the *Story of Sinuhe,* the story of an Egyptian who, accidentally learning of the violent death of King Ammenemes I, flees in fear to Palestine and there rises to a position of eminence and esteem. In the small compass of 350 lines, the author of *Sinuhe* manages both a skillful personal portrait and an adventure story. The *Story of Wenamun,* written during the XXth dynasty, recounts the travels of an Egyptian diplomat who might almost be a contemporary official.

The visual arts were among the earliest developed in ancient

119

Egypt. While Egyptian art discoveries have been confined mainly to tombs, many of the buried objects were articles of everyday use, and in the elegance and beauty of their design reveal the importance of art in the daily life of the time. Outstanding examples of ancient Egyptian art are the works of the Memphis sculptors; the Great Pyramid at Giza, which exemplifies the tremendous activity carried on in the construction of sacred buildings; exquisite pieces in jewelry, gold, and ivory; the drawings and paintings of the Theban artists; and masterpieces of heraldry and hieroglyphic calligraphy.

Egypt between the Persian and Islamic conquests. In the period between Egypt's absorption into the Achaemenid Empire of Persia in 525 B.C. and the Islamic conquest in the seventh century A.D., Egypt was successively influenced by the Persians, the Greeks, the Romans, and the Byzantine Empire. Of particular importance were the spread of Greek thought and the rise of Christianity, both of which were strongly felt in Egypt. With a few exceptions, however, Egyptians were not stimulated to any heights of philosophical speculation, and their contributions remained essentially concrete in nature. The elaboration in Egypt of Christian monasticism was a feature of this period, and the austerity and devotion of the Coptic-speaking Christians were famous throughout the Christian world.

Interest in the arts and letters, dormant and seemingly moribund during the Roman period, woke to life in Egypt under the influence of Christianity. Soon a whole literature, mainly translated from Greek into Coptic Egyptian, provided reading that included the works of Homer, Menander, Hesiod, Sappho, Pindar, and Aristophanes. Later, in the twilight of the Byzantine period, Egypt, which during the Roman period had been comparatively poor in writers, produced several of note.

Prior to the Moslem invasion, Egypt—particularly its urban elite —had for centuries been swept by diverse cultural currents. A Christian country, it nonetheless retained a lively memory of its pagan past, and the Greek classics continued to form the essential base of a liberal education for Egyptians.

Moslem Egypt. Converted to Islam following the Arab conquest, Egypt contributed little to the philosophical development of this creed or to the later theorizing on the nature of the Islamic social order. The imaginative cast of the Egyptian mentality, however, was reflected in Egypt's role in the development of Islamic mysticism. Among the great mystical poets of Arabic literature who were produced by Egypt, most important were Ibn al-Farid (born 1181) and al-Busiri (born 1213), whose panegyric of the Prophet, *Ode of the Mantle,* is considered the most perfect example of its kind.

Another significant Egyptian contribution to Islamic literature was the art of the story. Native Arabic writing prior to the Egyptian contribution was poor in narrative literature, and it had progressed little beyond the anecdote, in which it excelled. The stock of stories produced by Egyptians in the early Islamic period drew heavily on the past for themes. Strange tales and miraculous narratives were derived from Coptic tradition, and the literature of fantasy was employed to explain the many relics of Egypt's ancient glory. Soon the more recent Islamic heritage began to be exploited in the same way, and incidents in the lives of great men of the time were depicted with consummate skill. Stories of the ingenious roguery of city sharpers and thieves, usually with ironic reflections on the honesty and efficiency of the police, are also characteristic of Egyptian writing of that and subsequent periods.

Egypt had long been outstanding in the visual arts, and its contribution in this realm after the Moslem conquest was immediate and impressive. Egyptian craftsmen were recruited for service outside the country and were employed on the early mosques of Jerusalem and Damascus. Limited by religious tradition against representing the human body, graphic art in Moslem Egypt found an outlet in the development of geometrical design in every imaginable kind of material. Bookbinding, which reached a high peak of perfection in Egypt, gave full scope to the geometric motif. It was in calligraphy that geometric design found its fullest expression in magnificent reproductions of the Qur'an and in inscriptions decorating the walls of mosques and other public buildings.

Little has been written on the influence of the Ottoman Turks (1517-1914) on Egyptian artistic and intellectual development. Whether or not Turkish rule was a factor in the intellectual and artistic stagnation in the Arab world under the Ottoman Empire, the common Arab view is that the Turkish period was a repressive and stultifying one.

121

The Oral and Literary Tradition

Skillful use of the written and spoken word in set speeches, poetry, and formal prose stands at the head of the arts in Egypt and other Moslem countries. More than a means of communication, language, manipulated according to highly formalized canons of taste, becomes an end in itself. A well-worded speech, a proverb, a verse of poetry, or a recitation from the Qur'an may prove conclusive where logic has failed. As one student has stated it: "Upon the Arab mind the impact of artistic speech is immediate; the words, passing through no filter of logic or reflection which might weaken or deaden their effect, go straight to the head."

Telling and listening to stories is largely restricted to children and adolescents, although adults, who may say that story-telling is a waste of time, probably tell stories to their children more often than they will admit. Stories play an important role in preparing the children to understand the norms and attitudes governing family and community life. Folklore is also in some degree indicative of current tensions, conflicts, and frustrations in the society in which it occurs. A study of the tales told by children in the Egyptian village of Silwa reveals three basic themes which recurred in almost every tale. The first theme was a concern with food, especially meat. The second touched upon the Oedipus complex and emphasized masculinity. The third was the theme of revenge and retaliation. In these stories, the principal actor commonly achieves success by trickery and chicanery. In one tale, for example, the cock, who is represented as the weakest of all animals, succeeds through cleverness in besting the more powerful animals.

In adult life an extensive literature of proverbs and wise sayings is brought to bear in daily conversation. In their very banality, these sayings carry the force of immemorial usage, and they are highly effective counters in discussion and argument.

The Influence of the West

Western cultural penetration has brought about significant changes in the forms of literary expression, but has not diminished the status of that medium as the dominant artistic form. The major changes that have resulted from contact with the West are the abandonment of the traditional Islamic poetry for Western verse forms and the replacement of such traditional literary styles as the *maqama* (a type of strictly rhymed prose which lent itself to rhetorical virtuosity) by the novel and the short story. The drama is another artistic form borrowed from the West, and both essays and biographies have become important literary forms during the past 50 years. Taha Hussein's *The Future of Culture in Egypt* is a well-known series of essays on diverse aspects of Egyptian cultural life.

A significant change in narrative form is reflected in the attempt to concentrate more on over-all balance, unity, and coherence and less on inspired detail. This effort has not been completely successful, however; even the most Westernized authors feel compelled to present the reader with one climax after another, to the detriment of story coherence.

Contact with the West has enriched Egyptian literature, but it has not been an unmitigated blessing. The shift in emphasis from refined beauty of language to communication of information has made the old literary standards obsolete, but no coherent and generally acceptable set of new standards has been created to replace them.

Poetry

Of all literary forms, poetry has at once the greatest traditional value, the widest appeal, and the greatest emotional impact on the Egyptian mind. In a society which was always largely illiterate, poetry—along with the folk tale—was most easily committed to memory and transmitted by word of mouth. Moreover, traditional Egyptian poetry was designed to appeal to the emotions of the many rather than the critical taste of the few.

Western influence has altered both Egyptian poetic form and content. Three influential poets, al-Aqqad, Mazni, and Shukri, all born in the last decade of the nineteenth century, were quite well-read in Western literature, especially English. Admirers of the romantic movement in this poetry, they found the traditional forms inadequate for the times. Younger poets, grouped in the Apollo Society, headed by Dr. Abu-Shady, were even more outspoken in their admiration for the English romantics and the French symbolists. About 1945, Dr. Lewis Awad published a collection of verse entitled *Plutoland*. He was one of the first to abandon the use of the same rhyme throughout a poem. He also wrote verses

123

in the colloquial, and introduced forms new to Egypt, such as the sonnet.

Skepticism, disillusionment, and despair were keynotes of the newer poetry. In the *Biography of Satan,* by Mahmud al-Aqqad (which has been compared in theme to T. S. Eliot's *The Waste Land*), Satan looks on humanity as so worthless as to be beneath his attempts to corrupt it. The work symbolizes the poet's own loss of faith in life and his personal reaction to the influence of the West. As he wrote, "I was swept with an injurious skepticism . . . which shook all my basic beliefs . . . I could no longer see any wisdom or meaning in life. It became distasteful in all its forms and purposes."

Other poets followed a more positive road and wrote about the problems confronting their nation: social injustice, administrative corruption, and anti-Western themes were common in their works. Not only did such works feature a devastating criticism of contemporary life but they also sounded a call for action. One poem directed against the corruption of the wealthy concludes:

> Listen, my brother, crying is not enough;
> Only diamond cuts diamond.

Recently, Salah Abdel Sabour has expressed the poet's dilemma: "All real art is pessimistic, for art is an expression of man's longing to free himself from his own chains." He does, however, praise the present state of the art, writing, "Our poetry has been renewed, it has a fresh vision and a greater simplicity." This poetry displays an increasing boldness of form and an experimental interest. Rhymes are used, changed, and dropped at will; and imagery, symbolism, and metaphors feature this writing.

Salah Abdel Sabour, the literary editor of *al-Ahram,* is a towering figure in this field. In 1957 he published a collection of poems entitled *Al-Nas fi Beladi* (*One People Is My Country*), in 1961 a group called *Aqoul Laqoum* (*I Will Tell You*), and in 1965 a poem in free verse entitled *Ahlam al-Fares al-Qadim* (*Dreams of the Old Knight*). A sense of alienation pervades much of his work:

> The night, my friend . . .
> Lets suspicions loose in my small bed,
> And burdens the heart with blackness,
> And with the voyage of total loss in
> the sea of mourning.

124

Prose

The novel and the modern short story were unknown in Egypt prior to Western cultural penetration. These literary forms were quickly adopted by Egyptian writers, and were employed to treat the problems and perplexities resulting from the Western impact. The popularity of the novel and the short story in contemporary Egypt reflects the shift in literary emphasis from formal beauty of language to the communication of information and the discussion of problems.

In 1914, the late Muhammad Husayn Heykal wrote the first "modern" novel, *Zaynab*. Soon after, Tewfik al-Hakim moved into the field. His *Maze of Justice* recalls Gogol's *Dead Souls* in its criticism of an inefficient and corrupt bureaucracy. A stinging satire on the red tape and the inhumanity of the bureaucratic legal system in Egypt, it provides a vivid and realistic picture of Egyptian village life. One of the major themes of this work is the injustice that arises from the mechanical application of European law in a traditional Moslem community. A second theme is the ignorance and venality of an officialdom that uses its position to abuse and exploit a helpless peasantry. Human want, vengeance, and blood feuds also loom large in this portrayal of rural Egypt. In another work, *Awdal al-Ra'h* (*The Rediscovered Soul*), al-Hakim borrows the symbolism of the resurrection in the ancient Egyptian *Book of the Dead* to construct a novel whose theme is the reawakening of Egypt after the revolt of 1919. Western imperialism, and not Egyptian corruption and inefficiency, is made the culprit. This work made a deep impression on the student Gamal Abdel Nasser.

Majib Mahfuz, born at Cairo in 1912, is considered to be the leading novelist of the present generation. In 1956 and 1957 he published a trilogy, each volume bearing the name of a street in Cairo: *Bayn al-Qasrayn*, *Qasr al-Shawq*, and *al-Sokkariya*. The series traces the life of a conservative Moslem family of small shopkeepers from 1917 until 1944. In 1962 appeared his *The Thief and the Dogs,* a bitter tale in which injustice triumphs over the leading character, the thief.

Yusuf Idris, a physician turned writer and the author of a biweekly column of literary criticism for *al-Gumhuriya*, writes with detached humor and unsentimental pathos. His first novel, *Arhas Layli* (*The Less-Valued Nights*) explores the misery caused by overpopulation among the fellahin whose only activity away from

125

the fields is to produce more children. This work reflects a familiar theme, that of the dreary life of the peasants of the Delta. In the same vein, Abd al-Rahman al-Sharqawi wrote *al-Ard* (*The Earth*), the story of peasants exploited by landowners. According to Idris, prose writers have been compelled to create a modern Arabic to convey new thoughts and feelings.

An important novel by Fathy Ghanem, editor of *al-Gumhuriya*, has appeared in English translation under the title *The Man Who Lost His Shadow*. The story of a rising journalist is told from the points of view first of people with whom he came into conflict, and, finally, by himself. His own account ends, "Death is dead."

Writers of the short story have come into prominence more recently. Mahmud Taimur's *Comedy of Death* is a vivid portrayal of the greediness of man. In a different vein, his *Amm Mitwalli* is the tale of a humble peanut vendor who finds himself elevated to the position of a village saint as a result of the imaginings of the villagers. This story is characteristic of a genre which appeals to the Egyptian love of fantasy.

In 1956, Muhammad Sidqi published a collection of short stories, *al-Anfar* (*The People*), dealing with the lives of individuals in desperation and despair. A collection by Yusuf al-Siba'i, *Al-Saqq Mat* (*The Dead Water Carrier*), emphasizes detailed observation of character, lightened by humor. Stories by Yahya Haqqi were collected in *Iqra'* (*What Am I?*); most of these stories look at the problems of daily life prior to the revolution of 1952.

Other literary forms borrowed from the West are the autobiography and the essay. Egyptian autobiographical literature provides a fund of information on Egyptian life and the changes of the past 50 years. The essay has served as a vehicle for discussion both of the problems developing out of Western influence and of the past failures and future hopes of Islamic culture. Taha Hussein's *Kitab al-Ayyam* (*The Book of Days*), published in 1939 when the author was fifty years old, has been translated into eight foreign languages. The author, whose blindness did not prevent him from rising to the position of Minister of Education, vividly portrays life in an Egyptian family and scenes from student days at al-Azhar University. As mentioned above, Hussein has also written important essays. In the *Future of Culture in Egypt* he discusses, among other subjects, the failure of Egyptian methods of education and the impoverishment of Egyptian life stemming from this failure.

Another essayist of note is Ahmad Amin, recently deceased. His autobiography, *My Life,* establishes the background for a reading of his six volumes of essays, *The Outpouring of Thought,* which deal with the changes of the past 50 years and the problems of today—the hard lot of the peasant, the weakening of family ties and religious authority, and the deterioration of morals. Amin was also concerned with the dichotomy in modern Egyptian education between the national and the ultra-modern. He stressed the need for intellectual integration of the old and new as the best way to preserve and revive the Islamic heritage and called for language reform in behalf of the ideal of universal education.

Among lesser-known contemporary writers are Fikri Abaza, who deals with the problems of modern youth, Ibnat al-Shati, the female spokesman of the fellah, and Abd al-Hamid Fahmi Matar, who is the author of *Education and the Unemployed.*

In 1961, Husayn Fawzi published his *Sinbad Misri* (*Sinbad of Egypt*), a meditation in classical style on the journey of the Egyptian people throughout history, with emphasis on the persistence of the Egyptian personality. This work had a very powerful impact in intellectual circles.

Drama and the Theater

The Cairo Opera House was rushed to completion to coincide with the opening of the Suez Canal, and was inaugurated on November 1, 1869, with Verdi's *Rigoletto.* (His *Aida,* composed especially for this occasion, was not ready in time.) Continually active for nearly a century, its management offers such attractions as the Belgrade Opera, the Berlin Opera, and the Bolshoi Ballet.

Currently, the Higher Dramatic Institute trains actors, actresses, and specialists for the National Theater, the Musical Theater, and the Puppet Theater. In the modern Puppet Theater, the puppets have emerged from behind the screen, and are clearly visible to the audiences.

The contemporary theater in Egypt was borrowed from the West, but the medieval Egyptian shadow plays—now preserved by the Puppet Theater with modern themes—have contributed to forming Egyptian taste in the drama. Techniques common to the shadow plays, such as the reliance on vulgar words and gestures to incite laughter and applause, have carried over to the modern theater, as have such traditional themes as criticism of the rich, the highly placed, the foreigner, and occasionally such groups as the Copts or the Jews. One typical shadow play portrays the plight of the ignorant fellah who finds himself imprisoned and who is liberated only after his wife bribes the Coptic clerk with money, the village headman with money, and the district governor with her body.

In addition to foreign plays, many of which are produced in Arabic translations, the Egyptian theater offers three main types of indigenous drama. The first type is that played in classical Arabic: it has met with little success, not being able to compete with European plays. The second type is the Arab colloquial theater, which was until recently devoted to romanticized history and social drama; the third is the popular theater.

The historical plays of the colloquial theater glorify the Islamic past and the great days of ancient Egypt. In some of these dramas, Arab honor and courage overshadow the feeble virtues of the non-Arabs and also highlight their villainies. Typical of the social drama is *The Children of the Poor,* by Yusuf Wahbi. This play traces the story of a girl, Bamba, whose mother has been seduced by a wealthy cousin. To revenge his sister's honor, Bamba's uncle attempts to kill the seducer, but fails and is sent to prison. Released from prison, he becomes a drug addict, finally puts the now-syphilitic-Bamba to death, and goes insane. Other plays employ such themes as the plight of the fellah or the effect of Westernization on the family or on religion.

Tewfik al-Hakim, born at the turn of this century, is the doyen of Egyptian playwrights, and has had a great influence on other dramatists. After living in France for a number of years, he returned to Cairo and wrote four traditional comedies for a local theater. Unsatisfied with his own work, he wrote: "The play which our audiences used to applaud was either funny, full of jokes, exaggerated movements, personalities in caricature, or alternatively, a sad play full of tragic situations. In both cases we are far from the real theater. If we could get our audience to taste the natural kind of play, the one whose target is neither to make people laugh nor weep, the kind which presents to you life as it is, and people as they are, such an experiment would fill us with hopes for the future." Tewfik al-Hakim returned to Europe to study the theater, and, back in Cairo, wrote and published plays well before stages were found for them. They featured objective philosophical thought, metaphysical subjects, and symbolism, and in them dialogue was increasingly emphasized. These works included *Pygmalion, Sheherazadah, The Deal,* and *The River of Madness.* The theme of

Ahl al-Kahf (*People of the Cave*), is taken from a Sura of the Qur'an, which mentions the seven sleepers of Ephesus. In this play, the sleepers awake after 300 years, are deceived by the reality they find, and return to die in the cave. A recent work, *Toward the World of Tomorrow*, takes place in interplanetary space. A verse play by Salah Abdel Sabour, *Ma'ssat al-Hallaj* (*The Tragedy of al-Hallaj*) is greatly admired in present-day Egypt. Al-Hallaj was a renowned Moslem mystic who was put to death at Baghdad in the tenth century. Other active playwrights include Mahmud Taimur, Aziz Abaza, Rashad Roushdi, Numan Ashur, Alfred Farag, and Saad al-din Wahba.

The third type of Egyptian drama—the so-called "popular theater"—is well received by both the rural and the urban population. It is an admixture of local humor and showmanship, bolstered with the techniques of farce and burlesque. Popular themes are government corruption, the naiveté of the fellah, and the peculiarities of the various religious and ethnic groups. An example is al-Rihani's *Hasan, Cohen, and Marcus,* in which a Moslem, a Jew, and a Copt combine in a business venture. Hasan, the Moslem, is the handsome, confident, cultured, well-dressed front man, whose only expertise is in the public relations field. Cohen, the Jew, is the financial wizard, and Marcus, the Copt, is the practical operator, whose capacity for getting things done makes the enterprise a success. The popular theater also lends itself to the expression of antiforeign sentiment, and it has been used in this way in recent years in periods of particularly strong anti-imperialist feeling. Although much Egyptian comedy is broad farce, the works of a few playwrights are more subtle. An example is *A Tea Party,* by Mahmud Taimur, which in making fun of the uncritical imitations of Western ways conveys a warning of the dangers of this course.

Music

The National Orchestra of some 80 musicians is a comparatively new organization, as is the Choral Orchestra, while the Musical Theater produces operettas. Music, which was an essential accompaniment of the shadow play, is highly popular in the contemporary theater. Not only do musicals lead in drawing power but few performances of any type can be financially successful without some reliance on music. Formerly, Egyptian theater music was not composed with the atmosphere of the play in mind, but currently, serious efforts are made in this direction.

Music enters intimately into the lives of the people. Traditional melodies are heard in the cries of the street hawkers, the work chants of the fellahin, and the recitations of the Qur'an, and music constantly blares from loudspeakers in coffeehouses and other public places. The strength of the musical tradition in Egypt is evident in the ineffectiveness of Qur'anic prohibitions against music. Not only did music not decline under religious disfavor but it eventually penetrated religious practice in the *adhan*, the call to prayer.

Unlike Western music, much of which is the product of individual composers working according to fairly rigid rules, most music in the Arab world has been improvised by the performer, guided by a tradition rather than by formal theory. Unable to write down what he sang or played, the performer would transmit his pieces by ear to his followers, who in turn were free to introduce changes of their own. Even today, the ability to improvise and embellish a melody constitutes the criterion by which a performer is judged.

The traditional Egyptian orchestra consists of at least one woodwind, a drum, a tambourine, and a stringed instrument, the most common of which is the *rabab*, the one-string violin. More elaborate orchestras add other instruments, including the lute, flutes, oboes, and drums.

Like other aspects of Egyptian culture, music has been changed by contact with the West. Older rhythm patterns have been virtually supplanted by what is called the *masmoudi* rhythm, similar to a tango with the third beat omitted. Another development, which has only begun, is the attempt to introduce harmony into the traditional music. Western music, as such, has also been introduced into Egypt, and much Western classical, popular, and movie music is heard in Cairo and the other large cities.

Dancing

Only recently has there been a significant development of dancing in Egypt, where it has never been greatly esteemed as an art form. The most notorious form of this entertainment—the belly dance—is confined largely to the night clubs of the urban centers. The belly dance is also frequently seen in plays and motion pictures. Currently, the moralistic attitude of the government severely limits the amount of flesh exposed by these performers. In the villages, dancing accompanies weddings and festivals, and ritual dancing features funeral services.

The Reda troupe of dancers, later known as the National Troupe for Folklore, was founded in 1959 by Mahmud Reda, with his wife, Farida Fahmy, as the principal dancer: the group does folk dances based on traditional themes. Best known among several other groups is that led by Nelly Mazlum, which presents dances based on traditional and Pharaonic themes. Since the repertoire of folk dances in the Moslem centuries was very meager, these modern versions have been highly elaborated from scanty source material.

The Visual Arts

The visual arts have also been affected by Western influence. The old art forms still find their highest expression in the architecture of mosques, in calligraphy, in textiles, and in the intricately-patterned, colored tile work used for decoration. Alongside these traditional expressions, however, new forms have been introduced, especially in painting and sculpture. Although modern art in Egypt draws on the Moslem religious tradition, it is much more self-consciously focused on the sculpture and tomb paintings of the Pharaonic age, and, most of all, it shows the influences of modern Europe.

Among the better-known contemporary Egyptian artists are Mahmud Said, whose paintings of the labor of the Egyptian common people have attracted world-wide attention; Hamad Abdalla, an abstractionist painter; and Fadilah, the most prominent Egyptian sculptor, whose works show much pre-Islamic influence. Two main trends feature the present state of the visual arts. First, the younger artists are strongly concerned with abstraction and semi-abstraction. Second, a serious effort is being made to relate artistic production to the official view of the relation of people to the socialist state. Thus, themes for a sponsored competition in the plastic arts included: "The Farmer in the Field," "The Worker in the Factory," and "The Revolution in Ten Years."

In the field of architecture, there has been a sharp departure from the earlier influence of southern Europe, particularly the more grandiose structures of Italy, in the direction of the so-called "international style." Rural construction, where planned, shows a trend toward ancient Egyptian forms. An example is the new resettlement village of Gourna, designed by Hasan Fathi. Here Fathi has preserved traditional Moslem motifs for decoration, but has drawn on ancient Egypt for such functional features as brick barrel-vault roofs (which require no expensive timber) and a simple but effective air-conditioning system that sucks a draft over a bed of moist charcoal. The two controlling ideas in the erection of Gourna are simplicity, which will enable the fellahin to build their own houses, and the use of local materials—chiefly sun-dried bricks made from mud and straw. A similar approach appears in the planned communities of Tahrir province.

The Role of the Government

The government operates a very ambitious cultural program. Numerous cultural centers have been built, and more are planned. Each center has a theater, a cinema hall, a music room, and a library, and each sends out caravans to show films and distribute books. In the field of the drama, some 200 plays of distinction are being translated into Arabic.

The Ministry of Culture and National Guidance supervises the nationalized publishing firms and employs their facilities in a number of ways. The Arab Library is to comprise some 2,000 books, grouped under three headings: Revival of the Arab Heritage, Original Modern Books, and Translations. Already, the less literate readers have access to 17 different series of popular books. In addition, the cultural movement is supported by periodicals, such as *Culture, The Message, The Story, Theater,* and *Poetry.*

In an average year, about 3,500 books are published in Egypt, and of this number some 250 are translations from foreign languages. The largest number, about 1,000, are in the field of the social sciences, while publications in the fields of pure and applied sciences have increased from 340 in 1962 to 860 in 1964. Next in numerical order come works of literature, theology, history, and geography.

CHAPTER 11

Political Dynamics

The Dominant Political Tradition

THROUGHOUT RECORDED HISTORY, ONE OF THE MAIN FEATURES of political organization in Egypt has been its authoritarian character as represented by a highly centralized form of government and a strong chief executive. Among the numerous reasons that have been suggested as an explanation for this phenomenon is the fact that agriculture, which since time immemorial has been the mainstay of the Egyptian economy, is dependent entirely on Nile irrigation. Hence the need for a strong central government to control and regulate the distribution of the life-giving waters of the Nile. It should also be mentioned that Egypt is not unique in this respect. On the contrary, this form of political structure has been the prevailing traditional pattern in almost all countries of the Middle East for many centuries.

Another principal characteristic is the rather negative role that government has played in the life of the individual in Egypt. Until modern times—and especially before 1952—the government tended to be primarily an instrument for the exploitation of the governed by the governing—for collecting taxes for the ruler, providing him with cheap or free labor, and conscripting sufficient manpower for his numerous wars. Conversely, the governed have tended generally to regard the government as something to fear, to avoid, and to have as little contact with as possible.

A corollary and related feature has been the passive role played by the people in the government. On the whole, their participation has been limited mainly to being recipients of government edicts. As a result, the government was generally regarded by the people as an institution that was alien to them, different from them, and imposed upon them. Traditionally, therefore, it has been socially acceptable to try to cheat the government, to outwit and underpay the tax collector, and to escape military service. A great gap has existed between the government and the governed. Only since 1952 has there been a determined effort to bridge and close this gap and to introduce the concept that the function of the government is to be "for the people," if not of them.

Moreover, the government as a social institution has played a rather minor role in the life of the individual in Egypt. This vital function used to be and to a large extent still is assumed by the extended family and by religion—in this particular case by Sunnite Islam. Until recent years, and still to a large extent today, it was the family and the clan—not the state—that were the most important social units and therefore elicited the deepest loyalties of the individual. An Arab proverb illustrating this system of loyalties states: "My brother and I against my cousin. My cousin and I against the stranger." In turn, the clan assumed collective responsibility for its individual members. It protected the member, helped him in times of need, and provided for him in his old age. In this sense, what is regarded in the West as "nepotism" was a moral and social obligation. Indeed, a family member who did not help or give preference to a kinsman would be regarded as disloyal.

Islam, from its very inception, provided a complete system in which there was no separation between spiritual and temporal powers. It not only satisfied the spiritual yearning of its adherents but also regulated their daily lives, their personal conduct, and their social and legal relationships. Thus the individual tended to identify himself within the framework of a religious grouping. Several factors helped to reinforce this tradition. Whereas in the West the secularization of society began some four centuries ago, in the Middle East this process began only in the nineteenth century and is still continuing. Also, whereas in the West the nation-state began to develop as early as the sixteenth century, in the Middle East this concept is very new and is essentially a product of Western impact, which began in earnest in the nineteenth century.

Finally, the Turks, during their hegemony in the Middle East, introduced the *millet* system, which more or less divided society into various religious groups coexisting side by side. Each religious community was a self-contained social unit, with considerable autonomy in the administration of its internal affairs: its own canon law and canon courts regulated the personal relationships of its members, including such things as inheritance, marriage, divorce, the rights of children and parents, and so forth. Until recent years, canon and civil law were one and the same in Egypt, and to this very day, civil and criminal law are greatly influenced by Moslem religious law.

There is little question that today both religion and the family are gradually losing their hold on the individual and that his loyalty is more and more being transferred to the nation-state. This process is increasing in momentum in conjunction with secularization, urbanization, and industrialization, as the Egyptian government assumes more and more of the functions that these two social institutions used to perform for the individual.

Constitutional Development from Muhammad Ali to 1923

In the beginning of the nineteenth century, Egypt and the Middle East came under great political, social, and economic pressure from Europe. These influences introduced a novel social dynamism into Egyptian society. The ruling elite came under Western, especially French, cultural influence. More and more, the educated leadership began to think of political reform in terms of written constitutions, establishing representative bodies with the authority to control key items of public policy—such as the budget—and with some degree of executive responsibility to the legislature. The mass of the people were little influenced by these developments, and even the ruling groups moved little beyond the limits of their Islamic heritage. The Western impact, however, made it necessary to find legal and constitutional instruments suitable to the new forms of political and economic life which were taking shape.

Muhammad Ali to Lord Dufferin. Egypt was the first Arab country to be freed from Turkish rule, which was no more than nominal by the time of Napoleon's invasion (1798), and which continued to decline during and after the rule of Muhammad Ali. Even though Turkish cultural influence remained significant, the weakness of Turkey's control enhanced the opportunity for European influence to penetrate Egypt and further weaken Turkish power.

One manifestation of European influence was the creation of advisory councils to the ruler. Napoleon began the practice by establishing several advisory councils (*diwan*). One of these, the Special Council (*al-diwan al-khususi*), although appointive, represented several groups in the country: the ulama (religious leaders), the army, merchants, the Copts, and the French. Although these councils did not last, they provided precedents for the future.

Muhammad Ali produced a so-called constitution in 1826, which transformed the old Divan (diwan), the Executive Council of the ruler. He created the Advisory Council (*majlis al-mashwarah*), made up of 156 members: 33 high officials, 24 district or local officials, and 99 notables. Its function was to receive complaints, to put forward suggestions, and to advise in matters of administration, education, and public works. These limitations reflect the restricted concerns of the government, which were largely fiscal and judicial. He also reorganized the provinces under 12 provincial governments and attempted rather unsuccessfully to apply to officials in them new titles derived from France. It is clear that Muhammad Ali and his successors regarded the new government assemblies as personal creations, designed to advise the ruler to the degree he desired, and not as checks upon autocratic authority. But under Ismail, the assemblies began to assert claims revealing both the growing importance of Western ideas and the disposition of assembly members to view the authority of the executive as limited.

In November 1866, Ismail issued a decree establishing the Assembly of Delegates, made up of 75 members indirectly elected for a three-year term. Strictly limited by the decree to the consideration of domestic affairs, the Assembly could only advise; its advice would be accepted or rejected entirely at the discretion of the khedive. The khedive's exclusive right to convoke, adjourn, prorogue, or dissolve the body gave him ample powers to combat any show of independence.

The initial conflict between the Assembly and the government was over a financial question. In 1876, a delegate discreetly but firmly requested the government to reveal its past, present, and future financial objectives. Rather remarkably, the khedive in that year agreed that the continuation of a certain tax, the *muqabala*, would depend on the will of the Assembly. The body indicated that it appreciated this recognition of its authority and that it would proceed to use it. Its reply to the speech from the throne showed none of the fulsome flattery notable in former years. In 1879, in another reply to the throne, the Assembly asserted the principle of ministerial responsibility, the right of the people (*ummah*) to freedom, and the right of the Assembly to participate in making decisions affecting the future of the country. A new constitution of the Assembly proposed the same year by the Prime Minister called for the delegates to take an oath not only to the khedive but also to the *watan* (homeland). On down to the time of Lord Dufferin's work in 1882, the Assembly continued to demand greater authority in relation to the executive—a development accompanied by a declining representation in the Assembly of the *umdah* (village headman), on whose conservatism and compliance the executive was able to rely.

From Lord Dufferin to 1923. With the British occupation in 1882, Lord Dufferin, the British Ambassador to Turkey, was sent to Egypt to assist in reorganizing the administrative system. His report, drawn up on consultation with the London Foreign Office, was based on his own observations. The Viceroy's Council in India was also of some importance as a model in influencing his final proposals—which became the new Egyptian Organic Law. Dufferin proposed the establishment of two new quasi-parliaments. One, called the Legislative Advisory Council (*majlis shura al-qawanin*), was made up of 30 members, of whom 14, including the president and one vice-president, were to be chosen by the khedive and his government and 16, including a second vice-president, by the provincial councils and electoral groups representing the cities. The Council was consultative; it could discuss the budget and general legislation but could exercise no initiative. The only advance over earlier assemblies would seem to be that the Ministry was required to explain why it had not followed the advice rendered by the Council. The other body, the General Assembly (*al-jamiyyah al-umumiyyah*), was made up of 82 members, consisting of the ministers, members of the Legislative Advisory Council, and 46 delegates chosen by electors from the country at large. Candidates were required to be more than 30 years of age, literate, and to be paying at least £E 50 per year in direct taxes. Although the Assembly's functions were mainly advisory, its vote was needed for any new taxes, and it had to be consulted on loans, construction of canals and railways, and land classification. It could discuss and offer advice on any matter, and the government was required to explain its reasons for rejecting such advice. In addition to these national councils, Dufferin also successfully proposed the establishment of provincial councils.

This more elaborate administrative system was a British product, and not the outcome of any organic growth of parliamentary insti-

137

tutions in Egypt. Moreover, it did not reflect any confidence on the part of its author that the country was ready for self-government. The electorate consisted of 13.28 per cent of the population, and the delegates during the initial years were apathetic and ineffectual. Later, under the influence of the khedive, Abbas Hilmi II, the two assemblies followed his lead in registering nationalist opposition to British rule.

These assemblies and councils, although Western in form, often showed—to British consternation—the fundamentally Islamic premises of their members. Often a speaker had only to justify a position on religious grounds to gain the unanimous support of all Moslems in the Legislative Advisory Council. The assemblies performed one service of considerable importance, however, in constantly drawing attention to the meager appropriations for education under British rule. Leadership in the legislative bodies remained inadequate, for the country's political talent was not focused on them as significant instrumentalities. Often, as few as 1 per cent of the qualified electorate voted, showing an apathy that could not but be communicated to the bodies themselves. On one occasion in 1910, however, the Ministry yielded to pressure expressed in the General Assembly as well as in the country at large and dropped a proposed extension of the Suez Canal concession. Although the Assembly and the Council were not representative of the people in general, but rather of the privileged few, they gradually increased their pressure on the government for broader powers in the internal government of the country. More attention was given to their advice, and the British under Lord Kitchener, who became Consul-General in 1911, decided to establish a more popular assembly.

In July 1913, the Legislative Assembly (al-jamiyyah al-tashriyyah) was established. It included the ministers, 17 members nominated by the government, and 66 elected members. Among the nominated members, the Copts would be represented by four, the Bedouins three, merchants two, doctors two, engineers one, educational groups two, and the municipal interest by one. The government also appointed the Assembly's president and first vice-president. This body gained few additional powers and privileges. No projected law could be promulgated, however, without being submitted to the Assembly for criticism, and no new taxes could be applied without a vote of the Assembly. The Assembly could express opinions on government actions and formulate projects of its own. It could accept, amend, or reject any measure of the government; in case of disagreement, the government could after 15 days either prorogue the Assembly or publish the law, provided it explained its reasons. Certain subjects, such as the civil list, the public debt, and foreign obligations, were not to be discussed.

The electorate was enlarged to include about 2 million people, who elected elector-delegates, at a ratio of one delegate to every 50 voters. These delegates, in turn, elected the Assembly. Candidates for election to this Assembly initiated the practice of announcing campaign platforms, the first to do so being Sa'd Zaghlul Pasha, the rising nationalist leader. The establishment of the Legislative Assembly marked a closer collaboration of government and legislature, although it was never allowed to interfere unduly in matters which the government chose to reserve for executive decisions. World War I brought an indefinite postponement of the meetings of the Assembly.

The Constitution of 1923

Following the establishment of nominal independence in 1922 and the end of the British protectorate (which dated from 1914), a commission was created to prepare a constitution. On April 19, 1923, the first written Egyptian constitution was promulgated by royal decree. It was based largely on the Belgian model of 1830-31. Except for an interim period between October 1930 and December 1935, when a substitute constitution more favorable to the royal authority was in effect, this constitution remained in force until it was superseded by the decision of the revolutionary military junta in December 1952.

The constitution outlined a monarchical executive government, dominating a representative legislature. It provided for popular participation in administration and the making and execution of laws. However, the authority that was assigned to the chief of state (the king, or *melik*) and the chief of government (the prime minister, or *ra'īs al-wuzarā'*) preserved much of the executive's older power to block the legislature. Principles were embodied in this constitution that in application were mutually contradictory. It was stated that all power resided in the people; yet the king, in addition to his executive authority, was given legislative power conjointly with the new Senate and Chamber of Deputies. Each could take the initiative in legislation. Thus, the ideal of a mon-

139

archy limited by representative institutions confronted the actuality of provisions establishing strong royal authority. The king possessed a strong suspensory veto; he could prorogue Parliament or adjourn it for a month; in the interim, he could rule by decrees, subject to subsequent parliamentary ratification. He opened sessions by a speech from the throne to which the chambers replied. His ministers were collectively responsible to the legislature, he himself possessed enough discretion to be able to obstruct them in the fulfillment of this responsibility and to follow an independent course of his own. Such power in the hands of a stubborn, willful monarch was an important factor in the accumulated pressures that led to the military coup of July 23, 1952.

Two-fifths of the members of the Senate were appointed by the king, on the advice of the Prime Minister, who was often his creature. The rest were elected by the body itself. The Chamber of Deputies was elected by indirect ballot on the basis of universal suffrage. Each 60,000 inhabitants were represented by an elector, and the electors chose the members of the Chamber of Deputies, whose terms were for five years. The Chamber elected its own officers. The Wafd won most Egyptian elections after 1923, but the king was often able to prevent the leaders of the party from forming a correlative number of governments or maintaining them for any length of time.

Despite the severe limitations of the 1923 constitution as a popular instrument and as a check on the pervasive powers of an autocratic monarch, it was openly and blatantly violated on numerous occasions by the king. It was suspended altogether in 1930, and to all practical purposes it was nullified by the imposition of martial law during 11 out of the 15 years between 1937 and 1952.

Both the monarchy and the 1923 constitution were abolished following the military coup d'etat of 1952. They passed unlamented into oblivion, and their disappearance hardly caused a ripple in Egyptian life. The fact of the matter is that the 1923 constitution was an alien instrument exploited by the city politicians of Cairo, Alexandria, and other major towns. It hardly touched the lives of the bulk of the Egyptian people—the millions of fellahin who live in thousands of little hamlets in the Egyptian countryside. These were oblivious and apathetic to it. They could neither comprehend its provisions nor understand its ramifications. In their daily lives these millions continued, as they had for thousands of years before, to be governed by the unwritten common law—the customs, practices, and traditions of their clans, their villages, and their religious orders. Those were sources of law they could recognize and obey loyally, because they emanated from their own environment.

Constitutional Development under the Republic

Composition of the junta. On July 23, 1952, a small group of army officers, under the leadership of Colonel Gamal Abdel Nasser, overthrew the monarchy. Essentially the same group is still in power today, with Nasser as the unchallenged leader and president. This group called themselves the "Free Officers." It is claimed that the Free Officers Movement was organized as early as 1942, or even before. In any case, it came into more or less official existence in late 1949. The founding committee consisted of eleven members: (1) Nasser, the leader (2) Amer (3) Baghdadi (4) Sadat (5) Gamal Salem (6) al-Shafi'i (7) Zakariyya Muhyi al-Din (8) Salah Salem (9) Kamal al-Din Husayn (10) Hasan Ibrahim, and (11) Khalid Muhyi al-Din.

The Free Officers were united by many bonds. All came from middle-class backgrounds. All of the eleven founding members went to the same military academy. The first eight persons listed above entered the academy in the same year, 1936. Two more graduated a year later, and Khalid Muhyi al-Din, the eleventh, was graduated in 1940.

In political orientation, their membership included all hues of political opinion. Almost all had previously belonged to one political party or another. The majority were moderates, but some were members of the Moslem Brethren, and others were openly communist-oriented. No matter what their individual political views may have been, they were all united by two burning objectives: the expulsion of the British from Egypt—including all vestiges of foreign domination and influence—and the internal reform of the country.

When the Free Officers assumed power, the extremists among them of both the right and the left were either dropped or relegated to minor positions, while the moderates remained in control, holding a course slightly left of center. As time went by, however, this course moved further and further to the left. In seeking solutions to the problems of Egypt, the Free Officers were eclectic

141

and pragmatic in their approach, and relatively free from the bondage and straitjacket of political dogma.

After a brief struggle with General Naguib, Gamal Abdel Nasser emerged in 1954 as the undisputed ruler of Egypt. No matter what constitutions are adopted, and no matter what national assemblies are elected, Nasser and his close associates remain today the supreme rulers of Egypt. They and they alone have the power to give and to withhold.

Nasser was born on January 15, 1918, in the city of Alexandria, but his ancestral and spiritual home is Beni Murr, a village in Upper Egypt where his grandfather and uncles lived and where the boy Gamal spent many summers. Nasser's father was a lowly assistant postmaster, who was transferred frequently from one town to another.

Nasser graduated from al-Nahda Secondary School in Cairo in 1936. After attending law school for a brief period, he entered the Military Academy, from which he was graduated in 1938 as second lieutenant and posted in Manqabad, Upper Egypt, with an infantry company. He reached the rank of captain in 1943, and at the same time was appointed instructor at the Military Academy. During the Palestine campaign of 1948, he distinguished himself, particularly at the siege of Faluja, which became a symbolic landmark in his life. In November 1951, he was appointed instructor at the Staff College, and by the time of the revolution, he had attained the rank of lieutenant colonel.

Nasser's political activities began during his secondary school days, when he participated in many demonstrations. During one of these forays, he was clubbed by the police and spent a few nights in jail—the badge of honor for Egyptian students in those days. He is variously reported to have been a member of the Wafd, the Moslem Brethren, the Green Shirts, the Communist Party, and other political groups. There is no conclusive evidence to support any of these claims. In all probability, however, since he was a political "seeker" and activist, at one time or another he did come into contact with most of these parties. In fact, given the political climate in Egypt during 1942-52, it would have been difficult not to do so. At any rate, by 1949 Nasser had developed his own ideas, was independent of all existing political parties, and had founded his own organization—the Free Officers Movement.

Nasser has expounded on some of his experiences and ideas in a booklet called *The Philosophy of the Revolution*. In it, he describes conditions in Egypt before the revolution, his bitter experiences during the Palestine campaign and the effect they had on his political thinking, the growth of the "seeds" of revolution within him, and his constant seeking to find the correct and positive way to achieve his political goals. In one passage, he reflects that the geographic position of Egypt has imposed on it a leading role within three circles. He writes:

> We cannot look stupidly at a map of the world not realizing our place therein and the role determined to us by that place. Neither can we ignore that there is an Arab circle surrounding us and that this circle is as much a part of us as we are a part of it, that our history has been mixed with it and that its interests are linked with ours. These are actual facts and not mere words.
>
> Can we ignore that there is a continent of Africa in which fate has placed us and which is destined today to witness a terrible struggle on its future? This struggle will affect us whether we want or not.
>
> Can we ignore that there is a Muslim world with which we are tied by bonds which are not only forged by religious faith but also tightened by the facts of history? I said once that fate plays no jokes. It is not in vain that our country lies to the Southwest of Asia close to the Arab world, whose life is intermingled with ours. It is not in vain that our country lies in the Northeast of Africa. . . . It is not in vain that Islamic civilization and Islamic heritage, which the Mongols ravaged in their conquest of the old Islamic capitals, retreated and sought refuge in Egypt, where they found shelter and safety as a result of the counterattack with which Egypt repelled the invasion of these Tartars at Ein Galout.

Probably thinking of his own role, Nasser then reflects on the need for a hero:

> The annals of history are full of heroes who carved for themselves great and heroic roles and played them on momentous occasions on the stage. History is also charged with great heroic roles which do not find actors to play them on the stage. I do not know why I always imagine that in this region in which we live there is a role wandering aimlessly about seeking an actor to play it. I do not know why this role, tired of roaming about in this vast region which extends to every place around us, should at last settle down, weary and worn out, on our frontiers beckoning us to move, to dress up for it and to perform it since there is nobody else who can do so.

143

The first stage of constitutional development. When on July 23, 1952, the military junta overthrew King Farouk, he resigned in favor of his infant son. For a while, however, the fate of the system of government as a "constitutional monarchy" remained uncertain. Many believed that the military, after instituting some reforms, would hand over authority to the traditional civilian politicians and "go back to their barracks." This view gained some acceptance for several reasons: First, it was known that members of the junta were not certain as to their role after the "revolution," and, in their actions, they did indeed give the impression that their role was to be very temporary. Secondly, the junta asked a veteran and responsible politician—Ali Maher—to become Prime Minister and head a new civilian government. And thirdly, on August 2, 1952, the junta established a Regency Council—composed of Prince Abd al-Mun'im, Colonel Rashad Mahanna, and Baha' al-Din, Pasha Barakat—to act for the infant king and give royal assent to decisions of the junta, thus preserving the fiction of a constitutional monarchy.

On December 9, 1952, General Naguib, then titular head of the junta, declared the 1923 constitution abolished and announced the formation of a committee of lawyers to draft a new constitution which would determine, among other things, whether Egypt should or should not become a republic. Almost a month later, on January 16, 1953, all political parties were dissolved and their properties sequestered. At the same time, a three-year transitional period was declared, during which the members of the junta—which by now was called the Revolution Command Council or RCC—would rule the country by decree. On January 23, the Liberation Rally (Hay'at al-Tahrir) was established, ostensibly to fill the void created by the dissolution of the traditional political parties. No matter what the real objectives were, the Liberation Rally represented the first experiment by the RCC in the development of an all-inclusive, one-party system, controlled and directed by the government.

On June 18, 1953, the RCC assumed full control of the country. Without waiting for the report of the committee which was formed in December to draft a new constitution, the junta abolished the monarchy entirely and declared Egypt a republic, with General Naguib occupying the posts of President and Prime Minister at the same time. Nasser, who by now began to emerge as the real leader of the revolution, occupied the two strategic posts of Deputy Prime Minister and Minister of the Interior. As Minister of Interior, he controlled the country's police and the security services. In addition to their policy-making and legislative functions, the members of the RCC now arrogated to themselves also executive and administrative control, for most of the ministers in the new republican government were members of the Revolution Command Council.

The 1956 constitution. Exactly three years after the transitional period was declared, on January 16, 1956, President Nasser announced the long-awaited constitution, which turned out to be a synthesis of reformist ideas—in the direction of a welfare state—with Islamic and nationalist concepts. The preamble set forth the general tone of the document as well as the six basic principles that were to guide the Egyptian people. It stated in part:

WE, THE PEOPLE OF EGYPT,
> having wrested our rights to a life of freedom after an interrupted struggle against aggressive enemy forces from without, and the forces of exploitation within;

WE, THE PEOPLE OF EGYPT,
> inspired by the lessons of the past, and armed with the staunch determination of the present to lay down the broad landmarks of a future free from fear, free from want and free from subjugation; able to muster all our capabilities and potentialities for a massive positive effort toward building a welfare society wherein will be assured:

> The eradication of imperialism and its agents,
> The extinction of feudalism,
> The eradication of monopolies, as well as the
> control of capitalistic influence over the system
> of government.
> The establishment of a strong national army,
> The establishment of social justice,
> The establishment of a sound, democratic life.

Part I of the constitution (Art. 1-3) declares that Egypt is an independent and sovereign Arab state, a democratic republic, and an integral part of the "Arab Nation." Sovereignty belongs to the people, Islam is the religion of the state, and Arabic is its official language.

Part II (Art. 4-29) defines the "basic pillars of Egyptian society." Among these are the following: The family is the basic social unit

(Art. 5). Private economic activity is free, provided it does not harm public interest, does not violate public peace, or derogate from the freedom or dignity of the individual (Art. 8). The right to private property is guaranteed (Art. 11), but land ownership is restricted to a maximum limit specified by law (Art. 12). The state is to encourage the development of cooperatives and to regulate their activities (Art. 16). Family life, motherhood, and child welfare are protected (Art. 18). Egyptians have the right to state financial support in case of old age, sickness, or disability (Art. 21).

Part II (Art. 30-63) deals with "public rights and obligations." Egyptians are equal in their rights and duties, without any discrimination on the basis of race, language, religion, or belief (Art. 3). Freedom of thought is absolute. Freedom of worship, expression, scientific research, the press, and peaceable assembly is guaranteed within the limits of the law (Art. 43-46). Education is a right to all Egyptians (Art. 49), and elementary education is compulsory and free (Art. 51). Egyptians have the right to work (Art. 52) and to form trade unions (Art. 55). The law regulates the relations between employers and employees, on the basis of sound economics and social justice (Art. 54). All Egyptians have a right to medical care (Art. 56). Military service is compulsory (Art. 58).

The 1956 constitution gave the executive very broad powers. The chief of the state is the President of the Republic (Art. 64). He is nominated as candidate to that high office by an absolute majority of the National Assembly, and elected for a term of six years by direct ballot of the citizenry (Arts. 120-22). The President appoints and dismisses all ministers, as well as all other officials in the executive branch of the government.

The President, with his ministers, lays down and executes the general policy of the government. He has the right to propose laws to the National Assembly and to veto any law within 30 days, but if the same law is passed again by a two-thirds majority of the National Assembly, it then becomes law irrespective of the presidential veto (Art. 134). Between Assembly sessions or during times of national emergency, the president may issue decrees and regulations which have the force of law (Arts. 135-36). The president calls and terminates sessions of the National Assembly (Art. 72), and has the right to call the Assembly into extraordinary sessions as well (Art. 76). Finally, the President has the right to dissolve the Assembly entirely (Art. 111), in which case elections for a new assembly are to be held.

The National Assembly—consisting of one chamber—is the legislative branch of the government. Its functions are to propose, consider, reject, and adopt laws and regulations and to supervise the actions of the government. Members have the right to put questions to ministers, to interpellate them, and to open a subject for general discussion by the Assembly and to seek clarification concerning it from the government. The Assembly may also express its wishes and make suggestions concerning public matters to the government (Arts. 90-92). No member, however, has the right to interfere in matters that are the exclusive concern of either the executive or the judicial branch of the government (Art. 93). The government has no right to contract a loan or bind itself in any project involving the expenditure of public funds for any future year or years, without the prior approval of the Assembly (Art. 96). If the Assembly, by an absolute majority, takes a vote of "no confidence" in a minister, then the latter must resign from the cabinet (Art. 113). All treaties of peace, alliance, commerce, and navigation, and all treaties involving territorial adjustments, sovereign rights, or those that obligate the national treasury with expenditures not already in the budget must first be approved by the National Assembly in order to be binding (Art. 143).

Article 192 provided for the formation of a new organization, the National Union (al-Ittihad al-Qawmi) to replace the Liberation Rally created in 1953. This organization represented a further development in the experimentation with the government-sponsored, one-party system. Among the functions of the National Union were the screening and nomination of candidates for election to the National Assembly.

On June 23, 1956, a national plebiscite was conducted, which approved both the new constitution and the election of President Nasser to a six-year term. The eruption of the Suez crisis in late 1956 temporarily prevented additional constitutional developments. These were, however, resumed the following year with the establishment of the National Union, which came formally into being by presidential decree on May 28, 1957. President Nasser also became President of the National Union.

An electoral law promulgated in March 1957 provided for a National Assembly of 350 members, representing 350 single-seat constituencies. On May 18, the electoral campaign was officially opened, with elections to be held in July. Candidates for election had to be approved by a National Union executive committee,

147

composed of three leading members of the junta who were very close associates of President Nasser (Abdel Hakim Amer, Zakariyya Muhyi al-Din, and Abd al-Latif al-Baghdadi). The committee screened some 2,500 candidates who had applied, and rejected 1,182 of them, leaving 1,322 actual contestants from whom the six million registered Egyptian voters were allowed to choose the 350 members of the National Assembly. The 1957 elections were unique in at least one sense. For the first time, Egyptian women were allowed to vote and to stand for elective office. In fact two women —one representing Cairo and another, Alexandria—won their elections to become the first female members of the National Assembly.

It is obvious that the 1957 National Assembly—by virtue both of the very limited powers granted to it by the 1956 constitution and of the manner in which its members were screened, ensuring the elimination of all opposition—was intended to give formal support to a very powerful executive and to provide constitutional legitimacy for the regime. At any rate, the days of the 1957 Assembly proved to be numbered, for the union with Syria in early 1958 brought about its dissolution and the creation of a new and much larger assembly.

The Syrian interlude: February 1958–September 1961. On February 1, 1958, the leaders of Syria and Egypt, meeting in Cairo, signed documents merging their two countries into a new state—the United Arab Republic. In a plebiscite conducted on February 21, the electorates of Egypt and Syria approved both the merger and the appointment of Nasser as President of the new republic.

On March 5, 1958, President Nasser issued a temporary constitution for the United Arab Republic. The 1958 constitution was a much briefer document (73 articles) than its 1956 counterpart (196 articles). In both spirit and wording, however, it was an adaptation of the 1956 Egyptian constitution to take into account the inclusion of Syria.

This temporary constitution, unlike that of 1956, did not name Islam as the religion of the state. It made no reference to religion whatever.

Article 58 declares that the UAR shall consist of two regions— Egypt and Syria. Each region was to have a Council of Ministers (executive council) of its own. Thus, the UAR would have three cabinets—a central cabinet and two regional cabinets, all appointed by the President and responsible to him.

Article 72 provided for the formation of a National Union in language identical to that of the 1956 constitution. The provisions concerning the powers and limitations of the executive, legislative, and judicial branches of the government were more or less the same as in the earlier document, except that the President was given even greater authority.

Elections for members of provincial and local committees of the National Union were held in both Egypt and Syria on July 8, 1959. The considerable efforts that went into the attempt to form a National Union in Syria proved to be in vain, however, for the Union in Syria never got off the ground, and the project was abandoned entirely with the break-up of the UAR in 1961.

A joint UAR National Assembly, composed of 400 Egyptian and 200 Syrian representatives, finally came into being. Half the members were nominated by President Nasser and half by the National Union. During its brief existence, this Assembly proved to be as ineffective as its Egyptian predecessor, and when Syria withdrew from the union in September 1961, it was dissolved, leaving Egypt once more with no representative body.

The National Congress of Popular Powers. Following the withdrawal of Syria, President Nasser began to take steps for the formulation of a new constitutional framework for Egypt. Early in November 1961, he formally dissolved the National Union, and on the 18th of the same month, he issued a decree creating a Preparatory Committee for a National Congress of Popular Powers.

The Preparatory Committee was composed of 250 members, including university professors, lawyers, writers, leaders of women groups, members of cooperatives and unions, and religious leaders. The principal function of this committee was to debate and determine who should represent the people of Egypt in the forthcoming National Congress of Popular Powers. The Committee began its meetings on November 25th. Its sessions were held in public, and were also televised and very extensively reported in the Egyptian press. Apparently the debates and discussions of the committee were intended to be a nationwide seminar on the future political, economic, and social structure of Egypt. President Nasser presented his views and participated in most of the debates of the committee, and for the first time since 1952, some of his views were openly criticized and challenged.

149

Eventually the committee completed its deliberations and submitted its report on December 31, 1961. It recommended that the forthcoming National Congress be composed of 1,500 representatives, divided as follows:

	Number of Representatives	Percentage
Farmers	375	25
Workers	300	20
Professional unions	225	15
Employees	150	10
Nonunion workers	135	9
University professors	105	7
Students	105	7
Women's organizations	105	7
Total	1,500	100

Countrywide elections took place for the 1,500 seats in the National Congress, and also for the 250 members of the Preparatory Committee. Thus when the National Congress of Popular Powers began its meetings in February 1962, it had a total membership of 1,750 representatives. "Reactionaries" and members of wealthy families whose properties had been confiscated were not allowed to vote or to be represented in the National Congress. These people were said to be "isolated," not part of the "working people," and therefore had no right to participate.

The National Charter. On May 21, 1962, President Nasser presented a "National Charter" for the approval of the National Congress of Popular Powers. This charter was to be no ordinary constitutional document, but a national covenant among the popular powers—the working people of Egypt—defining the fundamental political, economic, and social principles which were to be both the bases and the goals of Egyptian society. This document was intended to provide the broad guidelines and to be the source of inspiration for all new constitutions and laws, the political institutions of the country, the administration of the government, and the organization of economic and social relations.

The document, about a hundred pages long, is divided into ten chapters. Chapter One, entitled "A General View," reviews the struggle of the Egyptian people for liberation. It concludes that the Egyptian revolution of 1952 with its manifold trends, even when measured against world revolutions, represents a new revolutionary experiment and is distinguished by:

1. A will for revolutionary change which rejects all restrictions and limitations on the rights and needs of the masses.

2. A revolutionary vanguard, which the will for revolutionary change enabled to seize power in the State and channel it from the service of existing interests to the interests of the masses.

3. A deep consciousness of history and its effect on contemporary man, on the one hand, and of the ability of man in turn to influence history, on the other.

4. A mind open to all human experiences, willing to benefit from them and to contribute to them.

5. An unshakable faith in Allah, His Prophets, and His sacred messages, which he sent to man as a guide to justice and righteousness in all places in all times.

Chapter Two, entitled "On the Necessity of Revolution," argues that revolution is the only way—"the only bridge that will enable the Arab Nation to move from what it used to be, to what it hopes to be." Arab revolution needs to arm itself with three capabilities:

1. Awareness that is based on scientific convictions springing from enlightened thought and free discussion.

2. Free movement that adapts itself quickly to the changing circumstances of the Arab struggle.

3. Clarity in the perception of goals, constant unremitting perseverance toward them, and the avoidance of being diverted by emotion into secondary interests that sidetrack the national struggle away from its path, and squander away a considerable part of its capabilities.

Chapter Two goes on to explain that long years of suffering and hope have finally crystallized the objectives of the Arab struggle: freedom, socialism, and unity. Freedom has now come to mean freedom of the fatherland, as well as freedom of the individual, and socialism has become both a means and an end in itself—namely, sufficiency and justice. The road to unity has come to mean the popular call to restore to its natural state of oneness a nation that was torn apart against its will and against its interests by its enemies; the popular call for peaceful endeavor to bring ever closer the day of this unity; and, finally, its unanimous acceptance as the crowning achievement of the popular call and the popular struggle. Very radical changes in the world of today require also changes in the means to achieve freedom, socialism, and unity. Friendship, bargaining, and compromise with imperialism is no longer possible as the road to freedom. Similarly, socialist action does not have to follow socialist theories propounded in the nineteenth century. The advances in the means of production, the growth of the national and trade union movements, and the increase in the possibilities of peace due to the growth of moral forces and the terror of atomic devastation make it necessary and, indeed, inevitable for the socialist experiments of today to be entirely different from those of a different and past age. The same is true of unity. The nineteenth-century examples of German and Italian unification cannot be valid today. Unity must be achieved by peaceful means and through popular unanimity, as a matter not only of noble ideals but of practical necessity to preserve national unity in times of trouble.

In Chapters Three and Four, entitled respectively "Roots of the Egyptian Struggle" and "Lessons of the Setback," Nasser reviewed the history and the struggle of the Egyptian people from ancient times to 1952. In conclusion, he argued that the quick and complete collapse of the old regime on July 23, 1952, proved without question that a new political, economic, and social structure would have to be built.

In Chapter Five, President Nasser expressed his views on the meaning of "True Democracy." True revolutionary action, he argued, by its very nature must be populist and progressive. "The value of a true revolution lies in its degree of popularity, in the extent to which it is an expression of the vast masses, in the extent to which it mobilizes their forces to rebuild the future, and also in the extent to which it enables these masses to impose their will on life." Democracy is thus the true expression of the revolution, being genuinely populist. Democracy means the sovereignty of the people, the placing of all authority in their hands, and the dedication of power to the achievement of their goals.

Similarly, he explains, socialism is the true expression of the revolution, being genuinely progressive. For socialism means the establishment of a society of sufficiency and justice, of work and equal opportunities, and of production and services. "Regarded from this viewpoint, both democracy and socialism are one and the same extension of revolutionary action. For democracy is political freedom, while socialism is social freedom, and the two cannot be separated. Without them, or without either of them, freedom cannot soar to the horizons of the awaited tomorrow."

To continue to paraphrase this chapter, people do not wrest their will from the clutches of usurpers to enshrine it in history museums, but rather to make of it the power capable of meeting their needs. Such a stage is the most dangerous in the experiences of nations. It is the point at which many popular movements, full of hope and great expectations, flounder and go astray. For after their first victory against external oppression, they wrongfully assume that their revolutionary goals have been realized, and leave the status quo without change—forgetting that the internal forces of exploitation are closely tied to the forces of external oppression, for collaboration between the two is a necessity dictated by mutual benefits and interests at the expense of the masses. Such popular movements always discover—often too late—that by their failure to institute revolutionary change in its economic sense, they have robbed political freedom from its true guarantee—leaving nothing but a false front, which soon afterward collapses because of the contradiction between it and the national reality.

Similarly, at this same critical stage in the national struggle, other popular movements also go astray because in their internal changes they follow theories that do not spring from the national experience. The recognition that there are natural laws for social action does not mean the acceptance of ready-made theories as adequate substitutes for national experience.

The real solutions for the problems of any nation cannot be imported from the experiences of other nations. No popular movement—in the implementation of its social responsibilities—can do without experience. National experience does not assume in advance the error of all previous theories or categorically reject all solutions reached by others, for that is nothing but blind fanaticism, especially since the will to social change, when it first assumes its responsibilities, passes through a stage akin to intellectual adolescence, during which it needs all the intellectual sustenance it can obtain. However, it also needs to digest this intellectual food and mix it with the secretions of its own living cells. It needs to know the world around it, but its greatest need is to practice life in its own habitat. For the experience of trial and error in the lives of nations—as in the lives of individuals—is the only path to maturity and clear vision.

Similarly, political freedom—that is democracy—cannot be merely the copying of constitutional façades. Following the popular revolutionary movement of 1919, Egypt fell under the great deception of a sham democracy. As soon as imperialism recognized Egypt's independence, the revolutionary leaderships surrendered to the pseudo-democracy of constitutional façades that had no economic contents. It is a self-evident, indisputable fact that the political system of any country is but a reflection of prevailing economic conditions and an expression of the controlling economic interests. Thus, when feudalism is the power that dominates the economy in any given country, then political freedom in that country means only the political freedom of feudalism, which controls the economy and dictates the political form of the state to suit its economic interests. The same is true when economic power is in the hands of exploitative capital.

Before the revolution, economic power in Egypt was in the hands of an alliance of feudalism and exploitative capital. It was inevitable, therefore, that the political institutions of the country, including its political parties, would be a true expression of this power and would represent and serve the alliance between feudalism and capital. Thus, the so-called democracy under such conditions is, in fact, no more than the dictatorship of reaction.

Nasser goes on to point out that the achievement of true democracy in Egypt should be guided by the following six basic principles:

1. Political democracy cannot be separated from social democracy. No citizen can be regarded as truly free to vote until and unless he has secured these three guarantees:

(a) He should be completely free from exploitation in all forms.

(b) He should have an equal opportunity for a just share of the national wealth.

(c) He should be free of all anxieties that undermine the security of his future.

2. Political democracy cannot exist under the domination of any one class. The inevitable and natural struggle among classes cannot be ignored or denied, but must be resolved peacefully through national unity and by means of dissolving class distinctions.

Experience has shown that the revolution must liquidate reaction, deprive it of all its weapons, and prevent it from being capable of launching any attempt to return to power and subject the state machinery to the service of its interests. Reaction has many means of resistance: it possesses the power of the state and, if this is taken away from it, it turns to the power of capital. And if this too is denied, it turns to its natural ally—imperialism. Thus, to achieve a peaceful solution for the class struggle, we must first of all, and before anything else, disarm reaction of all its weapons. The alliance of reaction with exploitative capital must be dissolved to pave the way for democratic interaction between the various working powers of the people—namely the farmers, workers, soldiers, intellectuals, and the national capital. The cooperation between the powers representing the working people is the legitimate substitute for the collaboration between exploiting capital and feudalism. It alone is capable of replacing reactionary democracy by true democracy.

3. It is national unity, created by the cooperation and alliance between those powers that represent the working people, which will be able to establish the Arab Socialist Union. This union is to be the authority representing the people, the driving force behind capabilities of the revolution, and the guardian of the values of true democracy.

These enormous popular powers that constitute the Arab Socialist Union, and which are responsible for unleashing its energies, require that the new constitution include certain basic guarantees:

(a) Popular political organizations, based on direct free elections, must represent truly and fairly the powers forming the majority of the population. Therefore, the new constitution must ensure that farmers and workers shall have half the seats in all popular and political organizations at all levels, since they form the majority, and especially since they are the majority that has long been deprived of its fundamental right to shape and direct its future.

(b) The authority of elected popular councils must be consolidated continuously and raised above the authority of the executive branches of the state, for that is the natural order, regulating the sovereignty of the people and guaranteeing that the people will always be the leaders of national action. Moreover, local government must gradually but resolutely transfer the authority of the state to popular authorities, for they are in a better position to feel and know the problems of the people and to find the proper solutions.

(c) There is an urgent need for the creation of a political organization within the Arab Socialist Union, the functions of which would be to recruit and organize elements fit for leadership, to help clarify the revolutionary motivations of the masses, to feel their needs, and to find proper solutions for these needs.

(d) Collective leadership is an imperative in the stage of revolutionary take-off. It is not only a guard against individual willfulness but also a reaffirmation of democracy at the highest level.

4. Popular organizations, especially cooperative and trade unions, can play an effective and influential role in promoting sound democracy. Farmers' cooperatives—in addition to their vital role in production—are democratic organizations able to spot the problems of farmers and find the right solutions for them. Moreover, it is high time for the formation of unions for agricultural workers. Industrial, commercial, and service trade unions, thanks to the great July [1961] laws, have now achieved a position of leadership in the national struggle.

5. Criticism and self-criticism are among the most important guarantees to freedom. The most dangerous obstacle to free criticism and self-criticism in political organizations is the infiltration of reactionary elements. By virtue of their economic domination, reactionary forces used to control the press. Freedom of opinion was thus deprived of its most effective instrument. The ownership of the press by the people was achieved by the press organization law, which at the same time ensured its independence of the administrative government machinery. The ownership of the press by the Arab Socialist Union, which represents all the working forces of the people, has delivered it from the influence of the ruling class. It has also liberated it from the domination of capital and the invisible censorship imposed on it by capital, which previously controlled the resources of the press.

6. The new revolutionary conceptions of true democracy should take into account the factors influencing the formation of the citizen, among the foremost of which are education, laws, and statutes. The object of education should no longer be to turn out employees for the government. Thus the curricula in all fields should be reconsidered in a revolutionary spirit and reformulated so as to enable the individual human being to reshape his environment. Laws must also be redrafted to serve the new social relationships established by political democracy. Moreover, justice, which is the sacred right of every individual, should never be an expensive commodity, beyond the reach of the citizen. Justice should be accessible to every individual, without material obstacles or adminis-

trative complications. Government statutes should be changed from their very roots, for most of them were drawn under the domination of one class. They should be transformed quickly and without delay to serve and uphold the democratic principles of all the people.

Chapter Six, entitled "On the Inevitability of the Socialist Solution," deals with the application of socialism to Egypt. According to this chapter, socialism, with its two pillars of sufficiency and justice, is the path to social freedom. Social freedom cannot be realized except through giving every citizen an equal opportunity to obtain a fair share of the national wealth. This does not mean merely the redistribution of the national wealth among the citizens, but foremost and above all, it means expanding and increasing this national wealth, so that it will be able to meet the lawful rights of the working masses. The socialist solution to the problem of economic and social backwardness in Egypt was never a question of free choice. It was a historical inevitability, imposed by reality, the broad aspirations of the masses, and the changing nature of the world in the second part of the twentieth century.

Progress through capitalistic means coincided with imperialism. The countries of the capitalist world reached the stage of economic take-off on the basis of returns from investments they made in their colonies. The wealth of India, of which British imperialism seized the largest share, was the beginning of the formation of the British savings that were used in the development of agriculture and industry in Britain. Similarly, the transformation of Egypt into a huge cotton plantation pumped vital blood through the arteries of the British economy at the expense of the starvation of the Egyptian peasant. However, those days of imperialist piracy, when the entire wealth of many nations was looted away without legal or moral restraint to enrich others, are gone forever, and we should stamp out their remaining traces, especially in Africa.

Other experiments in progress realized their objectives at the expense of increasing the misery of the working people, either to serve the interests of capital or under pressure of ideological application, which went to the extent of sacrificing whole living generations for the sake of others still unborn. The nature of the age no longer allows such things. Progress through the wholesale looting of other nations or through the forced labor system is no longer tolerated under the new human values.

Scientific socialism, then, is the only appropriate form leading

157

to the right path for progress. Those who call for freedom of capital as the way to progress are in grave error. In underdeveloped countries, capital in its natural development cannot effect an economic take-off at a time when the great capitalistic monopolies in the advanced countries have already achieved their full development through exploitation of the sources of wealth in the colonies. The huge development of world monopolies leaves only two alternatives for local capital in the countries aspiring to progress. It is clear in the first place that local capitalism is no longer capable of competition without high tariff walls paid for by the masses. Otherwise, in order to develop, local capitalism must tie itself up to the world monopolies, following in their footsteps, thus turning into a mere appendage and dragging its country behind it into this dangerous abyss.

On the other hand, the widening gap of underdevelopment that separates the advanced countries from those who are trying to catch up no longer allows the program of progress to be left to desultory individual effort, motivated merely by selfish profit. These individual efforts are no longer capable of facing the challenge, which calls for three conditions: (a) the accumulation of national wealth (b) placing all the experiences of modern science in the service of the exploitation of these national resources, and (c) formulating an over-all plan for production.

These conditions are concerned with the increasing of the national product. The other side of the coin, however, is fair distribution. This too requires the formulation of all-inclusive plans of social action to return the benefits and results of economic action to the masses, and create for them the society of plenty to which they aspire and for which they struggle.

Expansion of the national economy cannot be left to the haphazard ways of private capital; and the just distribution of the surplus of the national product cannot be accomplished through voluntary efforts, even though they may be well-intentioned and very sincere. Thus, the socialist solution is the only way out to economic and social progress. It is the way to democracy in all its political and social implications.

The control of the people over the means of production does not require that they all be nationalized, nor that private ownership or the legitimate right of inheritance that flows from it be abolished. Such control can be achieved in two ways:

1. The creation of a vigorous public sector that would lead to

progress in all fields and bear the main responsibility in the development program.

2. The existence of a private sector that would, without exploitation, participate in the development of the country within the framework of the over-all plan. Both sectors—the public and the private—would be under the control of the people.

More specifically, the general principles of division between the public and private sectors can be summed as follows:

1. *Production in general.* The major skeleton of production, such as the railways, roads, ports, airports, motive power (fuel, electricity, etc.), dams, means of sea, land, and air transportation, and other public utilities and services, should be in the public ownership.

2. *Industry.* The majority of the heavy, medium, and extractive industries should be part of public ownership. Limited private ownership may be allowed in this domain, but always under the control of the public sector. Light industries must always be beyond monopoly. Although this field is open to private ownership, the public sector must also play a role enabling it to guide this industry in the people's interests.

3. *Trade.* All import trade must be within the public sector. The private sector may participate in the export trade, but the public sector must have the main share—perhaps three-fourths to be undertaken by the public sector and one-fourth by the private sector. The public sector must have a role in internal trade. It should within the coming eight years be in charge of at least one quarter of the internal trade, to prevent monopolization and to open a wide field in internal trade for individual and cooperative activity.

4. *Finance.* All banking and insurance must be within the public sector.

5. *Real Estate.* Insofar as agricultural land is concerned, the agrarian reform laws have already limited individual ownership to 100 feddans. The spirit of the law, however, requires that this maximum limit include the entire family—the father, the mother, and minor children, so as to preclude the accumulation of ownerships within maximum limits and allowing a form of feudalism. This spirit of the law must prevail within the next eight years, during which families who own more than the maximum limit (100 feddans) are free to sell the excess to agricultural cooperatives or others.

As regards ownership of buildings, the laws of progressive taxation on buildings and the laws reducing rents place such ownership beyond exploitation. Constant supervision is still imperative, although the increase in public and cooperative housing will contribute in a practical manner to combating attempts at exploitation in this field.

Chapter Seven, entitled "Production and Society," deals with the development of the various sectors of the economy and the role of foreign capital, and with basic rights of the citizen, such as health care, education, work, security in old age, sickness or disability. It also deals with the vital role of religion in society, and of freedom of speech in its manifold manifestation.

Chapter Eight deals with "Socialist Application and its Problems"; while Chapter Nine discusses "Arab Unity" and how it should be achieved. Chapter Ten, the last, discourses at length on the basic principles of Egyptian "Foreign Policy."

On June 30, 1962, the Congress of National Powers approved the National Charter as proposed by President Nasser. Thus officially, at least, the charter became the basic document of the land, providing the fundamental political, economic, and social principles that guide Egyptian society today. In a certain sense, the charter represents the development of President Nasser's ideas during some ten years. On the other hand, once the particular references to Egypt are taken out, the document and most of its ideas read very much like the tracts written by Ba'th leaders such as Michael Aflaq some 20 years ago.

The 1964 National Assembly. It will be recalled that following the break-up of the union with Syria in 1961, the National Assembly was dissolved, leaving Egypt to be administered essentially by presidential edict.

In March 1964, 360 candidates became the new members of a new National Assembly. Of these, 350 were nominated by the Arab Socialist Union and elected by direct ballot in a nationwide election, and 10 were appointed by President Nasser. In accordance with the Charter, 115 members are farmers, 75 are workers, and 170 represent various other groups. The present National Assembly, unless dissolved by the President, should last until 1969, since its members are elected for five-year terms.

The 1964 Provisional Constitution. On March 23, 1964, President Nasser issued a provisional constitution, pending the drafting and adoption of a permanent constitution. Later, in 1967, a special committee set up to propose a draft for a permanent constitution held public meetings and public debates on the principles and provisions of such a document. Since a new constitution will be adopted at some future point, it would serve no useful purpose to discuss the provisional constitution in detail. In general, like all others before it, it provides for a very strong executive and a rather submissive national assembly. For the first time, however, a constitutional document declares that the UAR is "a democratic socialist state based on the alliance of the working powers of the people." The Arab Socialist Union is recognized, and Article 9 declares that "the economic foundation of the state is the socialist system." The President is given the right to appoint ten members of the National Assembly, and at least half of the members of the Assembly must be farmers and workers. In contrast to the 1958 provisional constitution, which ignored the subject entirely, there is a return to the declaration that "Islam is the religion of the state."

The History of Political Parties

The Nationalist Party. One of the early political organizations to develop in modern Egypt was the Nationalist Party (al-Hizb al-Watani), which appeared as part of the nationalist ferment stimulated in the 1870s by the great religious leader and reformer, Jamal al-Din al-Afghani. It was more in the nature of a movement held loosely together by nationalist sentiments and personal ties than it was a highly structured party. One of its principal objectives was to combat foreign domination of Egypt. The leadership consisted of professional politicians and religious leaders, in addition to some army officers, mostly from middle-class and peasant backgrounds. The role of the "native" officer corps foreshadowed the later developments of 1952.

In its platform, the party dealt with financial and constitutional questions. It declared Egypt's income and revenue adequate to meet required expenditures and debt obligations, and it demanded a change in the constitution of the legislature to make it conform more to European models. The demands were so moderate in tone that the khedive felt able to endorse the party's program.

In addition to the issue of foreign domination, various other internal problems helped to swell the ranks of the party. These included the water shortage of 1877; poor crops and increased taxation; the disgruntlement of "native" army officers, who resented the preferential treatment given to officers of Turkish and Circassian origin; and the disaffection of numerous civil servants, who were threatened by dismissals in the government's effort to economize.

For a time, the party continued to grow and prosper. It began to disintegrate, however, after 1882, with the British occupation of Egypt that year and the failure of the rebellion of Arabi Pasha, in which many of the party leaders were implicated.

The second Nationalist Party. The struggle for Egyptian independence was carried on by a new organization, which adopted the same name. The second Nationalist Party (al-Hizb al-Watani) was founded in 1907 by a young reformer and political leader named Mustafa Kamil.

Mustafa Kamil was born in 1874. He started his career in journalism, but through the generosity of a relative, he was able to complete his legal studies in France, where he also studied general politics, party organization, and propaganda. On his return to Egypt, he dedicated himself to the task of indoctrinating the people with a sense of their identity as a nation. The new Nationalist Party which he founded assumed not only the task of rousing Egyptian patriotism but also of convincing foreign powers that Britain's rule was immoral and that Egypt should be independent.

Kamil was well aware of the power of the press in political activity. He gained the support of some of the principal newspapers, and his party founded two of its own. He also emphasized the importance of schools and the need for education in modern subjects and foreign languages (English and French), as well as in Arabic and traditional Moslem learning.

Although the party functioned until the dissolution of all parties in 1953, it was unable to compete successfully with the more vigorous parties that emerged after the First World War, especially the Wafd. Following the death of Mustafa Kamil in 1908, no party leaders rose who were capable of taking his place. Moreover, the Nationalist Party relied chiefly upon appeals to the upper classes and the intelligentsia, an important factor in its ineffectiveness.

The Wafd. The Arabic word *"wafd"* (delegation) was initially applied to a group of leaders who proposed to present Egyptian demands for independence at the Paris Peace Conference after World War I. The leader of this group was Sa'd Zaghlul Pasha, who became one of the most venerated national heroes of Egypt. Later, al-Wafd al-Misri ("the Egyptian Delegation") became the name of the political party which grew out of this effort.

The principle of national self-determination enunciated by President Wilson aroused peoples throughout the colonialist world, not least of all the Egyptians. This principle, together with the imposition of the protectorate system, the hardships of the war, the deep-rooted and long-standing anti-British feeling, and the exile of Zaghlul Pasha and several of his associates, were some of the factors that finally brought about a state of open rebellion, which included mass strikes, demonstrations, widespread sabotage, clashes with the British authorities, and boycott of British goods. Gradually the movement, which included Moslems and Copts alike, began to acquire form during the campaign to raise money to send an Egyptian delegation to Paris.

Originally, the leaders and members of the Wafd did not consider themselves so much a party as a righteous instrument of national will. Under Zaghlul's leadership, however, the movement coalesced into a highly effective party, which, more than any other group, dominated the political life of Egypt from the First World War until 1952.

Zaghlul Pasha was of peasant origin. In his early years he participated in the Arabi Pasha Revolt, and like many aspiring young Egyptians, he studied law in Paris. At first pro-British, he came to the notice of the Earl of Cromer, who secured for him the position first of Minister of Education and then of Minister of Justice. An acute judge of men and a masterful orator, Zaghlul was the natural leader of the party he helped create.

Early in his career, Zaghlul became a member of the Legislative Assembly. From this forum he was able to lead in the demands for Egyptian independence, the end of the Capitulations, constitutional and educational reforms, and aid to agriculture. Upon Zaghlul's death in 1927, his place was taken by Mustafa Rasha Nahas Pasha. The stability of the leadership which characterized the Wafd contrasted with the instability of its membership, for the members drifted in and out as the personal popularity of the leader and interest in particular aspects of his program rose and fell.

The wide appeal of the Wafd clearly was a consequence not only of the personal appeal of its leaders but of the success of the

163

party in identifying itself as the principal proponent of Egyptian independence. This goal, which the party formally articulated as early as 1921, continued to be advocated throughout the years by Wafd spokesmen. So uncompromising was the party's stand that the Wafd almost alone among Egyptian political groups dared to oppose as unsatisfactory the British unilateral declaration of Egyptian independence in 1922.

In concentrating on the British issue, the Wafd tended to neglect the more complicated question of internal reform. Moreover, especially after World War II, corruption became widespread in its ranks, and many of its leaders exploited their government positions to enrich themselves through various financial schemes. Nevertheless, the party did establish an important precedent in Egyptian politics by cutting across class and religious lines to light the fires of patriotism and unite the people behind it.

The Wafd, along with other parties, was dissolved by the authorities in 1953; many of its leaders were tried and given jail sentences, while others were placed under house arrest. Although officially "nonexistent" today, there are unconfirmed reports that some of the Wafd's former leaders are in active opposition to the present regime. In any case, the hold that the Wafd had on the allegiance of the Egyptian masses is reflected in the fact that when Nahas Pasha, the party leader, died in August 1965, some half a million Egyptians marched in the funeral procession to the distinct displeasure of the authorities.

The Moslem Brethren. The founder of the Moslem Brethren (al-Ikhwan al-Muslimin) was Hasan al-Banna. He was born in an Egyptian village in 1906, and raised in a purely Islamic environment. At the age of 14, al-Banna was accepted in the Junior Teacher's School at Damanhûr, from which he received the "Certificat." He then enrolled in the government Dar al-Ulum College in Cairo. By his natural gifts, temperament, background, and training, al-Banna was destined to be a leader of men. He had a brilliant and a highly retentive memory, and was well known for his gift of remembering names and faces. He is reported to have memorized over 18,000 lines of verse and an equal number of lines of prose in addition to the entire Qur'an. As a speaker he was a spellbinder. His speeches appealed to the senses and emotions rather than to the mind. He moved his audiences with the cadence of his words, their rhyme and rhythm. He had those innate qualities of leadership that infused unquestioning loyalty in his followers: a towering personality, patience, understanding, and the ability to make quick decisions. In 1927, at the age of 21, al-Banna graduated from Dar al-Ulum in Cairo and was appointed a teacher in the government elementary school at Ismailia. Some six months later, in March 1928, the Moslem Brethren Society was born—composed of six friends and loyal students—and on April 11, 1929, it came into official being.

The fundamental thesis of the Moslem Brethren, from which all their principles and objectives emanate, is that Islam is a system which encompasses the whole totality of life. It embraces the here and the hereafter, the spiritual and the temporal. It not only defines the relations between Allah and man but also includes principles and laws to regulate moral, political, economic, and social life. Islam is not only a total system but also the only system that is completely suited to govern the affairs of the Moslem world and, indeed, eventually all of humanity.

Proceeding from this basic premise, the Moslem Brethren argue that their movement has within its framework and content all the good doctrines, ideas, and systems propounded in either East or West, in the past or in the present. Hasan al-Banna is reported to have instructed university student members to argue as follows in debating with communists: "If the communists argue with you and tell you that their principles are humanitarian, uphold the weak and the poor, call for equality between people, and establish social, economic, and political justice; then reply: This may be so, but our principles include yours and then some. There is no principle of which you boast, to which we have not an equivalent— similar and superior to it."

The source and guide of this universal system are the Qur'an and the Hadith. The Brethren, however, insist on a literal and strict interpretation of the Qur'an and reject ijtihad, or independent judgment. In short, the Brethren call for the establishment of a theocratic state, in which the Qur'an would be the constitution and its teachings the source for economic, social, and political relations.

The Brethren believe in both Arab unity and Moslem unity. Their fatherland is all Moslem lands. They argue that each individual should have three complementary loyalties. First, he should work for his country and favor it above all others. Second, he should support Arab unity as the second link in the chain; and finally, he should work for the realization of the Islamic League as being the ultimate circle which contains the entire Moslem fatherland.

The re-establishment of the caliphate is at the top of their program, for it is the symbol of Moslem unity. This, however, will require extensive preparation and numerous steps before the final one is taken: complete cultural, social, and economic cooperation among the Moslem countries; followed by treaties and alliances and the convening of assemblies and conferences; then the formation of a Moslem League of Nations; then the election of an imam who would be the focal point of the union of the Moslem world.

The political program of the Brethren also included the liberation of the Nile Valley, the Arab countries, and all parts of the Moslem homeland from every vestige of foreign domination, as well as assistance to Moslem minorities everywhere to secure their rights. In the economic field, they advocated raising the standard of living, the development of the national wealth and its protection and liberation, the realization of social justice among all individuals and classes, social security for all citizens, and equal opportunity for all.

The Moslem Brethren have been accused of being reactionary fanatics. This is true in one sense, but in another sense, it can be argued with some justice that the contrary is true. Indeed, at the very height of their power they were, in many respects, the most progressive group in Egypt:

First, the Moslem Brethren represented the first movement in the modern history of Egypt to attempt to deal with and solve the problems of Egyptian society in indigenous terms, comprehensible to and harmonious with its genius and historical experience. Most other political and social reform groups imported ideas and systems in toto from the West and attempted to graft them—without even adaptation—on Egyptian society. The result, generally, was the erection of hollow forms which hardly touched or had anything to do with the mainstream of Egyptian life.

Second, virtually all the political parties that were active between the 1930s and 1952 lacked positive programs of action—aside from advocating the expulsion of the British. In contrast, the Moslem Brethren not only had a comprehensive religious, social, economic, and political program but actually went to the masses, attempted to help them, recruited them, and gave them an active role in their movement. In a certain sense, the Brethren were the first genuine mass movement in the modern history of Egypt.

Third, in their own way, they attempted to regenerate Islam, dispose of the harmful accumulations that had attached themselves to it over the centuries, bring it into line with the spirit of the modern age, and reintroduce the moral theme into the fabric of social and political life in Egypt.

Fourth, they were fairly progressive in economic doctrine, and, in fact, veered somewhat to the left. They called their system Moslem socialism, and although they could and did find Qur'anic citations to support their arguments, it is quite evident that they borrowed most—if not all—of their ideas from the West, wrapped them in a coating of Qur'anic verses and presented them as Moslem socialism. Among other things, they advocated progressive taxation, inheritance taxes, land distribution, labor unions, social security, unemployment compensation, state ownership of basic industries, and limitations on wealth and on land ownership. These can hardly be called reactionary ideas.

And finally, although they denounced Western civilization as morally corrupt, spiritually bankrupt, aggressive, and in a state of disintegration, they were willing to accept Western science and technology. In their various industrial, agricultural, and commercial enterprises, they used modern machines and employed Western techniques and systems of business administration.

By 1932, Hasan al-Banna was able to establish a party headquarters and a school for girls in Ismailia, in addition to some ten branches in neighboring towns and villages, including Port Said and Suez. In 1933 al-Banna, who was then still a teacher, was transferred to Cairo, and the headquarters of the Brethren moved with him from Ismailia. From that date on, the Moslem Brethren entered a period of vigorous expansion. By 1948, they had some 500,000 to 600,000 active members, twice this number in passive members and supporters, and some 1,700 to 2,000 branches in Egypt alone. In addition to their political activities, they established schools, clinics, hospitals, mosques, and industrial and commercial enterprises. They encouraged sports, formed scout units for boys, organized a militia, operated military training camps, and, finally, organized and trained a secret military order—in addition to the militia—called al-Nizam al-Khass (Special Order). Also by 1948, the Moslem Brethren had established branches in most of the Arab countries. They claimed that they also had branches in Iran, Pakistan, Indonesia, and Ceylon.

The Moslem Brethren passed through three periods in their political activities before 1952. During the first period (1928-39), the government authorities paid them little attention and regarded them as primarily a religious organization, perhaps with political overtones—but still nothing to worry about. For instance, it was not until the late 1930s that the Egyptian Ministry of Education realized that al-Banna, the Supreme Guide of the Moslem Brethren, and al-Banna, one of the teachers in its schools, were one and the same person. For their part, the Moslem Brethren restricted their political activities to lecturing, writing unobtrusive articles, and sending "messages" to the successive cabinets, suggesting internal reforms based on the spirit of Islam. Very little attention was paid to this unsolicited advice.

The second period (1939-48) witnessed material changes. In this period, the Brethren reached the height of their power; but at the same time, it was the beginning of their decline. These were war years, and as such both the Egyptian government and the British authorities became far more alert to political organizations and political activity. By this time the Moslem Brethren had grown considerably in numerical strength and organization to become the strongest and largest mass movement in Egypt. They emerged from their relative obscurity, intensified their nonpolitical activities, and began to use terrorism and assassination for the achievement of their ends. What is more, their emphasis on the liberation of the Nile Valley made them implacable enemies of the British. Hasan al-Banna is reported to have instructed his followers to recite the following invocation at the end of all their prayers:

> O Allah, Lord of the universe, Haven of the fearful, Humbler of the arrogant, Leveller of the mighty, we beseech Thee to accept our prayers, listen to our pleas, grant us our rights, and restore our freedom and independence. O Lord, these British usurpers have occupied our land, tyrannized the country, and unleashed corruption in the land. O Lord, protect us against their machinations, confound them, split asunder their ranks, smite and afflict them with your might and those who support them, aid them, temporize with them or befriend them. O Lord God, turn against them, visit your afflictions upon them, humiliate their state, drive their authority from Your land, and thwart their machinations against any believer.

In October 1946, al-Banna issued a manifesto in which he called on all Egyptians to "Shun your British friends, boycott their businesses, withdraw from societies and clubs in which they are members, stop speaking their language and reading their books."

The Brethren were not only extremely active—politically and otherwise, publishing books and newspapers, organizing and leading demonstrations and strikes—but were also in a virtual state of permanent opposition to the eight governments that succeeded each other between 1939 and 1948. At times the authorities suppressed the movement, jailed its leaders, and confiscated its properties; while at other times, they left the movement alone. The Brethren, however, seemed to thrive on suppression, and the deeper in trouble they were with the authorities, the more members and supporters they seemed to attract.

During the Arab-Israeli conflict in 1948, contingents of Brethren volunteers fought with distinction under the supervision of the Arab League. There is some evidence that after the Palestine experience, the Moslem Brethren were preparing for a coup d'etat. The time must indeed have seemed ripe. For one thing, Egypt seemed to be in a state of total political and moral collapse. Farouk's scandals and escapades rocked the nation almost daily. Corruption permeated all levels of government, and disgust with the entire regime was rampant. Conversely, the Brethren were over a million strong, united in their faith and mission, with an excellent organization, well armed and well trained. During 1948 the Brethren greatly increased their terrorist activities.

Apparently the government felt that the threat of the Brethren was too serious to ignore, and it struck with a vengeance. On December 8, 1948, Prime Minister al-Naqrashi issued a military order dissolving the organization, and seized all its assets, properties, branches, office papers, schools, hospitals, clinics, publications, and business establishments. Hundreds were arrested and herded into prisons and concentration camps. Twenty days later, the Brethren struck back. On the morning of December 28, al-Naqrashi was shot dead by a Moslem Brethren student.

The third period (1948-52) may be called a period of reconsolidation and retrenchment. After al-Naqrashi's murder, the Abd al-Hadi cabinet assumed power. During the period of this government, the Brethren were subjected to extreme measures of harassment. Apparently al-Banna began to have second thoughts about the involvement of the Brethren in politics and terrorism, for he

169

saw the structure which he had spent 20 years building crumbling before his eyes. He began to consider seriously withdrawal from political activism and returning the Brethren to their prewar orientation—namely indoctrination, social welfare, education, and business. He had little chance to put his new program into action, however. In the evening of February 12, 1949, he was assassinated by the Egyptian political police.

After considerable bickering, the Central Committee of the Brethren decided to select an outsider to replace al-Banna as Supreme Guide, and its choice fell on Hasan Ismail al-Hudaybi. The choice was designed to meet the following conditions: (1) to lull Farouk into a sense of security (2) to help end the numerous cases against the Brethren in the courts, and (3) to end the internal rivalry among the leaders for the position of the Supreme Guide. Al-Hudaybi graduated from law school in 1921 and was appointed judge in 1924. He remained in the courts for 27 years, achieving the distinguished position of counsellor in the Court of Cassation. When he retired from office to become the Supreme Guide, he was 60 years old, in bad health, and failing in memory. In the same year (1951), he was struck with paralysis.

In November 1950, parliamentary elections were held in Egypt resulting—with the decisive help of the Brethren—in a sweeping victory for the Wafd Party. Farouk was then forced to recall Nahas Pasha, who formed a completely Wafdist cabinet which assumed power on January 12, 1950, and remained in office until January 27, 1952.

In February 1950, the government released all Brethren prisoners. In October 1951, al-Hudaybi—apparently with government blessing—was openly inaugurated Supreme Guide of the Brethren, and on December 15, 1951, the government released some of their properties, including their general headquarters in Cairo, some branch centers, and their publishing and printing establishments. By the opening months of 1952, the Moslem Brethren were nearly as powerful as they were before their dissolution in 1948, and certainly more powerful than any other political group in the country.

When the Free Officers overthrew the monarchy in July 1952, the Moslem Brethren welcomed the revolution, for they believed that the military were acting more or less on their behalf and that their day for assuming power had finally arrived. The Moslem Brethren were so confident of their position, in fact, that when the RCC (Revolution Command Council) invited the Supreme

Guide, al-Hudaybi, to meet with it, he kept the Council waiting for four days before he finally showed up.

There was some justification for the Brethren to arrive at this conclusion—erroneous as it turned out later to have been. They had infiltrated the army very thoroughly, so that many of the officers and other ranks were either members or supporters of the Brethren. What was more significant in this case was that about a third of the membership of the RCC, including President Nasser himself, had at one time or another been either members of or in close and very friendly association with the Brethren. Moreover, in the early days of the revolution, the RCC showed many indications of its desire to cooperate with the Moslem Brethren.

When Muhammad Naguib formed his first cabinet, the Brethren demanded that three of their members represent them as ministers in the new government. The RCC, however, accepted only one of the three nominees, a moderate reformer, Sheikh Ahmad Hasan al-Baquri, who was appointed Minister of Waqfs (religious trusts). The Brethren Supreme Guide, al-Hudaybi, then refused to have any part in the government and expelled al-Baquri from the movement for going against his wishes. The Moslem Brethren also demanded that a committee of their members should be formed to inspect and approve all draft laws prepared by the government. As was to be expected, this demand was bluntly rejected by Nasser and his associates in the RCC.

When the RCC dissolved all political parties in January 1953, the Moslem Brethren were exempted, after they had pledged themselves to refrain from political activity. By the middle of 1953, the RCC and the Moslem Brethren were in open conflict, and both were preparing for a showdown. The Brethren joined the communists and Wafdist elements in a loose, united front that was actively opposed to the regime.

When Nasser signed the agreement of 1954, providing for British evacuation of the Suez Canal, the Brethren started a violent campaign. In August, the Supreme Guide, al-Hudaybi, addressed an open letter to Nasser, calling on him to renounce this "treasonable agreement," and during a tour of the Arab countries, he openly denounced Nasser as being a "traitor to the national cause."

By the closing months of 1954, the country was in a virtual state of civil war. The Supreme Guide, al-Hudaybi, was arrested in early October, but the final showdown did not come until October 26, 1954, when a member of the terrorist wing (the Special Order),

Mahmud Abd al-Latif, a simple-minded tinsmith from Cairo, tried to assassinate Nasser while the latter was delivering a speech to a Liberation Rally in Alexandria.

The moment Nasser had been waiting for had come. Within a few days following the assassination attempt, most of the Moslem Brethren leaders were arrested, thousands of members were rounded up and interned, all assets and properties were confiscated, and, as the purge continued, more terrorist groups were uncovered and more caches of arms discovered and captured.

A special "People's Court" showed the Moslem Brethren no mercy. Abd al-Latif, the tinsmith who fired the shots at Nasser, was hanged, along with three other terrorists associated with the plot; but in addition—a development that caused shock waves throughout Egypt and the entire Arab world—two distinguished leaders of the Brotherhood, Sheikh Muhammad Faraghly and Abd al-Qadir Awdah, were also sent to the gallows. The Supreme Guide, al-Hudaybi, was sentenced to life imprisonment, and another leader, Sayyid Qutb, was sentenced to 15 years' imprisonment. Both al-Hudaybi and Qutb were released in 1964. The back of the Moslem Brethren as an effective political organization was broken in 1954; but to this day it remains a threat to the present regime in Egypt, especially as it has branches in various other Arab countries.

The events that took place during the summer months of 1964 and the security trials of 1966 indicate clearly that the Moslem Brethren movement is far from dead in Egypt. In July 1965, the Egyptian security police discovered that attempts to regroup the movement had been going on since 1959, that in 1964 Sayyid Qutb had taken control of the movement and had allegedly become the leader of its terrorist wing; and that in 1965, plans were being made to assassinate President Nasser and many of the top government leaders, to blow up various installations, and to take over the government.

Following the July 1965 discoveries, over 700 suspected Moslem Brethren were arrested in one raid after another. Eventually about half were released, while the rest—some 370—were sent to trial by the State Security Court. In decisions handed down between July 1966 and September 1966, seven were sentenced to death; many were given life terms; while the rest were given sentences ranging up to 15 years' imprisonment. Some of the sentences were accompanied by fines of over half a million dollars each.

Of the seven sentenced to die, three—Sayyid Qutb, Muhammad

Hawwash, and Abd al-Fattah Ismail—were executed on August 29, 1966. The sentences of the other four were commuted to life imprisonment. The executions caused demonstrations and protests in Morocco, Sudan, Tunisia, Jordan, Saudi Arabia, and Pakistan.

The Supreme Guide, al-Hudaybi (who is now over 74 years old), and one of his sons were sentenced to three years' imprisonment. A second son was given one year.

The Communist Party. The history of communism in Egypt is that of a movement rather than of an organized political party, for it did not begin to take roots until after World War II, and for some obscure reason (probably personal rivalries), it remains splintered even to this day into numerous minute factions that are almost always at odds with each other. Moreover, until recent years, the programs of the various communist factions—because of their concentration on the class struggle and absurd doctrinal disputations —had little relevance to the realities of political life in Egypt or to the needs of the masses. Furthermore, the majority of both leadership and membership consisted of non-Egyptians—Jews, Christians, Greeks, and other foreigners. It was not until the late 1940s that the movement began to become Egyptianized.

And yet, from this long travail, the communist movement has emerged today as an important element in the political life of Egypt—not because of its numerical strength or its organizational skill, but because it has been able to penetrate and permeate the intellectual environment of Egypt and, in this manner, to orient the entire socioeconomic political structure into a socialist path.

In 1920, three men founded the first socialist party in Egypt: Joseph Rosenthal, an Alexandria jeweler and the moving spirit; Husni al-Arabi, who later left the party and became a teacher of Arabic in Germany; and Anton Marun, a lawyer and the first secretary of the party, who died in 1924 in an Egyptian prison.

In 1922, the party was recognized by the Comintern, having accepted the "21 conditions" and changed its name to the Communist Party of Egypt. Although some claim that the party had some 2,000 members in 1924, reliable sources state that the membership did not exceed a few hundreds, most of whom were foreigners, and that even this estimate is based not on the payment of membership dues or ideological identification, but rather on a vague estimate of both activists and sympathizers.

The Communist Party was able to infiltrate some of the trade unions that were beginning to emerge in Egypt, and in the early 1920s it helped to organize some of the workers' strikes that plagued the country during that period. On June 5, 1925, the party was declared illegal by the government of the day and the entire leadership was arrested, along with most of the militant members—including Charlotte Rosenthal, wife of one of the original founders.

The Communist Party of the 1920s then ceased to exist—it seems to have simply vanished into thin air. Although small groups, mostly foreigners, were to be found in such cities as Cairo and Alexandria, communism to all practical purposes seems to have gone into a state of hibernation, between 1925 and World War II, and very little was heard of it during that period.

The war made the revival of communist activity possible. On the one hand, the Russians had become allies rather than enemies, and their defense of Stalingrad had won them great admiration. On the other, with the defeat of Germany, fascism was no longer fashionable. Anti-British feeling and anti-Western feeling in general was strong; conditions in the country were very bad and were to become even worse; and the intellectuals were in a state of almost total disillusionment.

Around 1941 or 1942, Marxist study circles were founded, which became the nuclei of the new communist movement in Egypt. Between 1942 and 1966 some 30 groups emerged, often changing their names and the titles of their publications, but all competing with each other to become the one and only true Communist Party of Egypt.

Out of these study groups, two communist parties emerged in 1942: the Egyptian Movement for National Liberation (EMNL), headed by Henry Curiel; and Iskra (the Spark), headed by Hillel Schwarz. A third group, the People's Liberation, founded by Marcel Israel, appeared in 1943. These groups were separated from each other not only by strong personal rivalries but also by questions of tactics. Iskra accused EMNL of activism at the expense of doctrinal purity; while EMNL accused Iskra of submerging itself in intellectualism. People's Liberation accused both of recruiting mainly from the minorities, and emphasized the need to Egyptianize the communist movement.

Between 1943 and 1945, numerous other groups came into being, such as al-Tali'ah (the Vanguard), the Marxist League, Citadelle, and al-Fagr al-Gadid (the New Dawn). By the end of the war there were approximately 1,000 active communists in Egypt, drawn

174

mostly from the minorities. Also by then, EMNL had emerged as the leading group, with Iskra second in importance.

In May 1947, EMNL, Iskra, and the Vanguard decided to merge into a new party called the Democratic Movement for National Liberation (DMNL). This union, however, was torn by personal rivalries and constant bickering among the various factions on questions of tactics and doctrine. The Palestine question, which by now had become the main issue of the day, also became the source of wide splits and deep antagonisms.

At the outbreak of the Palestine war, martial law was declared on May 15, 1948, and some 150 communists, including most of the leaders, were arrested and interned in concentration camps, which at that time held some 3,000 other detainees of various shades of political opinion and affiliations. With the imposition of martial law and the arrest of the leaders, the communist movement became dislocated and disorganized. From the long-range point of view, however, the arrests were a blessing in disguise. For it was in the concentration camps that many active nationalists met communists in the flesh for the first time in their lives, discovered that they were nice people after all, and that many of their objectives and even their ideas were similar or not too different from their own. It was in these concentration camps that communists established friendship with nationalist elements, and the foundations were laid for the United Front of 1951-52, in which Wafdists, Moslem Brethren, socialists, and communists joined forces, and through which the communists achieved their greatest success since the beginning of the movement.

All communist leaders were released in late 1949 and early 1950. Although the Communist Party as such was outlawed, front organizations, such as the Peace Movement and the United Front of 1951-52, were tolerated. In the summer of 1950, Henry Curiel and Hillel Schwarz were re-arrested, and Curiel was deported to Italy in August of the same year. In 1950, a new group appeared under the name of the Egyptian Communist Party.

The chaotic prerevolution years of 1951-52, during which the political structure of the country was disintegrating day by day, created the ideal climate for the growth of the communist movement. The membership of DMNL increased from 100 to 200 in 1950 to some 2,000-3,000 in 1952. Other smaller communist groups also made rapid gains.

With many DMNL leaders arrested or deported, branches were opened in Britain, France, Italy, and Austria. Due to this fact the leadership of the movement at this time began to pass to Egyptian hands. The foreigners had done their work well. They had prepared the ground and trained native cadres to carry on the work. The new leaders included Sa'd Kamil, a lawyer and a nephew of Fathi Radwan, and Sa'id Sulaiman Rifa'i, a mechanic who became secretary of the DMNL.

When the Free Officers overthrew the monarchy in July 1952, the DMNL—the largest and most influential communist group, hailed the coup d'etat as a popular movement engineered partly by its members in the army. Upon information supplied by the DMNL, the *Daily Worker,* organ of the British Communist Party, wrote that the Free Officers Committee included an almost equal combination of DMNL, Moslem Brethren, and Independents. A few days later, however, all foreign communist parties changed from open support to open hostility against the "Cairo fascist movement." This was also true of the various communist groups in Egypt itself. Only the DMNL continued to support the new regime.

Like the Moslem Brethren, the DMNL had some reason for its optimism and its support of the Free Officers. Some members of the military junta, such as Lt. Col. Yusuf Sadiq were openly communist; others, such as Major Khalid Muhyi al-Din, were believed to be communist; while still a third group was believed to have had relations with the communists at one time or another or at least to have been sympathetic to communist ideology. Even Nasser, it was rumored, belonged to this last group.

Relations between the new regime and the DMNL began to deteriorate in late 1952, and in January 1953 all communist groups, including the DMNL, were banned, along with all other political parties. Between 1953 and late 1955, several hundred communists were arrested, and some were given long prison sentences. The various communist groups declared open war on the government —attacking its domestic policies, the agrarian reform laws, and the 1954 Suez Canal agreement. As for the government itself, it was described as a fascist dictatorship.

The year 1955 was the great divide in Egyptian policy, which began to take a decidedly leftish turn with the Czech arms deal, the Bandung Conference, general rapproachment with the Soviet Union, and the nationalization of the Suez Canal in 1956. Thus during the period 1956-58 there was a comparable shift in the attitude of the various communist factions. They gave general support to the UAR government, but criticized its domestic programs and praised its foreign policies.

In the spring of 1956, following the declaration of the new constitution, many political prisoners, including most communists, were released from jail. At this time, which was a period of extreme tension between Egypt and the West, many communists and leftists were able to assume key positions in the press, radio, and in propaganda organizations.

In 1956, strenuous efforts were made to unite the various communist factions. Thanks to the mediation of the Italian Communist Party, a new central committee, representing the major factions, was elected at a meeting in Rome. The new organization called itself the United Egyptian Communist Party. Even then, full union was not achieved, because three groups refused to join. Renewed discussions and negotiations, which lasted some ten months, resulted finally in bringing into the fold most of the reluctant groups. On January 8, 1958, the new central committee of the enlarged United Egyptian Communist Party convened in Cairo. A new politburo and a new secretariat were elected, and a new program adopted.

Two events occurred in 1958 which brought the honeymoon to an end. In February 1958, Syria and Egypt merged to form the United Arab Republic. The merger was opposed by all Arab communists, and by the Syrian communists in particular. Khaled Bakdash escaped from Syria, and from his exile in Eastern Europe he conducted an unrelenting campaign against both President Nasser and the United Arab Republic. In the February 1961 issue of the *World Marxist Review*, he wrote: "The experience of the three years which have passed since the formation of the UAR, has taught all Syrians that the union imposed on them has no sound basis, and that the policy of the Cairo government is to wreak havoc under the slogan of Arab nationalism. This slogan is being used to further Egyptian nationalism."

The second event was the overthrow of the monarchy in Iraq in July 1958. Instead of joining the Egyptian-Syrian union, however, Qasim, the leader of the Iraqi junta, decided on a separatist policy. Moreover, for almost two years the communists were virtually in control of Iraq, while nationalist elements were hunted down, imprisoned, or killed.

Thus by the end of 1958 a virtual state of war existed between all the Arab communists and the Arab unionists headed by Nasser. Hundreds of communists and suspected communists in both Syria and Egypt were arrested and sent to jails or concentration camps. Nasser denounced the communists as foreign agents, enemies of Arab nationalism, and allies of Israel and Zionism. The communists for their part called him a fascist dictator. Nasser and the UAR were denounced not only in local party manifestos, but also in international communist publications such as the *World Marxist Review*. A 1963 issue of this publication, under the title "Save Our Lives! Persecution of Communists and Democrats in Egypt," claimed that:

> Four years have passed since the wholesale arrest of Communists began in the U.A.R.
>
> In November 1959, nearly 700 of those arrested were transferred to the notorious Liman Abu Za'abal camp, where they were subjected to fearful torture; the penal labour in this camp consisted of quarrying; men forced to carry boulders bare-footed, and deprived of rest and sleep; in addition, the prisoners were brutally beaten during the meal breaks. Worst of all was the complete absence of medical treatment after months of torture; wounds were not cleaned, nor was there any care for the cases of typhoid fever, malaria and meningitis. . . .
>
> When these facts became known to public opinion, the rest of the communists—hundreds of physicians, engineers, lawyers, teachers, trade unionists, workers and peasants—were transferred bare-footed, in rags, weak and nearer death than to life, to their present exile in the al-Kharija Oasis. Here they were joined by hundreds more from the other camps and prisons. Had the facts not been made known to the world the continued torture would have resulted in others contracting TB and other infectious diseases.

The state of open war between Nasser and the communists continued with varying degrees of intensity until the first half of 1964. Shortly before former Premier Nikita Khrushchev visited Egypt in May 1964, Nasser ordered the release of all communist detainees in the country. Khrushchev's visit is regarded as a turning point, for all Arab communists, including those in Egypt, soon reversed their position from violent hostility to open support of the regime. This reversal followed a *Pravda* article which appeared during Khrushchev's visit, urging Arab communists to cooperate with President Nasser and his socialist system.

178

At any rate, in April 1965 the Egyptian Communist Party, which was described as "our communist party, the Democratic Movement for National Liberation," decided to dissolve itself and instructed its members to join as individuals the UAR Arab Socialist Union, the only legal political organization in the country. This was probably the first time anywhere in the world that a communist party, of its own free will, dissolved itself and instructed its members to join another political organization. Two possible reasons—both speculative—have been advanced to explain this step. Some believe that during his 1964 visit to Egypt, Khrushchev reached an agreement with Nasser, whereby the communists would dissolve their organization and stop their underground activity. In exchange, Nasser would lift the restrictions on them as individuals, and allow them to join the Arab Socialist Union. This theory finds support in the above-mentioned *Pravda* article.

The second theory argues that the communists agreed to disband because they had become a small and ineffectual party after most of the members, who were Italians, Greeks, and Jews, had already left Egypt; and that the party would in fact gain by dissolving itself in that communists would be released from jail and be free to infiltrate the Arab Socialist Union.

The statement that the party issued declaring its dissolution explained that until 1961, President Nasser had concentrated on nationalist rather than socialist issues, but that with the socialist laws of July 1961, the regime began a socialist revolution. As a result, "Egyptian communists were no longer alone in raising slogans of socialism and socialist advancement. Other forces, sincere to the socialist cause, have emerged. This development has created a new situation faced by the Communist Party. . . . What has arisen is the need for interaction between all Egyptian socialist forces."

Significantly, the statement also declared that as members of the Arab Socialist Union, communists would not stop being Marxists. On the contrary, by seeking to discover the Egyptian path to socialism, communists would also be adhering to the "Marxist-Leninist line." The statement further proclaimed that differences had existed between Communists and Egyptian socialists, and that they "will continue to exist in the future about the necessary programs for settlement of political and social problems." However, the statement argued, "one basic fact remains: what joins all socialists (that is, including communists) together is by far greater

179

than what separates them." It noted that the National Charter "can be a basis for unity of action of all socialist forces."

No matter what the real motives were, the dissolution did not do the Communist Party any particular harm, and in all probability may have done considerable good. There is considerable evidence that communists have been able to take over sensitive positions in various levels of the Arab Socialist Union and in the various forms of mass media. Moreover, Egyptian communists, or at least popularizers of communist thought such as Khalid Muhyi al-Din and Ahmad Lutfi al-Khuli seem to have become steady contributors to the *World Marxist Review*—the monthly organ of the international communist movement.

The UAR authorities do not seem to be unaware of the danger, and despite the general atmosphere of amity, they are still wary. In January 1965, Heykal, editor of *al-Ahram* and one of Nasser's closest associates and advisors, wrote a long article in which he denounced communism as an alien movement which has no chance of survival in Egypt or the Arab world. The article caused a chorus of protests from communist publications throughout the Middle East.

By the middle of 1965, communists or communist sympathizers were in virtual control of the press. Only *al-Ahram* remained outside their influence. In late 1965, however, President Nasser removed Khalid Muhyi al-Din from his strategic position as chairman of Akhbar al-Yom House, which puts out a number of influential publications, including a widely-read daily and several weekly magazines. Several other "leftist" journalists were also removed from key positions in other publications.

In October 1966, the government began a campaign against communist influence in the ASU, and during that month some 20 to 50 Marxist intellectuals were arrested, including five prominent members of the ASU. These included Ibrahim Sa'd al-Din, Undersecretary of State, member of the ASU Secretariat General, and head of the Institute for Advanced Socialist Studies; Ahmad Lutfi al-Khuli, editor of *al-Tali'ah* (the Vanguard), the monthly socialist magazine; Amin Izz al-Din, member of the executive committee of the ASU Cairo section; and Muhammad al-Khafif, member of the ASU youth bureau.

Although the party that represented the majority of Egyptian communists did dissolve itself, this dissolution did not prevent

180

other communist factions from springing up. In December 1965, the authorities arrested 11 Egyptians and accused them of forming an underground organization called the "Arab Communist Party" for the purpose of overthrowing the government by force and establishing an "Egyptian People's Republic." The group was led by Mustapha Agha, a lawyer, and was reported to have been sponsored and subsidized by Peking. Significantly, several Chinese officials in Cairo, including the ambassador and the head of the New China News Agency, were recalled soon after the discovery of the group. On September 8, 1966, the State Supreme Security Court issued its verdict. Three of the members were acquitted, Mustapha Agha was given a life sentence with hard labor, and seven others were given jail sentences ranging from 5 to 15 years with hard labor.

Thus, as of March 1967, no communist party exists in Egypt. But this officially nonexistent movement wields considerable influence and continues to leave its imprint on the intellectual orientation of Egypt today.

CHAPTER 12

Theory and Structure of Government

THE CONSTITUTIONAL FRAMEWORK AND THE GENERAL PATTERN of the power structure in the United Arab Republic were discussed at some length in the preceding chapter. Although Egypt has had three constitutions since 1952 (1956, 1958, and 1964), and a fourth one is now in the making, the pattern of the system of government has remained essentially the same, and is not likely to change in its basic orientation. Egypt follows a republican "presidential" system, wherein the head of the state is a president with extensive powers. Today, the United Arab Republic is described officially as "a democratic socialist state based on the alliance of the popular working forces."

The government structure consists of three basic branches: the executive, the legislative, and the judicial. In theory, these three are separate and independent of each other; but in practice they are intermeshed, with supremacy assured to the executive. In addition, the Arab Socialist Union may be regarded as a new and fourth branch. For although it is described as a political party, still it is the *only* party allowed to exist legally in the country, it is sponsored and organized by the government, and it does in fact exercise some government functions. Moreover, the President of the Republic is also the President of the Arab Socialist Union.

The Executive

The President. The President of the Republic is the Head of the State, the Chief Executive, and the Commander in Chief of the armed forces. According to the 1964 temporary constitution, the President is elected by universal suffrage for a term of six years. An aspirant to this high office, however, must first be nominated as a presidential candidate by a two-thirds majority of the National Assembly. The Assembly can nominate only one candidate at a time. Thus the electorate is faced by only one candidate, and as in a plebiscite, it can vote only either for him or against him. In 1965, in a nationwide plebiscite, President Nasser was re-elected for another six-year term—and, according to official UAR sources, by 99.99 per cent of the total votes cast.

It is obvious that "presidential elections" in the UAR are no more than procedural exercises, for Nasser has been in power since 1954. Ritualistic as such "elections" may be, they do, however, serve some important functions. Even if in form only, they do establish the tradition of the supremacy of the electorate; they do establish the tradition of "voting" for the presidency; and probably most important of all, they do provide a constitutional means for legitimate succession without the use of violence. The fact is that if completely free elections were to be held in Egypt today, President Nasser would in all probability still win by an overwhelming majority of the votes.

The responsibilities of the President include, of course, the administration of the government machinery, the promulgation of laws, and the formulation and execution of basic political, social, economic, and other policies that affect the welfare and the security of the country and its people.

The powers of the President are pervasive indeed. Some of the important ones include the appointment and dismissal of vice-presidents, prime ministers, and ministers; the rights to propose laws and to veto laws passed by the National Assembly; and, under certain circumstances, the right to issue decrees and regulations which have the force of law. He may conclude treaties (some of which must be approved by Assembly before having any force), declare war (after approval of Assembly), declare a state of emergency, and appoint ambassadors and officers for the armed forces. He not only convokes the National Assembly and declares its sessions ended but also has the right to dissolve the National Assembly.

The vice-presidents. The President is authorized to appoint as many vice-presidents as he may see fit to assist him in the performance of his duties. Normally, there are four or five vice-presidents, each of whom is responsible for certain areas of government activity. One of the vice-presidents is designated First Vice-President, and it is he who succeeds to the presidency in case of the occupant's death or total incapacitation. For many years, this distinguished position was occupied by Marshal Abdel Hakim Amer, who was also Deputy Commander of the armed forces until stripped of these offices in June 1967. In September he committed suicide.

The cabinet. The actual administration of the affairs of the state are entrusted to a cabinet of ministers, usually called "the Government." Both the cabinet and its individual members are appointed and dismissed by the President. The cabinet is responsible to both the President and the legislative assembly. The National Assembly can force the entire cabinet or any one of the ministers to resign by passing a vote of "no confidence." In actual fact, however, no such vote has taken place in Egypt since the advent of the republican regime. A vote of "no confidence" is very seldom exercised by legislative bodies in the governments of the Middle East, mainly because such legislative branches are weak and are usually subservient to the executive branch.

In recent years, the UAR cabinet has become fairly large, as more and more ministries have been created, especially in the social and economic fields. In the appointment of persons to head the various ministries, there seems to be increased emphasis on specialization and technical knowledge. For instance, the veteran diplomat, Dr. Mahmud Fawzi, has been in charge of foreign affairs for many years.

The cabinet usually consists of a Prime Minister, who is the head, a number of deputy prime ministers for some of the more important functions, several ministers, and in some cases deputy ministers. The ministries are as follows:

Foreign Affairs	Agrarian Reform and Land Reclamation
Higher Education	Industry
Education	Interior
Treasury	Local Administration
Planning	Justice
Economy and External Trade	Labor
Supplies and Internal Trade	High Dam
Waqf and Social Affairs	Culture
Power, Oil, and Mineral Resources	Health
Housing and Public Utilities	Youth
War	National Guidance
Military Production	Communications
Agriculture	Tourism
Irrigation	Transport

The Legislature

The two-chamber parliament that existed in Egypt under the monarchy was abolished immediately after the present regime came to power in 1952. Today, the legislative branch of the UAR government consists of a unicameral National Assembly. In a real sense, this legislative branch has hardly had time to begin to function. From 1952 to 1956, the Revolutionary Command Council legislated by decree. The first National Assembly under the republican regime was established in 1956, but soon after it was created, the Suez crisis brought its activities to a virtual standstill. The union with Syria in 1958 made new legislative arrangements necessary, but the sudden breakup of the union in 1961 rendered obsolete the plans that were in process. In its legislative development, Egypt had to start all over again.

The present National Assembly began to function in March 1964. It consists of 360 members, of whom 350 were elected by direct secret ballot in a nationwide election and 10 were appointed by President Nasser. Members of the National Assembly are elected for five-year terms. Before any person can become a candidate for election, he must be screened, approved, and nominated by the Arab Socialist Union. More than half of those who applied for candidacy in the 1964 elections were struck out by the screening committee.

As is to be expected, the size of the National Assembly is determined by law in each election in proportion to the growth of the population in the country. The 1964 constitution, however, gives the President the right to appoint not more than ten members (Art. 49).

The composition of the National Assembly is of considerable interest. Although representation on the basis of geography and numbers is indeed taken into consideration, the most significant aspect seems to be representation on the basis of professional groupings—workers, farmers, engineers, physicians, students, teachers, women groups, etc. For example, the 1964 constitution (Art. 49) stipulates that at least 50 per cent of the members of the National Assembly must be representatives of workers and farmers, since these two groups comprise more than half the population of the country. Other professional groups are given proportionate representation.

The UAR National Assembly has in actual practice very limited powers. The significant point is not so much the power granted or not granted by the constitution, but the fact that the tradition of strong assertive representative bodies is not ingrained in the area. Despite its obvious limitations, however, the National Assembly plays an important role in the structure of the UAR government. Even its very existence, after a number of years of rule by the military, represents a step forward in the democratization of the country. Secondly, it provides a platform for the discussion of important public issues. Thirdly, it does exercise some influence over the government, and its opinions are usually accepted or taken into consideration unless there are basic differences of views. Finally, and perhaps most important of all, the peasant—who throughout the recorded history of Egypt has always been exploited, trodden on, and disfranchised—now receives the lion's share of representation in the legislative body.

Legislative acts. Laws passed by the National Assembly appear to average less than 200 annually. In practice, government is by decree. These decrees include UAR Presidential Decrees, Presidential Decisions, Prime Minister's Decisions, Decrees and Decree Laws, Arrêtés, Ministerial Arrêtés, and Arrêtés of the President's Executive Council. UAR Presidential Decrees average over 2,000 a year, Decrees over 3,000, and Arrêtés under 1,000. Through these decrees a vast body of legislative and administrative documents accumulates.

The Judiciary

The legal system in Egypt has been greatly influenced by French law and practice, partly because many of the early prominent members of the Egyptian legal profession were trained in France, and also because the colleges of law in Egypt are patterned after their French counterparts. In fact, the first director of the College of Law at Cairo University, which was established in 1868, was a Frenchman, nominated by Napoleon III.

Until recent years, several legal systems existed side by side in Egypt, each with its own courts, rules, and regulations. There were, for example, Mixed Courts and Consular Courts, which were established as a result of the system of capitulations. The Mixed Courts dealt with cases involving foreigners of different nationalities, or foreigners and Egyptians; whereas the Consular Courts dealt with cases involving foreigners of the same nationality according to their own laws. The Consular Courts in particular were in effect courts of foreign states with jurisdiction in Egyptian territory. Both of these courts were abolished in 1949, and all foreigners residing in the country were made subject to Egyptian law.

Probably one of the most interesting and radical developments in the legal system of Egypt—and one that is likely to have deep social ramifications—is the abolition of the *shari'a* and millet courts in 1955 (Law No. 462). These courts dealt with matters relating to personal status, such as marriage, divorce, inheritance, and so forth.

Both the shari'a and millet courts were based on religious law. The shari'a courts handled cases arising among Moslems, while the millet courts dealt with cases among the other religious communities, such as the Christians, the Jews, and the Copts. Each Christian denomination had its own court system, which was administered and presided over by its own religious leaders. They handed down decisions made on the basis of the canon law of their particular denomination, which were binding and enforced by the state. Among the non-Moslem denominations alone, there were some 14 such court systems. In 1955, the republican regime abolished all the shari'a and millet courts and transferred their functions to the regular state courts.

Thus, only the national court system remained. Since 1952, however, a rather large-scale movement has been under way to revamp Egyptian law itself. As described, the aims of this movement are to remove the "old residues," the deadwood and contradictions that had accumulated over the years, in order to simplify the law and the court procedures. It is further claimed that the over-all objective is to make justice available to the average citizen with speed and without prohibitive costs.

Administration of the law. According to the constitution, the judicial system is entirely free from the influence of the executive. Article 152 states that: "Judges are independent. They are in the administration of justice subject to no other authority save that of the law." Judges are appointed by presidential decree, after nomination by the Minister of Justice. Their appointments are for life, and they cannot be removed from office except for malpractice or obvious immoral conduct.

There are indications that in the future the personnel of the judiciary may be altered to make it less independent and to direct it to the interests of the state. The argument for such a change is that the earlier application of law built up an atmosphere of bureaucratic power and arrogance which isolated the judiciary from the people. Thus, a popular element should be introduced into the courts, so that laws may be interpreted in compliance with the aims of the socialist society.

The Ministry of Justice serves mainly in a housekeeping and an administrative capacity. All officials of the court system, including judges, are considered to be its employees, and all are supervised, regulated, and paid by it. This ministry also has responsibility for the construction and maintenance of courts and other related buildings. The ministry has substantive functions also, among which are the regulation of the legal profession and the drafting of laws. The various departments and functions of the Public Prosecutor are part of and under the jurisdiction of the Ministry of Justice.

The court system. Although there are a number of specialized courts —including state security courts, which deal with cases involving the security of the country—the national court system handles the vast bulk of all cases in Egypt. This system consists of four levels of tribunals, each of which has chambers for civil, criminal, labor, personal status, and various other types of cases. Aside from the informal village "courts," the lowest level of tribunal is the Summary Court (al-Mahkamah al-Juz'iyyah), which is usually presided over by one judge. The second level is the Court of First Instance (al-Mahkamah al-Ibtida'iyyah), followed by the Court of Appeal (Mahkamat al-Isti'naf), and finally by the highest court in the land—the Court of Cassation (Mahkamat al-Nakdh), of which there is only one. In 1960, there were 164 Summary, 19 First Instance, and 5 Appellate courts, as well as the one Court of Cassation. The number of tribunals today is probably much greater, especially of Summary and First Instance courts.

In addition to the regular court system, there is in Egypt today a system of administrative justice which follows the French and Italian models. This system is concerned entirely with disputes and cases between the government administration and its employees. The principal authority in the field of administrative justice is the State Council, which was established in 1946 and reorganized in

1955 under Law No. 165. The Council has two main functions: (1) it advises the government on questions of law, and (2) it has jurisdiction in administrative disputes. The legal section of the Council consists of three levels of courts: the Supreme Administrative Court, the Court of Administrative Justice, and the Administrative Courts.

Local Administration

In 1960, the Local Administration Law (No. 124) was enacted. It created a new Ministry of Local Administration, gave local jurisdictions considerable autonomy in the administration of their affairs, and tranferred to them many of the functions of the central ministries, especially in the field of social services such as health and education. This law represents quite a departure from former practice, which emphasized a very high degree of centralization of authority.

The law recognizes three local jurisdictions: the governorate (*al-muhafazah*), the town (*al-madinah*), and the village (*al-qaryah*). The governorate is a geographical area, comprising a number of towns and villages as defined by a decree of the President of the Republic. However, metropolitan centers with large populations and a high degree of industrialization and culture, such as Cairo and Alexandria and their suburbs, may also be given governorate status. The boundaries of the towns are fixed by a decree of the Minister of Local Administration; and those of the villages by a decree of the Governor. The law conferred on each of the three local jurisdictions a moral and juristic personality, and stipulated that each of them be governed by a local council.

The Local Administration Law conferred on the councils of the various local jurisdictions certain rights in educational, municipal, health, social, supply, communications, cultural, economic, and security affairs, as well as in combined projects undertaken jointly by several councils. It also imposed on them, in the fulfillment of their duties, the obligation to observe the general policy of the government as expressed in the directives issued by the various ministries. As a precaution, however, the same law also provided that in case of necessity, the governorate, town, and village councils may be dissolved by the President of the Republic, upon the recommendation of the Minister of Local Administration in agreement with the National Union (now, presumably the Arab Socialist Union). However, these councils may not be dissolved by a blanket decree, nor may any council be dissolved twice for the same reason.

The governorate councils. The United Arab Republic is divided today into 25 governorates, each of which is governed by a local council. The names of these governorates and of their capitals and their respective populations will be found in Chapter 4. A governorate council consists of the chairman, elected members, and ex-officio members representing the various central ministries. The chairman is the Governor, who is appointed by the President of the Republic. The elected members may be four or six, chosen from among the members of the executive committee of the National Union (now, presumably the Arab Socialist Union), one for every district or administrative division of the governorate. The ex-officio members represent the ministries of education, health, interior, agriculture, social and labor affairs, municipal and rural affairs, public works, communications, treasury, and supply. When the council discusses matters related to the functions of other ministries, such ministries may delegate representatives to take part in the proceedings, without, however, having the right to vote.

In addition to the powers conferred on all local councils, a governorate council is given the following further authority:

1. To assume responsibility for providing services in towns that have no councils. The council has also the authority to entrust the performance of such services to whomever it chooses and to confer upon him the necessary attributes in this respect.

2. In some cases, towns and villages may be in urgent need of certain vital projects, but unable to carry them out due to lack of competence or financial resources. A governorate council can then be authorized to undertake projects of a local character which town or village councils are unable to execute or administer.

3. When a village attains a certain degree of urbanization, it can apply to the governorate council for reclassification into a town. If the council approves the application, then the Minister of Local Administration issues a decree effecting the change of status.

The town councils. During 1960 and 1961, following promulgation of the Local Administration Act, 132 municipal councils came into being. There may be more today. The town or municipal council consists of a maximum of 20 elected members, chosen from among the members of the town executive committee of the National Union (presumably, now the ASU), and six ex-officio members, representing the ministries of education, health, interior, municipal and rural affairs, social affairs, and agriculture. The chairman is chosen from among the members of the council and is appointed by a decree of the President of the Republic.

The village councils. Following the enactment of the Local Administration Act, energetic efforts were made to establish village councils under the new arrangements. Because many of the villages are too small to warrant an elaborate setup, many—probably most—of these councils are organized so that each can represent and serve a number of villages. Generally speaking, each village council is designed to serve 15,000 inhabitants and, whenever possible, is located in the center of the area it serves.

In 1960/61, 373 such village councils were established; in 1961/62, 340; and in 1962/63, 239—bringing the total by the end of that year to 952 councils, which, according to official sources, served 82 per cent of the total population of the countryside. These same sources indicated that "the remaining 883 villages will be covered by the establishment of 140 village councils" by the end of 1964. Thus, it is safe to assume that in 1967 there were about 1,100 village councils.

The village council consists of a maximum of 12 elected members chosen from the executive committee of the National Union (now, presumably the ASU) in the village area, and six ex-officio members, representing the same ministries as those in the town councils. The law provides that any ex-officio member representing a ministry may be a member of more than one village council. The chairman is chosen from among the members of the council and is appointed by a decree of the Minister of Local Administration.

Finances of local councils. Since the governorate, town, and village councils assumed many of the responsibilities which had previously been vested in the central ministries, the question of providing financial resources adequate to carrying out these responsibilities became a vital consideration.

Local councils today have the following sources of income:

1. Taxes and duties. These include certain local property taxes, such as land taxes and taxes on buildings, which the central government relinquished to the local councils.

2. Revenues from the Joint Fund. A Joint Fund was set up, the revenues of which are divided among the 25 governorates. In turn, each governorate divides its share among the governorate, town, and village councils within its jurisdiction. The sources of revenues of the Joint Fund include an additional tax on customs and export and import duties; additional taxes on the revenues of movable funds, such as interest on debts, deposits and securities; and commercial and industrial profits.

3. Subsidies from the central government.

4. Nongovernment donations.

5. Loans. Each local council is authorized to borrow up to 10 per cent of its budget (with the approval of the Minister of Local Administration), and in some cases, up to 20 per cent (with the approval of the Vice-President for Local Administration).

6. Revenues from properties and projects owned by the local council.

The expenditures of the local councils during the first three years of the enactment of the Local Administration Law, were 177 million pounds in 1961, 139 million in 1962, and 148 million in 1963. Of these totals, the central government contributed as subsidies £E 75 million in 1961/62, 87 million in 1962/63, and 98 million in 1963/64.

Public Order and Safety

As already mentioned, the traditional role of the government in Middle Eastern society has for many centuries been a negative one —it has exploited the individual, levied heavy taxes on him, conscripted him into the army, and otherwise restricted his freedom, and at the same time made very little effort to help him or make his life easier. It is no wonder, then, that the attitude of the people toward the government has generally been one of deep distrust and suspicion, and that there has been a widespread lack of respect for the law, except from fear. To outwit the government, its laws, its functionaries and agents, has traditionally been a socially acceptable norm of conduct.

This attitude still prevails to a considerable extent in Egypt today, but it is beginning to decrease rather rapidly. This change is due in part to the active policies of the government in agrarian reform, labor relations, and the various areas of social services; and partly to the fact that the government is making a conscious, persistent effort to identify itself with the people—not only through positive social and economic action but in a variety of other ways, including the Arab Socialist Union, local administration councils, education, youth organizations, and propaganda.

Until the advent of the present regime, riots and demonstrations, especially by college and high school students, used to be a common form of violence and a prevalent means of political expression and of dissatisfaction with the government. The year 1954, when large student and other demonstrations were effectively suppressed, marked the end of an era in this respect. Since then riots and demonstrations, by students or anyone else, have disappeared almost entirely. Today such occurrences are very rare, and when they do take place, they are usually sponsored by the government.

The types of crimes that are common in the West tend to prevail mostly in urban and metropolitan centers, such as Cairo and Alexandria. In the countryside, tribal and clan feuds, quarrels over land and water rights, and crimes related to family honor are the most common.

Throughout the Middle East—Egypt being no exception—smuggling has for centuries been a profession that carries no social stigma. One of the principal commodities smuggled into Egypt—usually by organized gangs—is hashish. The addiction to hashish is quite common in Egypt, especially in the cities. In recent years, UAR authorities have launched a large-scale campaign to combat this habit, including the imposition of very severe penalties on smugglers and distributors.

The Ministry of Interior. The Ministry of Interior is the principal agency responsible for internal security and public order in the United Arab Republic. The functions of this ministry are wide-ranging, but according to official sources its main concerns in the field of public security are to:

1. Maintain public security; protect the people, their honor, and properties; maintain and defend morality; take care of juveniles; combat narcotics; guard the outlets and inlets of the country; control the entry, transit, residence, and departure of foreigners; organize traffic; combat fire; and organize civil defense.

2. Carry out various legal procedures, including the investigation of crimes and the collection of evidence for the prosecution in criminal cases; conduct other investigations prescribed by the law; and execute sentences pronounced by the courts.

193

Thus, the Ministry of Interior is responsible for the operation of the police and prison systems; regulation of traffic on the public highways and within cities, towns, and villages; regulation of all aspects of immigration; civil status identification (all Egyptians must have identity cards); civil defense; and fire fighting.

In 1961, following the passage of the Local Administration Law, many of the functions of the central ministries began to be transferred to local governorate, town, and village councils. This transfer, however, does not apply to public security functions, which remain under the full control and direction of the central ministry in Cairo. Security officials cooperate with local councils, listen to their suggestions, and try to coordinate their activities with their needs, but they are not responsible to them, nor do they take orders from them. They are responsible only to their own department. In other words, there is only one national police and public security system, which is administered and operated from Cairo. Local jurisdictions are not allowed to have police forces of their own. (Night guards in rural areas are the only exception to this general rule.)

In addition to the elaborate central headquarters at Cairo, there are 25 public security directorates, one for each of the 25 governorates in the UAR. The head of each directorate is responsible to Cairo. Under each directorate, there are divisions, subdivisions, and police stations in various parts of the governorate.

In 1965, the central ministry underwent considerable administrative reorganization, and at the same time the public security directorates in the governorates were also reorganized. In their organizational structures, they were divided into five different categories on the basis of geographic location, administrative situation, special social conditions in the area, and other factors. These categories were as follows:

1. Directorates of security in large cities;
2. Urban-rural directorates of security;
3. Rural directorates of security;
4. Directorates of security in the Suez Canal Zone;
5. Directorates of security in desert areas.

Criminal law and procedures. Criminal law in the United Arab Republic is based essentially on the French system, with modifications and adaptations to meet local needs and requirements. Since the advent of the present republican regime, however, this law has undergone considerable redrafting and revision. Until a few years

194

ago, the criminal law followed by the national court system was disregarded in some rural and tribal areas. A tribal, common, unwritten law, which had been developed through centuries of tradition, custom, and religious practice, was applied instead. In 1961, the government put an end to this, both as a matter of social policy (to unify the Egyptian people) and as a matter of equity. Today, all Egyptian citizens, regardless of their local customs and modes of living, are subject to the same national laws in both criminal and civil cases. This new policy will probably create considerable difficulties and even cause some hardships, but from the long-range point of view, its adoption was probably the wise thing to do.

Insofar as criminal cases are concerned, the function of the police is to apprehend the criminal and, in cooperation with the office of the Public Prosecutor, to investigate the crime and collect the evidence. The office of the Public Prosecutor, which is an autonomous department within the Ministry of Justice, prepares the case against the suspect and conducts it in the courts. There is no jury system in Egypt, so that the presiding judge in a criminal case has considerable discretion in the application of the law.

The Bureaucracy

Egyptian intellectual and cultural life, law, and education have all been deeply influenced by French thought and practice. It was British influence, however, that oriented and shaped the Egyptian civil service. The British were in effective control of the country for many years, and during their control they not only trained many Egyptians but established the traditions and practices that still form the basis of the Egyptian bureaucracy.

In terms of Middle Eastern society, the Egyptian bureaucracy is regarded as relatively efficient. In the years that preceded the overthrow of the monarchy in 1952, however, the civil service fell into great disrepute, primarily because the entire machinery of government had become rotten and corrupt. Nothing could be done without bribery; the government apparatus was overburdened with hundreds of officials who literally had nothing to do; and insofar as the public was concerned, it took days, weeks, or even years to get anything done.

Thus, when the present regime came to power, one of the most immediate and pressing tasks was to clean up the civil service.

And, indeed, there was a thorough purge. Not only were laws and regulations enacted to deal with various aspects of the state administrative machinery, including the complete reorganization of most departments, but also hundreds of officials were fired, bribery was severely condemned, and the public business began to be carried out with reasonable dispatch.

During the past ten years, the service has grown vastly in size, and the number of civil servants may even have doubled. In 1966, an informed estimate placed the number of the bureaucracy at 800,000. This is due partly to the great expansion in the activities of the state in almost every field and partly to the nationalization of the major industrial and business establishments in the country. Even though these organizations are regarded as business enterprises and are not treated as part of the state administrative machinery, their over-all supervision, coordination, and control require a large number of state officials.

Although the government has the right to hire and fire, there are regular legal procedures for dismissal, promotion, demotion, transfer, retirement, and imposition of penalties, in addition to established government grades and salaries. Nor can the government act in an arbitrary manner toward its employees, since any state official, even the lowliest, can (and does) take his grievance to the special administrative court system described above.

The Single-Party Structure

The establishment of a single-party structure in Egypt is considered in this chapter rather than in the preceding one, since it seems clear that the structure as planned will have powers equal to, if not superior to, those of the legislative and administrative branches of the government. The party will in effect itself function as a branch of the government.

The National Union. The National Union, established on May 28, 1957, was directed by a Supreme Executive Committee, headed by the President of the Republic. Its broad duties included drafting bills to be submitted to the National Assembly, based on proposals made by lower levels of the organization. Just below the National Union was the General Congress of 2,000 delegates, identified as "the supreme authority of the UAR," below which were the general regional congresses, each with an executive committee and a general committee, and the next lower tier of provincial congresses, each with an executive committee and a general committee. These provincial congresses recommended to the Supreme Executive Committee the names of potential candidates for the National Assembly. The next tier was that of the area committees, and, finally, at the bottom of the pyramidal organization were the National Union committees, with 4,000 elected members, some executive powers, and independent budgets. Through their executive committees, these National Union committees were responsible to the executive committees of the appropriate general regional congresses. At all levels, proposals made by the executive committees and approved at higher levels were to be executed by action committees in such fields as national guidance, public services, cooperatives, culture, education, and youth activities.

The announced goal of the National Union was to build a "socialist, democratic, cooperative society," and it was stated that it was not like a "single political party, which represents only a part of the people and has a monopoly on policy, but is an experiment in political education, open to all citizens." In actual fact, the tiered pyramid of the National Union was a close adaptation of the tiered structure of the Communist Party of the Soviet Union, formed according to the concept of "democratic centralism." By Communist definition, democratic centralism "guarantees complete inner unity of outlook and a combination of the strictest discipline with the widest initiative and independent activity of the party membership." Just as in the Soviet Union the Communist Party is more powerful than the government, so the National Union had powers superior to those allocated to the administration and National Assembly of the period.

In November 1961, President Nasser dissolved the National Union. This action was said to have been based on several grounds: the fact that everyone had been permitted to join, that lack of screening had led to its penetration by the bourgeoisie, and that it had not established a vanguard of revolutionary leadership.

The Arab Socialist Union. The National Charter emphasized the need to create a new organization to succeed the National Union. On July 4, 1962, the National Congress of Popular Powers charged President Nasser with the formation of a provisional committee to prepare the groundwork for the Arab Socialist Union. In accordance with the recommendations of the Congress, the Provisional

197

Higher Committee was formed in October 1962. One of the first steps it took was the promulgation of the Statute of the Arab Socialist Union, which includes its objectives, regulations, conditions of membership, and the different levels of its organization. The statute was issued on December 7, 1962.

Objectives. According to the statute, the basic objectives of the ASU are the following:

1. "To realize sound democracy represented by the people and for the people, and so that the Revolution will be by the people insofar as its methods are concerned, and for the people in its objectives."

2. To realize a socialist revolution, that is a revolution of the working people.

3. To safeguard the guarantees embodied in the Charter:

(a) To safeguard the minimum representation for workers and farmers in all popular political organizations at all levels—so that in the organizations of the ASU itself, farmers and workers will have at least a representation of 50 per cent, since they constitute the majority who has been denied its fundamental rights for so long.

(b) To insure the principle of collective leadership.

(c) To support and strengthen cooperative and labor union organizations.

(d) To establish, on sure foundations, the right of criticism and of self-criticism.

(e) To transfer the authority of the state gradually to elected local councils.

Duties. The duties of the ASU are:

1. To become a positive motive force behind revolutionary action.
2. To protect the principles and objectives of the revolution.
3. To liquidate any left-over influence of capitalism and feudalism.
4. To prevent the infiltration of foreign influence.
5. To prevent the infiltration of reaction.
6. To prevent the infiltration of opportunism.
7. To resist negativism and deviation.
8. To prevent improvisation in national action.

198

Membership. UAR citizens who are 18 years old and eligible to vote may apply for membership in the ASU. The candidate should be "a good, unexploiting citizen," not previously convicted on any criminal charges. He should believe in the Charter and be willing to participate in the activities of the ASU and to strive for the achievement of its objectives.

There are two types of memberships in the ASU:

1. Active members. These members are entitled to become candidates for membership in various organs of the ASU and to elect members in such organs. They also have various other privileges not enjoyed by others.

2. Associate members. Apparently these are passive members who do not enjoy the same privileges as the active ones.

Organization. In its structure, the ASU is supposed to be organized on the basis both of geography—that is the governorate, the city, the village, etc.—and of economic and social sectors (such as workers, farmers, trade unions, teachers, lawyers, doctors, professors, national capital, feminine groups, and students).

The "basic unit" (*al-wihdah al-asasiyyah*) is the base of the ASU structure. The basic unit is set up in a village or equivalent grouping or in a public organization. Each unit is made up of a "conference" (*mu'tamar*) and a "committee." The conference consists of the entire membership of the basic unit, and is regarded as the unit's highest authority. The conference must be held once every four months or at the request of the "committee" or of one third of its members.

Members of the committee of the basic unit are elected every other year. They in turn elect from among themselves a committee secretary and assistant secretary. The committee must meet at least twice a month. The committee undertakes the daily administration of the basic unit's activities. It also executes directives received from the Higher Committee of the Arab Socialist Union, to which it sends monthly reports. The committee of the basic unit has the right to form subcommittees from among its members.

Above the basic unit of the ASU are the following higher organizational levels:

1. The conference and committee of the ASU for the city, district, or public organization comprising more than one basic unit.

The conference at this level consists of the committee members who head the various basic units within the jurisdiction—city, district, etc.—and a number of other members in accordance with organizational decisions of the Higher Executive Committee of the ASU. The conference must meet every six months, or for extraordinary sessions at the request of the committee or one third of its members.

The conference elects from among its members a committee for a two-year term. The committee members in turn elect from among themselves a secretary and an assistant secretary. The committee must meet at least once every month. Its functions include the daily administration of the various activities of the ASU, the implementation of the resolutions taken by the ASU Congress, and the carrying into effect of the decisions and the directives of the ASU Committee at the higher level, as well as submitting monthly reports thereto.

2. The conference and committee of the ASU for the *markaz*. This conference consists of delegates representing all the basic units within the markaz jurisdiction. The tenure of delegates is two years. The conference must meet every six months, or in special sessions at the request of the committee or of one third of the conference delegates or of the members of the committees of the basic units.

The markaz committee is elected from among the conference delegates for a two-year term. The committee elects from among its members a secretary and one or more assistant secretaries. It must meet at least twice each month.

The functions of the committee include the day-to-day management of ASU activity, the implementation of resolutions of the markaz conference, and the implementation of decisions and directives of the governorate ASU committee, to which it sends monthly reports.

3. The conference and committee of the ASU for the governorate. This conference (or congress) is the highest ASU authority within the governorate. It consists of delegates from all the basic units in the governorate. The tenure of delegates is four years, and the conference must meet every six months or in special sessions at the request of the governorate committee or of one third of the conference delegates or of the ASU organizations in the governorate.

The governorate ASU committee is elected from among the conference delegates for a term of four years. The committee in turn elects its secretary and one or more assistant secretaries. It must meet at least twice a month. The functions of the governorate committee include:

(a) The implementation of the resolutions taken by the ASU governorate conference (or congress).

(b) The daily administration of the ASU activities.

(c) The implementation of decisions and directives from higher levels.

(d) The study of public political affairs as well as questions connected with public planning, within the limits of directives of the Higher Executive Committee.

(e) The choosing of leaders in the governorate and the organization of special training courses for them.

(f) The supervision of the activities of ASU organizations in all parts of the governorate.

4. The General National Congress and the Committee of the ASU for the Republic. The National Congress is the highest ASU authority in the republic, and according to the statute, it "shall be formed according to regulative decisions to be passed by the Higher Executive Committee." It has a term of six years, and it must meet once every two years or in special session at the request of the General Committee or of the Higher Executive Committee or of one third of the National Congress delegates.

The functions of the National Congress are:

(a) The study of the policies of the ASU and of its general plans and the issuance of resolutions concerning them.

(b) The study and discussion of the reports of the ASU General Committee.

(c) The revision and amendment of the ASU statute if necessary.

(d) The election and relief of the ASU General Committee members or reserve members.

The General Committee is the highest leading authority of the ASU during the intervals between the meetings of the National Congress. The General Committee is elected from among the members of the National Congress for a term of six years. The Committee must meet at least twice a year at the invitation of the Higher Executive Committee.

The functions of the General Committee are:

(a) The execution of recommendations and decisions of the General National Congress.

201

(b) Supervision of the execution of the program approved by the National Congress.

(c) The study of the principal issues of internal and foreign policy.

(d) Discussion of the development plan.

(e) Approval of subjects concerning the organization of the ASU.

(f) Examination and discussion of the reports of the governorate committees of the ASU.

(g) The election of members of the Higher Executive Committee and the election of reserve members to become members when necessary.

5. The Higher Executive Committee. The Higher Executive Committee is the executive arm of the ASU General Committee. It is elected by the General Committee from among the members of the General Committee, and presumably its tenure—like that of the General Committee—is six years. The number of members of the Higher Executive Committee cannot exceed 25 persons.

The Higher Executive Committee forms from among its members a permanent committee to carry out the daily work. It also forms from among the members of the General Committee a secretariat-general to take responsibility in all administrative and organizational matters.

The functions and responsibilities of the Higher Executive Committee are:

(a) Implementation of decisions and directives of the ASU General Committee.

(b) Assumption of the functions of the General Committee when the latter is not in session.

(c) Political guidance of ASU formations.

(d) Study of the reports received from ASU formations.

(e) Making decisions and taking action in all matters pertaining to individual members.

(f) The issuing of decisions and of executory and organizational regulations under the statute.

(g) Supervision of the ASU Institute of Higher Studies.

(h) Supervision of the administrative, political, and technical bureaus set up at the headquarters of the ASU.

The actual status of the ASU. Although more than four years have passed since the ASU was established, it is still in the process of formation. A great many of the "basic units" called for in various parts of the country have not been organized. For one thing, there seems to be difficulty finding leaders. By mid-1967, the National Congress that was called for by the Statute and required to meet every two years had never met, and the National Committee had never been elected.

The affairs of the ASU are still run by a "temporary" Higher Executive Committee appointed by President Nasser, who is also President of the ASU. The Executive Committee that was appointed by presidential decree on December 1, 1966, consisted of seven members, as follows:

President: Gamal Abdel Nasser.

Members: (1) Field Marshal Abdel Hakim Amer (2) Zakariyya Muhyi al-Din (3) Anwar al-Sadat (4) Husayn al-Shafi'i (5) Ali Sabri, and (6) Muhammad Sidqi Sulayman.

In 1965, President Nasser appointed Ali Sabri as Secretary-General of the ASU, but in June 1967 he assumed this post himself. The Secretariat-General consists of the following departments, each headed by a secretary:

1. Ideology and Indoctrination
2. Southern Area Liaison
3. Civil Service and National Capital Affairs
4. Maritime Area Liaison
5. Labor
6. Foreign Affairs
7. Arab Affairs
8. Members' Affairs
9. Financial and Administrative Affairs
10. Socialist Institutes and Training
11. Youth
12. Farmers
13. Cairo Liaison

By the summer of 1966, executive offices with more or less full-time staffs had been established in all the governorates.

On July 21, 1966, the Youth Organization of the ASU was formally established, although cadres had been in training since October 1965. The purpose of the organization is to prepare a new generation to lead the revolution and ensure its continuity and to discover young leaders and to train them in various aspects of political action based on establishing close links with the masses. The graduates from Socialist Camps join the ideological Education

Office for advanced political training, and graduates of both institutions are entitled to join the Youth Organization. Like the ASU, the structure of the organization is pyramidal, with its basic units in villages, schools, and colleges, and it also functions through a General Congress.

The Arab Socialist Union is characterized by a duality of organization. There is the mass political organization, which in 1966 had 6.5 million members, of whom 75 per cent were active members, and there is also the "political body," representing the revolutionary cadres. In August 1966, President Nasser stated that steps had been taken two years earlier to form a "secret political body," and that this group would continue to be secret for some time. A month later, Ali Sabri stated that members of the secret apparatus came from various fields of action.

> We select them on the basis of their experience in action. This saves us from pitfalls in the choice of people. We should be very careful and cautious in the screening process. . . . Members of the apparatus do not concentrate in any one field. They are distributed in various fields of official, legislative, and popular action. . . . Some believe that the apparatus is for collecting information. This is wrong, because it is directly connected with building of socialism by mobilizing the revolutionary masses.

Mr. Sabri also pointed out that the executive offices of the ASU in the various districts and governorates are not the "secret apparatus" referred to.

Regardless of the statutes and official pronouncements, the exact position and relation of the ASU vis-à-vis the government is not clear. On the one hand, it is described as a "political party"; but on the other, it is specifically provided for in the Charter and in the temporary constitution. It nominates all elected officials, such as members of the National Assembly and the elected members of local governorate, municipal, and village councils. Furthermore, all such elected officials must be active and leading members of the ASU. And finally, by definition, all top leaders and officials of the government must be members of the ASU. (The same rule applies to management councils, labor unions, youth groups, and various other public and professional organizations.)

The confusion among Egyptians as to the role of the ASU is reflected in the debate on the drafting of a new constitution. Some argue that the constitution "must give complete freedom to the

ASU to exercise its responsibilities" and that the "ASU's authority must be above that of the state's executive authority"; whereas others maintain that the ASU must have only a limited authority.

It may be noted that the ASU retains the pyramidal structure of the National Union, but that it reflects more concretely the political, directing apparatus of a Marxist-Leninist state. The ASU displays the democratic centralism of a communist party, with its political body comparable to the central committee of a communist party. In addition, President Nasser has established a Higher State Control Committee, stating that "the duty of this committee is to maintain surveillance over the counterrevolution everywhere." The communist counterpart of this committee is the Committee of Party-State Control. Finally, the ASU is described as a new power which is at the same time dictatorial and democratic—dictatorial for its enemies and democratic for its members, the popular working forces.

CHAPTER *13*

Mass Media

IN RECENT YEARS, GREAT EFFORT HAS BEEN DEVOTED to increasing the number of urban and local consumers of the mass media. Media operated or supervised by the government offer graded facilities, carefully designed to appeal to the various levels of the literate and illiterate segments of the population.

Traditionally, greater respect is paid to the written word than to the spoken one. Relatively few Egyptians can read, and for the illiterate majority the ability to do so conveys special knowledge and power. Writing in the Moslem world is not merely an essential means of communication: Arabic is the vehicle of the Qur'an, and even in its secular use conveys a kind of credibility to its subject matter. For the populace at large, classical written Arabic is the appropriate and compelling medium for important communications, although the classical language is directly comprehensible only to a minority, who must interpret it to others. However, the currents of change are strong. As noted elsewhere, President Nasser has since 1956 delivered his major speeches in colloquial rather than classical Arabic.

One out of every eight Egyptians owns a radio set. While the concentration of owners is greater in the urban areas, most farmers have access to radio through the village coffeehouse and through sets installed in public places by the authorities. Again, the level of comprehension of these programs increases as the percentage of time devoted to classical Arabic decreases. Newspapers continue to employ the classical medium, which poses problems for the less literate segment of the population, but still the press has a strong impact on the illiterate. A single copy of a newspaper is often read by a dozen or more people and read aloud to others. Farmers commonly hear the newspapers read aloud in the coffeehouses, and their concern with the prices of agricultural products may extend their interest to matters outside the village. Then, too, informal channels of communication are of special importance to the illit-

206

erate. In both rural and urban areas, the coffeehouses, shops, and mosques are transmission centers for news of all kinds, so that the output of the mass media is rapidly communicated and interpreted to many people. Information is not available on the relative effectiveness of the radio, television, and press in reaching the uneducated and semi-educated segments of the population.

The Press before 1952

Egypt has the oldest and most influential press in the Arab world. The first Arabic newspaper was established in 1800 as a propaganda aid to Napoleon's designs on Egypt, and it ceased publication with the defeat of the French forces. Its highly political nature and its short life were both prophetic of two features that were to characterize most later Egyptian newspapers. The press has since been divided between neutral independents and party papers, with the independents generally enjoying larger circulations. But whatever their political identity, all newspapers that have survived any length of time or developed a following have been firmly committed to Egyptian nationalism.

Muhammad Ali is credited with founding the second Arabic paper. He established an official gazette in 1828 called *al-Waqaa al-Misriya* (*Egyptian Events*). The first stirrings of indigenous and nonofficial Arab journalism occurred in Lebanon, where education was more advanced and the missionaries had imported printing presses. From Beirut, journalists emigrated to found newspapers in the freer atmosphere of Egypt, where Turkish censorship was less rigid.

Wadi al-Nil (*Nile Valley*) was founded in 1866, and in 1878, Salim and Bisharah Taqla, wealthy Christian Lebanese, established *al-Ahram* (*Pyramids*). Relatively few newspapers appeared before the 1880s, when they increased rapidly. Since then, Egypt has always had a comparatively large number of papers, many of which have suffered from poor quality, low circulation, and unsound financial status. In the early years of Egyptian journalism, when the cities were smaller, the literacy rate even lower than today, and advertising not extensively developed, no paper could hope to support itself on circulation and advertising income alone. The private wealth of the owner-editor often formed the most important source of financial support. If he was not independently wealthy, the owner often solicited funds from others, offering in return secret commitments of editorial or other support for the donor's personal or local interests. Sometimes subscriptions were "sold" to prominent individuals who wished to avoid any criticism or unfavorable publicity in the newspaper. Conversely, gifts might be made to owners or editors in the expectation that adverse comment would be averted. While Egyptian law prohibited foreign subsidies to newspapers, charges were made that such support existed. Until the abolition of existing political parties in 1953, party papers generally were privately owned, but received support from party subscriptions and contributions (and undoubtedly from occasional hidden sources as well).

The leading Cairo paper of these years was *al-Ahram*, often referred to as the *Times* of the Arab world. It stood outside the mainstream of Egyptian journalism in its emphasis on objective news coverage: it consistently avoided identification with any one political faction and never found it necessary to compromise its independence for financial backing. *Al-Ahram* did not hesitate to criticize the government, prominent personalities, and foreign powers, while abiding by a law which prohibited criticism of the monarch.

Among party papers, it is of interest to note that between 1945 and 1948 a number of Marxist papers appeared. Frequently suppressed, they included *al-Fagr al-Gadid* (*New Dawn*), *Omdurman*, *al-Tali'ah* (*Vanguard*), and *al-Gamahir* (*Masses*).

The Press: 1952-60

During this period, there were some 46 dailies, with a total circulation of approximately 500,000, and some 200 weeklies, with a total circulation of about 250,000. All the more important papers were published in Cairo or in Alexandria. The sizable foreign language press (French, English, Greek, and Armenian), which traditionally represented financial, commercial, and cultural interests, declined in importance.

After 1952, several well-established papers, such as *al-Misri* (*Egyptian*), ceased publication for political or financial reasons. In their places, *al-Qahirah* (*Cairo*), *al-Gumhuriyah* (*Republic*), and *al-Shab* (*Youth*) appeared as semi-official organs of the government.

In October 1956, the government sponsored a new paper, *al-Missa'* (*Evening*), with Khalid Muhyi al-Din as director. According to one source, its office was a meeting place for Communists, progressives, and intellectuals, and nearly half its contents were devoted to studies of Egypt in transition by local Marxists who were proposing socialist programs. In January 1959, some staff members were arrested in a roundup of local Communists, and in March the director and others of the staff were dismissed.

Nationalization of the Press

An official decree of May 24, 1960, entitled, "Organization of the Press" provided for the nationalization of all the more important dailies and weeklies, with their property vested in the National Union (and later in the Arab Socialist Union). Exempted from this decree was the publishing house Dar al-Tahrir (House of Victory) which published *al-Gumhuriyah* and *al-Missa'*. A note to the decree explained that the action was taken to prevent capitalist domination of the means of political and social orientation. Meeting with a group of journalists, President Nasser informed them that they were far behind the times and that they must carry out profound studies of contemporary society and its problems and propose solutions. He also criticized the earlier predominance of sensational, even pornographic, reporting, and the lack of relationship between the contents of the papers and the everyday life of the people. Following on the heels of the May 24th decree, a number of individuals were appointed to head the publishing houses and the newspapers. In April 1962, the press underwent another reorganization, and at various later dates journalists and editors regarded as unreliable were removed from their posts.

Publications now come under the control of the Ministry of Culture and National Guidance, and, at the working level, under the supervision of the Arab Socialist Union Press Committee. All active journalists must be members of the Arab Socialist Union.

The Current Press

Ten daily papers appear in Cairo: three in Arabic, three in French, two in Greek, one in English, and one in Armenian. Alexandria also has ten dailies: three in Arabic, three in Greek, three in French, and one in French and English. The majority of the dailies do not publish on Friday, but *al-Ahram* appears every day.

Al-Ahram, edited by Muhammad Hasanain Heykal, enjoys the largest circulation—some 133,000—and is widely distributed in other

Arab countries. The editor is a trusted associate of President Nasser, and his forceful editorials are eagerly read as reflections of official views and policies. It appears in some 12 to 16 pages, of the same dimensions as a standard-size American newspaper. Foreign and domestic news is about equally stressed, and features include fiction and articles—some translated from foreign languages—columns of interest to women and to children, sports, and a Tarzan comic strip. Advertisements are numerous, and obituary notices lengthy.

Al-Gumhuriyah is published in from 10 to 16 standard-size pages, and is regarded as appealing to a somewhat less sophisticated audience than *al-Ahram*. The third Arabic language paper at Cairo is *al-Missa'*, and the fourth is *al-Akhbar* (*News*).

The most important papers of the foreign-language press are the *Egyptian Gazette*, the *Egyptian Mail*, long a daily but now a weekly, and *Le Progres Egyptien*. The *Egyptian Gazette*, with a circulation of 20,000, comes out in four or more pages. The first page is entirely devoted to foreign news and the last to sports.

Foreign news and the reaction of the editors and writers to such news constitute the most lively section of the press, since criticism of certain foreign governments and individuals is strong and uninhibited. Domestic news tends to be rather bland and dull, with emphasis given to didactic articles. The major dailies subscribe to Reuters, AP, UP, and other commercial news services. With the exception of *al-Ahram*, advertisements do not fill a great deal of space in the press.

Periodicals

Periodicals flourish in Egypt; Cairo alone has some forty-five. Popular weeklies include *Akhbar al-Yum* (*Today's News*), with a circulation of 233,000; *Akher Saa* (*Final Hour*), with a circulation of 80,000; *Sabah al-Kheir* (*Good Morning*); and the satirical *Rose al-Yusuf*. The weekly illustrated *al-Musawwar* (*Pictorial*) is believed to have the largest circulation of any publication in Egypt.

Two periodicals promote the cause of Arab socialism. One, *al-Ishtiraki* (*Socialist*), provides indoctrination and studies on the background and development of socialism. *Al-Tali'ah* (*Vanguard*), which began publication in January 1965, is the monthly theoretical journal of the Arab Socialist Union. Edited by Ahmad Lutfi al-Khuli, earlier jailed as a Communist, its articles deal with such subjects as "Towards Unity of Socialist Forces," "Socialist Training for All," and "The Working Class between Unionism and the Political Movement."

Official Information Media

A characteristic selection from these publications might include *al-Jaridah al-Rasmiyyah* (*Official Gazette*), which appears every day except Friday; *al-Amn al'Amm* (*Public Security*); *al-Ta'bi'ah al-Ammah wa al-Ihsa'* (*Public Mobilization and Census*), a monthly; and *al-Kitab al-Sanawi lil-Ihsa'at al-Ammah* (*Yearbook for General Statistics*).

The News Services

The government-owned Middle East News Agency was established in 1955. It distributes news in Arabic and other languages to local and foreign customers, and it publishes the *Arab Observer,* an English-language weekly. In January 1967, the United Arab Republic Press Organization, publishers of *al-Ahram* and other papers, established the United Arab Press Agency. An important part of its activities are directed to the African continent.

The Government and the Press

The Egyptian press has traditionally been subject to both direct censorship and indirect pressure from the government, but the degree of official control has varied with the period and the regime. As elsewhere in the Middle East, freedom of the press has been guaranteed by constitutions only to be limited subsequently by laws. The administration of press laws has appeared to be not an attempt to restrict freedom of the press as an end in itself, but rather a practical expedient in the interest of maintaining an existing regime in power—presumably in the belief that under prevailing conditions in the Middle East, unlimited freedom of the press would render government impossible.

Traditional means of enforcing censorship have centered in the licensing system, whereby a government could suspend newspaper licenses for offenses under the press law of the penal code. A central licensing bureau maintained information on newspapers, their personnel, and their distributors. In effect it functioned as a postpublication censor of the press. When an item was found to be displeasing or potentially offensive to some official, it was usually possible to invoke one or another of the provisions of the press law to take the case to court. A paper was automatically suspended upon being brought into court on any charge of press law violation, and it remained suspended until the outcome of the trial. The grounds upon which charges could be brought were extremely broad; and it was not difficult to harass a paper out of existence or into conformity by a series of prosecutions, for even if the charges did not stand up in court, each case brought a temporary suspension of the paper.

On June 19, 1956, President Nasser proclaimed the end of press censorship. Since the nationalization of the major press outlets in 1960, censorship has been deemed unnecessary. Editors and journalists are assumed to be devoted to the aims and policies of the government. Censorship is, however, in effect. The imposition of martial law from July 1952 until 1964 had its reflection in the kind of material that was published. A concrete example is the Arrêté of the General Censor, No. 1, 1964, setting forth instructions to be followed in censoring foreign printed matter. Again, a Presidential Decree of May 8, 1967, revising a similar one of 1956, stated: "It is forbidden to publish or broadcast any news about the armed forces and their movements; and to give any information about their personnel; and, in particular, it is forbidden to report anything that is connected with the army and its strategy in any connection." As previously noted, the press attacks foreign governments judged to be unfriendly to Egypt, and abstains from reprinting material from foreign sources critical of the regime.

Rehabilitated Marxists, such as Ahmad Lutfi al-Khuli, are given free rein, under the conviction that they are first of all Egyptian-Arab nationalists and only secondarily Communists. The value of their services lies in the fact that their long years of study of socialism have given them the background to construct and interpret Arab socialism.

The Cinema

Films have been made in Egypt since the 1920s, and the country continues to be the major film producing center of the Middle East. In 1962, the film industry was placed under the General Egyptian Establishment for Cinema and later under the General

Egyptian Establishment for Cinema, Broadcasting, and Television. At Cinema City, outside Cairo, very modern facilities for film-making exist, and the Higher Institute for Cinema provides training in acting, photography, direction, production, sound recording, and set building. Some 50 feature films are turned out each year. Both current and older films find a wide market; as many as 800 film prints are sent annually to other Arab and Moslem countries.

Egyptians are very fond of the cinema. The locally-made films still tend to have the melodramatic or farcical themes and atmosphere characteristic of the silent film era in the United States and Europe. Rural audiences accept these films uncritically, both as a means of escapism and because the dialogue is almost always in colloquial Arabic. Until recent years, the upper-income groups showed a decided preference for foreign films, which comprised a large majority of the films shown in Cairo and Alexandria. More recently, however, a combination of the problem of foreign exchange and the attitude of the government served to reduce the importation of foreign films, and after June 1967, the importation of films made in "imperialist countries" was forbidden.

There are at least 400 movie theaters operating in Egypt, of which half are in Cairo and Alexandria. The authorities plan to build 4,000 small cinemas throughout the country, so that more rural communities may also enjoy didactic, documentary, and other films.

Radio and Television

Radio broadcasting is a government monopoly, with the Egyptian State Broadcasting controlled by the Ministry of Culture and National Guidance through the General Egyptian Establishment for Cinema, Broadcasting, and Television. Broadcasting over medium-wave and short-wave channels totals about 400 hours daily, and goes out in some 30 languages, including a number of African languages. As would be expected, broadcasting is concentrated at Cairo, although stations elsewhere operate their own programs or relay those of Cairo.

The announced purpose of the Egyptian State Broadcasting is "to proclaim the truth and advocate peace." Programs emanating in Cairo are as follows: (1) general programs (2) "With the People" (3) "The Second Program," which is designed to raise the level of national culture (4) the "Voice of the Arabs" (5) the

"Voice of the Sudan," and (6) local European programs, i.e. those in English, French, German, Italian, Greek, and Armenian. Best known outside of Egypt is the "Voice of the Arabs" program. Its strident attacks against imperialism and against some foreign governments (including certain of those of the Arab world) and its strong advocacy of various National Liberation Fronts reach a very large audience. Locally, there are at least 3.5 million radio sets, and there is a busy radio assembly plant at Cairo. The programs (already named) cover a very wide variety of material, such as news, Islam, music, plays, topical political subjects, Arab nationalism and Arab socialism.

The Egyptian television industry came into being in July 1960, and is now quartered in an imposing circular building, topped by a towering mast, in the heart of Cairo. The Cairo station, called Arab T.V., employs three channels, which are on the air about 30 hours a day. Two channels offer general programs, while a third, directed primarily to the populace of Cairo, aims at a higher intellectual level. Comparable to the Second Program over the Cairo radio, it offers operas, serious drama, lectures, and reports on research programs. Some ten theatrical groups and four ballet and folklore dancing troupes were established by the television organization: they appear on television as well as touring the country.

There are some 450,000 sets in operation, and a factory at Cairo assembles 300 sets daily. Each set pays an annual tax of £E 5.

CHAPTER 14

Foreign Relations

EGYPTIANS HAVE ALWAYS LIVED IN AN AREA which has figured in the strategic calculations of great empires and of aspirants to world conquest. For more than 2,000 years, Egypt was a prize or a pawn rather than an independent participant in recurrent struggles for power, and only recently has the country been able to pursue a foreign policy of its own making. The initial stimulus and some of the essential elements of modern Egyptian nationalism came from abroad. The Napoleonic invasion made Egyptians aware of their country's importance to Europe as a vital communication link with India and the Far East. During World War I, the British encouraged Arab nationalism as a weapon against the Ottoman Empire; in the same period President Wilson's Fourteen Points roused hopes for the end of British rule in Egypt and in the entire Middle East. During World War II, President Roosevelt recognized the right to independence of the Levant States. All of these occurrences are so many reference points in a process by which Arab nationalism was revived and through which it developed implications that passed from the local to the world arena.

The intensification since World War II of a global United States-Soviet rivalry has given strategically-placed Egypt a decisive position with respect to the balance of power in that area. Egyptian foreign policy is now inextricably involved with that of far stronger nations, and President Nasser's ability to help tilt the power balance in one direction or the other gives his country importance out of proportion to its actual strength. Egypt has taken on the militancy of a nation long dependent but now determined to be master in more than its own house.

President Nasser has demonstrated a capacity to interpret and to exploit the lessons of Egypt's historical experience of continuous foreign rule since the Persian conquest in the sixth century B.C.

He has also been able to take advantage of the decline of French and British power and its replacement by the competition of the United States and the Soviet Union for influence over the new Moslem nations in a vast area, extending from Morocco to Pakistan and Indonesia.

In the conduct of his policy, Nasser has displayed considerable gifts of political intuition and improvisation. He was in a position to exploit the emotions roused by defeat at the hands of Israel in 1948. He learned much from the new totalitarian pattern of empire-building that appeared in Europe between the wars. And he has shown that he understands the techniques which may be able to move Egyptian national sentiment from an exacerbated romantic nationalism to expansionist internationalism.

President Nasser came to power under the banner of social revolution; he has probably retained and expanded his power because of what were, for him, the fortuitous circumstances of a cold war. The first indications after the deposition of King Farouk in 1952 were that national reform, and not foreign involvements, would occupy the principal energies of the new leaders. Egypt firmly refused to participate in a Middle East defense pact, but it was not until 1955, when Egypt voiced shrill opposition to the Baghdad Pact, that Egyptian pronouncements became "neutralist" in the sense that has been identified as neutral against the West, i.e. neutral for the Communist bloc. Egypt's foreign policy is the product not only of the political intentions of the country's leaders but also of Egyptian historical experience, geographical situation, and cultural pattern. This context frames and in part poses the problems of Egyptian foreign policy; it also limits the available solutions.

Culturally, Egypt has been subjected to strong Western influence for a century and a half. In the course of that time, some of the traditional values and ways of doing things have persisted relatively intact; others have been changed or eliminated. Two examples relevant to the conduct of foreign policy may be noted. One traditional culture pattern in Egypt and elsewhere in the Middle East is the tendency to rely upon intervention in disputes. This pattern continues to be manifest in Egyptian diplomacy. Thus, in the Suez Canal dispute between Britain and Egypt in 1952, the persistence of the Egyptian Foreign Minister, Salah al-Din Pasha, in his efforts to obtain the third-party intervention of the United States illustrated the continued importance of this pattern in Egypt. On the other hand, the expulsion order applied in 1956 to British

216

and French nationals was officially explained as a necessary war-time security measure, but it is clear that an earlier regime would have regarded such action merely as the normal exercise of another Egyptian tradition—the arbitrary power of the political executive—and would have felt no such compulsion to justify it in terms familiar to Western diplomacy.

Geography is another important feature of the context in which Egypt's foreign policy is formed. Egypt's position at the crossroads of three continents is a fact of the greatest economic and strategic significance to countries far away from Egypt itself. While Egypt can without consultation adopt various policies with respect to the Suez Canal, it cannot avoid the consequences of the impact of its decisions on others. Again, within the context of geography, Egyptians may regard the Nile, together with its major tributaries—the Atbara, the Blue Nile, Sobat, and the White Nile—as a single complex, properly subject to unified political control in which the dominant voice should be Egyptian. Lacking the strength to achieve that end by force, however, Egypt can either frustrate itself and irritate its neighbors by verbal insistence on its maximum claims or it can accept the compromise gains to be had through international negotiation and mediation.

Among all the elements of the context in which Egyptian foreign policy is made and executed, one element stands out—the Egyptian reaction to the Western domination which began early in the last century and continued into the present one. Politically articulate Egyptians in general and the country's present leaders in particular look back on that period with anger and bitterness as a time of oppression and foreign exploitation. The material and cultural benefits that were realized tend to be forgotten in indignation at the thought of Egypt's dependent position. The achievement of independence and later the voluntary departure of British forces from Egypt did not basically relieve Egyptian feelings. The conviction remained that the country had won only the form and not the substance of national freedom, and in this there was something of the Middle Eastern capacity to cling to old resentments.

The military reoccupation of the Canal Zone by Britain and France, coupled with the Israeli attack in the autumn of 1956, gave new cause for hostility, but fundamentally the Egyptians were only confirmed in long-standing resentment, stimulated not only by the impingement of Western power but by consciousness of Western preeminence. Whatever the course of events, it seems clear that anti-Western sentiment, actual or potential, will for a long time to come constitute a component of Egypt's approach to foreign affairs.

Since World War II, the following issues have dominated Egyptian foreign policy: relations with Britain and France; the Israeli question; relations with other Arab nations; and relations with the United States and Soviet Russia. The struggle in the autumn of 1956 between Britain, France, and Israel on the one side and Egypt on the other marked a climax in the development of the first two issues.

The stage had long been set for that conflict. Britain and France, caught in the ebb tide of empire, were seeking to protect their remaining vital interests from further encroachments by independence movements in the area. Israel, viewed by its Arab neighbors as a dangerous interloper and a creature of Western imperialism, has confronted a uniformly hostile Arab world. Behind the specific issues of Israeli-Arab conflict is the profound cleavage between the essentially Western political, economic, and social patterns in Israel and the Middle Eastern patterns of the Arab peoples. Israel has had an impact on its neighbors out of proportion to the size of its population or the strength of its economy. Egyptian antagonism to Israel, until recently expressed mainly in political terms, has been going beyond anti-Zionism to a generalized anti-Jewish attitude.

Relations with Britain and France

The story of Egypt's contact with the West during the last 150 years has been dominated by relations with Britain. Until World War I, France was both an associate and a competitor of Britain in Egypt, particularly in economic matters, in which the French tended to press for a more stringent policy than Britain was willing to impose; but, while France's cultural influence upon Egypt overshadowed that of other Western countries, Britain dominated the politics of the area. Having compelled the expeditionary force of Napoleon to leave Egypt, the British were in a position to convince the Mamluks of the uselessness of resisting the drive of Western power into the area around Suez, which was again emerging as a great strategic crossroads. The British both exploited Muhammad Ali as a stabilizing force in Egypt and kept him from too strongly threatening the Turkish Sultan. The preservation of the Sultan's nominal authority was an essential feature of Britain's Egyptian policy until the Congress of Berlin in 1878, at which time it became clear that the Turkish sultanate could no longer effectively contain the pressure exerted by Russia, and that new means must be found for defending Suez.

Britain then took over Cyprus, moved to exert more direct control over Egypt itself, and acquired shares in the Suez Canal. The British occupation of Egypt and the subsequent events in Anglo-Egyptian relations during two world wars and afterward, culminating in the Suez crisis of mid-1956, reveal the critical importance of Egypt in Britain's strategic calculations. The British attitude was dramatically highlighted in the trying times of 1940-41; standing alone against Hitler's Europe, Britain nevertheless dispatched military forces to the Nile Valley.

Almost since the beginning of the British occupation of Egypt, and certainly since the first decade of the twentieth century, there has been conflict between mounting Egyptian nationalist aspirations and British determination to safeguard a strategic area and lifeline. Britain showed itself willing to make concessions, but with a caution and slowness which stimulated impatience to about the same amount as the concessions themselves whetted Egyptian appetites. The first important event marking Britain's reaction to Egyptian pressure was the British declaration of February 28, 1922, which abolished the protectorate and martial law and granted Egyptian independence, qualified by reservations that were to be negotiated later. These reservations, in which were forecast the outlines of future Anglo-Egyptian problems, left to British discretion (1) the security of British communications in Egypt (2) protection of foreign interests and minorities (3) the disposition of the Sudan, and (4) the defense of Egypt against foreign aggression (involving occupation). Negotiation on these reservations took almost 15 years to accomplish. Agreement was made difficult by the Egyptian insistence upon British evacuation and upon the unification under Egyptian control of the Nile Valley, including the Anglo-Egyptian Sudan. The threat posed by Mussolini's expansionist policy in Africa brought the two sides together into the agreement of August 26, 1936, whereby Britain was allowed to station troops in the Suez area for the defense of the Canal Zone and Egypt. The other British privileges claimed in the reservations were given up, and the question of the Sudan was held subject to further negotiation.

The treaty of 1936, at first hailed in Egypt as a great success, became increasingly unpopular as Egyptians began to realize that it allowed the maintenance of British forces in Egypt not only during World War II but afterward. In 1946, Britain's postwar Labor government received an Egyptian delegation in London to negotiate a settlement. The main points at issue were the perennial ones: (1) the role of Egypt and Britain in the event of war or aggression in the Middle East (2) the evacuation of British forces from Egypt, and (3) the unity of the Nile Valley. Agreement seemed to have been reached until it became apparent that the revised treaty would not be signed because of conflicting interpretations of the meaning of the Sudan Protocol. Egypt asserted that Britain had agreed to the permanent unity of the Nile Valley, whereas Britain insisted that the future of the Sudan must rest on "ultimate self-determination." The Egyptian attitude hardened with a change in government, and Britain, after offering to sign the treaty without the Sudan Protocol, asserted that the 1936 treaty was still in force.

In July 1947, Egypt brought the impasse to the United Nations Security Council, which refused to accept jurisdiction on the ground that the situation did not threaten international peace and security. Thereafter, Anglo-Egyptian relations drifted from bad to worse. The old issues bred new disputes, and one issue—that of Palestine —exploded into the Arab-Israeli war of 1948.

If Britain was more directly involved in the events of this period than were the other Western powers, still it was no more profoundly affected than they, for all the principal elements of Egyptian relations with the West in general were present. The attack on Port Said by Britain and France in October 1956 was the violent denouement of the unresolved conflict between Egyptian nationalism and Western vital interests.

The Suez Canal. Britain has long regarded the Suez Canal as vital to British survival, and the other Western powers, France in particular, have assigned it hardly less importance. These nations have, therefore, strongly objected to the assertion by any one power of a sovereign right to grant, withhold, or restrict the use of the Canal at will. The Egyptian claim to sovereign right over the Canal was particularly objectionable in British eyes, as it was asserted by a militant attitude.

Britain sought to base its efforts in the Suez controversy on the foundation of agreements embodied in treaties which are a part of general international law. Thus, the agreement of October 1954 between Britain and Egypt established the status of the Canal as an undertaking of international importance and recognized the applicability of the international Convention signed at Constantinople in 1888, which had established that the Canal should be free and open in time of peace and war to every commercial or war vessel, regardless of its flag. The signatories to the Convention, including the Ottoman Sultan on behalf of Egypt, agreed not to jeopardize the security of the Canal or to obstruct it. They agreed that no act of war should be committed in the Canal or within a radius of three miles of any of its ports. Other provisions dealt with rules applying to belligerents and the rights of the Sultan and Khedive.

Under the 1954 agreement on the Suez Canal Base between Britain and Egypt, Britain completely withdrew its forces from Egyptian territory, accepted the termination of the 1936 Treaty of Alliance, and retained the right to defend the Suez Canal Base in the event of an attack by an outside power on any signatory to the April 1950 Cairo Treaty of Joint Defense among the Arab League States. Egypt and Britain recognized "that the Suez Maritime Canal, which is an integral part of Egypt, is a waterway economically, commercially, and strategically of international importance, and [expressed] . . . the determination to uphold the Convention guaranteeing the freedom of navigation of the Canal signed at Constantinople."

Despite this accord, President Nasser acted on July 26, 1956, to nationalize the Suez Canal and to assert unilateral control of the waterway. Britain and France interpreted the move as a violation of the Treaty of Constantinople and as a direct threat to their vital interests. The United States, holding that some means of maintaining freedom of navigation of the Canal through a form of international supervision should be found, participated with Britain, France, and a number of other nations in negotiations to find a basis of compromise. Egypt refused to modify its position. When Israel sent military forces into the Sinai Desert for the professed purpose of destroying the bases from which Egypt had been raiding Israeli territory, the British and French invaded the Canal Zone, justifying the step as necessary for the protection of the security of the waterway. The Israeli forces thrust as far as the Canal Zone, overwhelming all resistance. The British and French advance south from Port Said was halted after a series of political reactions to their activity, including a threat of armed intervention by the

221

Soviet Union, swift condemnation by the United States of this aggression, and resolutions of censure by the United Nations, in which both the United States and the Soviet Union voted for the withdrawal of the military forces. In December, the Israeli Army pulled back from the Canal Zone, and the British and French withdrew their forces as an intervening United Nations security force arrived on the scene, and the work of clearing the Canal, which the Egyptians had blocked with sunken ships, was begun.

Egyptian hostility toward its attackers, however, was unabated. In January 1957, Nasser denounced the 1954 agreement with Britain, and continued to treat English, French, and Jewish property in Egypt as that of enemy aliens. Also in January of that year, President Eisenhower focused on another aspect of the Middle Eastern crisis by appealing to a joint session of the United States Congress for special powers—including the right to use troops—to deal with a possible military emergency that might result from Soviet penetration into the area. In the absence of a settlement that could somehow reconcile Egyptian national claims with vital interests that were broadly Western no less than specifically British, French, or Israeli, future conflict in the area seemed inevitable, and did indeed occur.

The Israeli Question

No problem affecting the Middle East and Egypt is as intrinsically difficult or pressing as that of Egypt's relations with the independent State of Israel. In November 1947, the General Assembly of the United Nations passed the Resolution on the Partition of Palestine, which led to the establishment of an independent Jewish state in this territory. With the creation of Israel as a sovereign state, there was established in the Middle East a political enclave that was vigorously Western in culture. Occupying territory which had been inhabited by Arabs for centuries, and sharing no significant community of values with the Arabs, Israel appears to its reluctant neighbors as a dangerous interloper. Moreover, the creation of the Jewish state led to the displacement of some 900,000 Palestinian Arabs, whose presence in bordering states and whose bitter determination to return to their homes is an incendiary factor in the area. Much of the postwar instability in the Middle East has resulted from this seemingly unsolvable problem.

Egypt has sought to make good its claim to leadership of the Arab world by a policy of violent opposition to Israel. It therefore took the brunt of the war with Israel in 1948. The revelation of Egyptian internal weakness at that time prepared the way for the 1952 military coup and complicated Egypt's leadership role in the League of Arab States.

Dozens of publications have examined the background and the details of the 1956 attack on the Suez Canal Zone by France, the United Kingdom, and Israel. Those that described the military aspects of the Israeli push through the Sinai Peninsula to the Canal must have been studied by the military leaders of the UAR.

President Nasser was comparatively mild in his repeated denunciations of Israel during the decade following the tripartite invasion. In a speech on November 26, 1965, he stated that a comprehensive Arab force was being built up against the racist and imperialist base in Israel, but that, "such preparations have not yet reached the point of committing a venture and bearing its consequences." This buildup included, for Egypt, the acquisition of massive supplies of arms and equipment from Czechoslovakia and the USSR and the manufacture of some military items within the country itself.

Other forces, however, were openly belligerent. The Palestine Liberation Organization, headed by firebrand Ahmad al-Shuqayri, was quartered at Cairo, where it used the radio facilities of the UAR for its "Voice of Palestine" program. A Palestine Liberation Army was brought into being. The People's Republic of China invited al-Shuqayri to visit Peking, gave him the kind of reception accorded to heads of state, asked him to assign a permanent representative to China, and offered to train members of the PLA. Many such members did go to Peking, and arms were sent from the People's Republic of China to the Gaza Strip, where the PLA numbered some 5,000 men. Al-Shuqayri called for the slaying of King Husayn after that ruler declined to allow units of the PLA to be stationed in Jordan, and as late as June 4, 1967, he renewed his demand that units be placed in Jordan and stated that he was planning to proclaim a Republic of Palestine. It was not clear to observers whether President Nasser used al-Shuqayri to push an extremely belligerent line or whether al-Shuqayri had escaped from his control. In this same period, that is from 1965 on, special guerrilla units were operating into Israel from Syria and Gaza.

In the spring of 1967, Egypt possessed a large, well-equipped army directed against Israel.* The total armed forces numbered 310,000, of whom 190,000 were regulars and the balance members of the organized reserves and of the national guard. The army itself comprised some 160,000 regular soldiers. Four infantry divisions were fully motorized, and there were additional infantry divisions, brigades, and parachute units. Two armored divisions had medium and heavy tanks, with a grand total of about 1,200 tanks, including some of British origin and well over 800 of Russian manufacture. Supporting equipment from Russia also included tank destroyers, surface-to-air missiles, ground-to-ground anti-tank missiles, armored personnel carriers, and advanced and early warning radar systems which fully protected Cairo, Alexandria, the Suez Canal, and Aswân. The navy had 11,000 regulars and 5,000 in its reserves, and the air force numbered 15,000 regulars and between 3,000 and 4,000 reservists. Soviet equipment included destroyers, escort vessels, submarines, torpedo boats, patrol boats with guided missiles, and other small craft, plus about 550 planes of various kinds and sizes.

Egypt had spent large sums developing its own rockets, under the technical direction of scientists from West Germany. Two were operational as early as January 1963, according to the Egyptian press. One was the Al-Zafir, alleged to have a range of 380 kilometers, and the other the Al-Qahir, with a range of 600 kilometers. Both could be launched from mobile bases. Later, the Al-Ra'id, a multistage rocket with a range of some 800 kilometers, came into production.

Guerrilla raids from Syria into Israel were frequent, as many as four a day, in the spring of 1967. On April 7, Israeli planes attacked Syria in reprisal, downing six Syrian planes. In his speech of May 1, President Nasser referred to this incident and, indirectly, to the charge that Egypt had not come to the aid of Syria as required by the joint defense agreement, saying that Syria had not

* As readers of this series may be aware, footnotes are generally not given with the text. On this particular subject, however, it may be helpful to identify the sources used for the material cited herein as follows: (1) A special study by Dr. Anis Sayigh, Director, Research Center, Palestine Liberation Organization, printed in the Beirut newspaper *Al-Jaridah* on May 22, 1967 (2) Ahmad S. Khalidi, "An Appraisal of the Arab-Israel Military Balance," *Middle East Forum*, 42, 3, 1966 (3) Mahmud ibn Sharif, *Our Modern Arab Weapons* (in Arabic), Cairo, 1965, and (4) articles in the *New York Times* of July 1967, describing Soviet military equipment captured by Israel.

asked for help. In his speech he scarcely mentioned Israel and made no threats against it.

Suddenly, on May 14, President Nasser moved large forces into the Sinai and put his country on a war alert. On the 17th he asked the Secretary-General of the United Nations to order the removal of the 3,400 man United Nations Emergency Force from their posts in the Gaza Strip, along the frontier in the Negev Desert, and at the Strait of Tiran on the eastern tip of the Sinai Peninsula. By May 20, Egyptian troops were at the Strait of Tiran, and on May 22 President Nasser announced to the world that this strait, which led into the Gulf of 'Aqaba and to the Israeli port of Elath at its head, was, and would remain, closed to all shipping destined to the Israeli port.

Activity, begun earlier, at the United Nations to head off a confrontation between Israel and the Arab states continued, while those states prepared for such a conflict. On May 30 King Husayn flew to Cairo and signed a treaty of defense with President Nasser: all the other Arab leaders expressed their common determination to face up to Israel. Indeed, many of their statements appeared to reflect a conviction that there would be a war. At Cairo Muhammad Heykal wrote that Israel had been forced into a situation in which she would be compelled to attack, and then Egypt would have to absorb the first blows prior to delivering the final blow to Israel. The exuberant al-Shuqayri, now welcome in Amman, said on June 1 that either Jordan or Israel might start the conflict, and he invited the reporters to be his guests in Tel Aviv. He added, "As for the Israelis born in Israel, any survivors would be allowed to remain in Palestine, but I think none of them will be left alive." On June 4 President Nasser said: "In 1956 the Israelis attacked us, knowing that Britain and France were with them in the battle. They spoke about the Sinai war and about their victories. We tell them today that we are facing them now, and that we cannot wait for this battle to begin in order to avenge the treachery of 1956, so that the world may know the Arabs and Israel better; so that the world may know that the Arab, the Arab soldier, is the brave fighting soldier and that the Arab people are a brave, sacrificing people." Also, the Sheikh al-Azhar called for a jihad against Israel.

Since present concern is primarily with relations between Egypt, the Arabs, and Israel, no effort will be made to describe the course of the brief war of June 1967. One result was, however, that the Arab states took a fresh look at their mutual relations and met to

225

consider postwar strategy. The Khartoum Conference, from August 30 through September 1, 1967, was attended largely by heads of state, although Algeria and Syria sent less highly placed representatives. Nasser, Husayn, and Faisal displayed marked cordiality toward each other. Saudi Arabia, Kuwait, and Libya agreed to make cash grants equivalent to $378 million to Egypt and Jordan: $266 million to Egypt and the balance to Jordan. The grants are payable in quarterly installments, possibly representing an unwritten guarantee that Egypt is to refrain from future interference in the affairs of the grantees, and they may be renewed and extended as long as the "consequences of aggression" remain. The conference also agreed on the immediate resumption of oil shipments to all the Western powers. Finally, President Nasser and King Faisal agreed to an immediate implementation of the Jidda agreement of 1965, with all Egyptian troops to be withdrawn from Yemen by the end of 1967. While there was no lessening of Arab hostility toward Israel, the conference was said to have taken a moderate, realistic position, as opposed to the extreme position of the Arab left, led by Algeria.

Egypt and the Arab World

In his 1955 publication: *Egypt's Liberation: The Philosophy of the Revolution,* Nasser wrote:

> We cannot look stupidly at a map of the world not realizing our place therein and the role determined to us by that place. Neither can we ignore that there is an Arab circle surrounding us and that this circle is as much a part of us as we are a part of it, that our history has been mixed with it and that its interests are linked with ours. These are actual facts and not mere words.

> Can we ignore that there is a continent of Africa in which fate has placed us and which is destined today to witness a terrible struggle on its future. This struggle will affect us whether we want or not.

> Can we ignore that there is a Moslem world with which we are tied by bonds which are not only forged by religious faith but also tightened by the facts of history.

> There is no doubt that the Arab circle is the most important and the most closely connected with us. Its history merges with ours. We have suffered the same hardships, lived the same crises and when we fell prostrate under the spikes of the horses of the conquerors they lay with us.

226

The Egypt of post-July 1952 aspired to the leadership of the Arab world and it has achieved this goal through the efforts of President Nasser. Such a claim was not without foundation. Arabicized rather than basically Arab, Egypt's population—the largest in the region—shares the Arabic language with its neighbors and counts itself "Arab." More sedentary and urbanized than any other country in the Middle East, Egypt has the largest city (Cairo), the greatest seaport (Alexandria), and the most extensive maritime contacts in the area. Across Sinai and the Red Sea it has easy access to the Fertile Crescent and the whole western littoral of Arabia. A distinct human and geographical unit since before the time of the pyramid builders, it contrasts with the recent and artificial entities into which most of the rest of the area is divided.

President Nasser has made this claim a reality. Longer in public office than any other Arab leader, a skilled orator with great personal magnetism, a relentless critic of imperialism and Zionism, and a fervent advocate of Arab unity, Nasser has no rival. At one time or another in recent years, however, Egypt has been at odds with the leadership of every other Arab state. In such cases, and, indeed, at almost any time, Egypt may call for the overthrow of other Arab heads of state. Muhammad Heykal, journalist and spokesman for President Nasser, has expressed Egypt's role in the Arab world in these words: "The Egyptian state is in close contact with all the systems of government which exist in Arab lands, although she differs from them in social points of view. The Egyptian revolution, represented by the [Arab] Socialist Union, has the right to be in close touch with all the popular forces of the Arab countries." To be quite specific, this statement means that Cairo welcomes the opening of an office there staffed by dissidents who seek the overthrow of the ruler of Oman, and that Egypt's "Voice of the Arabs" program may call on people in Arab countries—Jordan, for example—to rise in revolt against their governments. Such activity does have a pragmatic aspect, as when "enemies," such as ex-king Saud and King Husayn, suddenly become loyal allies.

No effective purpose would be served by tracing in full detail the relations of Egypt with all the Arab states; rather, certain trends and important incidents may be stressed. There is no doubt that Egypt under Nasser has been a sincere advocate of Arab nationalism and Arab unity, although there were no commonly accepted definitions of the meanings of these terms. In a speech of September 27, 1960, Nasser said: "We proclaim we believe in one Arab nation. The Arab nation always had the unity of language, that is, the unity of conception. The Arab nation always had the unity of history, that is, the unity of self-determination."

Earlier, in 1958, he had said that an Arab was someone who had Arabic as his language, lived or desired to live in an Arab land, and believed in his membership in the Arab nation. The provisional Constitution of 1964 states that the Arab nation has unity of history, language, conscience, and aspirations. Islam is not mentioned in these statements, and one could assume that a Copt or a Lebanese Christian would be accepted as an Arab. In practice, however, non-Moslem Arabs are not warmly welcomed within the Arab ummah, as Christian Arab writers and advocates of Arab nationalism have discovered.

During recent years, many concrete steps have been taken in the direction of Arab unity, usually with Egyptian initiative. A partial listing includes the Egypt-Saudi Arabia common defense agreement of October 1955; adherence to that agreement by Yemen in April 1956; a unified command for the forces of Egypt, Syria, and Jordan in October 1956; a collective solidarity pact among Egypt, Syria, Jordan, and Saudi Arabia in January 1957; a cultural unity agreement among Egypt, Syria, and Jordan of 1957; the charter of an Arab cultural unity agreement between the UAR and Iraq of 1958; and an Arab Common Market Agreement of July 1964, in which Egypt joined Jordan, Iraq, Kuwait, and Syria.

The most enduring and effective symbol of unity has been the League of Arab States. An initiative toward Arab unity was undertaken in 1943 by the then Prime Minister of Iraq, Nuri al-Said, with a proposal to the British Minister of State in Cairo that embodied the idea of a Greater Syria and of the eventual unification of all the Arab states of the Fertile Crescent. The Iraqi proposal met little response, and the next step was taken by Mustafa Rasha Nahas Pasha, Egyptian Prime Minister, who offered an alternative plan. Although Nahas proceeded in agreement with Nuri al-Said, his action appeared as an Egyptian bid against Iraq for leadership of the Fertile Crescent, and it carried the seeds of future conflict among the Arab states. The Egyptian initiative was successful, and an Arab Conference was held in Alexandria in the fall of 1944; represented were Egypt, Iraq, Syria, Lebanon, Transjordan, Saudi Arabia, Yemen, and the Palestinian Arabs. The outlines of the Arab League set forth in the protocol of this conference were somewhat less ambitiously realized in the actual Pact of the League of Arab States, signed at Cairo in March 1945. Later on, Sudan, Morocco, Tunisia, Algeria, and Libya joined the League.

The Pact was followed by a number of related agreements: the Cultural Treaty of the Arab League (November 1946), the Joint Defense and Economic Cooperation Treaty between the States of the Arab League (signed by members between June 1950 and February 1952), the Convention for Facilitating Trade Exchange and Regulating Transit Trade between States of the Arab League (September 1953), and the Convention for the Settlement of Payments of Current Transactions and the Transfer of Capital between States of the Arab League (September 1953). The obligation of the members of the League to act jointly to repel aggression against any one of them stands out among the provisions of the Pact (Article 6), and this obligation took concrete organizational expression in the establishment during the crisis of 1956 of a unified military command for the forces of Egypt, Syria, and Jordan.

Egypt has been the dominant voice in the League, whose headquarters are at Cairo. Most of the general meetings are held there, and successive Secretaries-General have been Egyptians. Harmony has not always prevailed at these meetings, but regional rivalries tend to be kept within bounds because of the fact that the Pact of the League provides for the protection of the sovereignty of its member states. The original vision of an organization that would be the vehicle of real Pan-Arab union has dimmed, but the League has accomplished a good deal. It has standing committees in the fields of administration, finance, defense, economics, cultural affairs, and, most notably, an effective committee for the boycott of Israel.

The United Arab Republic was born of an agreement between the presidents of Egypt and Syria on February 1, 1958. On February 5, it was accepted by the parliaments of both countries, and on February 21 approved by a popular referendum, which also welcomed Nasser as President. On March 5, the provisional constitution was promulgated.

Syrian politicians and army officers had taken the initiative in negotiations leading to this union, conscious of mass support for this initiative and looking for a way to handle serious internal dissensions among incompatible groups. The negotiators accepted Nasser's demands that all Syrian political parties be dissolved, that Syrians join the National Union, and that the Syrian army divorce itself from politics. In response to the creation of the United Arab Republic, on February 14, 1958, Jordan and Iraq joined in an Arab Union. This action, designed to ward off popular demand for accession to the United Arab Republic, was denounced by Nasser.

Friction soon arose between the two regions of the United Arab Republic. To the Syrians, it seemed apparent that Egyptians held most of the high government posts, and that thousands of army officers and technicians had moved into their region. On September 28, 1961, a military uprising took place in Syria, and on the following day a newly-formed revolutionary government withdrew from the United Arab Republic. President Nasser sent troops from Egypt to counter this development, but changed his mind before any conflict occurred.

After Syria's withdrawal, both sides put forth their complaints, only a few of which will be summarized here. The Syrians stated that their role had been to provide food for both countries, while obtaining industrial products only from Egypt. Syria's business community had been alarmed by the nationalization measures of June 1961. On the Egyptian side, President Nasser dealt at length with the breakup of the union in a speech delivered on October 16, 1961. Blaming the Syrians for its failure, he said, "I was wrong to believe that one could compromise with the bourgeoisie. The class struggle is a reality. 'Millionaires' have no place in our socialist society." He did acknowledge the error of not having made the National Union a vehicle for mass support of the union within the Syrian region.

The union between Jordan and Iraq was even more fleeting: the divisive forces among the Arabs were more influential than the voices calling for unity. Nasser himself had recognized this problem during the negotiations which led to the establishment of the United Arab Republic, when he said that a longer period of preparation was a prerequisite to lasting unity. In spite of the collapse of the union, Egypt clung to the name of the United Arab Republic, and this remains the official designation of the country.

Relations between Egypt and Saudi Arabia have grown increasingly unfriendly since 1952. Prior to that time there had been something of a natural bond in the hostility of both states toward the Hashemite rulers of Iraq and Jordan. But the socialist policies of President Nasser began to alarm King Saud, who also saw evidence that Egypt was planning to export revolution. Tied to the West by self-interest because of his country's massive oil royalties, he also cultivated closer relations with Husayn of Jordan and Faisal of Iraq.

Before Saud was deposed by his brother Faisal in November 1964, he was the target of numerous attacks in public speeches delivered by President Nasser. He was accused of stealing the country's oil royalties, of spending millions of pounds on a plot to have Nasser assassinated, and of conspiring with Zionism and imperialism. Nasser also referred to him as "the King of concubines and the harem." Yet in December 1966, on Nasser's warm invitation, self-exiled Saud moved to Cairo with all his wealth and all his suite, both male and female. Almost at once he became Nasser's mouthpiece, calling on the Saudi Arabs to overthrow Faisal, and in the following months he gave large sums of money to Egypt and to the Yemeni regime. This curious situation came about because of the confrontation between Egypt and Saudi Arabia over the Yemen.

On March 5, 1958, Crown Prince Muhammad al-Badr, son of Imam Ahmad of Yemen, signed an agreement with President Nasser of the UAR which established the United Arab States. This federation was to have a UAS Council as its governing body, a unified military force commanded by Field Marshal Abdel Hakim Amer, a unified foreign policy, and a permanent headquarters at Hodeida. In November 1961, Imam Ahmad issued a decree extending Yemen's adherence to the UAS for three years more, but in December the UAR withdrew from it. Nasser expressed friendship and admiration for Muhammad al-Badr, but in 1962 he invited political opponents of Imam Ahmad to come to Cairo and to speak against the Imam over the "Voice of the Arabs" program.

Imam Ahmad died on September 19, 1962, and was succeeded by Badr. A plot of Yemeni army officers to kill Badr came into effect with a revolt on September 26, but Badr managed to escape. One of the officers of the revolt, Abdullah Sallal, seized power and later named himself as President of the Yemen Arab Republic. Royalist opposition, supported by Saudi Arabia, was active, and by October an Egyptian military force was in the Yemen to secure the "revolutionary" regime. Friendly missions from Communist states followed.

Efforts to settle the conflict culminated in a meeting between President Nasser and King Faisal at Jidda in August 1965. This Jidda agreement called for an immediate cease-fire, for Saudi Arabia to stop its aid to the royalists, and for Egypt to withdraw its soldiers (estimated at 60,000) within ten months. A joint Egyptian-Saudi Arabian peace committee was to observe the terms of the agreement, and at a later date a peace conference would settle on an interim government. At this conference, held at Harad in November and December 1965, no agreement was reached between revolutionaries and royalists, and Nasser announced that Egyptian forces would remain in the Yemen indefinitely. This statement, subsequently repeated by other spokesmen for Egypt, reflected two concerns: (1) a concern for the stability of the revolutionary regime in the Yemen, and (2) a concern for the situation in adjacent territories. Yemen had not been pacified by Egyptian troops and planes; rather, increasing opposition from tribes there had forced a regrouping of these forces to hold smaller areas. This opposition came not only from the royalists but also from "republicans" who had become embittered over the heavy hand of Egypt, which controlled the politics of the regime and the economy of the country. In September 1966, Egypt managed to fly a large group of these republican leaders to Cairo, where they were placed in detention. The use of poison gas by Egyptian planes in 1967 against villages in the Yemen (as reported in the London *Times* of June 3, 1967) aroused adverse public opinion, while the withdrawal of much of the Egyptian force in June 1967 made the future hegemony of Egypt uncertain. After several tentative efforts at establishing a mass base for the regime, the Popular Revolutionary Union was established in 1967: it appeared to be a fairly close copy of the Arab Socialist Union.

Prior to making the decision to leave Aden and its hinterland in 1968, the United Kingdom had established a South Arabian Federation. This same area was called Occupied South Yemen by the Yemen Arab Republic and by Egypt. The Front for the Liberation of Occupied South Yemen (FLOSY) was set up in the Yemen, with the UAR training and financing terrorist activity in Aden and elsewhere. This activity was designed to intimidate moderates from taking part in any Federation government and to so prepare the ground that on the British withdrawal, a "revolutionary" force with close ties to Egypt could take over. Saudi Arabia sponsored a rival organization called the National Liberation Front (NLF), which clashed openly with FLOSY. In the fall of 1967, the government of the South Arabian Federation seemed on the point of dissolution, and the sponsors of FLOSY and NLF moved to end their mutual hostility.

232

In February 1967, President Nasser stated that Egypt will "stand beside progressive forces there against imperialism. We will stand beside the revolutionary forces in the Arab south and we shall give them arms." If the implication seems clear that Egypt plans to extend its influence from Yemen down through southern Arabia, the question arises as to whether it plans to bring these areas within the fold of the United Arab Republic. It is quite possible that Egypt feels that the incorporation of the Yemen Arab Republic within the UAR might work to isolate it from aid programs offered by a considerable number of nations, not all from the Communist bloc.

Moving toward the heart of the Arabian Peninsula, Egypt, relying in part on the voice of ex-king Saud, has called for the overthrow of Faisal. Saboteurs, allegedly in the pay of Egypt, distribute bombs, and, when caught, are executed.

On the other side of the Arabian peninsula is the Persian Gulf: it is flanked on the north by Iran, at its head by Iraq, just to the south by Kuwait, then by Saudi Arabia, and farther down by the Bahrein Islands, the peninsula of Qatar, then the Trucial Sheikhdoms, including Abu Dhabi, Dubai, Sharjah, Ajman, Umm al-Qaiwan, Ras al-Khaima, and Fujaira—barren areas strung along both sides of the peninsula named Trucial Oman. Further along, the sheikhdom of Masqat and Oman flanks the Gulf of Oman and stretches far inland. For a long time, the southern shore of the Persian Gulf sheltered the dens of pirates, who preyed on the shipping from the Indian Ocean up to the head of the Gulf. In the nineteenth century, the *Pax Britannica* was imposed on this region, and the British presence is still very apparent. Since the pirate dens have now given way to oil fields, the UAR has grown increasingly interested in the area. Egyptian teachers and technicians are active throughout the area, spreading the word of Arab nationalism and Arab socialism.

Within the area of the Persian Gulf, the expansionist aims of Egypt have come into conflict both with Saudi Arabia and with Iran, owner of the northern shore of the Persian Gulf and of a number of its islands. Radio propaganda from Cairo insists on renaming this body of water the Arabian Gulf and the southern province of Iran—Khuzistan—as Arabistan, the land of the Arabs. This propaganda is bitterly resented by Iran, which has been increasing its military forces in the area to counter any movements inspired by Arab nationalism.

233

Iraq shares with Syria a propensity for political instability, and, unlike Syria, has shown limited economic progress through the planned use of its vast oil reserves and water resources. Revolution came to Iraq in the blood bath of July 1958: the ruling family and the long-time Prime Minister Nuri al-Said were brutally slain. Before the revolutionist, General Abd al-Karim Qasim, was himself murdered, he had taken Iraq out of the Baghdad Pact (later CENTO) and engaged in a confrontation with President Nasser as to which of the two was the more ardent revolutionist and hence entitled to lead the Arab world. After his murder in February 1963, relations between Egypt and the new government of Iraq improved, especially as successive cabinets took severe measures to wipe out local Communists and, at a later date, invited troops from Egypt into the country as a stabilizing element.

Since the breakup of the UAR, Syria has rivaled Algeria as the most revolutionary in spirit of the Arab states and has established the closest ties with the People's Republic of China. President Nasser enjoyed very close relations with Ahmad Bin Bella of Algeria and was very much distressed when the latter was ousted from the government in June 1965. Nasser sent a mission to inquire after Bin Bella's safety and offered him political asylum in Egypt —a request that was refused. Egypt did, however, recognize the government headed by Colonel Houari Boumedienne—a government which has displayed more belligerency against Israel and the imperialist powers than President Nasser himself. Relations among Egypt and Libya, Tunisia, and Morocco have not been too cordial. In fact, at one point Egypt broke off relations with Tunisia after President Bourguiba called for a settlement of the Arab-Israeli conflict: Nasser referred to him as "that imbecile Bourguiba."

The record of Egypt's relations with Jordan during the past decade is one of almost unbroken hostility on the part of Egypt, marked by calls from the "Voice of the Arabs" for the overthrow of King Husayn. Husayn remained under attack because he was alleged to favor a settlement with Israel, because he obtained arms and budgetary support from the West, and because he was too close to Saudi Arabia.

Egypt and Africa

To President Nasser, Africa was the second of the circles of which Egypt was a part, and the role of Egypt was to extend its influence into "black" Africa. There Egypt has presented itself as the protagonist of areas still seeking freedom from foreign control and as a powerful opponent of imperialism and neocolonialism. The fact that Islam was having great success in proselytizing regions of Africa south of the Sahara brought into prominence the role of Al-Azhar as a training ground for Moslem leaders and as a source of teachers and activists.

President Nasser's efforts to rally the more radical of the African nations under his guidance—such as the Casablanca Conference of January 1961 and the All-Africa People's Conference held in Cairo in April 1961—ran into the opposition of African leaders. Furthermore, the rise of the Organization of African Unity, quartered at Addis Ababa, tended to diminish the amount of influence that any one person could exercise on the continent's affairs. Egypt still attempts to fan hostility toward Israel in those countries in which there is Israeli diplomatic representation. It cultivates friendship in countries in which Moslems are in a majority or represent a significant minority, and works to encourage anti-imperialist feelings. From Cairo, the "Voice of Free Africa" broadcasts in at least seven African languages. As an Arab state, Egypt is not really in harmony with black Africa, and its future role should be no more conspicuous than that of the past.

Egypt and the Moslem World

Egypt's role within the third circle defined by Nasser has been very limited. On the one hand, stress is placed on the compatibility between Islam and socialism, and graduates of Al-Azhar do indeed have influence throughout this world. On the other hand, President Nasser has vigorously opposed any Moslem organizations which were not within his control, such as the Islamic Pact sponsored by the rulers of Saudi Arabia and of Iran.

Egypt and the Rest of the World

Until the end of 1962, the new regime in Egypt showed interest in helping to establish a neutralist bloc, which would include India and countries of Africa and Asia. Nehru paid a third visit to Cairo in February 1955, and an official communiqué stressed the identity of the views of Egypt and India on international issues.

In April 1955, President Nasser took part in the Bandung Conference, where he came into contact with an atmosphere charged with hostility toward "imperialists led by U.S. imperialists," and reached the conclusion that "the only wise policy for us consisted in adopting positive neutrality and nonalignment." That same February, Nasser met Marshal Tito for the first time, and over the next several years the triumvirate of Nehru-Tito-Nasser made world news: Nasser's image in the Arab world and beyond was enhanced by his close association with these partners. The posture of non-alignment gained ground in the Arab world, and became specific in the decisions of these nations not to become involved in the Cold War.

Marshal Tito clearly had an impressive influence on Nasser. At this time he was out of favor with the Soviet Union, so that his freedom from restrictive dogma could be admired, while his in-dependent brand of socialism offered an attractive model to Egypt. In September 1961, Tito and Nasser staged the Belgrade Confer-ence of nonaligned nations, a meeting which deplored the effects of the Cold War on other countries, but did little constructive work. Nasser explained to the conference that Egypt's policy had passed through two phases prior to its present one of nonalignment: first, prior to 1955, nonengagement, and second, positive neutrality. Non-alignment—not so specifically defined by Nasser—included support to all national liberation movements, refusal to join military pacts with nonregional states, and refusal to grant military bases on na-tional territory to other states.

Egypt did attempt to remain nonaligned between East and West, but the atmosphere of the era was unfavorable to such a posture. With Egypt's heritage of hatred for the British occupation, it was natural for that country to join the Communist states and others in denouncing the West that had "created imperialism" and was now allegedly backing something called "neocolonialism." Hostile voices also emphasized the allegation that Western aid had strings attached to it, while aid from the Communist bloc was com-pletely disinterested. These and other factors served to nourish a growing spirit of hostility toward the United States, Britain, and France, fanned as it was by the fantastic lies and distortions of fact put out by the Egyptian press.

Relations with the Communist States

In May 1955, the USSR made a firm approach to Egypt with an offer to supply arms, and on September 27 of that year it was an-nounced that initially these weapons would be supplied by Czechoslovakia. That same December, the Soviet Union offered to participate in the international financing of the construction of the High Dam, as announced by Secretary of State Dulles, but this offer was rejected by Dulles. The first large Soviet loan to Egypt was extended in January 1958, and in April and May of that year, President Nasser visited the Soviet Union. In succeeding years, high-ranking officials of both countries shuttled back and forth between Moscow and Cairo. Nikita Khrushchev welcomed Nasser as the "national hero of the Arab people" and stressed that his country extended "disinterested aid to the Middle East" and "never pursued any selfish ends." He also made a reference to Israel, which is of interest in light of later developments: "We said (in 1956) that if Israel were to unleash a war against the Arabs, the Arabs would, in our opinion, start a holy war against the invaders. And such a war would inevitably end in the defeat of the aggressors." On this and on many subsequent occasions, Soviet spokesmen were to inform Egypt that the Soviet Union alone had forced the collapse of the tripartite invasion, ignoring the positive role played by the United States.

As long as Khrushchev was in power, he was not above lecturing Nasser from time to time. In March 1959, he criticized President Nasser's attack on local Communists, and was sharply rebuked: "Mr. Khrushchev's defense of Communists in our country is inacceptable to the Arab people." In 1961, Khrushchev criticized Arab socialism, and in May 1964, in Cairo, he lectured Nasser on the point that Arab unity and Arab nationalism were in error because they left no room for that unity of socialism which was a stage on the road to Communism. These disagreements did not slow the rate of Soviet aid, which, as noted elsewhere, reached a first crescendo with the agreements of December 1958 and August 1960 for the financing of the High Dam, and a second crescendo with the supplying of more than a billion dollars' worth of military equipment.

In general, the Soviet Union was well pleased with the course of events in Egypt. The country had enjoyed a "national-democratic" revolution, and, according to the *New Times* of December 1, 1965, had taken the anticapitalist road of development, and a "leftward shift" more favorable to the local Communists. Indeed, the "Arab" in Arab socialism seemed to be stressed less and less, and Nasser himself made references to "scientific socialism." What more, then, did the USSR want from Egypt? Probably nothing as

237

concrete as a military or naval base. Probably nothing more than an extension of Egyptian influence into the Arab and African worlds—an influence that would attack reaction and the status quo and encourage revolution and socialism.

The question of Israel presented a delicate problem for the leaders of the Soviet Union, since these leaders have never stated that Israel should be destroyed. It is well not to overlook the position of the Communist Party of Israel, which is not oriented toward Peking, so that its statements do not contradict Soviet policy. The basic line of the CPI is that the Israeli-Arab conflict is a national dispute that cannot be identified as a conflict between imperialistic reaction and the forces of progress in the Middle East. On June 4, 1967, the Central Committee of the CPI sent a letter to the Central Committees of Communist parties throughout the world. Among the steps recommended in this letter were the removal of the blockade that the UAR had placed at the Straits of Tiran, the withdrawal of military concentrations on both sides of the borders between Israel and the Arab countries, the stopping of terrorist penetrations into the territory of Israel, and the end of a policy of counteraction in the Arab countries.

Certainly the period of tension of May 1967, the brief Arab-Israeli war of June, and the long drawn-out aftermath presented the USSR with a serious dilemma. Not willing to push Egypt into war, and not prepared to intervene when conflict was joined, its posture was far less belligerent than at the time of the tripartite invasion. To recover face, to maintain its influence in the region, and to try to assure that Nasser and other leaders did not disappear from the scene, the leaders of the Soviet Union seemed to see no other course than that of assuming the burden of Egypt; that is of rearming the country and providing whatever food and financing were required to prevent economic collapse.

Egypt's relations with the other Communist states of Europe have been good: Czechoslovakia, Hungary, Poland, Rumania, and the German Democratic Republic—not diplomatically recognized by Egypt—have made large loans, and are increasingly important trading partners.

Egypt extended diplomatic recognition to the People's Republic of China in May 1956. Relations have not been particularly cordial, although Peking has avoided making a direct attack on Egypt. Tension has arisen over the alleged Chinese sponsorship of Communist activity in Egypt in 1965 and over the fact that Egypt retains its membership in the Soviet factions of organizations that have split into Chinese and Soviet elements.

The People's Republic of China shows no signs of a responsible policy toward Egypt and the Arab world; rather, it incites violence and promises the support of 700 million Chinese. The Peking press and radio of early June 1967 encouraged the Arabs to move on Israel, while on June 22, Premier Chou En-lai stated that the military setback of the Arab people was "only a temporary phenomenon," which would "only serve to arouse more incensed hatred among the entire Arab people against Israel, backed by U.S. Imperialism."

Ahmad al-Shuqayri, head of the Palestine Liberation Organization, is a favorite of Peking. On June 6, 1967, Chou En-lai sent to al-Shuqayri a lengthy cable, which included these words:

> Your Excellency has on many occasions stated that Palestine can be liberated only by armed struggle. I very much admire this clear-cut view held by your Excellency. The Chinese people's great leader Chairman Mao Tse-tung has taught us: "The seizure of power by armed force, the settlement of the issue by war, is the central task and the highest form of revolution. The practice of revolutionary struggle of the Arab people of Palestine will again prove this indisputable truth."

In a delayed reply to this message, al-Shuqayri asserted that: "The friendship of the heroic Chinese people and their support for the struggle of the Palestinian people and of the Arab peoples in general will always remain a distinguished landmark on the road of liberation and struggle." It may be hard for a distant observer to see just what Peking did, if anything, to come to the aid of the Palestinians and the Arabs. But logic has little relation to revolutionary formulas, and al-Shuqayri may be assumed to be of value to the Chinese, since he parrots the proper revolutionary line. Al-Shuqayri represents the Chinese voice, ready and willing to counter any Soviet voices calling for moderation in the national liberation struggle.

Egypt enthusiastically supports so-called "anti-imperialist" Communist front organizations and causes. The Afro-Asian People's Solidarity Conference, planned by the Soviet Union, was held in Cairo in December 1957, and was attended by representatives from 45 countries or areas, including both the USSR and the People's Republic of China. After issuing the customary denunciations of

the United States and other non-Communist countries, the conference moved to establish an Afro-Asian People's Solidarity Organization, with its seat at Cairo. An Egyptian, Yusuf al-Sebai, was
selected as its Secretary-General. In 1967 he still held that post, as
well as that of editor of a monthly published at Cairo, the *Afro-
Asian Bulletin,* which is loaded with articles stressing the "inhuman
crimes of U.S. imperialism."

In October 1962, an Afro-Asian Writers Permanent Bureau was
set up in Colombo, Ceylon, with a Ceylonese as Secretary-General.
As a result of the Sino-Soviet dispute, the organization split, with
the Soviet faction favored by India and Egypt. When the People's Republic of China announced that an emergency meeting
of the Bureau would be held in Peking at the end of June 1967,
the opposing faction convened in Cairo and dismissed the Ceylonese
Secretary-General, replacing him by Yusuf al-Sebai. The Chinese
faction held its meeting anyway, and received a message of greeting from Ahmad al-Shuqayri, while the Soviet faction met in Beirut
in March 1967. This latter conference adopted a lengthy resolution
on Palestine, which included a call for the liquidation of Israel.
Indeed, most of the speeches and resolutions of the conference had
very little to do with literature.

Egypt had also been represented at the First Conference for
Afro-Asian-Latin American People's Solidarity, held at Havana on
January 3-14, 1966. There, too, the Sino-Soviet dispute was in evidence, with the Chinese delegation protesting against establishing
a permanent Tri-Continental Solidarity Organization, as well as
the decision to have a second such conference in Cairo in 1968.
Peking's objections were believed to stem from the probability that
more of the Latin American representation was pro-Soviet than
pro-Chinese.

On October 24-29, 1966, a seminar on the subject, "Africa: National and Social Revolution," was held in Cairo. It was sponsored
by the Cairo periodical *Al-Taliah* and by *Problems of Peace and
Socialism,* a monthly published at Prague in several languages (the
English edition of which is called the *World Marxist Review*).
Aside from routine attacks on imperialism and neocolonialism,
such speakers as Khalid Muhyi al-Din stressed the importance of
ideological and economic collaboration between the socialist countries and the nations of Africa. The representatives included a
number from banned Communist and subversive parties and from
revolutionary "governments in exile." There were members from

the illegal Communist party of Morocco, the subversive Union of the Populations of the Cameroun party, and of the Supreme Council of the Congo Revolution. The seminar heard denunciations of the governments of Morocco, Ethiopia, Cameroun, and the Congo (K), and as a result, the *African Communist* (published in London) warmly praised the seminar as advancing socialist, i.e. Communist, objectives in the issue for the First Quarter, 1967. Finally, delegations from the Arab Socialist Union are welcomed as fraternal observers at the conferences of European Communist parties. Wittingly or unwittingly, Egypt seems to have become ensnared by Communist lines and policies served up under the guise of socialism.

Relations with Non-Communist States

Few non-Communist countries now have relations with Egypt that are of any real importance, although they may come under propaganda attacks. The major concern of the United Kingdom is to maintain its favorable trading position with Egypt. This task has been complicated by recurring breaks in diplomatic relations: one occurred after the tripartite invasion of 1956, and a second was initiated in December 1965 and remained in force through 1967—the result of a resolution by the Organization of African Unity on the Rhodesian situation. Relations with France, broken off in 1956, were renewed in 1963. Official opinion in Egypt appears to regard France as less of an enemy than either the United Kingdom or the United States, and it is well regarded as a continuing source of wheat.

For a number of years, Egypt had excellent relations with the German Federal Republic, suppressing its strong feelings over the massive reparations paid by West Germany to Israel. When the GFR recognized Israel, however, resentment came to the fore, and Egypt unilaterally severed diplomatic relations.

Since 1952, relations between Egypt and the United States have steadily deteriorated. The general outlines of these deteriorating relations are familiar. At first, American public opinion welcomed the overthrow of King Farouk and the appearance of a hard-working group, devoted to promoting the economic development of the country as well as freeing it from vestiges of foreign control. When Nasser said: "We had the courage, at the beginning of the revolution, to declare that we had no theory, though we did have

241

clearly-defined principles. We declared that we would proceed by trial and error to construct a theory," his pragmatic approach was much admired in the United States, as it clearly implied a freedom from foreign ideologies.

There may be some virtue in describing the course of American-Egyptian relations from an Egyptian point of view, in this case the view of Muhammad Heykal. From April to June 1967, Heykal ran a series of long, weekly articles on this subject in *Al-Ahram*. The series was summarized and extended after the Arab-Israeli war of June. According to Heykal, the spokesman of President Nasser, there have been four phases in American-Egyptian relations, each phase marked by a shift in aggressive policy and actions toward Egypt. During the first phase, from 1952 until 1955, the United States attempted to tame the Egyptian revolution. The second phase lasted from 1955 until 1958, during which time the main effort was to punish Egypt. In the third, from 1958 to 1962, the emphasis was on containment, and the fourth phase of violence culminated when the United States allegedly attacked Egypt in support of Israel. These suggested phases may be used as a thread on which to string a number of highlights. During phase one, the United States attempted to persuade Egypt to join the Baghdad Pact, while its refusal to supply arms to Egypt in 1955 led Nasser to turn to the Soviet Union.

On December 16, 1955, Secretary Dulles announced that the United States, the United Kingdom, and the International Bank for Reconstruction and Development had submitted an offer to finance the High Dam; a $1.3 billion project, of which sum Egypt would provide $760 million. In June 1956, a celebration was held in Cairo to mark the final evacuation of British troops from the Suez Canal Zone, as provided for by the Suez Base Agreement of 1954: Egyptian troops paraded through the streets with Soviet weapons. Dulles withdrew the American offer to participate in the financing of the High Dam on July 19, 1956, and shortly thereafter, similar actions were taken by the United Kingdom and the IBRD. The reasons offered alleged Egypt's lack of adequate financial resources and its failure to conclude agreements with other states through which the Nile River passed, but the Egyptians believed that the action was taken to punish the country for accepting Soviet arms and for recognizing the People's Republic of China. In a startling response, Nasser announced the nationalization of the Suez Canal Company, stating that the income from the Canal would be used to finance

242

the High Dam. The resulting counter response—the tripartite invasion—has been discussed elsewhere. For a time, Egypt did express recognition of, if not gratitude for, the firm stand of the United States at the United Nations in insisting on cessation of hostilities and the withdrawal of the invading forces. Heykal makes no mention in his articles of the American position, and, indeed, one could easily believe from them and from later statements by President Nasser that the United States had been a fourth party in the invasion.

According to Heykal, the fourth stage in the relations between Egypt and the United States began with the Egyptian military intervention in the Yemen. Disregarding the fact that the United States did recognize the new regime in the Yemen, Egyptian spokesmen stated that the United States was upset because of the presence of revolutionary forces in the heart of the Arabian Peninsula—forces which threatened Saudi Arabia and Aden.

Between 1946 and 1966, Egypt had been extended a total of $1,133.3 million in loans and grants. As noted elsewhere, the bulk of United States aid was for wheat and other food substances. An installment of $37 million in food grains was released at the very end of fiscal 1965, and no answer was given to an Egyptian request for supplementary shipments. An agreement concluded on January 3, 1966, provided for deliveries within six months of grain valued at $55,680,000, of which amount 25 per cent must be paid in dollars. In April 1966, Egypt requested a new food agreement in the amount of $150 million. No reply from the United States appeared to be forthcoming, however, and on May 1, 1967, President Nasser stated: "Some three months ago, we told the United States: We do not want your aid any more. You have kept us waiting one year for an answer. A dignified person cannot tolerate such things. Therefore, we have withdrawn our request for aid. We thank you, but also tell you that we are a dignified people."

On June 9, 1967, President Nasser announced his resignation, later retracted. In acknowledging the "grave setback in the last few days," he moved to shift the blame for this setback to "imperialist collusion." This alleged collusion included charges that "British aircraft raided, in broad daylight, positions on the Syrian and Egyptian fronts," and that "American and British aircraft carriers were off the shores of the enemy, helping his war effort." Nasser's charges were further elaborated by Heykal in *Al-Ahram* of June 23, 1967, in a lengthy article which includes these words:

243

"The direct aggression was U.S. air cover, which blanketed Israel during the days of aggression." Although this charge was specifically denied by King Husayn and never stated by the Soviet Union, still it was the reason given for Egypt's break in diplomatic relations with the United States. While it is difficult at this moment to believe that relations between the United States and Egypt will long be severed, the question remains as to what grounds exist for creating an atmosphere of mutual confidence, free of insults.

244

CHAPTER *15*

Labor

The Labor Force

THE LABOR FORCE OF EGYPT is largely rural, agricultural, and poorly educated. It is also overwhelmingly male, except in the rural atmosphere. In part, the lower proportion of women in the labor force is due to the traditional seclusion of women enjoined by Islam, notably in the towns. The nature of the economy and a lack of labor-saving devices also help to explain why women have rarely worked outside their homes. More recently, however, women have played an increasingly active role in clerical work, in the services, in factories, and in the professions. As noted elsewhere, the relative proportion of college-trained women to men displays a startling increase. In 1965, it was estimated that the labor force numbered 8.5 million people, of whom 60 per cent were engaged in agriculture—figures for this same year on female employment are not available. In 1960, women workers numbered about 615,000, of whom over a third were working in agriculture.

With the rapid growth of industry, large numbers of rural villagers have been seeking urban employment. The reasons for this population migration include a greatly widening gap between urban wages and rural income, the rapid acceleration of schooling in the villages resulting in rising aspirations, and the greater concentration of developmental and welfare expenditures in the urban areas.

Underemployment, sometimes called "labor inflation," exists both in agriculture and in industry. President Nasser has spoken about seasonal unemployment, stating that the farmer works only 180 days a year, and that this problem must be met by providing him with a job in industry. In industry, however, chronic underemployment has been met by assigning quotas of surplus workers to the larger industries. At the same time, underemployment is clearly preferable to unemployment. Official figures indicate that average annual unemployment is only about 4.5 per cent of the labor force.

A major problem is the lack of balance in Egyptian manpower resources. Unskilled agricultural and industrial labor is plentiful, as is the supply of white-collar workers and to a lesser extent certain categories of Western-trained professional people, but there is a shortage of semiskilled technical personnel and lower- and medium-grade professional people. In part, this imbalance stems from the historical composition of the Egyptian labor force, which was until recently made up of two major groups. One group—a small governing elite drawn from the ranks of the wealthy landowners and merchants, often of foreign extraction—held the initiative in the life of the country. In addition to controlling the economy, it also furnished the country with its political and intellectual leadership. The second group, constituting about 90 per cent of the population, was composed primarily of fellahin and a small number of craftsmen, domestic servants, and so on. Passive in its role, this group carried out the orders that came from above, and little individual initiative or enterprise was expected of it.

The Egyptian labor force in its traditional form was adapted to the needs of a particular social and economic situation. The Western impact dating from the last century has been progressively altering that situation, and with it Egypt's manpower needs. Knowledge of Western developments in such fields as industry, medicine, and communications gave many Egyptians a desire to participate in the benefits these techniques can provide. But the trained human resources necessary for the application of this new knowledge— and the creation of an economic order based upon it—were lacking, and the traditional division of labor militated in numerous ways against development of such resources. Illiteracy is a common and widely accepted state for the mass of the Egyptian population. The traditional tendency to look down upon anyone who works with his hands still persists. A portion of the Egyptian elite is Western-trained, but the persistence of conventional attitudes toward status and prestige deters many of them from putting their training to practical use. Even more serious is the fact that a corps of skilled workmen, which in modern society supplements the work of the professionally trained, takes considerable time to develop. In addition to those directly engaged in agriculture, many others earn their living from processing and marketing agricultural goods. Farming, largely a family enterprise, draws on the labor of untold numbers of women and children on a full- or part-time basis. Most rural women work in the fields and may do so throughout their lives except at intervals during the time that they are bearing children. Children begin to provide some assistance at about the age of five.

There is a strict division of labor between men and women. Men do all the plowing, cultivating, and threshing and all work in which draft animals are used. Women weed and carry fertilizer to the edge of the fields in baskets, then the men take it to spread broadcast on the ground. For a woman to take over a man's job would be highly disapproved, and a man would consider it degrading to be seen doing a woman's work in the field. The younger children, both male and female, assist the women in their tasks or are engaged as a group in picking cotton worms.

The labor force engaged in industry and commerce is discussed elsewhere. The remainder of the labor force is found in professional service, government employment, and domestic work of various kinds. The professional element—doctors, lawyers, engineers—has more than doubled in the past 20 years, but the number of qualified professional people in some fields is below the needs of the country. On the other hand, the bureaucracy, traditionally a haven for the educated and the partly educated, has been notoriously overstaffed. A final important labor category is that of domestic service. Because of the dearth of modern household equipment, the relative cheapness of labor, and the prestige value of employing servants, domestic servants reportedly number over 150,000.

Ethnically and religiously, the Egyptian labor force is highly homogeneous, more than 95 per cent of the total being Moslem Egyptians. The remainder are largely Greeks, Italians, Armenians, Jews, Nubians, Sudanese, Syrians, Lebanese, and Copts. The occupational distribution of these various groups differs from that of the Moslem Egyptians. Many of them, the Greeks and Armenians in particular, are found in the fields of commerce, handicrafts, and industry; while other groups—the Sudanese, for instance—monopolize the field of domestic service. The Christian Copts have had a high level of education, which has permitted them to occupy important positions in a number of fields. Their influence in the past has been particularly important in government. Today, however, many of them are being replaced by Moslems. There are Coptic farming villages in Egypt, but few of the members of the other minorities engage in agriculture.

247

The agricultural labor force. The primacy of agriculture in Egypt's economy makes the position of the Egyptian peasant—the fellah—one of major importance. The pressure of a rapidly increasing population and the division of landholdings, as a result of Moslem inheritance laws, into almost unworkably small plots contribute to making the livelihood of the fellah precarious. It is difficult to assess the income of those engaged in agriculture, but it is certain that the majority of the Egyptian peasants, whether small landowners, tenant farmers, or agricultural laborers, live in a state of malnutrition and debt. The reluctance of even the poorest industrial workers to return to agriculture suggests that the lot of the fellah is the least enviable in Egypt.

The unproductive utilization of human resources has been most common in the rural areas. When employed, the peasant usually works at his backbreaking task from sunrise to sundown. Many, however, find themselves out of work part of the year and dependent for seasonal employment upon the limited number of factories and other economic outlets that can be found in the countryside. The problem of seasonal unemployment has been partially overcome by the present system of crop rotation, which involves year-round cultivation, while the recently created rural social centers are attempting to combat underemployment by offering peasants an opportunity to develop handicraft skills and establishing co-operative outlets for their produce.

Within the limitations of the primitive tools and techniques he uses, which have changed little over the centuries, the Egyptian fellah is a skilled husbandman. Forced to get a living out of a small amount of land, he cultivates intensively and carefully. The attention he lavishes on his crops not infrequently goes to a disastrous extreme, as when he overirrigates in the early growing stages, apparently out of fear that the water supply will ultimately prove insufficient or in the belief that the amount of silt deposited on the land depends on the quantity of water used.

The low per capita output of Egyptian agriculture is undoubtedly due mainly to factors beyond the control of the fellah. The minute size of the plots of land cultivated, which prevents the application of more modern techniques and equipment, is probably the chief factor retarding greater productivity. It is estimated that at present there is a surplus unskilled labor force of about one million in rural Egypt. The experience of World War II, when large numbers of the fellahin migrated to the cities to provide needed industrial labor, indicates that this surplus could and would move into industry if given the opportunity. It is difficult at the present time to see how these problems can be overcome, even with extensive land reclamation and the movement of a large number of peasants from the land and into the cities. A more moderate solution is the extension of handicraft and small-scale industry into the countryside. Such a development would provide seasonal or part-time employment for the fellah, as well as produce goods greatly needed in the villages.

Though incapable of resolving his own difficulties, the fellah does not always welcome intervention from above. Despite growing enthusiasm for such measures as the Land Reform Act and minimum-wage legislation for agricultural laborers, the villagers have not lost their fear and dislike of the political authority of government nor of the economic power of the landlord. Such attitudes, rooted in the centuries of constant mistreatment suffered by the fellah, complicate even the best-considered government program. Visits to villages of persons whose missions are beyond the experience of the peasant and are therefore incomprehensible are regarded as intrusions and are viewed with suspicion, skepticism, and often unbelief.

However, the fellah has demonstrated a willingness to make adjustments if the measures offered show concrete results which he can comprehend, and if they do not basically conflict with traditional ways. Thus, DDT, offered as a means of eliminating typhus, met a hostile reception, but was accepted when the fellah discovered that the chemical put an end to the itching uncomfortably familiar to every villager. The replacement of subsistence-type farming by commercial crops was a step of major importance in Egyptian agriculture; it met little resistance, for it did not intimately affect the traditional methods. The peasant simply substituted one item for another, with little economic or functional difference to himself, and adapted himself to the circumstances by growing the new crops in the old way.

Wages. Presidential Decree No. 3309, 1966—Statute of the Workers of the Public Sector, made up of 91 articles—amended and supplemented earlier laws and decrees regarding employment. Included are such subjects as examinations for positions, promotions, committees on worker's affairs, wages, annual evaluation of performance, vacations, employee's duties and restrictions, investigation of employees, punitive measures, and retirement. Those articles concerned with restrictions, investigation, and punitive measures appear to enmesh the workers in strict measures of control.

The wage scale attached to the statute and given below is nearly identical with that first established in December 1962.

SCHEDULE OF SALARIES

Grade	Annual salary (in pounds)	Periodic increments or allowances (in pounds)
Superior	1,800, 1,900, 2,000	According to appointment resolution
Higher	1,400–1,800	75
First	1,200–1,500	72
Second	876–1,440	60
Third	684–1,200	48
Fourth	540–960	36
Fifth	420–780	24
Sixth	330–600	18
Seventh	240–480	18
Eighth	180–360	12
Ninth	144–300	9
Tenth	108–228	9
Eleventh	84–180	6
Twelfth	60–84	6

Thus, the lowest-paid worker earned £E 1.15 a week, an improvement over the situation in 1953, when the *average* weekly earnings of industrial workers was £E 1.80. Wages paid by private enterprises are reported to be somewhat higher than those paid by the state.

Working conditions. While the Labor Code of 1959 established a 48-hour week of 8 hours a day, exclusive of time out for meals and rest periods (usually totaling one hour), in 1961 a week of 42 hours was set for state-owned industries, and in 1964 the 42-hour week of 7 hours a day was extended to all workers. This decree also provided that workers could do 12 hours overtime in a week, at a premium above normal wages.

Youths under 12 may not be employed, and until age 15 they may not work more than six hours a day. Women are guaranteed against discrimination when they hold the same jobs as male workers. They are entitled to 50 days of maternity leave, at 70 per cent of their pay, and nurseries are to be provided for their children up to six years of age.

All workers are entitled to two weeks of leave on full pay each year and, after ten years with the same employer, a total of 21 days leave. During leave, they may not work for any other employer. Sick leave is also included in the regulations governing working conditions.

Friday, the Moslem day of rest and prayer, is observed as the weekly holiday. In addition, workers are entitled to leave with pay on ten public holidays—eight religious and two civil holidays.

Housing for workers is a special concern of the state, which finances construction by diverting a percentage of the workers' share of the profits of industry to the building of housing units.

Employment. In January 1967, all industrial concerns began to classify their employees in preparation for training programs. These categories appear to coincide with the wage scale grades given above. Top administrators are of Superior and Higher grades and Grade 1; the middle management is of grades 2 to 5; the specialists are in grades 5 to 7; the technicians are in grades 6 to 8, as are first-class foremen; office heads are not identified by grade, but may be grade 7; skilled laborers are in grades 8 and 9; clerical workers may be in grade 8, or higher, and unskilled workers are in grades 10 to 12. Training programs are of varying lengths. They involve 300,000 workers and are directed primarily at the higher grades.

These training programs appear to be one facet of the administrative revolution. President Nasser has spoken frequently of the need for such a revolution, which would take into consideration the moral and spiritual aspects of man and the fact that he needs incentive to work. Suggestions for carrying out the administrative revolution appear somewhat diffuse; they include getting rid of prerevolutionary laws that cause administrative confusion, publishing an exhaustive directory of administrative organizations, reducing the processing and routing of documents, decentralizing authority, and instituting training programs. Involved in this revolution are the Central Agency for Organization and Administration and the Arab Socialist Union. The ASU has worked out a philosophy of administrative revolution, which states that the administrations must be controlled by popular boards and that there must be self-criticism at all levels, in line with the fact that the essence of public service is humility and that government work does not mean personal gain.

Corruption was rampant within the government prior to 1952, and in spite of subsequent purges of officials this problem remains. As recently as March 1967, the Ministry of Planning drew up a plan to prevent bribery, misconduct, and irresponsibility on the public and private sectors. The plan was aimed at systemized social development, as is indicated by the fact that £ E 56 million was allotted for the plan. A current law provides that an official who attempts to delay work and to obstruct the interests of the public will be punished by imprisonment for not over six months. An official seeking bribes can receive up to 15 years, and those stealing government funds may receive as much as life imprisonment at hard labor.

In addition to the regularly employed workers in the public and private sectors, there are some 300,000 migrant workers. Largely landless villagers, these migrants have been hired by brokers as contract laborers. In an effort to put an end to this system, called a relic of feudalism, migrant workers who join unions are now provided with jobs through the employment offices in every district. For their expenses, these offices receive 8 per cent of the wages of the migrants.

Another type of worker is one who is employed by international or foreign organizations. Decree No. 126, 1966—To Implement the Regulations of Law No. 173 of 1958, Making it a Condition to Obtain Permission before Working in Foreign Organizations—sets out certain requirements. A request for such employment must be made by each individual to the Public Security Agency. It may be approved for a three-year period within the country and for one year abroad. If the worker goes abroad, he must remit monthly to Egypt a percentage of his salary in the foreign currency in which it is paid.

Professional associations, as distinct from trade unions, are said to have enrolled 300,000 members in 14 associations, such as those of engineers, teachers, doctors, lawyers, journalists, and agricultural specialists. Steps have been taken to democratize these associations and to tie them into the Arab Socialist Union.

Egypt has a very large bureaucracy—overwhelmingly large as it relates to the total population. Figures on the bureaucracy are elusive, since there appears to be no precise separation between the numbers of white-collar and blue-collar workers employed in clerical and managerial tasks in the numerous ministries and co-operatives, in the Arab Socialist Union and other organizations with comparable functions, and in nonindustrial organizations, such as the railroads. Traditionally, the Egyptian bureaucracy served as an employment haven for those with family and financial connections or political backing. As long as clerical or administrative positions were to be obtained in local or central government, it was rare for the educated Egyptian to enter the technical field. The high pay, social prestige, and political influence that accompany bureaucratic office have powerfully encouraged this trend. In general, the pay received even by those in the lower echelons of the civil service is higher than that of other Egyptian workers. The differential in the wages received by the white-collar workers on the one hand—and most civil servants fall into that category—and manual workers on the other is the difference between widely different standards of living.

The deference accorded the civil servant was correspondingly great. Not only was he envied as a man who does not have to work with his hands but he was also feared as an agent of an autocratic government. Although those bureaucrats who come into direct contact with the people may be resented, their authority commands outward respect and consideration. The political influence the civil servant has exercised, or was thought to exercise, has been an additional factor. Since many of the civil servants received their appointments through family or political influence, their allegiance was to family or political party and not to the government as such. Consequently, their primary concern was not to assist in the creation of an efficient and honest civil service but rather to promote personal and party objectives. Under this system, inefficiency and corruption flourished at the expense of the country.

The stated objective of the present government is the creation of an efficient, honest, and well-balanced civil service. In order to reduce the present high cost of the civil service and to eliminate the waste of manpower, the state is attempting to reduce the number of government employees to a maximum of 650,000 persons, from its estimated total of 800,000. Trusted army officers were introduced into the civil service to inspect and observe its operation, in order to eliminate corruption and inefficiency. Although these officers were viewed with suspicion because of their surveillance function, they appear to have achieved some success. Corruption has been reduced, and a promotion system based on performance has been introduced. The ultimate success of this effort will hinge upon the ability to replace the traditional network of personal ties in government with depersonalized patterns of administrative practice. The task clearly is not an easy one, for it involves changing attitudes and ways of doing things which are firmly rooted in Egyptian culture.

As noted elsewhere, the bureaucracy is a major target of the so-called administrative revolution. Commercial enterprise is fairly lucrative, and the numerous small entrepreneurs formerly enjoyed considerable independence. Both merchants and their employees enjoyed the prestige which in Egypt attaches to nonmanual work. While the majority of Egypt's merchant group was made up of owners or employees of small shops, street hawkers, and traveling merchants, all of whom depend on their individual sales for their income, there has also been a small class of salaried workers employed in the larger commercial establishments. Most of the small, one-man, commercial establishments in Egypt were and still are owned and operated by Egyptians, but the larger commercial establishments were generally owned and staffed by members of the ethnic minorities. Jews ranked high among the employees of city retail firms. Greeks and Armenians also played an important role. Greeks were particularly active in the sale of foodstuffs and in the operation of restaurants and cafés; the majority of small stores in the rural areas also were operated by Greeks.

Egypt's professional element has increased very rapidly in the past 20 years, and at an accelerated pace in the last decade. Despite this growth, the country still lacks a sufficient number of professional people. Even in regions where doctors or engineers are in sufficient supply, supporting staff is lacking. As a result, physicians are required to perform tasks which should be handled by nurses, and engineers must undertake repairs and services which should be carried out by skilled workmen.

Forced labor. Forced labor no longer exists, but it should be of interest to trace the origin, development, and decline of this practice. Slavery and other forms of forced labor were important throughout Egyptian history, until quite recently. The pyramids of the Pharaohs and the nineteenth-century canals built by Muhammad Ali are reminders of it. The system has left its mark on the people as well as on the landscape, and the fear and hostility which exist in the villages toward government authority is in no small part the aftermath of centuries of experience with forced recruitment. Forced labor has been known in almost every epoch. Of the reign of Thutmose III, in the middle of the second millennium B.C. (about 1500-1400 B.C.), one historian writes:

> Year after year did this Pharaoh's war galleys, mooring at Thebes, disembark an unlimited supply of captive manpower, and the imagination can perhaps be inspired to call up a mental picture of long files of oppressed Israelites assisting the vast army of captives from other countries to raise some of those gigantic temples whose ruins remain to remind us of the Old Testament epoch.

The use of enslaved captives by the Pharaohs is portrayed in the relief on the walls of the temple of the god Amon at Karnak, showing Amon leading rows of captives. In periods of expansion, the ancient Egyptians relied heavily on captive labor; in times of decline and defeat, the Egyptians themselves were subject to the slave levies of their conquerors.

The Arab conquest of Egypt had little effect on the employment of forced labor. Under Saladin and his successors, captives were converted to Islam, and some of them were formed into an elite corps of warriors. So great became the power of these slaves, the Mamluks, that they were able to overthrow the government and found the Mamluk (or Slave) dynasty, which ruled Egypt until its conquest by the Turks in 1517.

The founder of modern Egypt, Muhammad Ali, also placed great reliance on forced labor in his program of modernizing the country. One writer observes that "the fellahin, under the lashes of the Pasha's overseers, were made to work even beyond the limits of human endurance. It is said that 20,000 of his unpaid labourers died during the construction of the Mahmoudia Canal."

In evaluating the accomplishments of Muhammad Ali, the same writer says that "he had shown not the slightest regard for human life or human suffering; his subjects had been flogged and driven to toil, unpaid, on his public works; his concern had been for Egypt and not the Egyptians." The practice of utilizing forced labor was continued by Muhammad Ali's successors until its abolition in 1893.

The institution of corvée, or forced labor, was abolished in Egypt in 1893 by the Earl of Cromer, the British Consul General and Agent. Despite this formal abolition and subsequent Egyptian confirmatory legislation, the use of forced labor was not completely eliminated in the country. Its persistence may be attributed in part to long tradition, and in part to basic factors in the economic life of the Nile Valley. The corvée system appeared again in 1917, when it was used by the Egyptian government as a method of recruiting labor for wartime transportation services. This was only a temporary compulsion, however, which could wring crops and labor, but little else, from the peasantry.

The Ministry of Labor

In 1959, the Ministry of Social Affairs and Labor was created, to be followed, in 1961, by a separate Ministry of Labor. Presidential Decree No. 1201, 1964, reorganized the Ministry of Labor and defined its duties. It was to study and devise the labor policy in accordance with socialistic principles, and especially to provide the people with opportunities for stable and remunerative labor and to insure such labor relationships as would help to increase production and raise the standard of living.

The structure of the Ministry of Labor includes 12 General Administrations: Wages and Industrial Relations, Manpower, Labor Inspection, Trade Unions and Workers' Culture, Industrial Safety, Foreign Labor Relations, Statistics and Research, Accelerated Vocational Training, Legal Affairs, Finance, Administration, and Local Government Affairs.

Regional directors manage regional labor offices, which have administrations similar in function to the 12 General Administrations: Manpower, Labor Inspection, Wages and Labor Relations, Trade Union Workers' Guidance and Education, Industrial Safety, and Foreign Workers' Permits. The most important of these administrations is that of Manpower, which in 1965 had nearly 100 offices. These offices make surveys of labor availability, maintain registers of the unemployed, operate employment exchanges, and forward reports to the central Manpower Administration.

Other organizations, or bodies, provided for by the Labor Code operate through the Ministry of Labor. Joint Consultative Boards provide for worker participation in management, described as full participation in the responsibilities of management in the fields of production, finance, marketing, and personnel. Also, there are Joint Advisory Boards for each industrial sector, Local and Regional Advisory Committees, Industrial Progress and Professional Training Committees, Joint Committees on Dismissals, and Joint Committees for Fixing Wages.

The Reconciliation and Arbitration Section of the Wages and Industrial Relations Administration of the ministry supervises Boards for the Amicable Settlement of Labor Disputes. Established in 1964, there is one board in each governorate. The boards operate through Conciliation Committees and Arbitration Boards. The latter Boards take up problems not resolved by the Committees and have authority comparable to Civil Courts of Appeal.

The Labor Code

The Labor Code was promulgated as Labor Law No. 91 of April 1959. The provisions of this lengthy document are contained in seven books: Preliminary Provisions; Apprenticeship, Vocational Training, and Labor (including individual and collective labor contracts); Organization of Work; Trade Unions; Conciliation and Arbitration in Labor Disputes; Labor Inspection and Judicial Police; and Penalties. Some of the amendments to the Labor Code are mentioned elsewhere. Subsequently issued were a great many laws, decrees, and orders which broadened and detailed the provisions of the Labor Code on such subjects as workers in industry, management-labor relations, conditions of employment, wages, workmen's compensation, and social security. Enforcement of the Labor Code and of related documents is the responsibility of the Technical Inspection Section of the Wages and Industrial Relations Administration of the ministry.

Social Security

Social Insurance Law No. 63 of 1964 replaced the earlier law, No. 92 of 1959, on this subject. In part, the law puts into effect Article 40 of the draft Constitution of 1964, which says that the state shall guarantee fair treatment to all Egyptians according to the work they do, by means of limiting working hours and establishing wages, social insurance, health insurance, insurance against unemployment, and the right to rest and to vacations.

The law is administered by the General Organization for Social Insurance, itself under the supervision and control of the Ministry of Labor. Coverage is extended to occupational injury, health insurance, unemployment insurance, old-age pensions, disability pensions, death benefits, and survivor's insurance.

Occupational injuries and medical care on the job are provided

257

for by the employers. For health insurance, the worker contributes 1 per cent of his monthly wages, and another 1 per cent for unemployment insurance. If unemployed, he receives 50 per cent of his previous wages up to 28 weeks. The worker also contributes 8 per cent of his monthly wages for disability, death, and survivor's insurance. The contributions of the employers are larger: 4 per cent of wages for health insurance, 2 per cent for unemployment insurance, and 14 per cent for the other benefits listed above. Old-age pensions begin at age 60; they and the disability pensions have a top limit of £E 100 a month and a minimum of less than £E 4 monthly. Workers in agriculture are not covered by this law, but through their agricultural cooperatives. Government employees are covered by separate legislation.

Organization of Labor

Trade unionism, which was imported from Western Europe in the early 1900s, developed slowly in Egypt. Underlying the early development was the traditional pattern of authority that existed between the family and the government. The Egyptian worker, whether he was a tenant farmer or a craftsman, looked to his landlord, master craftsman, labor leader, or in recent years his government, for protection and guidance.

In the landlord-tenant relationship, the role of the fellah was a passive one, and, although there was considerable variation in the exact terms of the relationship, it was invariably the landlord who took the initiative. He determined all matters relating to crop rotation, harvesting, and the division of the crop. The peasant's dire need for land and his lack of other opportunities deprived him of the ability to reject the arrangement imposed by the landlord.

Since wealth in Egypt was based on land, and since the wealthy ruled the country, the landlord class played a dominant role in the formulation of Egyptian political and economic policy. Formerly, the landlord accorded varied types of protection to his tenants, such as assistance in time of sickness or death in the family, guidance in personal problems, and the adjustment of disputes. These advantages to the tenants have, however, disappeared with the growth in the past century of a class of merchant-landlords whose residence in the cities and use of absentee control through overseers have diminished their sense of obligation to the peasant.

The traditional craftsman-artisan relationship was similarly based on the authority of the master and the protection he could offer the artisan. The master's authority resided in his power to employ, his role as ultimate judge of the quality of a piece of work, and his determination of wages and working conditions. The artisan executed the patterns set out for him and accepted without question the commands of the master. The authority of master over worker was further enhanced by the formation within each city of separate trade or craft corporations, which were headed by the most influential of the masters. Each group of masters determined policy in regard to working conditions, wages, and standards of workmanship, and the workers were without much recourse from their decisions. Also, ties of religion, family, and pride of workmanship reinforced the relationship between masters and craftsmen and bound them together in a sense of mutual interest and shared objectives. In the personal atmosphere of the guild pattern, the workman found security in relation to the outside world and opportunity to advance in his profession.

In some measure, the traditional combination of authority and protection has now been transferred to the newer forms of labor relations that have arisen with the growth of modern industry. And, at least in part, the inner drama of the Egyptian labor movement is the attempt to apply effectively the old patterns in a new situation.

Trade union development. Before the enactment of the Trade Union Law of 1942, the right of workers to organize was not recognized by the Egyptian government. Nevertheless, considerable union organization had taken place, and the pattern of union activity had already been established. In the late 1890s, a number of "friendly societies" were organized among the better-paid workers. These served as a transition between the traditional craft system and the modern union, the first of which was organized in 1899 by the cigarette workers. The early initiative toward the creation of Western-style union organizations came from the workers—French and other foreign skilled workers in particular. By 1911, 11 unions existed, with a membership of over 7,000.

Denied the right to strike during World War I, these unions had little influence. Their influence grew in the immediate postwar period, however, as they moved into the realm of political action through a policy of cooperation with the existing political parties. In the early period, the Egyptian Socialist Party, which in the early 1920s adhered to the Communist Third International, was favored by many unions. Later, the allegiance of most workers was given to the Wafd Party. The numerous strikes of these years were more important for their role in establishing the principle of political action by unions than for the achievement of concrete economic benefits.

Official recognition of the right of workers to organize came in 1942 from the Wafdist government, which apparently hoped to exercise some control over the existing unions and to channel their activities along lines acceptable to the government. The Wafd hoped at the same time to hold and enlarge union political support. The right to strike, which was granted at this time, was hedged about by numerous restrictions. Recognition was to be accorded only to those unions which subjected themselves to considerable government supervision. Public employees, hospital workers, and agricultural workers were not permitted to form unions.

The fear that labor organization might escape government control and fall under Communist or left-wing influence was a constant preoccupation of post-World War II governments, a fear which was confirmed in the labor unrest that immediately followed the war. The strikes that took place at this time were inspired in part at least by the left-wing-controlled Workers' Committee of National Liberation (commonly referred to as the Workers' Congress). They were ruthlessly but not quickly suppressed. There followed a period of close government supervision of union activity, somewhat ameliorated by an attempt to eliminate the causes of grievance among the workers by means of investigation, reform, and the expansion of social benefits.

In December 1952, the new government issued, by decree, the Trade Union Act No. 319, which among other things extended the right to organize to agricultural workers and to certain others. The effect of a 1954 amendment to the Act was to prohibit strikes among employees of the Ministry of War and all administrations subordinate to it, including workers in munitions and arms factories. The new legislation permitted the formation of a federation to represent each group of unions whose members were from the same craft or industry, and further permitted federations and individual unions having 1,000 or more members to join in a single national confederation. It also maintained the 1942 provisions for government supervision. One provision, which made management subject to punishment for claiming to represent a union or otherwise interfering in union activities, suggested that the efforts of employers to control the labor movement through company unions and other devices were in conflict with the aims of government in this regard.

Political and religious influences. Although Trade Union Act No. 319, like earlier labor legislation, forbade unions to "deal in political or religious matters," the trade union movement in Egypt had always been deeply involved in politics and religion. As a general rule, the majority of unions depended on the aid of political leaders, who in turn directed union activities in the interest of their parties. As early as 1923, Abbas Halim—a prince of the royal family —formed a rudimentary Labor Party, which was suppressed by the government at that time. Although it reappeared in the 1930s and again during World War II, it never was an important force in Egypt. The composition of its leadership was drawn to a large extent from the upper class, making it suspect in the eyes of the workers; the encouragement given it by the government during the labor unrest of 1946 was another reason for suspicion on the part of the workers.

Other political parties and pressure groups also vied for the support of the labor unions. Through covert activities, the Communists made a continuous effort to infiltrate and influence union activities; left-wing leadership of the Workers' Congress was but one example. The Communists also sought to gain influence by clandestine support of such extremist religious groups as the Moslem Brethren, which represented itself, among other things, as the defender of the working class.

The late president of the Moslem Brethren, Hasan al-Banna, went so far in 1946 as to break from his former affiliation with the Wafd, in an unsuccessful attempt to organize a political movement based on working class support. Before the suppression of the Wafd in 1953, it was the most successful party in winning labor support. It had carried out a number of investigations of working class conditions, and its paper, *al-Wafd al-Misri*, gave extensive coverage to labor problems. As has been mentioned, it was a Wafd ministry that passed the law granting workers the right to organize, as well as much of the social legislation favorable to them.

Strikes. An important element in the unprecedented wave of strikes that swept Egypt from 1945 to 1948 was the agitation of the politically-oriented Workers' Committee of National Liberation, which had been organized in early 1946. The long and violent labor disturbances at Shubra al-Khayma and the September-October 1947 strikes at Mahalla al-Kubra—over both of which the Workers' Congress exercised leadership—appear in retrospect to have been part of a general pattern of labor agitation by political leaders. The strikes were based, however, on the felt grievances as well as the nationalistic sentiment of the workers, and in both cases the Workers' Congress sought to associate itself with such Egyptian nationalistic and patriotic front organizations as the Democratic Movement for National Liberation. The anti-British strikes of February 21 and March 4, 1946, which brought together both left-wing and conservative unions, were certainly more nationalistic than economic in nature.

Although labor agitation has been curbed since the strikes that followed the coup of 1952, the use of the strike as a political weapon was confirmed by the events of 1954. Coincident with the Naguib-Nasser struggle for power, a series of strikes was staged to protest Naguib's plan for scheduling national elections on July 15, 1954. It was later reported that these strikes were carefully planned by political leaders to support those within the Revolutionary Command Council who desired to postpone the scheduled elections and to replace Naguib by Nasser. The main industries affected were transport (including taxis and railways), motion pictures, and petroleum—services which affect the daily lives of a maximum number of people. The pledge made by Arab trade union leaders to President Nasser in 1956 to sabotage oil pipe lines in the event of an attack by the West on Egypt indicates not only the continuing role of nationalism as a factor in labor action but also a drive toward unity in Arab trade unionism.

The present status of trade unions. The Labor Code, Law No. 91 of April 1959, included provisions relating to the formation of trade unions. These provisions provided for a complete change in the structure of the unions from many small unions to 59 large industrial-type unions.

Presidential Decree No. 62, of April 1964, together with a number of related ministerial orders, set the number of trade unions at 27 and extended the right to join unions to all workers, including public servants, agricultural workers, and those in establishments which employed fewer than 50 workers. Law No. 62 of May 1964 then completely revised and amended Title IV of the Labor Code, the section of the Code that dealt with unions.

According to revised Title IV, only one General Union may be formed for each of 27 listed occupations and industries. Each establishment or group of workers forms a trade union committee, with its own executive board. In regions where there are at least ten trade union committees, a general union may establish branch, or area, unions. Delegates from each of the trade union committees attend the annual meeting of the general union. In each establishment, full-time shop stewards represent the workers. Workers who are 15 years of age or older may apply to join a union, and no applicant can be refused except by a two-thirds majority decision by the executive committee of the trade union committee. The monthly dues of members may or may not be deducted by the employer.

The 27 general unions are federated with the General Federation of Labor, established in or about 1964. Its predecessors were the All-Egypt Trade Unions Congress, from 1954 to 1957, and the Egyptian Federation of Labor, which dated from 1957. Members of the general unions are represented in the general assembly of the General Federations of Labor.

Figures on the membership strength of the trade unions tend to be elusive—they are estimates rather than official figures. In 1952, membership was claimed to be 266,178; in 1958, 275,000; in 1961, 301,310; and in 1963, 408,566. However, figures given (ca. 1964) by each of the general unions, when totaled, produced a membership of just over one million. This latter figure includes 350,000 members of the General Trade Union of Agriculture, 200,000 in the GTU of Textiles, 40,000 in the GTU of Chemical Industries, 58,000 in the GTU of Food Industries, 46,000 in the GTU of Building Industries, 46,000 in the GTU of Railways, 40,000 in the GTU of Business and Management Services, and smaller numbers in the other general unions. Decree No. 31, of August 1966, established an Agricultural Union—apparently the twenty-eighth general union —to be composed of agricultural engineers.

The Trade Unions Section of the Industrial Relations Administration of the Ministry of Labor enforces the provisions of the Labor Code that concern unions. In 1963, it established regional offices for the guidance and education of the members of the unions.

The theory of the trade unions. According to the National Charter of 1962, the unions, along with other popular organizations, are to play an effective and influential role in promoting sound democracy and assuming a position of leadership in the national struggle. The Charter also states that trade unions can exercise their responsibilities through serious contributions to intellectual and scientific efficiency, and thus increase productivity among the working forces. The Arab Socialist Union has its own labor organization, but claims that it assists the unions and calls for their assistance in realizing the objectives of the Charter.

A lecture delivered in Cairo in 1964 underlined the functions of the syndicates (unions) in socialist (communist) states as they exist in theory. Such unions have a number of functions: (1) to play an important role in ideological and political training (2) to stimulate production (3) to collaborate with the state apparatus in sharing in the planning of production (4) to supply services, such as health and housing, to their members, and (5) to represent these members. Most, if not all, of these functions appear to be reflected in Title IV, revised, of the Labor Code. Article 160 states that the unions should increase the productivity of their members and that they should supervise the material, cultural, and social advancement of the membership.

According to Title IV, the total income of the unions and of the committees within each general union is to be distributed as follows: 30 per cent for administrative expenses; 30 per cent for health, social, cultural and training programs; 25 per cent for collective services; 10 per cent to the General Federation of Labor; and 5 per cent to the reserve fund of the general union.

International relations of the trade unions. The General Federation of Labor is affiliated with the Confederation of Arab Trade Unions (CATU), established in 1956 with Egyptian backing. In 1961, the GFL joined the All-African Trade Union Federation (AATUF). As between the International Confederation of Free Trade Unions (ICFTU) and the Communist-controlled World Federation of Trade Unions (WFTU), the GFL carries on formal relations with the latter through a series of solidarity conferences. Egyptian officials of the CATU give advice and support to their Aden affiliate, while the General Trade Union of Mining, Quarrying and Petroleum is an active member of the International Federation of Petroleum Workers (IFPW). Egypt became a member of the International Labor Organization in 1936.

CHAPTER 16

Public Health and Welfare

EGYPT IS A COUNTRY in which the great mass of the population is undernourished, ill-clothed, and inadequately housed. It is also a country in which for centuries vast social inequalities permitted a small elite group—often foreign in origin—to enjoy a life of ease and plenty.

The poverty of the rural population did not, however, lead to any considerable social unrest. The fellah would cheat his landlord and steal from him, but seldom did he feel sufficiently sure of himself to challenge his authority. The government was viewed as an agent of oppression, and little was expected from it in terms of social welfare. This resignation of the masses is explained in part by their relative weakness vis-à-vis the landowning and governing classes, and also by the fact that historically, Egyptian agricultural production kept the population somewhat above the bare subsistence level.

Efforts to improve the general health and welfare took specific form near the end of the nineteenth century and gained momentum in the years following World War I. It was not until after the revolution of July 1952, however, that a government came into power which undertook coordinated, costly programs in these fields. As will appear, the problems relating to public health and welfare are vast. Their alleviation will depend in large part on the success of the government in convincing the long-neglected farmers and workers that the state is no longer the people's taskmaster, and in securing their active cooperation in the various programs.

The Standard of Living

Official figures on the average national income per capita may be accepted with some reservations, as they appear to reflect a great leap forward in the years immediately following the revolution of

1952. Thus, income for 1953 is given as £E 37.1, and for 1960 a £E 50.2. In 1965, the figure stood at £E 59.8. The question tha remains is the relation of this latter figure to those of other coun tries, since the conversion factor may either be the official rate o $2.30 to the £E or the selling rate of the £E in world markets which was $1.35 in 1967. However, according to the United Na tions' comparative figures on the per capita income in Middle Eas countries, Egypt and Iran fall within the $100 to $190 range, whil the Sudan is below $100.

As of 1966, the family budget for those with an income of les than £E 120 annually was spent as follows: 71.3 per cent for food 12.1 per cent for entertainment and pleasure, 11.8 per cent fo clothing and household equipment, 3.4 per cent for transportatior and communications, and 1.4 per cent for education and sports Families with an income of more than £E 480 and less than £I 1,200 spent 52 per cent on food, 8.8 per cent for entertainment anc pleasure, 19 per cent for clothing and household equipment, 9.8 per cent for transportation and communications, and 10.4 per cen for education and sports. The above breakdown of family budget contains no category for the rent of housing. In the long-established villages, the fellahin occupy mud huts rent free or build such shel ters on barren, unclaimed land. Within the listed categories, com paratively large amounts are spent on kerosene for fuel and light ing and on weddings and funerals.

While the average per capita income has shown a slight rise ir each of several successive years, it is not at all certain that the standard of living is also rising. The only pertinent indicator woulc appear to be the consumption index for the principal cereals. Ir the late 1920s, the per capita annual consumption was 309 kilo grams, in the late 1930s it was 245 kilograms, and in 1965 it stooc at 213 kilograms.

Diet

According to figures compiled in 1966, the Egyptian family witl an annual income of less than £E 120 spends 71.3 per cent of thi income on food: 41.4 per cent for cereals and starchy products 18.8 per cent for meat, fish, and eggs; and 11.1 per cent for milk and dairy products. In contrast, the family with an income of ovei £E 480 but under £E 1,200 spends 52 per cent of this income or food: 16.9 per cent for cereals and starchy products; 22.2 per cen for meat, fish, and eggs; and 12.9 per cent for milk and dairy products.

The average daily calorie intake per person in Egypt is estimated to be 2,877 calories, of which 70 per cent is obtained from cereals. This rather scanty, low-protein intake results in deficiency diseases, such as anemia, rickets, pellagra, and protein malnutrition. The difficulty of providing a higher protein diet is formidable, since the total numbers of dairy cattle and animals available for slaughter show a very slow annual increase. The relative amounts of fresh vegetables and fruits consumed reflect a high per capita increase, however.

Lacking both variety and abundance, the diet of the majority of Egyptians is dominated by a single staple, *bettai* (cornmeal bread). In the south, millet, rice, and wheat are more widely used as a corn substitute. Vegetables and fruits are readily available. These include onions, eggplant (the potatoes of the Middle East), tomatoes, turnips, cucumbers, green peppers, lettuce, green beans, lentils, vegetable marrows, citrus fruits, and dates. At most, 10 per cent of the average Egyptian's caloric intake is obtained from these products; to them may be added eggs and a coarse variety of cream cheese made of goat or buffalo milk preserved in salt water.

Meat is an expensive delicacy, rarely enjoyed by the fellah. A prosperous peasant family may have meat once a week; the poorer families see it only at festival times or when an animal has been killed by accident. Pork, considered unclean and prohibited by Qur'anic injunction, is eaten only by Copts and the nonindigenous minorities. Fish is increasingly available. Urban dwellers consume larger quantities of meat and fish than do the villagers.

Water and tea are the main beverages of the fellah. Coffee, more expensive, is better known in the cities than in the countryside. Water, drawn directly from the irrigation ditches, is invariably contaminated, and as a rule little effort is made to purify it. The black tea consumed by both adults and children has been described as the national drug of Egypt. Concentrated by being boiled into a thick, black syrup, it is a powerful drink, detrimental to both stomach and nerves, and low in nutritious value.

Carbonated beverages are increasingly popular, both in towns and villages. The consumption of alcohol is contrary to the teachings of Islam, and most alcoholic beverages are too expensive for all except the wealthy few. However, the fact that the production of beer has risen from 10 million liters in 1952 to 25 million liters in 1965 suggests widening public consumption.

As a rule, the peasant eats three meals a day: one at sunrise before leaving for work (*fitr*); one about 10 A.M. in the fields (*ghada*); and one at home at dusk (*asha*). In the fields, the fellahin may be seen at their midmorning meal, sitting cross-legged on the ground, eating with their fingers from the common bowl, and drinking from a bottle passed from hand to hand. The evening meal, the chief one of the day, consists of hot food cooked over an oil stove or in the household oven, heated by means of cakes of strawed animal dung.

Sanitation

The shortage of pure water is a major health problem in Egypt. Cities and villages depend largely on the Nile for their water supply, and cities have filtration and chlorination plants. In recent years, filtering pumping stations have been installed in some places where subterranean water is available, and filtering stations have been built along the Nile, providing at least 7,000 villages with potable water. Even where potable water is available, however, the fellah is more likely to drink the untreated waters of the Nile —either his wife finds it inconvenient to go to the pump, or the small fee for pure water seems too much, or, even if he is not one of the many who believe that raw Nile water will enhance his fertility, he may believe that it is pure by reason of the river's flow. Even more polluted than the Nile are the irrigation canals—which are laden with human and animal waste—but they continue to be a major source of water supply.

The general sanitation of all but a few "model" villages is extremely poor. Dust beclouds the air of narrow alleys strewn with offal and rubbish. The village birka (reservoir) is usually a greenish pool of stagnant water, which provides drinking water, a bathing place for the children, and a laundry for the women. There is also the inevitable village dump, where dirt, dung, and carrion are constantly being heaped and left for the birds and the village dogs. Sewage disposal facilities in the villages are few and primitive. Pits dug near the houses serve as latrines, as do the irrigation ditches in the field.

The handling of food is another source of illness and contagion. Foods displayed in the shops are exposed to dust and flies. Fruits and vegetables are frequently grown in soil on which raw sewage has been used as fertilizer; they are often washed in the polluted canals en route to the market. Massive efforts are being made to improve the handling of food products. Dairy herds are inspected, and several large pasteurization plants are now in operation. Slaughtering is carried out under controls, and the capacity of cold storage units for local and imported meats continues to increase.

Disease

Nature and man have made Egypt one of the most disease-ridden countries in the world. In spite of recent improvements, not only does Egypt still have a low life expectancy rate and a high infant mortality rate but also the majority of those who survive suffer from malnutrition and chronic illnesses.

Overpopulation is a major contributing factor to Egypt's health problems, but there are numerous and varied other factors. The fellah who is confined to a small parcel of land or employed as a farm laborer ekes out a living at subsistence level. Malnutrition leaves the mass of the population vulnerable to the multitude of diseases that abound in Egypt. Overcrowding, another result of population pressure, contributes to the prevalence and severity of the epidemics which sweep the country. A climatic factor is present in the sandstorms, which contribute to chronic eye irritation and respiratory diseases, and in the sudden temperature changes, which dispose persons in the coastal area to respiratory ailments. Finally, the heavily populated Nile Delta abounds in numerous forms of animal and plant life—including malaria-carrying mosquitoes, lice, rats, snakes, and ragweed—which take their periodic toll in the form of discomfort, sickness, and death. Natural factors are reinforced by human failings. The ignorance, apathy, and superstition of the majority of the population are serious obstacles to the achievement of even a modest level of personal hygiene and to the successful application of the techniques of preventive medicine.

Egyptians, with the exception of the urban middle- and upper-class groups, view problems of health and disease in radically different terms from those which prevail in the modern Western nations. For the mass of the Egyptian peasantry and urban workers, disease is not a temporary suspension of good health. Rather, chronic illness of one kind or another is almost the norm, so much a part of existence as to be taken for granted. Although endowed with a robust physique and hardened by heavy labor, the fellah usually falls prey at an early age to one or more of a number of debilitating diseases. So long as he can continue to work, he is not prone to consider himself in need of medical attention. Having learned to live with illness, he is not likely to seek medical help—which in any event is available to relatively few—until he is no longer able to follow his daily routine.

Traditional religious beliefs powerfully affect popular views about health and disease. Accepting that there is no mediating power between the Creator and His creation and that all things and events proceed from Allah's universal and absolute will, the majority of Egyptians tend to see sickness and death as manifestations of this Divine Will. Pagan beliefs and superstitions have persisted within the framework of Islam in the countryside, and many of these relate directly to sickness and health. One of the most widespread folk beliefs is that jinns (spirits) have power to do men good or evil. Another is that the "evil eye" brings sickness and death to its victims. As a result of the persistence of these ideas, sorcerers—preferably Copts, who are thought to have power to control or ward off these forces—are much in demand. Children are commonly safeguarded against the evil eye by a blue bead hung on a thread around the neck. Sometimes a favored son is dressed as a girl in order to trick the evil eye. The preliminaries to childbirth include various practices designed to bring the child full health and happiness, and it is widely believed, for example, that if an expectant mother occupies her time gazing at pictures of good-looking men her child will surely be a handsome son.

The rural Egyptian is prey to an impressive array of debilitating or fatal diseases. Prominent among these are bilharzia, hookworm, trachoma, tuberculosis, venereal diseases, typhoid, paratyphoid, typhus, diarrhea, enteritis, and malaria. Less common—but more difficult to control—are yellow fever, meningitis, pneumonia, leprosy, and, occasionally, bubonic plague.

Chief among Egypt's debilitating diseases is schistosomiasis, commonly known as bilharzia. Currently about 80 per cent of the rural population suffer from this infection. Among the farmers, bilharzia spreads primarily from their habit of relieving themselves in the irrigation canals or on the canal banks. The eggs of the parasite that causes the disease are passed by the human subject, hatch into larvae which penetrate the body of a snail, and after a period of further development enter human beings through the skin. In the body, the parasite, a blood fluke, attacks various organs, causing low vitality and lassitude. Bilharzia is most widespread in the Delta, where the extensive system of perennial irrigation favors the disease-producing organisms by keeping the ground moist throughout the year. The incidence of bilharzia is several times higher among men than among women—apparently because men spend the greater part of the day working barefooted in the irrigation canals. In spite of intensive research over many years, no drug has been developed which completely controls this infection.

Other common disease-producing parasites are ankylostoma—the earth parasite—hookworms, roundworms, and beef and mutton tapeworms. The incidence of hookworm infection varies throughout the country but averages about 50 per cent. Roundworm infection is common in the south-central portion of the Delta, and a fluke that is transmitted to humans in mullet and certain other fish is prevalent around the lakes of the northern littoral.

Trachoma and other eye diseases are pernicious ailments in Egypt. Dust, heat, glare, and blown sand, helped out by flies and dirty fingers, combine to inflame and infect the eyes. Approximately 90 per cent of Egypt's population suffer from eye diseases, and an estimated 2 per cent are blind. Acute purulent conjunctivitis is equally prevalent, and a large number of young children are affected repeatedly, with resultant damage to the cornea. The reciting of prayers, accompanied by the rubbing of saliva into the eyes, is still the popular remedy for these eye conditions. Experience has shown the treatment of trachoma with penicillin ointment has only a temporary effect in lowering its incidence unless there are parallel improvements in local hygiene.

The tuberculosis rate, although not definitely known, is believed to be high. Bovine tuberculosis is highly endemic among the local cattle, but human infection from this source is no doubt restricted by the almost universal habit of boiling all milk.

Typhoid and paratyphoid are endemic in all parts of Egypt, and serologic tests performed in a village near Cairo in 1949 produced data which, if representative, suggested an infection rate of 1,400 per 100,000 population. There are indications that the incidence of typhoid and paratyphoid has increased in urban areas in recent years as a result of rural migration to the cities.

Syphilis, gonorrhea, chancroid, and other venereal diseases are

271

widespread; it is estimated that about 20 per cent of the population are infected. The Egyptian government attempts to control prostitution by licensing brothels and prostitutes, but the medical inspection of prostitutes is impossible, since any woman may avoid examination by claiming to be married.

Malaria is mildly endemic throughout the Nile Valley, and on occasions has reached serious proportions in parts of Faiyûm province, the Suez region, and the western oases. The infection rate has averaged from 1 to 5 per cent in Upper Egypt and from 3 to 10 per cent in the Delta, with the area of greatest incidence there being the vicinities of the rice fields and lakes. A series of intensive campaigns to spray all villages with DDT has been so successful that malarial infection is fast disappearing from the country.

Typhus fever, a louse-borne disease, is endemic in the Delta region, and its incidence has been particularly high in the Beheira and Gharbîya regions. The migration during World War II of a number of workers from these regions to Cairo, Alexandria, and the ports of the Suez Canal led to an increase of typhus in these centers. In recent years, typhus has been considerably reduced by the use of DDT.

Bubonic plague, which flared into epidemic proportions in Alexandria in 1899, is always a threat in Egypt. Throughout the country the crevices in the stone embankments of the canals and the numerous dovecotes in the fields and on the roofs of houses provide excellent shelter for rats, the carriers of the fleas that transmit the plague. The rise in incidence of the plague each August and September is attributed to the fact that the rats flee from the embankments in those months, in order to escape the floods, and take refuge in the adjacent houses.

Medical Care

Traditional practices. Until recent years, those wanting medical care were denied it either by poverty or by lack of local facilities. And even when hospital treatment was available, the fellah was reluctant to go to a hospital, fearing to leave his wife and children and apprehensive about his ability to maintain the family while away. Most often he placed his trust in providence and on the *mizayen* (barber-surgeon) or some other folk practitioner for treatment.

In hundreds of villages, the mizayen continues to be the most prominent medical practitioner. His is a practical rather than a magical skill, and, in addition to his tonsorial duties, he treats wounds, pulls teeth, dispenses purgatives, performs circumcisions, administers vaccinations, and serves as village coroner. Another important professional personage in the village is the midwife, whose calling is transmitted from mother to daughter. Crude as the methods of the midwife may be, her position is doubly secured —both by the lack of doctors and by Egyptian ideas of modesty, which for most country people would make the performance of the midwife's duties by a man unthinkable.

As stated, villagers and the uneducated in general invoke the aid of magic and sorcerers in meeting their health needs. The village sheikh, an older man noted for his learning and wisdom, is widely believed to possess magical remedies and fertility charms. No clear distinction seems to be made here between the efficacy of magic and prayer. Thus it is common for the sheikh to be asked to write a prayer or a Qur'anic text on a piece of paper, which is then placed in a jar of water. When the water is drunk by a childless couple, it supposedly has power to make them fertile.

These various village practitioners—mizayen, midwife, sorcerer, and sheikh—seem not to be in competition with one another; each performs a special function and caters to a particular need. The pattern is one that would allow, without any great resistance, the introduction of still another practitioner—the modern doctor and medical specialist. This has been borne out by the experience of mobile hospital units in Egypt; it has been demonstrated that the fellah is capable of accepting modern medical treatment if it is brought to him. Once the confidence reposed in the folk practitioners is transferred to the physician, the peasant submits himself to even the most painful treatment in the blind faith that every ailment must have its cure.

Hashish, a narcotic drug produced from the hemp plant, has long been a scourge of the country and is smoked by millions of men. On the one hand, its use serves to break the monotony and lack of excitement of daily life, and on the other, it acts as a palliative for the aches and pains from which the fellahin suffer. The Egyptian government is determined to stamp out the use of hashish and other narcotics, however, and gives very severe sentences to those caught dealing in such drugs or smuggling them into the country.

Modern medical care. The National Charter includes this statement:

> The right of each citizen to medical care, whether treatment or medicine, should not be a commodity for sale or for purchase. It should be a guaranteed right unrelated to price. Medical care should be within the reach of every citizen, in every part of the country, and under easy conditions.

Without any question, the government is sincerely devoted to achieving this objective.

The Ministry of Public Health. This ministry was established in 1936. Among its principal divisions are the Departments of Preventive Medicine, Rural Health, Social Hygiene, and Endemic Diseases Research and Control. In 1960, the Ministry of Public Health charted a new course of decentralization of government health services, when it set up 20 autonomous medical regions. At the same time, it placed emphasis on planning, training of personnel, and the maintaining of statistical records. The budget of this ministry steadily increases: in 1952 it was £E 10.1 million; in 1963, £E 28 million; in 1964, £E 31.2 million; and in 1965 it was £E 44.3 million. In addition to its annual budget, the ministry benefits from projects financed by development plans.

Medical personnel. In 1950, there was one doctor to every 1,000 inhabitants in the cities and one to every 13,000 rural inhabitants. In 1960, there was said to be one physician to every 2,000 persons. In 1964, there were 13,000 doctors, up from 10,000 in 1960, but because of the population increase the figure of doctor to persons had gone down to one for every 2,300 persons. Currently, the country's six medical colleges graduate about 1,000 doctors a year, of whom over 20 per cent are women. These colleges attract outstanding students, since the profession has high prestige, along with an income much higher than that for most other occupations.

In 1966, there were 1,775 doctors in the rural areas, averaging one doctor for each two villages. At this time the Ministry of Public Health announced that it was preparing a new program for the political training of rural doctors under the Arab Socialist Union. According to the statement of the Minister:

> The successful doctor must interact completely with the inhabitants of rural areas from the cultural, social, and political points of view, since he is the person most capable of reaching the hearts of the

people. . . . His medical work should be accompanied by political work in order to achieve a great aim of the pledge he has taken, namely to develop the Egyptian village to the urban level.

Medical facilities. Official statistics on the number of hospitals in Egypt merge hospitals, mobile units, and other units and sections into a grand total of health units serving urban areas, but it would appear that in 1965 there were over 400 hospitals, with a total of 62,158 beds. Of this latter figure, 45,228 beds were in institutions operated by or for the Ministry of Public Health, 8,408 beds under other government departments, and 8,522 beds in the private sector.

Medical care is free in all government hospitals and public health clinics. The larger hospitals are operated either directly by the Ministry of Public Health or by the country's seven colleges of medicine. Thus, the medical colleges at Cairo operate the Kasr al-Aini Hospital, al-Manal Hospital, the Children's Hospital, and the Shubra Hospital for Women. In these government hospitals, the doctors receive a nominal salary in addition to their income from teaching in the colleges. There are also two categories of privately-operated hospitals and clinics: those owned by Egyptian doctors and those operated by one of the minority groups or by non-Egyptians. The Ministry of Public Health also operates special hospitals and mobile units for ophthalmic diseases, endemic diseases, tuberculosis, leprosy, skin and venereal diseases, and mental disorders.

Since 1956, an enormous, continuing effort has been made to provide medical facilities for the entire rural population. The target figure is 2,500 rural health units, with the aim of having a unit located no more than five kilometers distant from any settlement. In 1966, some 1,618 such units were in operation, staffed by 1,775 doctors, and providing about 8,000 hospital beds. The units vary in degree as to the kinds of preventive and treatment services provided, and many are directly associated with the agricultural cooperatives.

Health education offices are located in each governorate, and each office is provided with mobile units. The villagers are shown films on personal and social hygiene, on narcotics, water pollution, and fly control. Widespread campaigns popularize preventive measures against bilharzia and other diseases, and the social centers of the agricultural cooperatives supplement the work of these offices.

The Ministry of Public Health Laboratories, founded in 1885,

275

operates several facilities for the production of vaccines and serums for immunization against smallpox, cholera, typhoid and paratyphoid fevers, diphtheria, and tuberculosis.

Several medical research facilities come under the general guidance of the Supreme Science Council, while the National Research Center has concern for research in medicine as well as in many other fields. The Institute and Hospital of Endemic Diseases, established in 1932, undertakes research and establishes programs for the treatment and control of these diseases, and the Ophthalmic Institute, founded in 1935, is the central point for research and programs relating to the indigenous eye diseases of Egypt. The World Health Organization of the United Nations cooperates with a variety of measures for the treatment and control of disease, including the nationwide campaign to eliminate malaria.

Public Welfare

The traditional theory. Public welfare in the Moslem tradition is based on the principle of mutual responsibility of all members of the community. This principle, drawn from the Arab past and expounded in the Qur'an, has been honored in theory and often neglected in practice, but its fundamental tenets have never been challenged. Islamic theory recognizes natural inequalities among men and sanctions differential rewards for different degrees of talent. At the same time, however, it looks with disfavor upon class distinctions based on wealth and imposes a moral obligation on the wealthy to assist the less fortunate members of the community.

Almsgiving (zakat), one of the five pillars of Islam, represents a means of applying this ideal of mutual responsibility among members of the community. The giving of alms is a moral obligation, and the amount given is left to the discretion of the giver. At times in history, however, zakat has been imposed as a compulsory tax on property, including money and merchandise. Even soldiers' pensions were not exempt. The exact amount of this imposition varied, but generally it averaged 2½ per cent. It was collected through regular officials and administered from a central treasury to support the poor, build mosques, and help defray government expenses. Precedents for government taxation for public welfare purposes are, therefore, not lacking. The principle of almsgiving was defined, moreover, not as charity but as the duty of those who gave and the natural right of those who received. In addition, free-

276

will offerings (sadaqat) are given, as a means of expiation, to the poor, the needy, orphans, and travelers.

Waqfs, or bequests, are another reflection of early public welfare measures. Under this system a man could establish a secular endowment for his heirs or a religious one for charitable purposes. The endowment could not be sold or otherwise alienated, but had to be held in perpetuity, with only its yield utilized for its beneficiaries. Secular waqfs no longer exist, and the religious waqfs have all been taken over by the government, their funds being managed by the Ministry of Waqfs and Social Affairs.

Supplementing, but at times conflicting with, the principle of communal responsibility, is the ideal of family solidarity, which was firmly established in the Arab world long before the advent of Islam. In the Qur'an this ideal took the force of a moral duty. The sense of obligation to family has always been far stronger in Egypt than the feeling of community responsibility. Thus, a wealthy man would bequeath his property to a charitable waqf on the condition that it be used for charitable purposes only after his line had become extinct.

Despite modern welfare programs, it is clear that almsgiving, waqfs, and the self-help of the family have not lost their traditional importance in Egypt. A United Nations survey of poor Egyptian rural families indicated that 10 per cent of their total income was derived from relatives and more than 6 per cent from private or institutional charity. Urban indigents derived 13 per cent of their income from relatives and 3 per cent from institutional charity.

The modern approach. The old family and village welfare practices continue, but they have not sufficed to meet the needs of a rapidly expanding population nor to answer the problems created by industrialization and urbanization. Many families and whole villages in Egypt are too poor to render effective assistance to their members in time of trouble. Neither the knowledge nor the material means needed for the solution of the problems posed by modern developments is available within the confines of the family or the village.

During this generation, attempts have been made, mostly on the initiative of Egyptians trained in Western countries, to alleviate the widespread and growing misery of the Egyptian population by adopting modern public welfare techniques. These attempts have been characterized by increased activity on the part of the central

277

government and a relative decrease in the importance of private welfare institutions. Along with this change has come an attempt to widen the scope of public welfare activities and to provide comprehensive coverage. A step in this direction was the creation in 1953 of the Permanent Council for Public Welfare. Originally composed of the Ministers of National Guidance, Waqfs and Social Affairs, Municipal and Rural Affairs, Public Health, and Education, the Council is responsible for coordinating the activities of private and government welfare agencies. A second important change is the stress on rehabilitation and self-improvement, as contrasted with direct relief. Still another change has been the concentration of welfare activities among the long underprivileged fellahin.

Local service organizations. Inaugurated in 1936 by the Egyptian Association for Social Studies, the Rural Social Centers program represents an attempt to deal simultaneously with the three basic and related problems confronting the fellah: poverty, ignorance, and disease. The experimental efforts of the Egyptian Association proved so promising that the program was taken over in 1939 by the newly-created Ministry of Social Welfare. Since then, the number of rural centers has increased—by 1950 there were over 125 centers. In 1965, there were 5,270 local service organizations, of which total nearly 3,000 were in urban areas. These statistics do not indicate which of the local service organizations in rural areas are actually Rural Social Centers, but there are over 300 of these centers, each serving about 15,000 people. Since 1954, the Ministry of Agriculture and the Ministry of Education have cooperated in the staffing of the centers.

The Rural Social Centers reflect some modern, Western trends in public welfare philosophy and techniques. Financed largely by the central government and staffed by members of the central administration, the centers nevertheless encourage local initiative. The government will consider the creation of a center only upon the request of a community, and will provide financial assistance and trained personnel only after the community has demonstrated the seriousness of its interest by itself contributing £E 1,500, two feddans of land, and labor.

To carry out a concentrated attack on all aspects of village backwardness, the Ministry of Waqfs and Social Affairs assigns to each center—when the limited number of qualified personnel permits—an agricultural social worker, a health and welfare nurse, a doctor, a qualified laboratory assistant, and a club leader. The duties of the agricultural social worker include operation of a demonstration plot, distribution of improved seed, education of the peasants in the control of plant insect pests, training in improved methods of livestock raising, and encouragement of agricultural diversification. In addition he promotes rural and home industries—utilizing local materials—thus permitting the fellah to make beneficial use of his unemployed time.

The health services of the centers emphasize both the cure and the prevention of disease. They try to persuade the women to have their children at the clinics, where proper care can be given. As an inducement, the mother is provided with free food for one week after childbirth, and the baby is given two sets of clothing. Moreover, each child born at the clinic is eligible for regular medical care up to two years of age. The health service also carries on extensive campaigns through posters, lectures, and films to educate the fellah in disease prevention.

The social and cultural services of the centers include a program of elementary education for adults and various clubs designed to channel the leisure of the peasants along constructive lines. The centers also attempt to provide education in self-government. All male members who contribute to the center participate in the election of a council. The council appoints members to a number of committees concerned with community functions; there is a committee for conciliation of disputes, plus committees for charity, for economics and agriculture, for education and recreation, and for health and cleanliness.

Although some of the centers have been criticized for lack of achievement, they have clearly had success in raising agricultural incomes and improving health conditions. More important, perhaps, is their promise for the future. By their emphasis on local initiative and local self-management, they help to arouse new awareness and new interest on the part of the fellah. The potential effectiveness of the program is indicated by the fact that wherever a center has been established, surrounding communities quickly begin to take interest and ask for a center for themselves.

Other welfare activities. In addition to the local service organizations, there are over 900 associations and organizations working in the field of environmental and home industries. Other welfare activities are carried on through combined public and private action.

One of the most important of these is concerned with the problem of juvenile delinquency. Private organizations receiving financial assistance from the government have established centers in Cairo and Alexandria to assist the courts in dealing with juvenile offenders. Special juvenile courts handle cases pertaining to minors, and, although there are no special detention facilities for juveniles, the Prison Department has a new social service division which devotes particular attention to juveniles. During their confinement in prison, minors receive school instruction and are also given vocational training.

The government operates a number of orphanages, a psychological clinic, nursery schools, and a school for the training of social workers. The work of these institutions is supplemented by the efforts of private organizations, and Egyptian women have been particularly active in these activities.

The Arab Socialist Union Youth Organization engages in voluntary labor in order to improve rural conditions—building roads, filling in ponds and swamps, and constructing water and lighting facilities.

Under a broader definition of welfare, the government keeps the cost of basic foods at a low level through such measures as subsidies on flour and other materials, and price and profit controls imposed on food processors.

Public housing. The Ministry of Housing and Utilities controls the Egyptian Public Foundation for Construction and Building and the Egyptian Public Foundation for Housing and Development. Under the First Five-Year Plan, £E 161.5 million was allocated for public housing, and under the Triple Plan the figure was £E 119.1 million. These sums were nearly all for urban housing: residential units and apartment buildings rented at an average monthly rental of about £E 1 per room.

The task of providing adequate and sufficient public housing remains an enormous one. The location of new industrial plants in or near the already crowded cities and the influx of workers to these areas have complicated the task. In addition, the cities were already burdened by slum areas. While some such areas have been cleared for new housing, Cairo has quarters that are veritable rabbit warrens; narrow lanes are flanked by decaying structures that lack decent sanitary facilities.

Serial reports give figures on the construction of new housing units for government employees and workers with low income, but totals on all units are difficult to find. It is believed that between 1952 and 1963 about 71,500 "dwellings" were built by the government. At Cairo, the government has encouraged the trade unions to purchase state-owned land and to construct housing for their own members; several such quarters have arisen.

Rural housing has improved only in areas where the government has built new villages; by the end of 1963, about 30,000 houses had been built in these villages. Farmers are, however, encouraged to obtain loans from the agricultural cooperatives for the improvement of their own dwellings.

Birth control. In his speech on the National Charter, President Nasser stated:

> The population increase constitutes the most dangerous obstacle that faces the Egyptian people in their drive towards raising the standards of production of their country in an effective and efficient way. . . . Attempts at family planning with the aim of facing the problem of increasing population deserve the most sincere efforts, supported by modern scientific methods.

Again, in a public speech delivered in July 1966, he said:

> I wish you would listen to the Prime Minister, who is the chairman of the committee on birth rate control, on this matter, and that you would apply the plan which he laid down for social evolution. This means that the family which has several children cannot secure a dignified and acceptable living for all the children. . . . I do not want you to lose control of the birth rate. Then we would find that we had lost control of the [development] plan.

There was no opposition to the birth control program, which began in 1963, from any source, including the Moslem religious leaders. In 1964, the Ministry of Waqfs and Social Affairs began to set up throughout the country clinics which were associated with the existing rural social centers, to supply oral contraceptive pills. As has been the experience in India and other countries plagued with very high birth rates, such programs are difficult to organize and even more difficult to administer. Material is not available from Egypt to indicate whether devices or measures in addition to oral contraceptive pills are in use, nor is there information on the relative success of the program. In 1967, the Ford Foundation made a grant of $480,000 toward this program.

CHAPTER 17

National Economic Goals

THREE GENERAL GOALS DOMINATE THE ECONOMIC POLICY DECISIONS of the present Egyptian government: (1) improved living standards for the present generation (2) industrial development for the sake of future generations, and (3) international prestige and independence. The first two goals probably existed in amorphous form in the minds of at least some of the revolutionaries. The third did not become crucial to domestic economic policy until after Nasser had successfully nationalized the Suez Canal and defied the major powers of Western Europe, but it may have been an inevitable outgrowth of centuries of Egyptian humiliation at the hands of foreigners. These three ideas compete for the money needed to realize them; in competing, they contribute jointly to most of the foreign and domestic economic difficulties Egypt has experienced since 1952.

Economic progress and policy in Egypt are influenced strongly by considerations of domestic and international politics. Economic growth itself is important to Nasser's image at home and abroad. Domestic stability, however, is even more important, and economically desirable policies often have been abandoned in the face of incipient discontent. Military preparedness and prestige have taken precedence over civilian requirements for many years. Almost a quarter of the total amount budgeted for current government services is allotted to the armed forces. And the reluctance to penalize a worker whose performance is inadequate results in an inability to reward the one whose performance is outstanding; the absence of economic incentives has been perhaps the single greatest weakness of the Egyptian economy in recent years. By the end of 1966, even Soviet economists were urging Egypt to increase the use of incentives in both industry and agriculture and to abandon the practice of hiring redundant workers in government-owned factories.

When the Free Officers seized power, neither Nasser nor his associates had much notion of economic policy. They were determined to eliminate the worst excesses of the monarchy and to provide better opportunities for the lower classes, but they were equipped with no specific formula for accomplishing their ends. "Arab Socialism" as a concept evolved only slowly, and its outlines have never been defined clearly. The new leaders were generally aware of the most obvious socioeconomic ills of Egypt—markedly unequal distribution of income, extreme poverty, a paucity of schools and hospitals, and extortionist rates of interest on small loans. The coup group came largely from the small cities and rural areas, where such factors were most apparent, and their military service in small garrison towns had increased their awareness of Egypt's difficulties. Most of them undoubtedly wanted to change these things for the better, but they had never discussed what to do, or how.

In the years before the revolution, Nasser and his intimates deliberately discouraged any talk of specific programs they might adopt in the future. They agreed on the need for change, without elaborating on the details. This approach was designed to maintain cohesion among all members of the group. Nasser was convinced that many revolutionary movements throughout the world had fragmented and foundered before seizing power because the members squabbled over future policies. He wanted all energies directed toward attaining power; the methods of its use could be determined after that first hurdle had been surmounted.

The new government, therefore, made the economic decisions of its early years in a pragmatic—and largely conservative—manner. A land reform program initiated in 1952 was the only drastic innovation in the 1952-56 period, and even that was but a successful version of earlier abortive attempts. In all other fields, the regime moved slowly and carefully to restore economic and fiscal stability to the shambles created under Farouk.

Economic History

The Egypt the new government came to control was not markedly different from the Egypt of 1920. It was then, and it remains, primarily an agrarian country. The two factors that make Egypt unique among underdeveloped nations—a monetized, export-oriented economy based on long staple cotton and a national cohesiveness and ease of communication and control bred by the unifying

283

force of the Nile—had long been established. Western influence and subsequent Western control in the nineteenth century had set in motion a process of change in the traditional agricultural economy that still continues. The rudiments of modern industry had been installed.

The period between 1880 and 1914 was one of rapid development for Egypt as a whole, but not for industry and not for the individual peasant. The modernization of the irrigation system brought an agricultural revolution. The cotton crop was increased by 250 per cent in bulk, and its value increased fourfold. Increased national income permitted large new investments, almost all of which were devoted to projects that either facilitated the export of cotton or served the needs of the urban upper class: a good railway network was laid out, harbors were built, the principal cities were provided with public utilities, and the banking system was developed. But the poorer classes were forgotten—the rich became richer; the poor, poorer. And the British-dominated government actively discouraged the establishment of industrial facilities that might compete with imports from Britain.

World War I marked the end of the period of expansion. Soil exhaustion began to lower yields, and the wide-scale use of imported and highly expensive chemical fertilizers, though bringing yields back to and even above the previous level, increased the cost of cultivation. Internally, cotton prices rose, while externally a sharp fall in world prices for cotton led in the 1920s to a deterioration in Egypt's terms of trade. Some factories were built, and tariffs that were almost prohibitive were imposed on imported manufactures in the mid-30s, leading to an increase in industrial production. This increase was not, however, sufficient to offset the decline in agriculture—and in fact the real national income of the 1930s was below that of the previous decade. These factors, combined with the rise in population, resulted in a distinct decline in the standard of living.

World War II held up Egypt's economic development, created new problems, and, even though it provided certain assets (particularly sterling assets), did little to alter the fundamental problems of the economy. Agricultural production and foreign trade were depressed, and improved health facilities led to ever-increasing population pressure. However, Allied military expenditures gave Egypt a foreign exchange cushion of £E 400 million at the end of the war—an ample endowment, which was rapidly dissipated in the subsequent years. It also relieved Egypt of the overwhelming foreign debt problem that had persisted for almost a century and had denied the country any revenue whatsoever from the Suez Canal for the 1881-1935 period.

The British occupation of Egypt in 1882 was facilitated by the country's inability to meet financial obligations that had been incurred by Ismail Sidqi Pasha. The foreign debt had reached £E 117 million when annual export income was only about £E 13 million, and foreign obligations absorbed over half the total budget. Britain's postoccupation efforts were directed at fiscal reforms, especially the imposition of balanced budgets. Foreign debt service was the overriding consideration, since nonpayment of foreign debts might invite the intervention of other major powers into a domain profitably controlled by Britain. Otherwise, the United Kingdom was concerned primarily with insuring the flow of low cost raw materials to England.

Nor did Egyptian governments after 1923 exhibit any greatly enhanced concern for economic development. Private entrepreneurs —Egyptians, citizens of foreign origin, and foreigners—were more active. The Misr Bank, established in 1920, started companies to run hotels and to engage in shipping, publishing, and insurance, while the so-called Misr Group financed and largely controlled the production of textiles, pharmaceuticals, chemicals, cement, and edible oils. In 1922, the establishment of the Federation of Egyptian Industries, composed of management engaged in productive enterprises, gave some added impetus to industrialization.

1952-61—From Conservatism to Government Ownership

After the new regime came to power, its leaders showed no more interest in socializing the economy than they did in political socialism. As late as 1958, Nasser was speaking about a "controlled capitalistic economy," a goal or objective spelled out in the Constitution of 1956. In fact, well through 1956, orthodox methods were the basis of efforts to achieve economic stability and to develop production, as well as to initiate a program of social welfare.

Farouk's legacy to the Free Officers included massive, chronic deficits in both the balance of payments and the domestic budget. At the end of World War II, Egypt possessed sterling reserves of over £E 400 million. By the end of 1951, this nest egg had been reduced to only £E 233 million, and the country had little to show for its overspending. Cotton prices had been manipulated beyond the limits of a Korean war boom, and prices plummeted after 1951, cutting deeply into foreign earning power.

The new military regime, sharing the horror of every history-minded Egyptian at the idea of foreign debt, reacted in a classic conservative manner, reducing government expenditure at home and curtailing spending abroad. Concurrently, taxes were increased, and export promotion schemes were adopted. In consequence, Egypt experienced a small budget surplus in 1952/53 and a small current account surplus in the balance of payments in 1954.

Outside the strictly fiscal sphere, the revolutionary character of the new regime was somewhat more apparent. The land reform program was adopted and enforced. Foreign investment laws and mineral concession legislation were liberalized in an attempt to attract foreign capital. Domestic industrial regulations were revised to afford greater protection for domestic industry and to encourage the flow of investment funds into industry instead of agriculture, real estate, and the government. And the government began to take an activist role in social services and in development. The Council for National Development was established, with a membership which included representatives of the Bank Misr and the Federation of Egyptian Industries. These experienced capitalists exerted considerable leverage. At this time, the government insisted that the state was to be a partner with established industry, and that it would take the initiative only when necessary—especially in capital-intensive heavy industry.

An abrupt change occurred in 1956, triggered largely by external events. The regime had made notable progress during the previous few years, but its leaders undoubtedly had come to feel that Egypt's economic and social problems were so severe as to demand drastic treatment. They could not forget their twin desires for development later and better conditions now. And they clearly were attracted by the panacea of socialist planning that was rapidly becoming the watchword of the underdeveloped world. But both the timing and the precise direction of an almost total inversion of economic policy were determined primarily by the great power minuet of the Cold War.

The sequestration, termed Egyptianization (i.e. government seizure and protectorship) of foreign-owned property began after the

Israeli attack on Gaza in February 1955 and went into high gear after the 1956 invasion by British, French, and Israeli forces. In 1955, Egypt began seeking weapons to strengthen the demoralized army. When the United States refused to sell the desired equipment on acceptable terms, Egypt took up a Soviet offer, in which Czechoslovakia was the ostensible supplier. The U.S. countered with an international plan to finance the much-wanted Aswân High Dam, but Egyptian intransigence on the Soviet arms deal and other international issues led the U.S. to withdraw the offer of aid for Aswân. Nasser, in turn, nationalized the Suez Canal Company, while guaranteeing the Canal's status as an international waterway and promising full compensation to Canal Company shareholders. Negotiations on these matters had been underway for three months when the Anglo-French-Israeli invasion started on October 31, 1956. The invasion itself was short-lived, but it led to sequestration of British, French, and Jewish property.

Finding itself in control of substantial assets, especially in the banking and insurance fields, the regime began establishing the machinery for control. Concurrently, the Soviet Union provided a $175 million credit to finance industrial projects that naturally fell under government control. In two separate agreements, Moscow also agreed to finance the $325 million foreign exchange cost of the Aswân High Dam and related electric power facilities. After Egypt worked out arrangements for compensation of Canal Company owners, relations with the Western world improved, and development aid began flowing from the United States, West Germany, and other Western countries. These funds, too, tended to be channeled through the government and thus to spur the growth of the public sector. In 1960, the crisis in the Belgian Congo found Egypt on the radical side—Belgian attempts to suppress the Congolese radicals led to seizure of Belgian property in Egypt. During this same period, all foreign banks, insurance companies, and commercial agencies were ordered to convert to locally-owned joint stock companies within five years.

By about 1960, the government apparently had given up on the idea that private capital, either domestic or foreign, could be attracted in sufficient quantities to finance the ambitious program of industrial development that it considered necessary. Instead, it moved abruptly from government participation with private capital in industry to government control of most facets of the economy outside agriculture.

287

The nationalization, as distinctive from "Egyptianization," of properties was marked by the take-over by the state in 1960 of privately owned banks, and in July 1961 additional sweeping measures were carried out. On February 13, 1960, the Bank Misr was taken into public ownership; later on it and its companies became the Misr Organization, a so-called national-socialist institution. Decrees of July 1961 nationalized the cotton trade, shipping lines, most remaining banks, insurance companies, and 44 basic companies in the fields of manufacturing, transport, and power. Varying amounts, half or less, of the assets of 233 other companies were seized. Complaints from members of the business community resulted in the imprisonment of some of them and the sequestration of the property of several hundred others. These measures, of which only a few have been cited, gave the state full ownership of the infrastructure, financial institutions, and heavy industry, as well as a controlling interest in external trade and most large corporations. By 1965, more than half the total national wage bill was paid by the public sector.

Earlier laws that were intended to attract local and foreign capital to industry had failed to produce the desired results. Private capital remained in stock companies or was diverted to a rash of apartment house construction. In 1956, a law was passed which required permits for the construction of housing units, and in 1958, rents were arbitrarily reduced on units built in recent years. In 1954, the first step was taken to limit the rights of management over stock companies, and in 1959, limitations were placed on the dividends of these enterprises. The tax rate went up to 90 per cent on all incomes over £E 10,000, and higher taxes came into effect on rental properties.

The Economic Organization, which had been established in January 1957, continued to function through 1961. It took over the management of state-owned industrial and commercial properties and of sequestered properties, and it named directors to the boards of privately-owned companies. In March 1961, two parallel organizations were created: the Misr Organization and the Al-Nasr Organization, with the latter controlling 24 companies. In December 1961, these three organizations were placed under the newly-formed Supreme Council for Public Organizations. Still later, all state-owned or state-controlled properties were merged into groups of companies under Egyptian Public Organizations—or, according to variant translations, Egyptian General Foundations or Egyptian General Establishments—administered by the various ministries.

The national economic structure was summarized by President Nasser in the National Charter of 1962, and a restatement of some of his points may point up the reasons for taking actions already described.

The infrastructure, such as railways, roads, ports, power, irrigation, sea, air, and land transport and utilities and services should be under public ownership, as should the majority of the heavy, medium, and extractive industries. The import trade and perhaps three-quarters of the export trade should be within the public sector, which must also have an increasing role in internal trade. All banking and insurance must be within the public sector.

Finally, Nasser stated in 1965: "Industry, and heavy industry in particular, becomes the real source of hope for the achievement of the comprehensive advance which is Egypt's goal."

Planning and Investment

Given the existing realities of a densely settled and rapidly growing population, an already highly productive agriculture, and a paucity of natural resources, it was obvious to the regime that Egypt's only° hope for future prosperity lay in industrialization. Their initial efforts in this direction, as in other fields, concentrated on the encouragement of private capital. The Council for National Development was asked to recommend policies and projects that would promote economic development. By July 1953, the Council had produced a four-year plan for public investment that was immediately implemented by the regime, and direct government investment increased rapidly. The emphasis, however, was on such traditionally government-dominated activities as irrigation, drainage and land reclamation, and transportation and electric power. In January 1957, a National Planning Committee was set up, whose purpose was to prepare a long-term plan for social economic development, with the emphasis still on combining public and private effort. This committee formulated a plan for industrialization that was put into operation in 1958, but the planners realized, and the government soon learned, that industry could not be planned in a vacuum. The 1957 plan may never have been intended as more than a temporary expedient; in any event, unimplemented portions were incorporated into an over-all development plan for the 1960-70 period.

The resulting plan encompassed the Egyptian fiscal years 1961-70, with Fiscal 1960 used as the base year. It initially was divided into two segments: the First Plan (FY 1961-65) and the Second

FRAMEWORK OF THE FIVE-YEAR PLAN

Sector	Investment (million £E)	Increase in production (million £E)	Increase in income (million £E)	Increase in employment (1000 persons)
Agriculture, irrigation, drainage, and High Dam	392	162	112	555
Electricity, industry, and construction	578.7	727	266	204
Transport, communications, and Suez Canal	271.8	29	20	7
Housing and utilities	223.4	15	13	9
Services	111	143	102	251
Increase in inventory	120	......	......	......
Total	1,696.9	1,076	513	1,026

Source: Hassan Abdallah, *U.A.R. Agriculture*.

Plan (FY 1966-70). Its basic aims were to increase national income by 40 per cent in the first five-year period, and to double it by the end of the ten-year period. Contrary to previous statements, this plan included provision for substantial participation by the government in the ownership of industrial facilities. And, with the nationalizations of 1961, the government came into possession of many of the facilities initially planned as assets of private enterprise.

In terms of over-all goals, Egypt did better than most similarly situated countries during the First Plan period, and particularly during the first four of the five years. Gross Domestic Product (GDP)* (Table 1) reached over 98 per cent of the plan target and

* Gross Domestic Product, which is the commonly used measure of aggregate national income in Egypt, measures aggregate output at factor cost, including excise duties and consumption taxes or subsidies. Gross Domestic Product less factor incomes paid abroad equals Gross National Product. In Egypt, where foreign ownership is small and foreigners do not make up a substantial share of the labor force, the discrepancy between GDP and GNP is small. All national income figures used herein are GDP.

might have exceeded the goal had a crop failure not occurred in 1961. Actual investment (Table 2)—available only in terms of current prices—totaled £E 1,513 million—almost 96 per cent of planned investment (which had been calculated in constant prices). Employment exceeded plan goals by over 5 per cent (Table 3), and wages totaled some 16 per cent more in FY 1965 than had been foreseen by the planners.

The performance of the various sectors with regard to plan goals indicates some of the more serious weaknesses underlying growth during this period. Agriculture and industry both lagged far behind plan targets, while targets were exceeded by substantial amounts in construction and in "other services." The rapid growth of the construction sector apparently indicates very great activity in one of the few sectors left largely in the hands of private entrepreneurs. The inflated growth of the services sector, however, is primarily a reflection of the rapid growth of the government bureaucracy. Since government normally is calculated in economic terms by summing the salaries of government employees, additions to the government payroll automatically increase national income. They do not, however, automatically increase national production.

A sectoral breakdown of actual versus planned investment (see Table 2) further supports the conclusion that much of the growth was due to overemphasis on the "services" sectors and to a high level of investment in industry that earned less than the anticipated return. Although agriculture per se received its full allocation, expenditures on irrigation and drainage fell far short of targets. The Aswân High Dam turned out to be more expensive than anticipated, although some expenditures originally included under electricity may have been transferred to the Dam, thereby distorting the picture. The amount of investment devoted to services was well in excess of plan targets, and the discrepancy between plan goals and actual investment in the sectors falling short of targets would be far more marked if the data for actual investment were available in the constant prices upon which the plan was based.

The most critical deviation, however, was in the volume of foreign borrowing necessary to implement the goal. Initial plans called for domestic savings to rise to 20 per cent of GDP by Fiscal 1965 and for foreign loans to decline throughout the five-year period, so that repayments would exceed borrowing in the final year of the plan. According to Nasser's speeches and various newspaper reports from Cairo, however, borrowing abroad to finance investment under the plan actually totaled about £E 417 million, or over 27 per cent of total investment. The totals increased annually until 1965, and went up again in 1966.

Also noteworthy is the fact that the rate of growth slowed appreciably in the fifth year of the plan period. By the fall of 1964, Egypt's shortage of foreign exchange was becoming acute. Growth up to that time had been financed, like other programs, largely by drawing down foreign assets and by utilizing foreign loans. The influence on the policies of the Nasser government in its first ten years of the foreign exchange assets left over from the Farouk regime is incalculable; the availability of large balances in hard currency permitted the revolutionary regime to pay for many programs that might otherwise have been abandoned as too costly. In 1961, however, a crop failure occurred that led to the exhaustion of this legacy. And the abrupt growth of Egypt's foreign debt followed almost immediately. Between 1962 and 1964, in particular, Egypt ran up large short-term debts with Western commercial banks. Such funds, which normally should be used only to finance seasonal needs, were devoted to investment in long-term projects. They did not, therefore, earn an immediate return that could be used for their retirement; instead they mounted steadily. In late 1964, saddled with growing debt service requirements and unable to obtain long-term loans of sufficient size from Western governments, Egypt was forced to adopt an austerity program that concentrated particularly on import curtailment. The results for growth were immediate, especially in the industrial sector. Industry's contribution to GDP had been growing by about 10 per cent annually; in fiscal 1965, it increased only 4.2 per cent. GDP, in turn, increased only 6.9 per cent.

Until several months after the expiration of the First Plan, official pronouncements continued to refer to a Second Plan of five years' duration that would reach the original national income targets. Egyptian planners themselves knew better, and eventually it was announced that the Second Plan would be stretched out to encompass seven years (FY66-72), but with the original goals essentially intact. Various problems persisted, despite the regime's desire to ignore them, and the next change involved temporary abandonment of the Second Plan. Instead, Egypt would adopt a three year "Accomplishment Plan" for the period FY68-70 to fulfill all the original goals of the Five-Year Plan, with some additions and adjustments for recent developments such as unexpected pe-

292

troleum discoveries and the continuing high level of foreign borrowing. Since even the latter plan has been abandoned in the aftermath of the June 1967 war with Israel, any detailed discussion would be meaningless. Unlike actual investment in the First Plan, however, which averaged £E 303 million annually, the Seven-Year Plan called for annual investments of £E 452 million. Even the three-year accomplishment plan called for investments of £E 368 million each year. The national income target of the achievement plan, now expressed in FY 1965 prices, was £E 2,483 million. In terms of the FY 1960 prices, in which the Ten-Year Plan originally was formulated, the new 1970 goal amounted to about £E 2,305 million, compared to the £E 2,510 million set as the 1970 target in the original plan.

The goal envisaged in the accomplishment plan would have been a formidable accomplishment even under normal circumstances, but the entire Egyptian economic picture changed in the wake of the Israeli war. After only a few weeks of new planning by a somewhat changed lineup of personnel in the economics and treasury ministries, a revised budget was published for the fiscal year ending June 30, 1968, that cut all expenditures except defense to the bone and allocated £E 232 million of public funds to investment. It was expected that £E 16 million would be invested by the private sector. The sectoral allocation of investment, which emphasized small-scale projects that would be expected to yield a rapid return, was roughly as follows:

	million
Aswân High Dam	£E 10.0
Electric power	50.0
Agriculture, irrigation and drainage	47.0
Industry (plus added funds from reserve)	48.5
Petroleum	19.0
Textiles	9.0
Chemicals	8.0
Foodstuffs	6.0
Transport & communications	28.5
Education	7.0
Housing	22.0
Health	1.6
Other ⎱ Reserve fund ⎰	25.4

293

The change in emphasis in the above allocations is obvious. Agriculture, which had received only 17 per cent of investment under the First Plan, would receive over 20 per cent. Industry, which had received almost 30 per cent, now would get less than 20 per cent. And the "services" sectors appear to have virtually disappeared from the calculations. Funds to finance investment were expected to include some £E 65.8 million in foreign loans, while the capital repayment obligation on previous foreign loans was estimated at £E 49.8 million.

Somewhat surprisingly, in view of speeches made earlier in 1967 on the prospect of refusing to pay debts to countries that attempted to "exert economic pressure," considerable stress was laid on the necessity for fulfilling all foreign debt obligations. By September a new plan for 1970-75 was being prepared, which was supposed to emphasize minimal foreign borrowing and controlled consumption.

Domestic Consumption

The imbalances that developed during the period of the First Plan are traceable primarily to the second major goal of the current government—i.e. improved standards of living for the present generation. It is a truism, but nonetheless true, that income and expenditures must somehow be equal, even if some of the income is deficit financing. In its reluctance to deprive the present generation of the "fruits of the revolution," the regime permitted consumption expenditure to outstrip plan estimates by large amounts, thereby greatly increasing the necessary total of foreign borrowing to finance investment and simultaneously increasing inflationary pressures in the economy, as the government borrowed from domestic banks to pay ever-increasing bills for wages and services on the domestic front. The money supply increased faster than the total output was able to expand. Plan estimates had anticipated an increase in savings from about 13 per cent of total production in fiscal 1960 to some 20 per cent by 1965. Instead, the actual rate of savings actually shrank somewhat between 1960 and 1962 and never exceeded 14.4 per cent (see table on "Development of Consumption, Savings, and Investment," below). In fiscal 1966, savings amounted to only 11.2 per cent of total output. The same problem may be expressed in terms of wages, which rose about 10 per cent annually, and productivity, which appears to have increased about 3.5 per cent each year. In essence, the population had more purchasing power in its hands than there were goods available for purchase. This could have been avoided if the regime had been willing to resort to high taxes or to permit prices of basic necessities to rise. But both domestic political considerations and apparently sincere ideological convictions blocked any such moves. The result was a growing demand for imported goods, which fell into the luxury class in Egyptian terms, and a growing deficit in the trade balance.

A major factor in the increase in consumption was the rate of population growth, which has been an important consideration to Egypt's policymakers for many years. Since 1820, the land under cultivation has merely doubled, while the population has increased ten-fold. Almost a million new mouths must be fed each year. Egypt's agricultural productivity already is among the highest in the world, making improvement correspondingly difficult, while the lot of the peasant remains precarious. Even a successful birth control program would take many years to slow the rate of population growth. And the gargantuan Aswân High Dam will only help to slow the increasing pressure of population on land.

Like many other countries today, Egypt is the scene of a struggle between modern techniques and traditional methods. On the whole, the country has benefited from the impact of the new ways; land reclamation, the scientific development of irrigation, and the introduction of new farming techniques have brought bigger crops, but there are many more millions of people among whom the crops must be distributed. The rate of population growth has absorbed much of the growth in national output.

Government Expenditure

Maintenance and enhancement of prestige on the international front did not become important, or costly, until Nasser had successfully carried off the nationalization of the Suez Canal Company. Egypt, which had been only a pawn in big power politics, and a minor one at that, suddenly became important. To a nation that has been in the backwash of history since the dawn of the Christian era, this new status offered nearly irresistible appeal. Suddenly Nasser joined Tito and Gandhi in the "big three" of nonalignment, and the establishment of an international image became another goal competing for Egypt's scarce resources. Militarily, too, the desire for strength that would be a significant factor on the international

DEVELOPMENT OF CONSUMPTION, SAVINGS, AND INVESTMENT
(in million £E)

Year	Local production*	Consumption	Savings	Investments	Foreign borrowing†	Per cent of consumption to production	Per cent of savings to production
1960-61	1409.3	1249.2	210.1	225.6	15.5	85.6	14.4
1961-62	1513.3	1348.6	164.7	251.1	86.4	89.1	10.9
1962-63	1684.6	1489.0	195.6	299.6	104.0	88.4	13.6
1963-64	1887.9	1651.1	236.8	372.4	135.6	87.5	12.5
1964-65	2050.6	1962.2	288.4	364.3	75.9	85.9	14.1
1965-66	2216.4	1967.6	249.1	363.6	114.5	88.8	11.2

* Gross Domestic Product at market price.
† Investment minus domestic savings.
Source: Al Ahram, July 25, 1967, p. 5.

CHANGES IN LAND PER CAPITA
(*Selected Years, 1945-72*)

	Cultivated area* (in million acres)	Popula- tion (in millions)	Cultivated acres/ capita
1945 (approximate)	5.73	18.0	0.318
1952	5.67	21.5	0.264
1960	6.02	25.8	0.233
1965	6.23	29.8	0.209
1968 (projected)	7.58	32.5	0.233
1972 (projected)	7.58	36.6	0.207

* Includes post-1965 reclamation only if related to Aswàn High Dam.

scene added to the burdens being supported by the economy. Government overspending at home, which supported primarily the goals of increased welfare now and greater development for the future, was joined by government overspending abroad. Balance of payments data indicate that Egypt was spending the equivalent of $85 million each year for "government foreign expenditures"— i.e. to support elaborate embassies, multiple trade and cultural delegations, and such costly ventures as the war in Yemen. The latter, which probably was entered into as a short-term venture that would reap returns in prestige, turned into an affair lasting at least five years, as far as Egyptian involvement was concerned, and undoubtedly costing a substantial sum of money for troops, arms, and transportation. Egypt began a small foreign aid program of its own, probably designed to promote Egyptian exports and to counter Israel's similar efforts in Africa. Participation in international trade fairs became common, rather than extraordinary.

Foreign Economic Relations

The same history of humiliation that caused Egypt to seize its chance for a major role on the international stage has also influenced its attitude toward foreign bilateral economic relations in a way that is otherwise inexplicable. Until the revolution, Egypt had been dominated by foreign powers, for largely commercial interests, with foreign debts used as the wedge for entry. In consequence, Egyptians are more than ordinarily sensitive to what they consider "strings" or "conditions." Within this context, the Egyptian government tends to resent any bilateral arrangement that carries conditions other than simple repayment. Debts in themselves are bad enough in Egyptian eyes, given the history of the Canal, and Egypt has been conscientious in attempting to meet its foreign debt obligations on time. In fact, both the compensation payments due to the former owners of the Canal Company and the indemnities due to the Sudan to finance Sudanese expenditures resulting from the flood effects of the Aswân High Dam were paid in full a year ahead of schedule. In the past several years, whenever Egypt has found its debt obligations outstripping the money available for debt service, the regime has resorted to renegotiation rather than default. Any request by a foreign power for concessions or internal changes in addition to a debt obligation causes an unrealistic, but nevertheless sincere, overreaction from Cairo. The current Egyptian regime also shares the tendency of many problem-ridden governments of underdeveloped countries to look for foreign scapegoats as an excuse for their own shortcomings and failures.

The Wheat Problem

Strained relations between Egypt and the United States and the drawdown of U.S. agricultural surpluses led the latter country to suspend loans for the purchase of wheat, flour, and other foodstuffs that had been extended to Egypt in substantial quantities since 1955. By the early 1960s, the U.S. was selling Egypt annually about $140 million worth of wheat and flour that was paid for in local currency, most of which was then reloaned to the Egyptians for development projects. These products came to account for 12 per cent of all Egyptian imports, and their sale for local currency eased the drain on foreign assets. The final shipments under a three-year agreement were made in 1965; a limited agreement was signed and implemented in early 1966. Since that time, Egypt has been faced with a new problem in international finance.

Egypt can treat its wheat problem only by treating the general foreign exchange problem—by reducing over-all spending for all consumer goods, by increasing the quantity and quality of its own products, and by postponing some of its more grandiose development plans until income more nearly equals expenditures. The wheat problem is primarily a function of Cairo's numerous competing needs for foreign exchange. It has been exacerbated by changing consumption patterns and by world politics. Egyptian agriculture is, on balance, a net earner of foreign exchange. In 1965, foreign sales of raw and processed agricultural products totaled about $525 million. Purchases of agricultural products and related goods and services cost only about $350 million—including $142 million for wheat and flour, $140 million for other farm products, $43 million for fertilizers and insecticides, $20 million for farm equipment, and a small amount for technical assistance, etc. Thus agriculture brought some $175 million into the country. Huge imports of other goods for consumption and development, however, left Egypt with an over-all trade deficit of $328 million.

Wheat has become the best-known factor in this imbalance for several reasons: it is the largest single import, it is essential to maintain normal consumption and dietary patterns, and it has been available on easy terms until recently. Corn is more important than wheat to the rural diet, but city dwellers typically eat large amounts of bread made from wheat. Consumption has increased very rapidly as a result of population growth, movement of population to the cities, and rising incomes combined with artificially-fixed low prices. Government policy has been to encourage domestic production sufficient to cover rural needs with only a small surplus for sale in the cities. In the 1960s, total consumption reached 3.5 million tons annually, of which about 2 million tons had to be imported. Until 1965, this requirement did not pose a serious foreign exchange problem, because the U.S. provided about 1.5 million tons each year for local currency. Egyptian financial managers came to rely on this supply; when it was decreased and later terminated they faced what was in effect a tremendous new demand on the country's scarce foreign exchange resources.

The solution does not lie in a reordering of agriculture in favor of cereals. To grow all its own wheat needs, Egypt would have to divert almost all the acreage now devoted to export crops—and thus sacrifice almost all export earnings. A feddan planted with rice, onions, sugarcane, fruit, or winter vegetables can earn a higher domestic return—or a higher foreign exchange return—than a feddan planted with wheat. Nor would increased domestic consumption of rice be efficacious. Although a ton of rice and a ton of wheat are roughly equal in nutritional terms, Egypt can sell rice for about $95 a ton and buy wheat for about $75 a ton. Instead, Egypt must reserve a portion of its foreign earnings to purchase the wheat it needs.

299

Economic Conditions in Late 1967

The First Plan (FY 61-65), although it fell short of its extremely ambitious goals, raised the aggregate growth rate to the respectable level of between 5 per cent and 6 per cent per year. Prior to 1952, economic expansion had failed to keep pace with population growth. Until the Israeli war, the Suez Canal had been running smoothly, and its revenues were more than double those prior to nationalization. Other foreign earnings also were growing, although they were not adequate to cover overambitious spending programs. (See below, "Major Sources of Foreign Earnings.")

Education and social welfare programs had been introduced and expanded, and the literacy rate was increasing. Population was shifting from rural to urban areas, and the employment was shifting from agriculture to industry (see Table 3).

Agriculture still is the dominant activity, and most farmers live in the Nile Delta—planting, irrigating, and manicuring their tiny holdings—raising cotton for sale to government agencies and foodstuffs for the family and the nearby markets. Today's farmer, however, has a slim chance of living in one of the new villages made up of concrete block houses provided with electricity. There is a better than even chance that the farmer's young children will attend school, at least for a few years, learning the reading and writing skills that their parents never had the chance to acquire.

Transportation, communications, and services provide employment for another third of the working population. In contrast to agriculture, where the role of the peasant and the methods of farming have changed little from generation to generation, the services sectors are striking for the contrast between new and old. The transportation worker may be a Suez Canal pilot, a flier for United Arab Airlines, a taxi driver, or a locomotive engineer; on the other hand, he may be at the helm of a Nile barge or at the reins of one of the donkey carts that crowd the streets of the towns and cities. With the growth of tourism, tour guides, travel clerks, museum guards, palace custodians, and hotel employees make up a significant segment of the labor force in the services sector.

In industry, Western methods are replacing the work of small artisans and craftsmen, except in some of the highly skilled working trades. These workers, together with fair numbers of the landless peasantry, are being gradually absorbed by the expanding factories, and Egypt now has for the first time in its history an industrial

MAJOR SOURCES OF FOREIGN EARNINGS
(in million U.S. $)

	1952	1955	1958	1961	1963	1964	1965	1966	1966 (First six months)	1967
Total	549	575	635	692	748	804	903	924	538	545
Suez Canal revenues*	76	92	121	147	164	179	198	219	108	120
Receipts from tourism†	43	65	41	66	62	86	102	100	50	50
Raw cotton exports	362	307	312	297	278	268	336	330 }	380	375
Other exports	68	111	161	182	244	271	269	275 }		

* Accruing to foreign shareholders until 1958. Data for 1967 estimated.
† Official estimates, except 1952, estimated on the basis of comparative number of tourists. Figures for 1965, 1966, and 1967 are arbitrary estimates.

working class—together with the problems characteristic of the growth of that group. The productivity of workers in industry has risen, but it is still very low as compared with advanced nations. It is low for a number of reasons: (1) government employment practices (2) a high degree of absenteeism and of rapid turnover (3) lack of technical skills and (4) health problems of the workers.

One of the important and growing salaried occupations is that of bureaucrat. Most government employees are counted in the services sector, but almost all industry is government-controlled, and a sizable number of industrial employees are in effect government administrators. These executives have replaced most of the former management, much of which was foreign, and the change usually has not been for the better in terms of efficiency. The government itself, as well as government-run enterprise, suffers from overemployment, red tape, and inertia. Corruption, however, is not the major problem in Egypt that it is in most other Near Eastern countries. The sincere puritanical streak in the leadership has made an impression, and a large police establishment makes its presence felt. Scandals do occur, and small gifts change hands, but in Egypt inefficiency and incompetence are far more prevalent than graft.

Modernization is a firmly established trend, but its effects are uneven. Visual evidence of the coexistence of old and new is plentiful. Leaders of government and industry, together with members of the bureaucratic establishment generally, have adopted modern ways, but the rest of the population is changing only slowly. The regime has encouraged adoption of external evidences of modern life, but the galabia is still worn by many workers in construction and industry and is the almost universal garb of the rural male. Merchandise travels to rural markets and city shops by truck, donkey cart, or even on the backs of camels. The mixture of old and new is perpetuated both by shortages and by tradition. For example, trucks and their components involve expenditures of scarce hard currency. Donkeys and camels usually do not.

The Future Direction of Economic Policy

Immediately following the war with Israel, Egyptian economic policies and programs apparently were very much up in the air. Income had been seriously hurt by the loss of revenues from the Suez Canal and from tourism, while expenditures had been increased by both military demands and the costs of conducting international trade without the Suez Canal for a transportation route. These effects, however, had been offset to a great extent by foreign assistance, largely from other Arab countries. The government's pronouncements put great stress on the high productivity of the private sector as compared to the public sector, and assurances were given that Western tourists were welcome and Western investment was desired. The new budget even included an allocation for "removing the bottlenecks" from industrial production, and numerous articles began to appear underscoring the necessity for incentives and rewards in the economic sphere. Whether these various statements portend a new direction in the government's policies or whether they are merely concessions to the pressures of the immediate situation remains to be seen. If Egypt is to have a chance for substantial development and for release from its foreign exchange shortage, its leaders must make some choices among the goals they have pursued in such a headlong and expensive manner for the past 15 years.

CHAPTER *18*

Agriculture

ALTHOUGH AGRICULTURE'S DOMINANCE OF THE EGYPTIAN ECONOMY has lessened somewhat as diversification has progressed, over half the total labor force remains strictly agrarian, and agriculture still provides over 25 per cent of the national income. Raw and processed agricultural products constitute 80 per cent of total exports, and farm output supplies the cotton gins and the yarn and textile mills that employ almost half of Egypt's industrial labor force. More than half of the commercial firms, wholesalers, and retailers are kept busy handling local agricultural produce.

The cultivated area is highly productive, but is limited to less than a quarter acre per capita—a tenth as much as in the United States. Total agricultural production has increased 20 per cent since the mid-50s, and food production has increased 23 per cent; population has grown so rapidly, however, that per capita output has barely been maintained.

In the struggle to support a large population on the limited land available, Egyptian agriculture has become thoroughly organized and controlled, relatively well administered, and highly productive. Because of intensive farming and multiple cropping, yields per acre are very high for almost all crops. Each cultivated acre produces an average of 1.7 crops per year, and over 99.5 per cent of the cultivated land is under irrigation. More fertilizer is used in the Nile Valley and the Delta than in all other North African countries combined, and the rate of application per acre is far higher than in either the United States or the United Kingdom.

A number of other factors, in addition to methods of cultivation, contribute to this unusually high productivity: (1) an agricultural labor force with centuries of experience in settled farming (2) ease of communication between government and farmer, growing out of geographical cohesiveness and a tradition of government control

(3) a good "growing" climate, with abundant sunshine, and (4) fertile soil that has been constantly replenished by deposits of silt from the Nile.

Egypt's land is worked by millions of fellahin, most of whom live at bare subsistence level. Rural villages are essentially crowded clusters of farmhouses, from which the villagers go out daily to their own small parcels of land or to the larger holdings of local or absentee landlords. The village pattern of settlement is common throughout the Middle East, but it does not reflect the same social or physical conditions everywhere. In Egypt, a highly centralized system of irrigation, based on the control of a single river, the Nile, rests on the cooperation and disciplined labor of the village unit. The practice of squeezing houses together on the poorest land (or the desert fringe along the upper Nile) saves scarce land. And, even if the peasant chose to break away from the deeply-rooted tradition of village life, he could hardly live away from his fellows, for much of the land is fragmented into plots too small to maintain independent homesteads.

The squalor of the fellah's physical surroundings, the resemblance of his simple tools to those of his forebears, the techniques he employs in working the land, all make it easy to think of him as impervious to change. Yet if the social organization of agriculture and the village institution have changed little over the centuries, economic and technical change have in fact occurred, and these have affected the peasant—increasingly so in recent years. He has accepted new crops and become dependent on them. He has persisted, however, in trying to grow them in old ways, and traditional cultivation techniques exist side by side with modern methods. Because the fields now must produce more—and more varied—crops, and because water now is available at all seasons, he works sporadically the year around instead of seasonally (i.e. if he is not a landowner and if he is lucky enough to find employment). In 1967, the government estimated that the average wage worker in agriculture was employed only 180 days of the year.

Throughout most of Egypt's history, the fellah has been treated by his rulers as an expendable economic resource. Successive Egyptian governments—most of them alien—used the food supply and tax revenue they extracted from the peasant to perpetuate themselves. The victim of countless oppressions and indignities and living in unrelieved monotony and poverty, the fellah had been brought, as General Naguib wrote in 1955, "too low to be able to help himself without a great deal of compulsory assistance from the government."

Since 1952, however, comprehensive and determined efforts have been made to improve the lot of the peasant—described as the backbone of the revolution—through agrarian land reform, land reclamation, agricultural cooperatives, increased supplies of fertilizers, and improvement of health services and sanitation measures.

Farming Practice

Farming practice in Egypt is slowly and unevenly changing under the impact of modern knowledge. Where government experts are given a free rein, mechanization and scientific soil treatment almost completely exclude the older ways. However, in spite of the government's ambitious land redistribution program and its avid encouragement of the use of mechanized and scientific methods, the fellah is not easily turned from the traditional procedures he has learned from his elders. The exceptionally high yields obtained by progressive landowners and the government experimental stations show that the old methods of cultivation are laborious, wasteful of seeds and natural fertilizers, and comparatively less profitable, but these facts must be doubly proved to the peasant, whose fatalistic acceptance of any existing situation has been ingrained through centuries of dependence on the flow of the Nile. Furthermore, most of the fellahin are as suspicious of agricultural machines as they are of any other innovation. Progress in agriculture also has been hampered by the prevalence of absentee landlords, illiteracy, land fragmentation, and open drainage, which wastes land. The tools most fellahin employ are few, simple, and differing only in minor respects from those their ancestors used in Pharaonic times. Their draft animals are the cow, the buffalo, and sometimes the camel, and these they hitch to primitive plows, scoops, furrowers, drags, and threshing sledges. Hand tools are the hoe and the sickle, with which vast quantities of grain and clover are still cut.

In 1965, a total of about 6 million feddans was under cultivation in Egypt, giving a total crop area, with rotation, of about 10.4 million feddans. This was close to the 1963 figures (see Table 4). About 3.5 million of the cultivated feddans were in the Delta, and the remainder were about equally distributed between Middle Egypt (Giza, Beni Suef, Minya, and Faiyûm) and Upper Egypt (Asyût, Girga, Qena, and Aswân). Less than a tenth of Egypt's productive soil remains under basin irrigation; with the help of continuous warmth and maximum sunlight, allowing only short periods for fallow, almost all of the cultivated area can produce crops throughout the year. There are three growing seasons: a winter season (*shitwi*), accounting for almost half the total crop area; a summer season (*seifi*), with about 36 per cent of the crop area, and an autumn season (*nili*), with only about 17 per cent. Cultivation is most intensive in the Delta; on the land closest to the Nile branches and main irrigation canals, crop area is almost double the cultivated land area.

Berseem (clover) and wheat are the chief winter crops, occupying 80 per cent of the 4.8 million feddans cultivated. Horse beans rank third, with almost 10 per cent, and barley, lentils, fenugreek, onions, and a wide variety of vegetables are also grown in this season.

About 3.9 million feddans are cultivated in summer, over 60 per cent of which are in the Delta. Cotton is the leading crop, occupying about half of the crop area. Rice, sorghum, and corn are also widely cultivated, and large quantities of sugar, melons, sesame, and peanuts are grown.

To date, only about 1.6 million feddans have been planted in the fall—the season when flooding historically has prevented cropping in the basin areas of Upper Egypt. By far the greater part of the fall crop consists of corn; most of the remainder is put to sorghum and vegetables. Fall planting has begun to expand, however, and will grow rapidly as the storage capacity of the Aswân High Dam comes into use.

The length of the seasons varies somewhat between the upper valley and the northern Delta. There is a considerable overlapping of the seasonal crops, and the high winter yield is largely due to the fact that winter is the only cropping season for land not yet under perennial irrigation.

In most areas, cultivation follows a two- or three-year rotation. In the two-year cycle, the plot is halved, and each portion generally grows two crops. In the three-year cycle, the area is divided into thirds. One portion alternates clover and cotton, one grows beans or clover in winter and corn or rice as a nili crop, and one is sown with wheat, barley, or flax in winter and corn or rice in the flood season. Each half or third is alternated through successive years. In Middle Egypt, sorghum replaces the corn or rice grown as the nili crop in the Delta. In the far south, sugarcane is the main crop

307

and usually dictates a four-year cycle. In the first year, cane occupies a quarter of the land; in the second year, a half; and in the third and fourth years, cane covers three-fourths of the area. The remainder grows winter crops, followed by cotton, or lies fallow in winter and grows corn during the remainder of the year.

Some 75 per cent of the soil of the Delta and the Nile fringe is alluvial—level, deep, and black, but lacking in nitrogen. Other soils include clay alluvial, sandy, and gravelly-sandy—all of which are suitable for irrigation.

Major Crops

In the 1965 harvesting year, field crops accounted for 71.8 per cent of Egypt's gross agricultural revenue. Vegetables brought in 9 per cent, fruit 5.9 per cent, and poultry, livestock, and livestock products accounted for the remaining 13.4 per cent. Cotton accounted for a third of the value of field crops, or slightly less than a quarter of the total farm revenue. The most important change in the relative importance of crops has been a steady increase in rice acreage and production. Rice is now the second largest export crop, although raw cotton continues to average almost 55 per cent of total exports by value, and cotton yarn and textiles account for a further 15 per cent (see Table 5).

Egypt occupies a unique place in cotton production. Although growing less than 5 per cent of the total world crop, the country is the third largest cotton exporter, trailing only the United States and Mexico. Egypt produces almost a third of the world output of long staple cotton and about 40 per cent of extra-long staple. Grown on 16 per cent of the crop area, production varies widely (between 336,000 tons and 518,000 tons during 1960-66). In the 1964-66 period, output averaged about 500,000 tons, equivalent to about 2.2 million 480-pound bales. Of this total, about 30 per cent is locally processed and manufactured into yarn or textiles.

For 30 years, the Cotton Research Board of the Ministry of Agriculture and the Royal (until 1952) Agricultural Society of Egypt have been working successfully on the improvement of existing varieties of cotton and on the development of new ones. The quality of long-staple cotton deteriorates after only a few generations, and introduction of entirely new varieties is necessary every few years. Other experiments have led to improved growing methods, such as earlier sowing and closer spacing, and the ruling that prohibits the mixing of varieties within a small area of land or in the ginneries has reduced the incidence of hybridization. Farmers must obtain their seed from the Ministry of Agriculture, where it is sorted and controlled with great precision. Thanks to these measures and to the increasing control of cotton pests and diseases, the yield of Egyptian cotton rose by more than 50 per cent between 1919 and 1940. A plateau was reached during World War II, largely as a result of the disruption of world trade. With foreign transactions suspended, land was switched from cotton to soil-exhausting cereals for domestic consumption, and fertilizer imports also were curtailed. Little progress in cotton technology was made until the late 1950s. Between 1959 and 1965, however, yields increased by a further 15 per cent.

Cotton is by far the most profitable of the three main field crops. It is labor-intensive in a land where labor is cheap. It offers no temptation for diversion by tenants or hired workers. It is not perishable. And it is "light on the soil" as compared with the cereals. Government agencies maintain strict controls over all aspects of cotton production and marketing. No more than a third of any one holding may be planted with cotton, while at least a third of the area must be given over to wheat. Both the variety to be planted and the date of planting are centrally determined for all areas of the country. There is a guaranteed market for all the cotton at government-determined prices, and incentive payments are made for superior quality and for careful sorting and cleaning.

Food-grain crops—wheat, corn, rice, sorghum, barley, and millet—occupy almost half the cultivated area (see Table 6). Wheat production averages 1.5 to 1.6 million tons on 1.4 million feddans; while corn, planted on 1.6 to 1.8 million feddans, recently has experienced a considerable increase in production—from an average of about 1.8 million tons in 1960-64 to 2.1 million tons in 1965 and 2.4 million tons in 1966. Corn and wheat together occupy about 65 per cent of the area planted to grain; rice acreage has been increasing rapidly, and now accounts for over 20 per cent of the total; the remainder of the grain acreage is devoted to sorghum, barley, and millet.

Wheat of the spring type is grown throughout the country and harvested in late May or early June. Any excess over family requirements that the farmer wishes to sell is purchased by the government at support prices. Sales quotas are established for farmers in the few areas that normally grow more wheat than is needed in the surrounding territory. Corn is the principal staple food in the villages and is produced almost entirely for rural consumption. Most domestic wheat also is consumed outside the cities; requirements in urban areas, where wheat is the staple diet item, are met almost entirely from imports.

Rice production, centered in the northerly section of the Delta, requires large amounts of water between April and August, when the natural flow of the Nile is at its lowest. As the Aswân High Dam has begun to store flood water for use in this season, the government has begun to expand the acreage allotted to rice. The announced allotment for 1967 was 1.2 million feddans; production of 2.3 million tons was anticipated.

Grain sorghum, called *durra*, is the fourth most important food grain, and it is also used for fodder. Barley, on the other hand, is of minor importance in the human diet, but is important for livestock feed.

Egypt's clover, the quick-growing, vivid green berseem, is peculiar to the country and has been known since Pharaonic times. Its dual purpose as a stock food and a fertilizer makes it indispensable, and each year some 2.5 million feddans, more than 20 per cent of the total crop area, are planted to it. Berseem, Egypt's staple animal fodder, is cut and fed green in the winter or dried for summer feed, and every farmer, large or small, grows it in proportion to his stock-feeding needs. Though used sparingly for green manure, there is no doubt that its faculty for fixing nitrogen from the atmosphere has played a major part in the continuing high fertility of Egypt's soil. A winter crop, sown usually in October, berseem grows very rapidly and is ready for cutting in seven weeks, yielding between six and eight tons to a feddan.

After many ups and downs, Egypt's sugar industry survives today in a healthy condition; from the 30,000 feddans in the depression period of the 1930s, the area devoted to cane has now reached 140,000 feddans and is scheduled to occupy 167,000 feddans in 1968. From an annual production of 6 million tons of cane, about 470,000 tons of sugar are refined. Prices received by the growers for cane as well as those paid for sugar by the consumers are all controlled by the government. Climatic conditions and good drainage in the Nile Valley, particularly in the most southerly provinces, are ideal for sugarcane growing, and in this region it has become the principal industrial crop. The plantations in Qena province provide 60 per cent of the country's total production, while mills in Aswân province and in the Qena neighborhood produce three-quarters of the raw sugar output. It is a common practice to leave the cane stubble in the ground to sprout a second crop, and even a third crop may be produced this way, although the yield is poor and unprofitable. Sugarcane quickly exhausts the soil and requires heavy artificial fertilization and a three- or four-year rotation. Nevertheless, a good crop is so highly profitable in proportion to acreage, that the industry has been more than able to hold its own.

Cottonseed oil provides some 85 per cent of the total edible oils, as well as more than half of the vegetable oils used in industry. Peanuts are the second most important source of oils. Important quantities of cottonseed and soybean oils are imported.

All the common varieties of vegetables are grown in Egypt, and the yield is high and the quality generally good (see Table 7). Except for onions and melons, however, vegetables are raised primarily for city consumption and for export. Onion production averages 670,000 tons, well below the production of tomatoes, which attains 1,250,000 tons. Potatoes are an increasingly important crop, although seed stock must be imported annually. Other major vegetables include melons, cucumbers, cabbages, marrow beans, and eggplant. Large quantities of tomatoes, potatoes, onions, melons, and cucumbers are exported, principally to European countries. A truck farmer near Cairo or Alexandria can realize returns of over £E 1,000 ($2,300) per feddan.

Egypt has a wide range of temperate zone, suitable for both subtropical and tropical fruits. These are generally of high quality, and, since they ripen early, are in good demand in European markets (see Table 8). Intensive efforts have been made to increase production, and the area in orchards has increased from about 35,000 feddans in 1930 to some 180,000 feddans. The production of oranges and other citrus fruits has risen to 480,000 tons, and a sizable proportion of the crop is exported. Other important fruits include dates, grapes, bananas, mangoes, and guavas. Coffee, cocoa, tea, and a few spices are almost the only food crops not cultivated in Egypt.

Egypt has over 6 million date palms, fairly evenly distributed throughout the Valley, the Delta, and the oases. Most of the 385,000-ton date crop is eaten locally; even the Saite date, which is among the world's finest, gets no farther than the tables of Cairo and Alexandria. The date requires little cultivation. It is tolerant of soil and water salinity, and all the manuring it gets is from plowedin stubble and decomposing undercrop. The only attention date palms receive is artificial pollination (usually the female flower is dusted with pollen from the male flower by boys who climb the trees) and an annual pruning. The trunk of the date palm is a supplementary source of lumber, of which Egypt is in very short supply.

Cut flowers, essential oils, and medical plants are the major nonfood crops, aside from cotton and cottonseed. A number of farms specialize in preparing flowers for city florists and for export. Some $230,000 worth of cut flowers are exported annually, and considerable opportunity exists for improvement both in the size and the handling of flower crops. Rose oil, mint oil, and orange oil are produced primarily for export to Western Europe. A single large government farm in Al-Jīzah produces jasmine for Egyptian perfume factories and for an export market, with revenues of nearly $1 million a year. Senna, henna, geranium oil, and a number of other pharmaceutical and cosmetic plants thrive in the warm, arid climate. Tobacco was produced on experimental plots at Tahrir in 1965, for the first time since tobacco cultivation was prohibited in 1890.

Land Tenure and Agrarian Reforms

In 1952, before the introduction of agrarian reform, over 94 per cent of all landowners shared only 35 per cent of the cultivated land, while the remaining 6 per cent of the owners held 65 per cent. While 188 landlords held over 1,000 feddans each, some two million farmers owned one feddan or less. About 67 per cent of the land was leased by landless peasants. With increased population, land prices had soared from £E 119 a feddan in 1930 to £E 430 in 1947. By the time of the revolution, rents sometimes exceeded the entire value of the crop that could be produced on the land. Comparatively few of the large owners worked their entire estates themselves, and many of them regarded the land, on which a luxurious villa was a characteristic feature, as a place to which to repair to escape the city heat. The current expression was not "I'm going to the farm," but "I'm going to the villa." Most landlords were city merchants, industrialists, or wealthy professional men. For them, as for their counterparts elsewhere in the Middle East, real estate was a major vehicle for capital investment, owing both to the traditional prestige connected with land ownership and to the generous returns in rents and income from cash crops. Absentees for the most part, they left the management of their domains in the hands of managers or bailiffs, whose underlings dealt directly with the peasant tenants.

Some landlords were in the habit of retaining for their own use a fraction of the land they owned, farming it through a manager; the amount of land thus retained varied with the profitability of the crops in any particular year, and it is not clear what proportion of the total cultivable area was worked by the owners. Figures compiled during recent studies differ widely, but the figure probably varied between 25 and 40 per cent.

No moderately prosperous smallholder group stood between the big landowner and the peasantry, for whereas those holding 5 to 50 feddans were more likely to be in direct contact with the peasant, and therefore to have firsthand knowledge of his plight, still their attitudes and pattern of relationships with the peasant were essentially those of the larger landlords. Agrarian reform has not fundamentally altered this relationship. The big landlord, shorn by the new laws of a portion of his land, and the smallholder, striving to become a bigger one, are in the main still very much landlords, and the tenancy and hired labor systems preserve their essential character. However, the rent and credit provisions of the land reform laws have greatly strengthened the position of the tenant with regard to the landowner.

The conditions governing tenancy in Egypt are of three kinds. First, and least complicated, is the cash payment system, which—not surprisingly in a country where the peasantry is perennially in debt or short of cash—is the least fully developed. It is found almost exclusively on state domains and in the immediate vicinity of the larger cities, where truck farming can be profitably carried on.

A second and more widely-spread practice is the payment by the tenant of all or part of his rent in kind. The rent is fixed according to the quality of the soil, and the owner usually undertakes to buy the crop at going prices. Should the tenant or the owner at any time during the agreement wish to change the payment plan, this is usually arranged without difficulty. If, for example, a tenant agrees to pay his landlord a cash rental plus 5 kantars of cotton (1 kantar = 110 lbs.), he may, on agreement, substitute cash for the total or for any fraction of the crop payment.

The third, and previously the most general, practice is *métayage*.

Under this arrangement, the landlord provided the costs of cultivation and got the bulk of the crop; while the tenant did the work and received the lesser share. This type of contract was usually made for one crop only. A tenant took over for a single cotton crop; the landowner provided seed, fertilizers, and draft animals; met the taxes and half the cost of picking; and received in return about five-sixths of the crop. This proportion decreased as the services provided by the landowner were reduced, though it was only rarely that the landlord received less than half, even if the tenant paid all the expenses, including taxes. Métayage became much more widespread with the inflation of land values following World War II. Even now, this method of financing and repayment remains legal, but reform laws prohibit the payment to the landlord of more than half of the return after all expenses have been paid.

Under all forms of tenancy, the landlord or his agent regulates matters of water, drainage, and rotation. He also supervises gathering of the crops and has them deposited in his granary as collateral for rent. The landlord usually takes full advantage of his knowledge of the markets in dealing with his tenants.

Land reform was not an idea unique to the present regime, but all previous attempts in that direction had failed. Redistribution had been tried, at various times, with unfavorable results, and in the last days of the monarchy there were evidences of a growth of social and political consciousness, which led among other things to a demand for a reform of the Egyptian system of land tenure. A bill which would have limited the future acquisition of land to 100 feddans was overwhelmingly defeated by a parliament dominated by rich merchants and industrialists, most of whom had invested heavily in land. The most that the would-be reformers could obtain from the government at that time was a law which required owners of large estates to provide better housing and social services for their tenants and laborers. Even this was largely nullified by the inadequacy and corruption of the supervisory machinery.

The Agrarian Reform Law was promulgated on September 9, 1952. An explanatory note to the Law explained its social objectives:

> There are social justifications which must not be overlooked because the distribution of wealth in Egyptian rural districts is at variance with any concept of justice. . . . The unequal distribution of agricultural wealth gives rise to social evils. One of the worst effects of these evils is the enslavement by a minority of the big landlords of the peasants and the direction of the country's general policy

according to their personal interests, which in no way conform with the principles of democracy. . . . The time has now come for reform in Egypt to be carried out with a view to rebuilding Egyptian society on a new basis that will secure for every individual a free and honorable life, close the wide gap between landowners, and remove the deep-rooted class barriers with their attendant social and political unrest.

The law was to be administered under the Ministry of Agrarian Reform and Land Reclamation by the General Agency for Land Reform, supported by an Executive Agency and a Judiciary Committee. Its specific goals included the redistribution of land held in excess of maximum amounts, the regulation of relations between landowners and tenants, the organization of multiple purpose cooperatives, the prevention of land fragmentation, and the safeguarding of the rights of agricultural workers.

An individual could retain a maximum of 200 feddans, while transferring an excess of up to 100 feddans to his children. Surplus lands would be purchased by the state for seven times the basic land tax, equal to ten times the rental value, plus the value of trees and fixed and other improvements. Compensation was by treasury bonds, carrying 3 per cent interest and maturing in 30 years. The acquired lands were to be resold in lots of not fewer than two feddans or more than five feddans, and the plots must be farmed by the purchasers. The resale value was established as the purchase price, plus 15 per cent for state expenses, and was to be payable in 30 installments at 3 per cent interest. The law prohibited the division of lands into less than five feddan plots.

Later on, other laws and decrees amended the terms of the original bill. Law No. 127 of July 1961 limited to 100 feddans the holding of any individual or organization; while the National Charter of May 1962 stated that by 1970 the holdings of any one family must not exceed 100 feddans. Law No. 168 of 1958 reduced the interest on the compensatory bonds to 1.5 per cent and stretched their maturity to 40 years; while Law No. 128 of 1961 halved the price of the distributed land to recipients. Law No. 138 of 1964 again halved the price of the lands; while Law No. 104 of that same year canceled compensation due from the state on account of land expropriation. The argument put forward to justify the cancellation of all payments to former owners was that such action was not in accord with the new socialist framework and that the annual income from 100 feddans was more than ample for a family.

By 1966, about one million feddans had been expropriated and 700,000 feddans had been redistributed to some 290,000 families, comprising 1.5 million individuals.

Distribution of both seized and reclaimed land (both handled by the Land Reform Authority) has put farms in the hands of 410,000 new owners since 1952 and has increased the average size of the smallest farms by 50 per cent. However, many small farms remain uneconomical in size. The average smallholding in 1952 was 0.8 feddans—by 1965 it still was only 1.2 feddans. Even if the 6,420,000 privately owned feddans were evenly distributed among the existing owners, each farm would contain barely 2 feddans. Since the reform law calls for distribution of no less than 2 and no more than 5 feddans to a recipient, it appears likely that 2 feddans is considered to be the minimum holding necessary to provide a family with a bare living. Such is the magnitude of Egypt's land and population problem. Nevertheless, land reform has transferred control of the majority of the available land from the absentee aristocracy to the resident smallholder and has left a larger share of farm income in the hands of the producers.

LAND OWNERSHIP IN EGYPT

Farm size (feddans)	Before 1952 land reform		1965	
	Thousands of owners	Per cent of total land area	Thousands of owners	Per cent of total land area
Under 5	2,642	35.4	3,033	57.1
5-9.99	79	8.8	78	9.5
10-19.99	47	10.7	61	8.2
20-49.99	22	10.9	29	12.6
50-99.99	6	7.2	6	6.1
100-199.99	3	7.3	4*	6.5
200 & over	2	19.7		
Total	2,801	100.0	3,211	100.0

* 4,210 owners of 100 feddans each.

The rental and credit provisions of the land reform laws undoubtedly have had more impact on the average peasant than the ownership regulations. The 1952 law fixed the maximum rent ceiling at seven times the basic land tax; together with the tax law, this provision prevented the landlord from charging any more than the assessed annual rental value of the land (and landlords had, of course, striven to keep the valuations low in order to minimize their taxes). For sharecropping rents, the law limited the landlord's share to no more than one-half the returns after expenses. Over a million families, totaling some 4½ million persons, have benefited from a great reduction in rents through these regulations. The program also promoted cooperatives to handle purchasing and sales for the small holdings and fragmented farms and provided for low cost credit to be made available to tenants and sharecroppers. Loans now are made with only crops for collateral; in the past, a loan could not be obtained unless the land was pledged as security.

According to Egyptian statistics for 1966, owners who had received land under the program retained £E 53 more per feddan farmed than they would have received as tenants in 1952, due to both improved productivity and the advantage of owning rather than renting. Those who remained tenants were said to have benefited to the extent of £E 42 in increased income per feddan, because of productivity and lower rents.

The socialist government has been disturbed by the activities of a group newly classed as agricultural capitalists—owners of between 20 and 100 feddans, whose land is intensively worked by mechanized equipment and hired laborers. These "feudalists" and other landowners who through devious means had managed to keep large holdings were among the objects of a decree of June 1966. This decree established a Committee for the Elimination of Feudalism, headed by the then vice-president, Field Marshal Abdel Hakim Amer. The broad powers of the committee included the confiscation of land, the banishment of feudalist elements from the villages, and the abrogation of individuals' political and public rights. The anti-feudalist campaign did not last long, and it apparently had little real effect, although it may reappear in the future. Some consideration also has been given at intervals in the past to lowering maximum land holdings to 50 feddans. Such a move is not likely while Egypt remains confronted with the problems created by the June 1967 war. If it does eventually occur, it will require redistribution of about 7 per cent of the land area.

Irrigation

It has been said that the harnessing of the Nile has given Egypt the equivalent of the rainfall of the Mediterranean in winter, of the American Gulf of Mexico in spring and early summer, and of the

317

monsoon in late summer and autumn. Mastery of the river is achieved by two main types of irrigation: basin irrigation, in which the water is supplied by a single flooding during the high-water period of the Nile, and perennial irrigation, which regulates the flood and furnishes controlled amounts of water at all times. As we shall see, basin irrigation is giving way to perennial irrigation. Modern Egypt is almost literally the creation of the irrigation engineers, who maintain a highly complicated and efficient irrigation system and plan and execute its further development. Large-scale irrigation was begun by Muhammad Ali in the early nineteenth century, but the greater part of the credit for building the present installations and for developing the maintenance techniques must go to the British, who from the time of the occupation until 1946 provided the directors, senior planners, and executive officers of the Egyptian government's Department of Public Works. Today, however, the engineering staff and planning staffs are either graduates of the Egyptian School of Engineering in Cairo or Egyptians who have been trained abroad and who are serving under the Ministry of Irrigation.

All dams, barrages, regulators, and the 15,000 miles of public canals are owned and maintained by the government, which carefully controls the distribution of water, thus obviating inequities which might otherwise result from local and sectional rivalries. The main canals remain full at all times, but outlets to each farm are opened only on a fixed schedule—5 days out of 15 in the summer.

The Irrigation Service maintains ten Inspectorates—four in the Delta and six in the Valley—each of which is divided into districts of about 40,000 feddans in the charge of a district engineer. The recommendations and complaints of farmers are brought to the attention of the Irrigation Service through the Provincial Councils, to which two members are elected from each of the districts into which the provinces of Egypt are divided. Two inspectors-general, one in Upper Egypt and one in Lower Egypt, receive the reports of the ordinary inspectors and coordinate plans for the seasonal water budgets and programs of control at the various barrages, taking into account the acreages under the principal crops, the specific needs of these crops, and the amount of water available at any given time.

Basin irrigation. The earliest form of agriculture on any large scale in Egypt consisted of a simple scattering of seed in the mud left

behind on the river banks after the annual Nile flood had subsided. Basin irrigation followed as the population grew and as better control of the crop area became necessary. Basin irrigation,
which is slated to disappear by the early 1970s, has few mechanical
requirements. First, the land is divided into compartments by building an earth bank along the river and crossbanks leading outward
to the edge of the bordering desert. These main strips are subdi-
vided into individual holdings and fields by other banks running
parallel to the river line, and the basins thus formed are connected
directly with the river by regular canal systems. When the Nile
rises to flood proportions in mid-August, the sluices of the Nile
barrages are opened, and water floods the basins to depths varying
between three and six feet. The land is allowed to remain inundated for 40 to 60 days, then water not absorbed by the soil or
evaporated is drained back into the river.

With this procedure, the basins were entirely dependent on flooding and devoted exclusively to one winter crop. Recently, however,
a good deal of summer irrigation has been achieved by pumping
from wells within the basins themselves. This modification of the
simple flooding practice has proved of particular value in the case
of land put to cotton. Since cotton cannot be picked until late
August, flood irrigation was delayed until after harvesting, and
without the wells the ground could not be saturated for a long
enough period to give the best results for the second crop.

Perennial irrigation. Perennial irrigation, as practiced in Egypt, involves a complicated system of storage reservoirs; barrages across
the river to maintain the flow into the network of main, branch,
and distributary canals during the annual low-water period; subsidiary regulators within the canals; and drainage lines. Perennial
irrigation is generally preferred to basin irrigation, since it increases
the total potential crop yield per unit area and makes possible the
cultivation of a wider variety of crops. Such important crops as
rice and sugar, which require a constant supply of water during
their growing seasons, can only flourish under perennial irrigation.
The perennial system soon will expand to include all land now
under basin irrigation, and further desert land is being added to
the cultivated area. The Egyptian government has long been aware
of the problems attending the maintenance and extension of drainage, fertilization, and general soil care, and its long experience in

319

dealing with such matters is evident in the plans being worked out for future irrigation undertakings.

Though envisaged by Napoleon during his occupation of Egypt between 1798 and 1801, canal-fed perennial irrigation in Egypt really began in 1816, when Muhammad Ali dug a deep canal from the Delta branches of the Nile to provide water for the summer irrigation of his cotton and sugarcane plantations. It was Muhammad Ali also who took the first step in the development of the present system of storage reservoirs and barrages, when in 1835 he commissioned French engineers to draw up plans for a twin barrage across the heads of the two Delta branches of the Nile, some miles to the north of Cairo. Construction began in 1843; but the Viceroy's impatience to have his plans completed resulted in faulty construction, and the barrages did not function satisfactorily until rebuilt and strengthened in the early years of the British occupation. Six subsidiary barrages have since been built—three in the Delta, at Zifta (1903), Muhammad Ali (1939), and Idfina (1951); and three between Cairo and Aswân, at Asyût (1902), Nag Hamadi (1930), and Isna (1908). In 1900, there were only about 700,000 feddans in the Delta under perennial irrigation from canals. In Lower Egypt today, some 3.5 million feddans are canal irrigated. The 1.5 million feddans under canal irrigation in the Nile Valley (including the Faiyûm Oasis) are almost entirely a development of the past 50 years.

Aswân High Dam. The completion of the first Aswân Dam in 1902 (heightened in 1912 and again in 1933) and the Asyût barrage six years later permitted rapid development of Egyptian agriculture. Together, these works made it possible vastly to increase the area of perennial irrigation in the Nile Valley and to maintain a scientific programing system for the supply of water to the Valley and the Delta throughout the year.

The initial proposal for the construction of the Aswân High Dam (Saad al-'Aali) at a site four miles upstream from the original Aswân Dam was made in 1947 by Greek and Italian engineers living in Egypt, and this plan was revived after July 1952. In December 1958, following withdrawal of a Western financing offer, the USSR agreed to provide the equivalent of $100 million in credits for the first stage of construction, and a subsequent Soviet commitment raised the total Soviet aid to $325 million out of the estimated total cost of $735 million for dam, power plant, power

320

transmission lines, and compensation payments to the Sudan. Related expenses for irrigation works, roads, etc. are expected to cost an additional $250 million. Soviet engineers prepared the designs, and construction began in 1960 with 1,000 Soviet technicians on the site, supervising 40,000 Egyptian engineers and workmen. At one time, the number of Russians reached a peak of 1,800; by 1967, there were some 640 Russians and 19,000 Egyptians remaining at the site.

The dam began storing water in 1964 and started to prove its value almost immediately. The flow of the Nile that fall was the highest in many years, and the Delta area was saved from severe flooding by the Dam's ability to slow the flow of water. The water stored became vitally important in 1965, moreover, when the Nile's flow was among the lowest on record. Construction of the Dam itself has been scheduled for completion in October 1968, with the first electric power to be generated in January 1968 and the electric power installations completed by 1971. The installed capacity of 2.1 million kilowatts will triple the 1963 electric power capacity of the country.

The High Dam stretches across the Nile Valley for two miles and will reach 366 feet in height. Its reservoir will reach 300 miles to the south, with depths up to 500 feet, flooding much of Nubia. The huge size of the reservoir insures that it will take many, many years before the settling silt markedly lessens its effectiveness.

The High Dam is first and foremost an electric power project. Its secondary function, however, is of great importance. It will store the water which was lost to the sea during the annual Nile flood, eliminate the fear of flood in low-lying areas, and provide water during seasonal periods of low water and when the flood itself is low. The flood will be controlled to supply proper amounts for the various crops at the right times, and the Dam's tremendous storage capacity will curtail the free flow of water during the flood season, thus lowering the ground water table and reducing the danger of waterlogging of the soil.

The result will be to bring up to one million feddans of new land under irrigation and to permit conversion of some 973,000 feddans to perennial irrigation. Of this total, some 538,000 feddans had been converted by June of 1965.

Since the flooding Nile will no longer rise over the fields bordering the river valley to deposit on them a film of nourishing silt, great amounts of chemical fertilizers must be substituted. Power from the dam will serve the Kima nitrate ammonia fertilizer plant at Aswân. The power of the Dam will come from twelve turbines, each with a capacity of 175,000 kilowatts, and transmission lines will carry the power to Cairo and other industrial centers.

Since no tributary joins the main Nile within Egyptian territory, the country contributes none of its flood water. Thus, international cooperation in the exploitation of the river is vital for Egypt. The Nile Waters Agreement of 1959 between Egypt and the Sudan, which replaced an agreement of 1929 between Egypt and the United Kingdom, allocates to Egypt 55.5 billion cubic meters out of the river's annual average flow of 84 billion cubic meters at Aswân. The Jebel Aulia Dam (1937), located on the White Nile, just south of Khartoum in the Sudan, stores water for Egyptian agriculture, and other dams closer to the sources of the rivers are contemplated. Through these measures, supplemented by the tremendous capacity of the High Dam, annual storage is being effectively replaced by long-term storage of water.

Lift and pump irrigation. Water for the perennial irrigation of small areas, both within the basin compartments and elsewhere where canal irrigation is not provided or cannot be guaranteed throughout the year, is still provided by lifting from wells or canals or from the river itself, by various antiquated hand- or animal-operated devices or by mechanical pumps.

The earliest water-lifting device, the shadoof, unchanged since primitive times, consists of a pole attached near one end to a crossbeam. From the long end of the pole a bucket or water skin is suspended, and to the other end a lump of mud or a stone is attached as a counterweight. The operation consists simply of lowering the bucket into the water, then lifting it with the aid of the counterbalance. Wasteful and tedious, this method allows two men, working from sunrise to sunset, to water only one feddan in four days.

More efficient, though nonetheless time-consuming and wasteful, is the Archimedes' screw, a cylinder about ten feet long, containing a broad-threaded screw. When lowered into the water at an incline, it can be made, by rotating the screw with a crank, to lift water into a trough connected with a field ditch. Two men working in shifts with the device can water only about three-quarters of a feddan a day.

The third device, the *saquia,* is much more elaborate. In its common form, it consists of a vertical wheel with wooden cogs on its rim, meshing with a cogged horizontal wheel to which water buckets are attached. The mechanism is moved by a draft animal (often blindfolded), which walks round and round, hitched to the end of a shaft on the horizontal wheel. As the filled buckets of water rise they tip and empty into a trough.

Some 100,000 acres in the Nile Valley are watered by pumps driven by steam, diesel power, or electricity, most of which are owned and operated either by the government or by the larger landowners. This method is, however, to be found in relatively small areas which border immediately on the river and are too high to be reached by canals except at the height of the flood; it is also found to some extent in both the Nile Valley and the Delta on land usually watered by canals from gravity flow. In the latter areas, pump irrigation is as a rule limited to the early part of the flood, when the demand for water is so great that all canals cannot be supplied with enough to reach all parts of any particular section of the system. Lift and pump irrigation will gradually disappear as perennial irrigation becomes universal.

Drainage. The complicated network of canals and ditches required for successful perennial irrigation demands that close attention be paid to adequate drainage. The soil deposited by the Nile through the ages is a clayey silt which is not sufficiently permeable to allow water to seep down quickly to its lowest layers. In basin irrigation, the problem does not arise, but with the perennial system, unless there is an efficient system of artificial drainage, waterlogging near the surface can occur, with the consequent accumulation at root level of noxious chemicals.

In the middle and upper Nile Valley, drainage has been less difficult than in the Delta, for by the time perennial irrigation was instituted in the Valley, the need for good drainage was well recognized. In the Delta, where drainage of the low-lying land is a problem in any case, difficulties have been enhanced by the fact that canal irrigation was in operation before the important role of drainage was fully realized. Even today, the greater part of the Delta is drained by the wide-ditch method, which is wasteful of land and water, time-consuming, and expensive to maintain. Experiments are now being made with small-bore tiles of porous cement laid below root level and inclining very gradually to the main drains. The initial capital outlay, however, is so great that there is little prospect of any broad development of tile drainage for some time, except perhaps in the government-sponsored reclamation projects.

Land Reclamation

Land reclamation is the responsibility of the Ministry of Agrarian Reform and Land Reclamation. Subordinate authorities are divided up both functionally and, in some cases, geographically. Reclamation is defined as consisting of three stages: plans and surveys, capital improvements, and supervision of initial cultivation. Engineering surveys are made, and plans are formulated, by the Egyptian Public Organization for Land Rehabilitation in most areas and by the Egyptian Public Organization for Desert Rehabilitation in desert areas that depend on underground water. Once plans have been made, the capital improvements are carried out by the Egyptian Public Organization for Land Reclamation until the land is ready for cultivation. The supervision of the initial cultivation is conducted by the Egyptian Public Organization for Planting, Developing, and Exploiting Reclaimed Lands.

Two geographically-oriented coordinating bodies exist. The Tahrir Authority oversees the activities of the various organizations in its territories, and the Authority for Development and Rehabilitation of Bahariya and Faiyûm Governorates does the same job for its area. Fully-developed lands are turned over to the Egyptian Public Organization for Land Reform, which handles the actual redistribution of new land and the initial settlement of the new owners. The organization is further complicated by the participation of foreign aid missions and foreign corporations such as Italconsult, which work as subcontractors. Reclamation is a long and laborious process; in 1965, 478,000 feddans had passed through the "improved" stage and 137,000 feddans were in the process of improvement. Some 482,000 feddans remained in the planting and development stage. As a general rule, reclaimed land does not begin to earn a profit until the fifth year of cultivation. When returns exceed the costs of cultivation by enough to support a family, the land is released to the Land Reform authorities.

Proposals have been made to the government that all reclaimed land be placed under public ownership: a decision on this issue supposedly will be made at the first National Congress of the Arab Socialist Union.

324

The total reclamation program includes constructing irrigation canals and ditches, building drainage ditches, laying irrigation and drainage pipes, building barrages, and constructing houses and other buildings. Within the reclaimed areas, each farmer receives a plot of two to five feddans, a house, cattle, and implements, for which he pays in annual installments, and a loan from the local cooperative. For each area of 4,500 feddans, a school, a medical unit, a veterinary unit, and premises for three cooperatives are provided. For each area of 13,500 feddans, the ministry constructs a market, a mosque, a club, and premises for the town council and for a branch of the Agricultural and Cooperative Credit Bank.

The average cost of rehabilitation of land—from reclamation to the production of crops—amounts to £E 249 per feddan: £E 125 for reclamation, £E 49 for the initial stage of construction, and £E 75 for the period until the first crops are brought in. During the First Five-Year Plan, almost 550,000 feddans were taken up for reclamation, at a cost of about £E 145 million. During 1965-72, 658,000 feddans were scheduled to be recovered (86,000 in FY 1967), of which 90,000 feddans would be outside of the Nile Valley proper. It should be noted that all statistics cited above, and elsewhere in these chapters, should be viewed with some reserve, since official, semiofficial, and general publications issued in Egypt contain conflicting figures.

The pioneer among the reclamation projects was the Tahrir Authority (originally Tahrir province). Situated on the western edge of the desert, it became the training ground for subsequent projects. By 1966, some 143,000 feddans had been improved, and about 90,000 feddans were producing fruit, grain, and vegetables by means of irrigation from the Nile and from subterranean sources. Model farming villages are scattered throughout the area. The project was very costly, so that it may be many years before financial returns equal the expenditures.

The Wadi al-Jadid (New Valley) comprises a vast depression some distance to the west of the Nile and includes the widely-scattered oases of Siwa, Bahariya, Farafra, Dakhla, and Khârga. There are very large tracts of level, sandy soil, and underground water is available, including some artesian wells. Some half century ago, the private Corporation of Western Egypt built a rail line to Khârga and attempted to expand the area under cultivation through wells: the project failed. During the First Five-Year Plan period, some 79,000 feddans in the five oases were reclaimed, and

325

it has been estimated that eventually the depression region could support three million as compared with its present population of some 100,000 people. In such case, electric power eventually might come from the exploitation of the Qattara Depression, situated in the northern section of the general area. The lowest point in this depression is 440 feet below the level of the Mediterranean: it has been proposed that a canal be dug from the sea and power stations installed at the point where the water would plunge into the depression. The cost of this project is estimated at $300 million.

The Wadi al-Natrun is a depression of over 200,000 feddans lying just to the west of the desert road between Cairo and Alexandria. Some 6,000 feddans have already been reclaimed and irrigated by underground water. Other areas in which reclamation is proceeding include the northwest coastal section, the Faiyûm region, the Mariut district, the western edge of the Sinai Peninsula, and the Nubian resettlement zone. Located south of Aswân, the latter, called "Nubaria," now houses some 17,000 families who were moved from their former homes in the region flooded by Lake Nasser.

The National Charter aptly sums up the vast goals of the land reclamation program: "The horizontal expansion of agriculture into arid lands, and the operations for the reclamation of new lands must not halt for a single second. Green areas must expand daily on the banks of the Nile. A day shall come when every drop of the Nile shall be able to flow over its banks and generate an ever-dynamic life."

Productivity and Marketing

Efforts to increase drastically the productivity of Egyptian agriculture face a number of problems. First and foremost, productivity already is very high, making improvement correspondingly difficult. Furthermore, reduction in the acreage of berseem planted in rotation would tend to lower the yield of other crops and place livestock feed in still shorter supply; whereas a reduction in the area under feed grains would result in a decline in the small herd of livestock, and a reduction of the area under cotton is economically unfeasible. Most farm units are too small for efficient use of machinery except through cooperatives.

On the positive side, crop yields may be expected to increase as the result of the ever-expanding local manufacture of fertilizers and of the wider use of pesticides. Scientific seed selection and more careful sorting methods for perishables also can improve the quantity and quality of Egyptian produce. A promising sign is the trend toward high-value products, such as fancy fruits and vegetables. Notable gains also have been made by experimental changes in the planting seasons for certain crops.

Agricultural Finance

In 1902, the Agricultural Bank of Egypt was established, with the participation of the National Bank of Egypt, and the agricultural cooperative movement, initiated in 1909, was able to obtain loans from the bank at 3 per cent as compared with the 5 per cent charged to private individuals. In 1923, the liquidation of this bank began, a process completed in 1936.

In 1923, the first law concerning cooperatives was promulgated, and in 1927 and 1929, additional laws were passed, bringing cooperatives under government supervision and placing £E 350,000 (at that time $1,400,000) at their disposal with the Banque Misr. Under the terms of this loan, cooperatives could borrow at 4 per cent and relend to their members at 7 per cent.

The response was not immediate. The fellah, suspicious of anything in which the government had a hand, would not desert the village usurer until his reticence to participate in a scheme which he did not understand was overcome by the zealous propaganda of the umdahs and other village notables and by the promises of government publicity teams. When it became clear to the fellah that cheap credit was really available, there was a rapid swing in favor of cooperatives, and by 1931 about 540, with a total membership of 53,000, were in operation.

In 1931, the Agricultural Credit Bank (Banque du Crédit Agricole) was established, with a capital of £E 1,000,000, in which the share of the government was 51 per cent. Its policy of advancing money both to individuals and cooperatives hit the cooperatives hard, and their growth had slowed down almost to a standstill by 1939. It was during this period of decline that the big landlords began to join the cooperatives and quickly secured control of them. The peasants, on the other hand, preferred an uncomplicated loan from the new bank, if they could get it, and many of them left the incomprehensible and demanding cooperatives for the simpler if less advantageous procedures of the bank or the moneylender.

During World War II, the cooperatives once again received support and encouragement from the government, and they enjoyed unprecedented prosperity until 1945. Cooperatives were heavily relied upon for the distribution of supplies and fertilizers, and membership increased from 78,000 in 1939 to about 770,000 in 1944. The end of the war brought another decline in interest, and from 1945 until 1953 there was no increase in the membership of the cooperatives and little increase in their transactions. A further reason for the decline was the fact that during the World War II period the cooperatives for agricultural supply and loan were by far the most numerous (1,654 out of 2,004 in 1948), and marketing activities, which would have been of the greatest help to the peasant, were negligible—with only six marketing societies in operation in 1949.

In 1944, the cooperative movement in Egypt was reorganized, and government control was extended. The Agricultural Credit Bank was also reorganized to permit the cooperatives to share more fully in its activities. By 1948, when the name of the bank was changed to Agricultural and Cooperative Credit Bank (Crédit Agricole et Coopératif), it had a capital of £E 1,500,000, of which £E 250,000 was newly subscribed by rural and consumers cooperatives.

After 1952, the bank offered special privileges to members of the multi-purpose cooperatives, while all beneficiaries of the Agrarian Reform Law were obligatory members of these cooperatives. The Agricultural and Cooperative Credit Bank was completely nationalized in 1961, and in the same year, Presidential Decree No. 1250 stipulated that the bank was not to charge any interest on its loans. Later on, credit was extended exclusively to the cooperatives.

In 1964, the bank was transformed into the Egyptian Public Organization for Agricultural and Cooperative Credit, and the new organization was charged with central planning in these fields. At the same time a number of rural banks which had been established by the Agricultural and Cooperative Credit Bank were transformed into independent banks, with a Provincial Agricultural Credit Bank in each governorate.

A law of July 1956 amended the one on cooperatives passed in 1944 and placed them under the Egyptian General Agricultural Cooperative Organization. By 1964, there were some 4,000 local co-

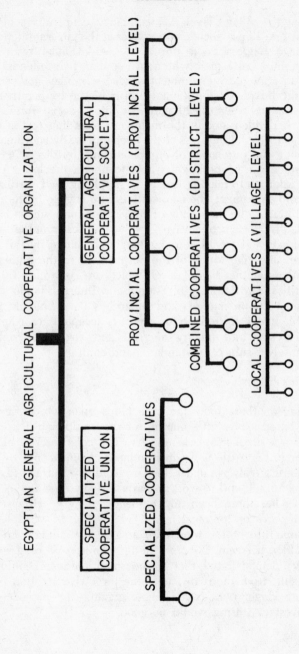

Source: Hassan Abdallah, *U.A.R. Agriculture*

operatives at the village level, 127 combined cooperatives at the district level, and 19 provincial cooperatives at the governorate level.

Each village cooperative is run by a board. Four-fifths of its membership must be farmers who own less than five feddans, and it includes an appointed government official who may not be dismissed by the board. Of the annual profits of the cooperative, 25 per cent goes into reserves, 20 per cent into a social fund, and 55 per cent is divided among the members, according to the contribution of each to the business of the cooperative. By coordinating and combining the purchases of equipment and fertilizers needed by each farmer, the cooperative is able to obtain the lower price per unit. In addition to making loans and supplying seed, fertilizers, pesticides, and equipment, the cooperatives also engage in the marketing of produce. The marketing of rice, cotton, and onions is entirely handled by these cooperatives. Produce moves from the farms by pack animals and trucks, and for longer distances, by rail and by barges on the Nile. Much of the output goes to the numerous country markets at the district level, which are controlled by the local authorities. The Ministry of Supply and Internal Trade operates eight major grain markets and supervises the wholesale fruit and vegetable markets. Produce for export is accepted according to standards for size and quality at fruit and vegetable packing houses, themselves subject to standards and controls.

Livestock

Concentration on those food and cash crops upon which Egypt's economy is based leaves little margin for the production of fodder for more than a small livestock industry. The chief interest of the small farmer in his cattle is as draft animals. Animals sold by the farmer for meat are always males, the cows and cow buffaloes being kept to provide milk and to work in harness. Only on a few of the larger estates has there been any tendency to raise cattle solely for dairy purposes or for meat.

As it is, one-fifth of the total crop area is put annually to the principal fodder, berseem. Government agronomists and progressive farmers have demonstrated that if the small producer could be induced to shift from the two-year to the three-year rotation plan, thus allowing longer periods for fallow grazing, the prospects of increased livestock raising would be good.

The table below gives the approximate number of the various livestock species over a 25-year period. Progressive increases are shown, but these have barely kept pace with the extension of total acreage resulting from irrigation projects, and they have not meant any significant increase in the amount of meat available for human consumption.

LIVESTOCK IN EGYPT
(*in thousands*)

	1927	1937	1947	1957	1962
Cattle	739	983	1,321	1,390	1,609
Buffaloes	757	958	1,240	1,395	1,579
Donkeys	570	1,142	1,125	950	1,027
Camels	179	154	196	157	n.a.
Horses	37	31	27	45	49
Mules	21	22	12	11	11
Sheep	1,232	1,918	1,875	1,259	1,596
Goats	622	1,310	1,475	723	848
Pigs	20	36	50	17	18
Total	4,177	6,554	7,321	5,947	6,797

Source: Egyptian National Census, 1947, and Food and Agricultural Organization Yearbooks.

The water buffalo is the most popular farm animal. Hardy, resistant to disease, tolerant of the climate, and docile, it works well at the plow or the water wheel. It has greater endurance than the cow and gives more and richer milk. The raising of sheep and goats is a secondary source of wool, meat, and milk to the small farmer, and, though some flocks are run on scientific lines on the larger farms, most of Egypt's sheep live *au pair* with peasant families. The few nomads left in Egypt have the largest flocks (some 10 per cent of the total).

The sheep are of the fat-tailed type: their wool is not of high quality and is generally used for making carpets and coarse cloth. Comparatively few pigs are raised, and these are consumed exclusively by the Coptic and European elements of the population, since Islam forbids the raising as well as the consumption of pork. Even so, the local supply is insufficient, and a fair amount of preserved and processed pork is imported. The donkey, used both as a mount and a carrier of produce, is Egypt's principal beast of

331

burden. Seen in thousands, it is the fellah's inseparable companion. The camel, though used to some extent as a draft animal, is really a desert creature, none too well suited to conditions in the Delta. As a carrier, the camel is giving way to the truck, but the camel population of the Delta and the Valley remains around 200,000. There are few horses and mules outside the urban centers, where they are mainly used for heavy carting. They, too, are being used less frequently than formerly, and their disappearance as carriers is only a matter of time.

The main source of Egypt's limited domestic meat supply consists of surplus cattle and buffaloes, some camels, and sheep raised for the purpose, which animals are slaughtered by the peasants or sold on the hoof at village markets. Some meat is imported, but its consumption is confined to the wealthier elements. Domestic dairy products are consumed in the rural areas, and city requirements are met from imports. In only a few districts are there creameries and cheese factories to cater to the urban consumer. The average production of buffalo, cow, and goat milk is about 1.6 million tons. Of this, more than half is made into butter, about 30 per cent into cheese, and only 10 per cent is consumed as fresh milk. Egyptian buffalo milk has a butterfat content of 6 to 8 per cent, or more than twice that of American cow milk. Poultry is everywhere underfoot and overhead in the villages and countryside. Chickens, geese, ducks, turkeys, and pigeons have the run of the farmyards, eating what they can pick up for themselves. As a result, they tend to be stringy and tough, and eggs are small and far from abundant. Chickens far outnumber all other types of poultry, and serious efforts are being made to improve the breed through the importation of foreign stock.

Forests

There are no natural forests in Egypt. Stress is placed on growing timber trees along the edges of the many thousand kilometers of canals, drainage ditches, and roads. Casuarina, eucalyptus, poplar, acacia, and other varieties are planted, with saplings supplied, in part, by the Ministry of Agriculture. Because of the scanty supply of wood, paper and cardboard are manufactured from local supplies of rice straw, cotton stocks, and sugarcane pulp and also from imported wood pulp.

332

Fisheries

Egypt's fisheries employ some 300,000 individuals, and the annual yield is about 155,000 tons. About 55 per cent of the fish come from the Mediterranean and the Red Sea, 32 per cent from the lakes in the Delta and from the Faiyûm areas, and the remainder from the Nile. Consumption averages about 11 pounds per person a year, which is only one-third of the world average. Consumption is confined principally to the areas immediately proximate to the fishing grounds, since refrigeration capacity is very limited. There is an active sardine canning industry, and frozen shrimp and natural sponges both are fairly important export items.

The lakes in the Delta are mostly salt, and the fishermen there are professionals. The fellahin do not fish to any extent, nor do they eat much fish. There are many wholesome varieties of fish in the country, and in view of the generally low protein intake of the average Egyptian, attempts are being made to encourage fish consumption and to increase availability by various fishing, restocking, and hatchery projects.

Income from Agriculture

According to Egyptian agricultural officials, the total value of agricultural production reached £E 707.3 million in the year ending June 30, 1966, compared to £E 581.6 at the beginning of the Five-Year Plan. Net income from agriculture, after deducting costs of production, totaled £E 490 million—an increase of £E 85 million over the base year of the plan. The number of wage earners increased 12.5 per cent, to about 3.6 million workers; the total wage bill, on the other hand, soared by 70.4 per cent.

CHAPTER *19*

Resources and Industry

THE NASSER GOVERNMENT HAS WROUGHT MANY CHANGES in the size, composition, and organization of the relatively good industrial base inherited from the Farouk regime. At the time of the Revolution, Egypt was much more advanced economically than any other country on the African continent except the Union of South Africa. By 1952, there were more than 700 manufacturing and mining establishments, each employing more than 50 persons. These concerns contributed about 10 per cent of the GDP and employed about 4 per cent of the working population. In addition, there were some 2,730 small firms (of 10-50 workers). The principal industries were food processing, cotton textiles, tobacco, petroleum, and chemicals. The country had two oil refineries, three cement factories, two fertilizer plants, a small paper industry, three small steel plants based on scrap, and a moderately diversified chemical industry.

Industrial production, measured in current value of output, is today almost quadruple the 1952 level and has been increasing about 8 per cent annually over the past few years. During the First Plan period, output increased over 75 per cent, and the rate of increase exceeded 10 per cent annually. In some industries, notably chemicals and electric power, the pace was even more rapid. Some of the value increase, however, stems from higher unit prices rather than from increased quantity of output. Value added has risen less rapidly than total value of output, reflecting rising costs of raw materials and components. In a number of fields, growth since the 1961 nationalizations has lagged behind the 1952-61 rate of increase. Despite obvious progress, industry suffers acutely from mismanagement, bureaucratic chaos, shortage of skilled workers, excessive employment at government urging, and lack of raw materials and spare parts.

Growth has been based both on accelerated exploitation of domestic natural resources and greatly increased investment of both domestic and foreign capital. Foreign funds, except for investment in the petroleum sector, have come almost entirely from government-to-government loans, exacerbating the tendency toward centralized control of industry. And the availability of heavy capital goods from foreign countries, especially from those in Eastern Europe, has permitted Egyptian planners to indulge their leanings toward highly sophisticated mechanical industries at the expense of agriculture-related industry.

Spinning and weaving and food processing, which utilize primarily Egyptian agricultural products, remain far and away the major industrial sectors, but the engineering and electrical equipment factories and a number of other industrial establishments are heavy users of imported components and raw materials. In the headlong drive for industrialization and development, industries that are not agriculture-based often have glamour and appeal out of all proportion to their economic justification. This has been true in Egypt, where agricultural conditions give the country a tremendous competitive advantage in fields that either consume farm produce or provide the materials needed by agriculture. Favoritism toward relatively heavy industry probably has retarded industrial growth and certainly has aggravated Egypt's foreign exchange difficulties. With the realities of the situation forced to their attention in the aftermath of the 1967 war with Israel, Egyptian policymakers finally seem to be listening to Egyptian economic planners on this score. Investment plans for 1968 devote proportionately more attention to food processing, fertilizer production, and the manufacture of agricultural implements than has been true in the past. Whether the trend will continue when (and if) the foreign exchange situation becomes less stringent is another matter.

Organization of Industry

Since 1952, the government has acquired ownership of as much as 90 per cent of the basic means of industrial production. Within all fields of production, numerous state-owned industries are grouped within a number of Public Organizations. In the area of industrial production may be found the Egyptian Public Organization for Chemical Industries, the Egyptian Public Organization for Food Industries, the Egyptian Public Organization for Spinning and Weaving, the Egyptian Public Organization for Petroleum, the

335

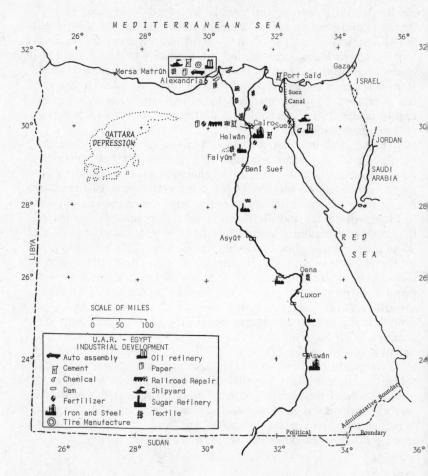

Egyptian Public Organization for Building Materials and Ceramics, the Egyptian Public Organization for Military Factories (with plants that produce primarily civilian consumer durables), the Egyptian Public Organization for Cooperative Production and Small Industries, and others too numerous to mention. An Egyptian Public Organization for Iron and Steel Industries was established in January 1967 to bring under one agency all the major production units for iron and steel and the supplier industries for iron ore, limestone, dolomite, and coke. Each Organization oversees a number of plants of diverse size and ownership. For example, in 1966, the Egyptian Public Organization for Food Industries controlled 29 companies producing foodstuffs, soap, cigarettes, ammonia, and beverages. It included local bottling plants for Coca Cola and Pepsi Cola, as well as canneries and sugar refineries. Many of these units have some substantial, but unknown, degree of private ownership. The Chemical Organization oversaw the activities of 27 companies producing plastics, pencils, paint, paper, and rubber products, as well as items more usually included in a definition of chemicals. Some 30 plants and mills came under the Egyptian Public Organization for Spinning and Weaving. As can be imagined, the structure of these numerous holding corporations and their far more numerous companies, subsidiaries, and affiliates has resulted in an expanding bureaucracy, whose individual members are often more concerned with advancing their own status than with devotion to the socialist state. The individual company manager, who may be running the same plant he ran under the private enterprise system, now finds himself increasingly frustrated by the echelons and echelons of civil servants through whom he must filter his requests before he can make and implement even relatively minor decisions.

The 1961 industrial census, taken at about the time that most industry was nationalized, recorded 884 establishments with over 50 employees and 3,172 smaller firms; both totals undoubtedly have risen substantially since that time. The 4,056 recorded enterprises employed 400,000 persons—over 6 per cent of the labor force. Since industrial employment figures for 1960 totaled 602,000 workers, some 200,000 must have been employed in very small plants, cotton gins, and handicrafts. Another 12,000 or so were employed in electricity. An integrated steel mill had been added to the pre-revolutionary industrial base, along with many metal fabricating plants (e.g. plants that produced steel castings, forgings and pipes, aluminum cable, and copper foil); plus one petroleum refinery, three motor vehicle assembly plants, many consumer durables factories, and several new textile mills and chemical plants. Many of the plants that existed in 1952 were greatly expanded by 1961.

According to Egyptian statements, 1,440 industrial projects were scheduled to be completed during the First Plan. Six months before the end of the plan period, 786 had been completed, and 41 had reached the "running-in" stage. Another 121 were under construction, and 126 had been postponed or canceled. The bulk of the

337

new industry is centered in Hilwân and the other suburbs of Cairo and near Alexandria. Each of these locations provides a favorable combination of transportation, electric power, labor force, and proximity to large domestic markets. Alexandria, along with Suez, Port Said, and Ismailia, also has benefited from the availability of port facilities for ready export. Considerable new activity also is arising around Aswân in anticipation of the power output of the new High Dam.

By 1965, the industrial sector (broadly defined to include manufacturing, mining, petroleum, and electric energy) employed some 843,000 workers and produced goods valued at £E 1,662.7 million (see Table 9). Actual investment in industry and electricity totaled £E 516.5 million during the First Plan period. In that same time span, aggregate industrial wages rose from £E 91.2 million to £E 154.3 million, and the average wage rose from about £E 148 to almost £E 183 per annum. This 24 per cent wage boost, however, was accompanied by an increase of only about 10 per cent in productivity per worker.

In the past, several factors had impeded Egypt's industrial development. Until 1933, tariffs were fixed by international convention at only 8 per cent of the value of the imported item, affording no protection for domestic industry from foreign competition. Economic matters were handled largely by British civil servants, who held an ingrained belief that government had no proper role to play in industry. In addition, the British were naturally more concerned with Egypt's role as a supplier of raw materials and a market for British finished goods than with building a healthy, self-sufficient economy. Dependence on foreign capital for most investment hampered diversification, because of the emphasis on low-risk enterprises, such as food processing. The dominance of the landowning class in Egyptian government circles, and the consequent legislative favoritism accorded the producers of raw agricultural goods, limited industrial development by focusing attention on basic produce rather than processing and the manufacture of finished goods.

In addition, what might be called "the failure of entrepreneurship"—the absence of an industrial middle class with a tradition of modern business and industrial techniques—hampered early development. The Land Reform Law of September 1952 and its subsequent revisions were designed to channel large-scale private investment into industry. Instead, however, private funds were devoted largely to real estate speculation, and it soon became clear that private capital and savings could provide only a minute portion of the tremendous cost of the industrial programs considered necessary by the state. Few members of the former landed aristocracy were willing to take an active role, either financially or managerially, in activities they saw as only a variation on peasant handicrafts.

Raw Materials

Egypt's most important mineral resource is petroleum. From a net oil importing country, Egypt is well on its way to becoming a net exporter, while meeting its own ever-increasing demand for oil and oil products. Prior to World War II, the exploitation of Egyptian oil resources by foreign companies was subject to severe pressures. Legislation during the years preceding the abdication of King Farouk raised oil royalties to a level which ultimately proved to be prohibitive, discriminated against foreign companies in regard to licenses, and limited the companies' power with respect to control of operations and the transfer of profits. So restrictive were the conditions during this period that the major foreign companies refused to accept them. Standard Oil of New Jersey abandoned its licenses and withdrew from Egypt, and Socony Vacuum and Anglo-Egyptian Oil suspended all exploration operations.

Legislation passed after July 1952, however, in effect canceled earlier legislation regulating foreign business and created conditions more favorable to foreign investment. The Mines and Quarries Law No. 66 of February 1953 opened oil concessions to foreign firms on an equal footing with Egyptians and liberalized existing provisions relating to profit transfers. The new policy brought about a revival and expansion of both foreign and domestic activity.

The exploration, production, refining, and marketing aspects of oil are supervised by the Egyptian Public Organization for Petroleum. This organization controls eight domestic firms, including the Egyptian General Petroleum Company (EGPC), the Al-Nasr Petroleum Company, the Eastern Petroleum Company, and the Suez Petroleum Refining Company. Most are wholly state owned, but Eastern Petroleum is a joint venture of the EGPC and ENI (Ente Nazionale Idrocarburi) of Italy. Al-Nasr and EGPC also participate with foreign companies in the development and exploitation of new fields.

339

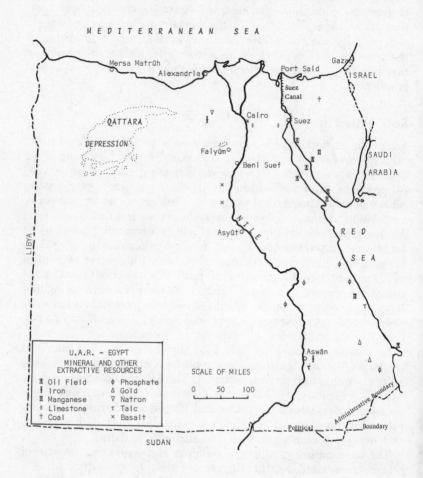

Crude oil production began in 1910, with total output of only 27,000 barrels; it has climbed fairly steadily, totaling 6.3 million tons in 1965. Especially noteworthy increases have occurred in the 1960s. It was expected that the slight decrease in 1966, stemming from depletion of older fields, would be reversed in 1967 through the exploitation of new fields in the Gulf of Suez.

CRUDE OIL PRODUCTION
(*in million tons*)

Year	
1952	2.6
1960	3.6
1961	4.2
1962	5.1
1963	6.2
1964	6.3
1965	6.3
1966	6.1
1970 forecast by UAR:	30.0

The companies producing crude oil through 1966 were: (1) Eastern Petroleum Company of Egypt, jointly owned by the EGPC and the International Egyptian Oil Company (a subsidiary of ENI, the Italian state agency) (2) General Petroleum Company, wholly owned by EGPC (3) Al-Nasr Petroleum Company, 14 per cent private and 86 per cent state owned (including 29.5 per cent previously owned by Shell Oil and British Petroleum, which were nationalized in 1964); and (4) Al-Nasr and Mobil Oil Egypt operating together, with minority participation by Mobil, which is wholly owned by the Socony Mobil Oil Company of the United States. Eastern Petroleum Company controls six fields, including the three that have been the largest producers in recent years, all in the Gulf of Suez area. Al-Nasr/Mobil operate three fields in Sinai; Al-Nasr itself and EGPC have fields on the western side of the Gulf of Suez. The fields under Israeli control as a result of the June 1967 war were those of Eastern and the Al-Nasr/Mobil combine. They had accounted for roughly two-thirds of Egypt's total crude production in 1966.

The Gulf of Suez Petroleum Company (GUPCO) began producing in April 1967. It is jointly owned by EGPC and Pan American Oil, which is a subsidiary of Standard Oil of Indiana. Pan American was awarded a 2,500 square mile concession in the Gulf of Suez area in 1963, and by 1965 had made a major discovery offshore, about 150 miles south of Suez. GUPCO was established

341

to exploit this Morgan (or Al-Murjan) field and began producing at the rate of about 60,000 barrels per day, reaching 80,000 barrels by the middle of the year. Production apparently continued throughout the one-week war, with crude being piped to the western shore of the Gulf. Plans call for an output of at least 150,000 barrels per day by 1968 and that output may be doubled by 1970. Pan American also has a 27,400 square mile concession in the Western Desert that has not yet proved out.

The Western Desert Producing Company (WEPCO) is scheduled to begin producing from its 36,000 square mile concession in the Western Desert, just south of the World War II battlefield of Al-Alamein, in January 1968. Like GUPCO, it has an American partner—the Phillips Petroleum Company. Although indications are very favorable, the size of the field has not yet been ascertained, and initial production targets have been set at about 50,000 barrels per day. If ENI is successful in its new 10,500 square mile concession area in the Delta and Red Sea, exploitation will be handled by the existing joint company, Eastern.

The three foreign companies are obligated to invest $67 million on exploration in the period (varying from 9 to 12 years) following their receipt of concessions in 1963. As of 1963, total capitalization of the Egyptian petroleum industry was estimated at $246 million—of which 16.2 per cent was foreign investment.

Two refineries have been in operation since 1922, and a third was added in 1956. All have been expanded since they were built. Combined output capacity in April 1965 totaled about 7.6 million tons per year—double the 1956 figure. Throughput has risen dramatically, from 2.5 million tons in 1952 to 3.8 million tons in 1960 and 8.3 million tons in 1965. The oil refineries are among the most efficient establishments in Egypt, usually operating at over 98 per cent of capacity. The country is self-sufficient in all refined products except lubricants and some special fuels. Imported refined products accounted for less than 2 per cent of total supply in 1965. Plans call for capacity of 13 million tons by 1972.

The Al-Nasr Petroleum Company refinery in Suez is the oldest and largest in Egypt. When nationalized in 1961, its capacity was 3 million tons per year, which had been increased to 3.85 million tons by 1965 and was scheduled to reach about 5 million tons by 1968. The nearby refinery of the Suez Oil Processing Company, originally the only state-owned refinery, has a capacity of 2.65 million tons; it is a subsidiary of EGPC. Vacuum distillation units are in operation at both refineries in Suez; a thermal cracking unit is used at Al-Nasr, which also has a heavy lube oil plant. Original construction at the Alexandria Petroleum Company in the Alexandrian suburb of Mex (or Al-Maks) was completed in 1956; capacity was scheduled to reach 2.2 million tons in 1967. The Mex facility was built to run imported crude, and still refines only a small proportion of domestic crude. The 13 per cent share originally owned by California Texas Oil Corporation was purchased by EGPC in 1961, but there is still some cooperative and private ownership.

The combined output of the three refineries in 1965 is shown below, in thousands of tons:

Motor gasoline	855
Kerosene and turbine oil	888
Distillate fuel oil	943
Diesel oil	290
Residual fuel oil	4,691
Asphalt and other	192
Total	7,859

Total production of natural gas probably comes to about 7 billion cubic feet. Small amounts are used in a new power plant near the eastern shore fields along the Gulf, where it is produced, but most is flared or reused in the production process.

Crude oil is delivered to the refineries by tankers. Offshore fields are connected to shipping terminals along the coast of the Gulf, on both east and west. Product pipelines convey refined products from Suez to the Cairo/Hilwân area and from Alexandria to the Delta. Other transport is handled by river barge and by truck.

Egypt's mineral industry, aside from petroleum, is not a significant contributor to the economy, and the trend appears to be toward a declining role. Total production of unprocessed minerals, including construction materials, accounts for less than 1 per cent of the GDP. The more common metallic and nonmetallic materials are present in quantities such that Egypt could become largely self-sufficient as a mineral producer. At present, however, most proved and exploitable reserves have not been developed sufficiently to meet local needs. The industry suffers from insufficient capital and a dearth of exploration and research activities. Here, again, the desire to be modern and to manufacture probably has

343

mitigated against the investment of funds in such prosaic activities as removing ores from the ground.

Although Egypt remained a net exporter of minerals, at least until 1965, sales have declined while imports have risen. The export balance was only $2 million in 1964, compared to $7 million in 1963. Data for 1965 seem to indicate net imports, but they may not be complete. Iron, coal, and cement have enjoyed a relatively favorable position in the allocation of investment, because they are essential to expansion of the domestic economy, but exploration—requiring little hard currency outlay—forms the bulk of the activity in other minerals. Total investment in minerals during the First Plan amounted to only about $9 million, about 5 per cent of total investment in industry during the period.

Phosphates rank first among the exploited mineral resources. Mining is carried on at two locations along the Red Sea coast, primarily for the export market. Areas near the Nile between Isna and Idfu provide most of the raw material for domestic industries. The largest proved reserves, near the Dakhla and Khârga oases in the Western Desert, are not exploited because of transportation difficulties. In 1965, production totaled 594,000 tons—little larger than the 1952 output of 527,000 tons, and substantially below the levels of the previous three years. Total production of selected minerals is shown in the table below. Exports have been hampered by increased competition for world markets and by rising costs of production in Egypt, while domestic requirements also are rising as local facilities for the production of phosphate fertilizers and insecticides are being established and expanded.

PRODUCTION OF SELECTED MINERALS 1952, 1961, 1964, 1965
(*in tons*)

	1952	1961	1964	1965
Phosphates	527,204	626,530	613,237	593,699
Iron ore	....	422,145	447,213	507,010
Manganese	191,008	278,447	328,011	182,145
Kaolin	....	27,180	62,796	42,275
Talc and steatite	4,600	5,956	16,821	39,628
Asbestos	60	230	1,578	2,926
Salt	498,393	517,220	674,555	494,121
Sodium nitrate (natron)	3,050	3,190	4,652	4,218

Source: *Federation of Industries Yearbooks.*

Iron ore is found to the east of Aswân, in Sinai, and in the Western Desert. Proven reserves are over 225 million tons, of which 150 million are relatively low-grade deposits near Aswân. Production rose fairly steadily to the 1965 level of 507,000 tons. Domestic ores are used in the manufacture of iron and steel at Hilwân, but output is insufficient to supply local needs, and expansion of the Hilwân plant will further increase the gap unless new deposits can be exploited in the near future. Known deposits at the Baharìya Oasis in the Western Desert contain a higher percentage of iron and a much lower percentage of silicon than the Aswân ores, but their exploitation awaits long-planned but uninitiated construction of a railroad across the desert—a project that presents formidable technical problems.

Coal deposits have been identified in the al-Maghara district of Sinai, in a layer two meters thick at depths of between 300 and 400 meters, and mining was scheduled to begin in 1967.

Manganese almost equaled phosphates in value terms in 1964, but output dropped 45 per cent in 1965. Local consumption, in a newly-built ferro-manganese plant, is small, and most production is for export. With world prices falling, export earnings dropped more than 60 per cent between 1965 and 1966. Mines are located in Sinai and in the Eastern Desert, and most of the ores are of low grade.

Egypt's salt industry supplies all of the country's requirements and provides a surplus for export. The largest operations are at Port Said and nearby Port Fuad, but salt pans also are found as far east as Alexandria. Total 1965 output of 494,000 tons was valued at about $3 million; exports earned about $768,000. The industry dates back to ancient times and still uses solar evaporation of Mediterranean water. Seawater is channeled inland on the high tide, undergoes preliminary evaporation in basins, and then is gradually released into evaporating pans. Flooding continues for about eight months and builds a salt layer about eight inches deep. The remaining four months of the year are devoted to harvesting, purification, packaging, and shipping operations. Japan traditionally has been the major buyer; other substantial purchases have been made by Yugoslavia, Guinea, and the United States.

Sulphur is mined in the Ras Jamsah area at the south end of the Gulf of Suez and is recovered as a by-product from the petroleum refinery in Suez. Open-pit mining of sulphur crystals began in 1955, when total output amounted to 615 tons. A full-scale sulphur flotation plant at Ras Jamsah was completed in 1960, with an annual capacity of 60,000 tons. Mine output reached 45,000 tons in 1961, dropped off to 31,000 tons in 1962, and dropped to only 4,750 tons in 1963. The reason for the sudden decrease is not clear, but production apparently ceased entirely in 1964 and has not been resumed. Production of petroleum by-product sulphur has remained in the neighborhood of 2,500 tons per year since 1959. The fertilizer industry is the largest single consumer of sulphur, using it to produce sulphuric acid required in the manufacture of superphosphate fertilizers. Up to 85 per cent of domestic requirements are fulfilled from imports of pyrite, elemental sulphur, and sulphuric acid.

Production of milled talc and block steatite has climbed steadily, and the 1965 output was almost 40,000 tons, compared to less than 6,000 tons in 1961. Deposits of asbestos are extensive in the Eastern Desert, and production has reached 3,000 tons. Various products such as ilmanite, a source of titanium oxide; magnetite; zirconium; and monazite, a source of thorium, are recovered from the so-called "black sands," which are brought down by the Nile and then washed back ashore on the Mediterranean coast.

Quarry products exceed minerals in value and provide the country with its domestic needs and an export surplus. Some 3 million cubic meters of limestone—used in the manufacture of steel, fertilizers, cement, and lime—are lifted annually. Sandstone quarries yielded 221,000 cubic meters in 1965. Gypsum is found at many sites, and most of the annual production (220,000 cubic meters in 1965) is exported. Dolomite, granite, and marble are abundant, as are deposits of clay (kaolin), used in pottery and in the manufacture of numerous other items.

Food Processing

The processing of food products comes under the Egyptian Public Organization for Food Industries, which directs some 30 large companies. The output of the food industries was valued at £E 284.1 million in fiscal 1965, compared to £E 122.3 million in 1952.

Sugar production typifies the monopolistic form of recent industrial development. Raw sugar production averages about 400,000 tons. Two firms, the Egyptian Sugar and Distillation Company and the Al-Nasr Sugar Manufacturing Company, control all stages of the refining process. Well over 27,000 workers are employed in a refinery at Hawamdieh, the largest in the world, and in crushing plants along the Nile at Kous, Idfu, Kom Ombo, Armant, and several other locations. One firm also owns the country's major alcohol plant, at Tourah. Only the molasses industry is outside this two-firm complex. The refinery industry, which processes both domestic and imported sugar, is quite efficient and turns out a relatively inexpensive product, which is sold to the Ministry of Supply. The Ministry, in turn, sells sugar at a very large profit, which covers more than half the cost of maintaining low prices for other consumption items such as wheat and soap.

Other food-processing industries include grain milling and rice bleaching; vegetable, fruit, fish and meat canning; macaroni and biscuit production; dehydration of onions and garlic; and the manufacture of starch, glucose, and oils for cooking and for soap manufacture. Other products include dried and frozen meats, food pastes, malt, ammonia, yeast, vinegar, fruit juices, and cigarettes. Beer is manufactured from local barley, with part of the malt and all of the hops imported. Limited quantities of various wines are produced, and three large factories cater to the local demand for soft drinks.

Output of the foodstuffs industries has been greatly diversified since 1952. Frozen and canned shrimp, canned sardines, pasteurized milk, rice bran oil, and acetic acid are among the new products. Output of almost all these items has increased substantially. In value terms, the major items are tobacco products (all processed from imported tobacco), cheese, cotton seed oil, vegetable oil, margarine, sugar, white rice, and bottled soda water. One of the major obstacles confronting the food industries as a whole is the lack of adequate refrigeration facilities. Practically all of the present refrigeration capacity is located in Cairo, Alexandria, Port Said, and the larger towns. In the rural areas, refrigeration is practically unknown.

Manufacturing

Textile manufacturing comes under the Ministry of Industry, which supervises the Egyptian Public Organization for Spinning and Weaving. More than 30 companies are directed by this organization. In terms of the value of production and the number of workers employed, textile manufacturing is Egypt's largest industry. The value of the finished products was £E 362 million in 1965 as compared with £E 85 million in 1952 (see Table 9). Exports were valued at £E 37 million, and imports at only £E 13 million: the value of exports is increasing rapidly. About a fourth of the industrial labor force is currently occupied in various phases of textile production. Although hand looms are found everywhere in Egypt, there is an increasing concentration on mechanized spinning and weaving at the textile centers of Mahalla al-Kubra, Damanhûr, Damietta, Tanta, Cairo, and Alexandria. Cotton yarn and cotton textiles account for nearly 70 per cent of production by value. In descending order come wool yarn and textiles, silk textiles, artificial fiber textiles, blankets and carpets, and jute textiles. Raw jute, largely imported from Pakistan, is manufactured into burlap and twine in two factories. The hosiery and knitwear industry has developed very rapidly, and now meets almost the country's total requirements.

Paper is produced by six companies—all but one in Alexandria—using rice straw, sugarcane pulp, waste paper, and imported wood pulp as the basic raw materials. Types include cardboard, wrapping paper, and writing paper. The major output of the leather industry is footwear, but it also turns out belts, bags, and gloves. Two firms produce cigarettes and other tobacco products. While the supply meets local demand, and Egyptian cigarettes are widely exported, all of the raw tobacco must be imported. Over 13,000 million cigarettes are manufactured annually.

The Egyptian Public Organization for Chemical Industries, under the Ministry of Industry, supervises 27 companies, and the Egyptian Public Organization for Drugs, Chemicals, and Medical Supplies has an additional 10 companies. The chemical and pharmaceutical industry has been registering the greatest gains in the manufacturing field. Its growth appears to have been maintained in the past several years, while many other economic sectors were falling behind their 1952-61 pace. Egypt's highly intensive agriculture depends on the availability of fertilizer. Domestic production doubled in the 1960-64 period, but declining imports and growing requirements have perpetuated shortages. For 1963, demand (optimum use per cropped acre) was estimated at almost 2.1 million tons; local production provided 809,000 tons and imports 409,000 tons, leaving a shortfall of about 850,000 tons. The industry set new records in 1964, however, producing a total of 1,043,000 tons—a 29 per cent increase in volume. The major producing plants are at Hilwân, Aswân, and Suez. Ammonium nitrate, calcium nitrate, and superphosphates are produced. Imports in 1964 also increased, and total consumption amounted to almost 1.5 million tons, falling short of the estimated demand by about 700,000 tons. Newspaper reports claim total production of 1.2 million tons. Development plans call for greater emphasis on high-concentration products and for a total domestic output of 4.2 million tons per year by 1972.

Almost all basic chemicals have registered annual gains. In 1964, 194,228 tons of sulphuric acid were produced, compared to 113,020 tons in 1963. The 70 per cent increase was attributable primarily to production from a new unit. Hydrochloric acid output doubled in 1964, to 4,000 tons, the increase coming from a new unit at the Kima fertilizer plant. Output of carbon disulphide, produced largely by Misr Rayon for its own use, rose from 2,800 tons in 1963 to 3,300 tons in 1965; glycerine output rose from 4,100 tons in 1963 to 4,500 tons in 1964; nitric acid production increased from 286,000 tons in 1963 to 448,000 tons in 1965. Chlorine and caustic soda followed the general trend; chlorine output rose from 4,000 tons in 1963 to 4,970 tons in 1965, and production of caustic soda increased from 17,556 tons to 18,861 tons.

The pharmaceutical industry, under the supervision of the Egyptian Public Organization for Drugs, Chemicals, and Medical Supplies, continues to be one of the better performers. Production has increased consistently, reaching a total value figure of £E 22 million in 1965—an increase of almost 40 per cent in one year. Diversification also has been striking. In 1952, 342 products in 10 major groupings were produced; in 1965, there were 1,369 products in 34 classifications. Local production now covers about 70 per cent of total consumption, compared to 10 per cent in 1952, and consumption stands at more than 6 times the 1952 level. Foreign capital participation in drug manufacturing is unusually large for present-day Egypt. All distribution is carried out by Egyptian government firms, but one American firm and two Western European firms also maintain manufacturing facilities. Also included in the "chemical" category are a number of loosely-related industries, such as glass, plastics, tires, and matches. Gains in these fields have not been as spectacular as in chemicals and medicinal preparations, but most have made substantial progress.

The Egyptian Iron and Steel Company—the white elephant of Egyptian industry—is located on a 1,000 acre tract at Hilwân, some 15 miles south of Cairo. The mill initially was constructed between 1955 and 1958 by a West German firm, at a cost of £E 27 million. Equipment from other suppliers has been added since that time. Production has never reached 200,000 tons of steel, although rated capacity is 315,000 tons, and the mill employs about 10,000 workers. All the difficulties of Egyptian industry are here gathered under one group of roofs. The Aswân iron ore used as an input is poor. High cost coking coal must be imported. Quality control is almost nonexistent; hot steel billets are a safety hazard at every turn; faulty products litter the premises. Despite all this, the mill has been due for expansion, although plans have repeatedly been scaled down in size and postponed in time. The USSR agreed to provide some £E 70 million in credit for the facilities needed to increase output to 1.2 million tons of steel; the original target date of 1970 has been postponed, at least until 1973. Following the Israeli war, the steel project was the one major industrial target that was publicly stricken from the development plan for the foreseeable future.

Hilwân is also the site of several of the plants operated by the Egyptian Public Organization for Military Factories. These plants produce largely consumer durables and an assortment of metal sheets, pipes, and wires. They include the Hilwân Nonferrous Metals and Military Products Company, which turns out aluminum and copper products. The Hilwân Company for Military and Commercial Cast Iron Equipment produces such items as heavy castings, diesel engines, and sewing machines.

Other factories turn out an ever-increasing range of finished metal products, almost too diverse to enumerate. Many fall under the Egyptian General Organization for Engineering Industries, supervised by the Ministry of Industry, which oversees 21 companies. Included are factories assembling motor vehicles and producing diesel engines, motorcycles, bicycles, weaving equipment, batteries, transistors, steam equipment, precision parts, transformers, electric motors and fans, meters, radios, television sets, refrigerators, stoves, water pumps, telephones, and wood products. Nearly all the factories making such products have been constructed since 1952, and semiofficial statements point out that Egypt now manufactures 3,000 different articles which were formerly imported. These same statements, however, fail to mention that many of the articles are based in no small measure on imported components, and that many of the factories in the "mechanical and electrical equipment" category are little more than assembly operations.

Also under the Ministry of Industry is the Egyptian Public Organization for Construction Materials and Refractory Articles, which supervises 12 companies. Three modern cement plants operate at

Hilwân, one at Turra, and one at Alexandria. Favored by the presence of vast deposits of limestone and clay, the cement industry has soared in recent years. In 1951, production was 1.1 million tons, and in 1965 it came to 2.3 million tons. In spite of the huge amounts of cement required for construction of the High Dam and many other projects, Egypt has continued to be an exporter. Such cement products as pipes, electric transmission posts, and cement bricks are manufactured, and factories in this group also turn out tile, gypsum, and, in recent years, high-temperature refractory bricks for the steel and glass industries.

Construction

The construction industry is relatively well developed, and continues to have a relatively large measure of private ownership. Local contracting firms carry out much of the work at the High Dam and have undertaken projects in a number of neighboring countries. Raw material supplies are adequate, but input prices have been rising. Despite greatly increased expenditures, however, the housing shortage has defied solution. The flow of population into the cities has outstripped new urban construction, and controls have been ineffectual. Construction of thousands of new units in rural areas has been offset by both population growth and transfer of large numbers of people into new areas, such as reclaimed lands and the Nubian resettlement villages.

Power Sources

In the past, Egyptian power was derived largely from domestic and imported oil. While imported coal also was once in wide use, its high cost led to a shift toward oil as needs expanded and domestic oil production increased. Thermal plants now provide the power for more than half of Egypt's installed horsepower in industrial enterprise. The Suez Petroleum Refining Company produces large quantities of "mazout" (residual fuel oil) for industrial use. To date, the bulk of the electric power has come from a number of large thermal plants and many small diesel units. The only source of hydroelectric power has been the old Aswân Dam. Some 18,000 workers are employed in producing and distributing electricity.

All major power facilities are owned or controlled by the state and are operated under the Ministry of Electric Power, which controls the planning, expansion, and new construction of power stations, and the distribution and sale of electric energy. The government has far-reaching plans for the almost total electrification of the country. The state concerns engaged in this effort are the Public Authority for Electrification of the UAR and its subsidiaries —the Egyptian Public Establishment for the Execution of Electric Projects, the Egyptian Establishment for Production and Transfer of Electric Power, and the Egyptian Public Establishment for Distribution of Electric Power—as well as the High Dam Authority.

Both installed capacity and production of electric power have increased significantly since 1952. At the end of 1964, installed capacity totaled 1,423,000 kilowatts. Output in 1965 came to 5,475 kilowatt hours; 49.2 per cent from state-owned plants, 15 per cent from industrial plants, 32.2 per cent from the old Aswân Dam, and the balance from small privately-owned plants. By 1967, a network of power lines stretching north from Aswân was nearing completion, and power from the new Aswân High Dam was scheduled to flow to Cairo in January 1968. A huge transformer station at Cairo will relay power on to the Delta. When the 12 huge turbines of the High Dam reach full capacity in 1972, the potential power output will be almost triple the 1963 production.

Electric power facilities have been geared to satisfying the needs of industry, large urban areas, and agricultural irrigation. Industry is by far the largest consumer, and in recent years has utilized more than three-fourths of total output.

The Industrial Structure and the State

Statute No. 32, 1966, for the General Organizations (Public Foundations) and Companies of the Public Sector, replaced earlier statutes issued on this subject. According to the 92 articles, herein very briefly summarized, each minister is to execute the general policy of the state through his authority to supervise and control the General Organizations that are subject to him. Each General Organization shall have an administrative board, with a chairman appointed by the President of the Republic. The capital of each General Organization shall consist of the government's share in the capital funds of the economic units (companies) attached to it, and funds added and allotted to it by the state.

The companies of the public sector under the General Organizations are defined as economic units established for the implementation of economic projects in accordance with the development plan for the achievement of national goals in building a socialist society. Regulations pertaining to the companies are published in the *Journal of Companies,* issued (in Arabic) by the Ministry of Economy. Each company has a board of not more than nine members and of an odd number of individuals: the chairman and half of the members are appointed by the President of the Republic, and the other half are elected by its employees.

The General Organizations come under the Ministries of Industry (the largest number), Economy, Communications, Supply, Housing, Labor, Agriculture, Agrarian Reform, and Public Works. After the accounts of each company within a General Organization for a fiscal year have been audited by the Bureau of the Budget, a proposed budget for the new fiscal year is reviewed and approved, with changes as ordered, by the appropriate ministry. For example, the Ministry of Industry reviews the proposed budgets of 102 companies.

Government support of industry takes a number of forms: high tariffs on competing products, tariff-free imports of approved capital requirements, generous allowances for depreciation, ready credit, and subsidies on exports. In addition, primarily to conserve foreign exchange, the government published in 1964 a list of items which could be imported only on government orders or with the approval of the government. Those items relating to local industry included textiles; articles of iron, steel, and copper; cement; sugar; soap; paper; and dairy products. In 1967, the Ministry of Economy announced the creation of the Councils of Merchandise, one council for each of the General Organizations or categories of items. These Councils decide to import what the country needs at the least price possible and to accomplish the aim of the export policy by selling the exports at the best possible price. These decisions apply to the individual companies within each large category.

The present regime is faced with a dilemma in disposing of some industrial products. Deliberate policies of overemployment and higher wages have led to high production costs, especially for consumer durables which incorporate many imported components. During the early 1960s, easy credit terms were available, and the goods were sold at home. By 1965, however, consumption spending was growing so rapidly that little was left for investment. As part of a program to retard consumption, credit sales of consumer durables were suspended. The desired result was achieved, but attempts to export such items fell flat, because Egyptian prices were too high and the Egyptian reputation for quality was too poor. As supplies began accumulating in warehouses during 1966, the authorities finally decided to resume installment sales of refrigerators, heaters, stoves, television sets, bicycles, and washing machines.

The state continues to stress the fact that it is proper to introduce incentives into the socialized industries, and that this step has been taken. On the one hand, it is stated that since a fourth of the profits of the companies in the public sector is distributed among the workers, it is in their own interest to increase production. On the other hand, since the workers sit on the boards of directors of these companies, they feel a sense of participation and responsibility. As an aside and in this latter connection, the trend within the companies appears to follow the model of Yugoslavia, where the workers manage the factories. Unfortunately for the concept of an incentive system, however, the authorities have not yet been able to deny a profit-sharing bonus to the workers in a company that does not make a profit.

The National Institute of Managerial Development at Cairo, founded in 1961, has a special role in industrial development. Applicants for a four-week course at the Institute must have had at least five years of managerial responsibility. Some 1,500 persons had taken these courses by 1966. The Institute also offers research and consultative services. It is supported by the government and by grants of nearly $1 million from the Ford Foundation and about $1 million from the United States Agency for International Development.

Industrial Prospects

Egyptian industrial production has increased steadily at a rather satisfactory rate of almost 10 per cent annually. Output of numbers of items has declined, however, and the causes of decline are common to all industry. It appears that industrial gains could have been even more spectacular with more care and less emotion. The problems of the Hilwân iron and steel complex have been outlined —they account for falling output of some steel products and also for declines in output of industries depending on Hilwân for products. The motor vehicle plants, which are essentially assembly operations, have done little or no work for over two years. They depend almost entirely on imported components from hard currency suppliers, and little hard currency has been available. Thus the plants have stood idle, but fully staffed, for months at a time. To make matters worse, their supplies come from West Germany (with whom diplomatic relations were severed by Egypt in 1965) and from Ford Motor Company (target of Arab boycott action in 1966). The Arab boycott has created difficulties for other industrial establishments, including the Coca Cola bottling plant, and an ingrained suspicion of foreign capitalists has delayed negotiations with oil concession-aires and other prospective investors.

Egypt's industrial future is very much up in the air. Attitudes toward types of industry and toward foreign financing, either private or official, have swung widely with changes in international relations, domestic politics, and foreign currency assets. As of late 1967, the dominant political philosophy in Cairo apparently was pragmatism—with emphasis on obviously profitable and rapidly productive projects that could be financed from any willing source. Reports released in August 1967 of industrial achievements in the year ended in July emphasized the unusually high productivity of the private sector, and there was much discussion of the need to encourage and support "national capitalists."

Financing, however, was available primarily in the form of credits from Communist countries for facilities they could supply. And the USSR and other countries of Eastern Europe tend, in both attitude and capacity, toward mechanical and capital goods industries. Western Europe and the United States have a clear technological and marketing edge in petrochemicals, petroleum exploitation, and "fancy" foods. Western investment, however, would come largely from private funds. Any major breakthrough in that area depends on Egyptian willingness to accept a renewal of foreign ownership within Egypt and on Egyptian ability to convince Western investors that their capital is relatively safe.

CHAPTER *20*

Public and Private Finances

As a MOSLEM COUNTRY, EGYPT HAS A HERITAGE of Moslem principles influencing the organization and administration of public finance. These principles and their application have long conditioned both the actions of government and the attitudes of the people in this sphere. In the course of the last century, under the impact of the West, the original Moslem principles of public finance were almost entirely replaced by borrowed Western forms more suitable to the financing of a modern state. Yet some of the old tradition persists in the application of the new principles and practices.

The real condition of public finance in Egypt, as in other Islamic countries, tends to be obscured or disguised in public information and statistics. The success of tax collection, especially of direct taxes such as income or estate taxes, cannot be determined by noting the provisions of the law or reading official pronouncements about such matters. Tax collection in the rural areas, which comprise most of the country, remains partially in the hands of local officials such as the sheikhs, and these function more as representatives of their own community and family interests than as agents of the government. The temptation they face to serve local interests rather than the government inevitably hinders the tax program. In the villages it is also difficult, if not impossible, to determine the size and extent of landholdings as a source of income, and hence the actual income of individual landowners. City dwellers, too, are accustomed to misrepresenting income and assets in order to escape the payment of taxes. These practices are so universal that the citizenry sees nothing immoral in them, and behind this attitude lie centuries of Moslem experience with taxes and tax collecting. In the Arabic language the word for tax, *dariba*, derives from the root *drb*, meaning to hit or strike. The word at once reveals something of the Arab's feeling toward taxation in general and suggests

356

the justification for avoiding taxes when possible, just as one would avoid a blow. For the Egyptian, taxes have traditionally been regarded—as has the government itself—as something inimical to individual or family interests, a necessary evil to be endured. Nevertheless, the government's figures show that in the year ended June 30, 1966, tax collections exceeded anticipated revenues.

The orthodox Islamic concept of public finance, which existed for 1,200 years as an ideal in Egypt and in the Arab world, permits or enjoins the (Islamic) state to levy a tax (zakat), in order to employ the surplus of the well-to-do for the benefit of the poor. The principle of its application was that the more capital and labor are involved in the accumulation of income, the less the income should be taxed, and that articles should be taxed in inverse proportion to their perishability and in direct proportion to their capacity for production, growth, and reproduction. Thus fruit or fresh garden produce would not be taxed, nor a mule as contrasted with a mare. This concept of taxation was linked inextricably with religion. It was clothed with the sanctity of orthodoxy, and was meant to apply in a relatively static social order. Change was not extolled but decried, except for political and territorial expansion to bring more persons into the Moslem fold, within which all were supposed to enjoy the benefits of the leveling system of finance directed at goal of equality—the state in which all Moslems (theoretically) find themselves on the pilgrimage to Mecca.

Quite naturally, the actual practice of government in the Islamic world fell far short of the ideal. The rich, in league with government, generally managed to grow richer at the expense of the poor. Thus, in practice, inequality was served, and a wide gap between the rulers and the vast mass of the people was maintained and expanded. Powerless to ease their heavy financial burdens, the peasantry hated and feared their governors and relied on Allah to do justice.

In contrast with the Moslem ideal, fiscal practice in the Islamic state was largely directed at two closely related public goals: military preparedness and territorial expansion. The religious sanction for this policy was the enlargement of the ranks of the faithful by the expansion of Moslem rule, but the consequence of a budget almost exclusively devoted to maintaining and improving an army was the creation of a military caste or aristocracy. This ran counter to Islamic principles of equality, but the financial policy of the state was designed to conform to these objectives of preparedness

357

and expansion. Peacetime goals of the state involving public finance were of secondary significance. Military demands upon the public treasury became voracious and eventually began to destroy taxable capacity. The early military caste throughout Islam was drawn primarily from the militant Bedouin, whose claims were satisfied to the neglect of the needs of the settled population. The only way for conquered non-Moslems to escape even greater burdens of taxation than were imposed on the Moslem majority was for them to accept the religion of their conquerors. In Egypt the main tax load was carried by the rural population. In the course of time, the tax-collecting function was transferred to intermediaries or "tax farmers." This practice led to the development of a kind of Moslem feudal system. The intermediaries became feudal overseers, owing obligation directly to the government and spreading corresponding obligations among those below them, but retaining a divided loyalty, one to the government and one to the local community and the local retainers with whom they might very likely have family relationships.

Much of this institutional history continues to have importance today. The old system of tax farming has its modern counterpart in the employment of local sheikhs as intermediaries in collecting taxes, with all the associated conditions of divided loyalties and special interest. Much has changed, however. The government is taking an increasingly direct role in tax collection, and taxes on the rural population now constitute only a small fraction of government revenue.

Domestic Finance

Until recently, Egyptian budgets seem to have been drafted as much to obscure as to reveal the true state of the country's finances. Muhammad Ali felt no obligation to make public the condition of the treasury or its revenues and expenditures. Moreover, in his capacity as Pasha, his privy purse was not held separate from the public treasury. Later, the same arbitrariness enabled the Khedive Ismail to pursue what proved to be a ruinous fiscal policy. Ismail's government did make financial reports to the Assembly of Delegates, but these reports are now known to have been blatantly falsified. Government secrecy and deception in such matters were of course not new in Egypt, which has known so much of authoritarian and alien rule.

With European intervention came the establishment and maintenance of an internally sound but highly circumscribed system of public finance. Imposed primarily in the interest of servicing Egypt's debts to European creditors, the system brought financial stability, but its stringent attitude toward spending resulted in the serious neglect of such vital services as public education. Throughout this period, the government played only a minimal role in encouraging or financing development.

Upon termination of the British protectorate in 1922, the Egyptian government found itself in a generally favorable financial situation, as the result of over two generations of conservative government finance. Only minimal economic advances had been registered in the interim, however. For some time thereafter, government spending continued to remain within the limits of revenue, but budgets again were manipulated to conceal the diversion of funds to private pockets. Eventually, government spending again became profligate, especially under Farouk. Corruption and waste persisted up to the time the revolutionary group took over in 1952. Since that time, a real attempt seems to have been made to alter the old system of deception, official corruption, and diversion of public funds by individuals in high places. The new regime, intent upon maintaining its prestige and retaining public confidence, is striving to ensure that monies are expended for the purposes intended. Recent financial problems have arisen not from corruption but from the attempt to do too much too fast.

Upon the abolition of the Capitulations in 1937, Egypt came into full control of its financial affairs. The sources of public revenue were limited, as they continue to be, by such basic factors as the weak development of a middle class, a high degree of dependence upon agriculture, and an embryonic, although growing, industrial plant; but the government could now resort to direct taxation of income, estates, and inheritances. Under the Capitulations, foreigners in Egypt could not be directly taxed without the consent of their governments, and as long as immunity for foreigners existed, no Egyptian government dared impose direct taxes upon Egyptians. The situation has changed, but the old attitudes persist, and it will no doubt be a long time before Egyptians at large view the payment of direct taxes as a public duty rather than an imposition. Despite widespread evasion, however, such taxes have become an increasingly important source of revenue.

The Western models on which Egypt has drawn in public finance

359

were produced by a process of economic and social evolution in Europe, which more and more has demanded sound and efficient accounting, the payment of taxes in keeping with the law, and expenditure for publicly-stated purposes. In the West, this concept of public finance, particularly with respect to sources of revenue and objects of public spending, has been associated with a private enterprise system and the development of a strong middle class. While neither private enterprise nor the encouragement of a strong middle class are part of the socialist program of the government, the general principles of Western public finance will certainly be retained.

Sources of Revenue

The traditional Moslem theory of taxation, which based taxes on the nature of the source, characteristically worked to the advantage of certain groups at the expense of others. The system ignored the question of ability to pay and equality of obligation, and individuals with the same incomes might be taxed at different rates, depending on the sources of their incomes. Direct taxes, collected from a property-owning or income-earning individual, have only recently become important sources of revenue. Under the Capitulations, only two forms of direct tax existed: a land tax, assessed on the basis of the estimated rental value of land, and a building tax, based on an estimated annual rental value of built property. In 1899, the land tax was set at 28.64 per cent of the estimated rental value of land; the average rental value for these assessments was £E 3.595 per feddan. Despite rising returns and rising land values, the Capitulations prevented any modification of this tax until 1939. In that year, taxes were imposed at the rate of 16 per cent of the estimated rental value, and the average value was calculated at £E 5.715 per feddan. A maximum tax of £E 1.64 per feddan also was included, which obviously worked to the benefit of owners of the best land, since only the first £E 10.25 of value was, in fact, taxed. Any implicit incentive for land improvement, however, was minimized by the inability of an owner to make major improvements without large-scale assistance from the government. Subsequently, steps were taken to lighten the burden on the smallholder, and in 1949 the rate of taxation was reduced to 14 per cent and the ceiling of £E 1.64 per feddan was abolished. Landowners whose taxes would total up to £E 4 per year under this formula are now exempted; those who would be assessed between £E 4 and £E 20 are exempted from the first £E 4. Under these guidelines, very few smallholders actually are subject to the land tax. Of the 3,211,000 landowners in 1967, 2,575,000 were exempted from all land taxes. An additional tax, called a "defense tax," was added to the basic tax rate in 1956 and underwent subsequent upward revisions, reaching 10.5 per cent of the annual rental value of the land as of January 1966. A tax for financing the costs of local government was added in 1963, amounting to 15 per cent of the basic tax, and following the June 1967 war with Israel, an additional surtax, labeled the "national security tax," was added, which amounts to 25 per cent of the defense tax (or 2.65 per cent of the annual rental value). The effect, of course, has been to raise the basic rate to 29.225 per cent on the rental value of land that is subject to the basic tax itself. Exempted smallholders, however, remain tax free.

From 1954 to 1961, building taxes amounted to 10 per cent of the taxable value (annual rental value, less 20 per cent allowance for maintenance) on all buildings earning annual rents over £E 18. A progressive rate of from 10 to 40 per cent of taxable value, rising with the average value per room, was introduced in July 1961. Buildings with rental value below £E 3 per room were exempt. This measure obviously was aimed at discouraging both rent increases and continued investment in luxury-class housing. It was followed later in 1961 and again in 1965 by forced reduction of rents in the lower price ranges. The surtaxes mentioned above have all been applied to income from real estate, although at different rates.

Egypt's first income tax law, passed in 1939, established flat rates on three of the four taxable categories of income: 7 per cent on dividends and interest; 7 per cent on profits of financial, commercial, and industrial enterprises; and a tax on professional (law, medicine, education) income, calculated as 7.5 per cent of the rental value of the office space occupied. Wages and salaries were taxed at from 2 to 7 per cent, with only the first £E 60 exempt. Until 1950, agricultural profits were wholly exempt unless earned by joint-stock companies. The role of powerful influence groups—especially landowners and professionals—in the formulation of the above tax structure is self-evident.

Between 1939 and 1952, some revisions in the basic structure were made. Taxes on the basic sources of income were raised four times, reaching 11 per cent on professional income and 17 per cent on dividends, interest, and profits in 1952. The exemption on wages and salaries was raised to £E 100 for the unmarried and £E 150 for the married, and the rate on higher incomes was increased to 9 per cent.

By 1950, even Egyptian lawmakers could no longer overlook the fact that large amounts of income remained wholly free of taxation, while the burden fell most heavily on those least able to pay. King Farouk's easy spending policies also spurred the search for new sources of government income. In consequence, a general income tax on revenues from all sources was adopted on after-tax income above the first £E 1,000 annually. A sliding scale of from 5 to 50 per cent was applied; the rates were revised to 8-70 per cent in 1951 and again to 8-80 per cent in 1952. Although the £E 1,000 exemption appears high, incomes also remain subject to the four basic forms of tax, exemptions to which remain low: £E 150 for a bachelor, £E 200 for a couple, £E 250 with one or more children.

No major tax changes were made from 1952 until June 1961, when the general income tax rate was increased sharply. Rates on upper-level incomes were raised again in 1966, and Egypt came to have one of the most progressive rates of taxation in the world. The first £E 1,000 remains exempt from the general income tax; amounts above £E 10,000 are taxed at the rate of 95 per cent (see schedule below). Rates in the basic income categories have also been

GENERAL INCOME TAX SCHEDULE AS OF JANUARY 1, 1966

Net income	Percentage
1. Up to £E 1,000 exempt	
2. From £E 1,000 to £E 1,500	8
3. From £E 1,500 to £E 2,000	9
4. From £E 2,000 to £E 3,000	10
5. From £E 3,000 to £E 4,000	15
6. From £E 4,000 to £E 5,000	30
7. From £E 5,000 to £E 6,000	40
8. From £E 6,000 to £E 7,000	50
9. From £E 7,000 to £E 8,000	60
10. From £E 8,000 to £E 9,000	70
11. From £E 9,000 to £E 10,000	80
12. Above £E 10,000	95

Incomes also are subject to additional taxes depending on source (see pages 363 to 364). Other taxes are deducted before calculating net income subject to the General Income Tax. For net incomes less than £E 2,000, exemptions of £E 50 per dependent are allowed up to a maximum of £E 200.

raised, and some have been placed on a sliding scale, with a maximum rate applying to taxable incomes over £E 2,000. Including the defense taxes and the national security taxes that have been imposed, the basic tax rates, as of late 1967, can be summarized as follows:

	Basic tax %	Local taxes %	Defense tax %	National security tax %
On taxable* incomes from:				
Agricultural land (rental value)	14	2.1	10.5	2.65
Buildings				
Dwellings (rental value)	10-40	2-8	5.0	2.5
Other (rental value)	10	2-8	5.0	2.5
Dividends, interest, and profits	17	1.7-2.55	10.5	5.25
Professions	11-22		10.5	5.25
Wages and salaries	2-22		1.5-6.0	0.75-3.0

*Exemptions:

Buildings: 20% of rental value

Buildings with rental value up to £E 5/room exempt from basic tax

Buildings with rental value up to £E 3/room pay only the national security tax

Agricultural land: All income if total assessment is less than £E 4, the first £E 4 if income is no more than £E 20

Wages, dividends, professional income, etc.: £E 150-250

An inheritance tax was first adopted in Egypt in 1944, ranging from 2 per cent on the first £E 1,000 to 10 per cent on bequests over £E 50,000. The prevailing rates for children, spouses, and parents (with £E 500 exempt on bequests up to £E 4,000) are from 5 per cent on the first £E 5,000 to 22 per cent on any amount over £E 10,000. The tax rate doubles and exemptions are canceled for bequests to foster parents, nephews, etc., and the rate quadruples for more distant relatives. In addition, there is a tax on the entire estate; the first £E 5,000 is exempt, and rates range from

5 per cent on the next £E 5,000 to 40 per cent on estates valued at over £E 60,000.

All the above levies are grouped in Egyptian revenue estimates into a general category labeled "taxes on income and wealth." They were expected to bring in £E 108.2 million in 1967, compared to £E 70.8 million collected in 1964. Rates of collection have improved noticeably in recent years. Receipts in FY 1957 were only half the amount budgeted, whereas in FY 1965, collections actually exceeded budget estimates by a small amount.

Despite the growing importance of various forms of direct taxation, indirect taxes remain the largest single source of income to the government. Customs fees and other import and export duties, as well as specific taxes on various consumer items, fall into this category. In total, indirect taxes were budgeted to bring some £E 232.9 million into the Treasury in 1967, compared to £E 200.5 million gathered in 1964. The largest producers of revenue, they are also the cheapest and easiest type of tax to administer.

Customs duties are the country's largest revenue producer; rising imports and increases in tariffs have combined to increase them to about £E 170 million annually. Customs duties are computed either ad valorem (at a specified percentage of the delivered value of the goods) or at a specified rate per unit of weight, volume, number, or surface size. They are graduated in such a way that smaller charges are assessed on raw materials required for local industries, higher charges on the importation of semimanufactured goods, higher still on luxury items, and highest of all on goods competing with local industries. The Customs Administration administers excise duties and certain charges accessory to customs duties, such as quay dues and portage and weighing fees. Almost half the total income from customs duties stems from levies on tobacco and cigarettes. Stamp fees are required for certification of a wide variety of legal documents, including those passed between the government and private parties and those covering transactions among private parties.

Other revenue sources in 1967 included an anticipated £E 14.9 million for legal stamp fees and an income of £E 73.3 million from charges for services rendered by various government bodies, such as the transportation and broadcasting authorities. More than half this revenue is income to the Ministry of Supply for commodities it sells; on the other side of the ledger, however, the expenditures of the Ministry to keep the prices of basic commodities down have meant that the Ministry runs at a substantial loss.

Allocation of Expenditures

As the role of the state has expanded to include ownership of production facilities, the budget structure has undergone many changes. At present, the annual budget comprises two main parts (see Table 10). The services budget includes both current expenditure and investment outlay in traditional government sectors such as defense, justice, education, and health; whereas the production budget includes current operating costs and capital investments in government-owned enterprises such as manufacturing firms, the Aswân High Dam, the Suez Canal, and United Arab Airways. In some sectors, expenditure is divided between the two budgets. Normal outlays for administration and maintenance of agricultural facilities are included in the services budget, for example, while outlays for major reclamation works appear in the production budget. The latter budget appears in several guises. The largest version totals "uses of funds" in a gross manner that adds together all the purchases of each entity, including payments to its own parent organization and its own subsidiaries. The smallest version nets out all interbudgetary transfers.

The totals of the state budget have risen very steeply in recent years. In 1956/57, revenues amounted to £E 276.3 million and net expenditures came to £E 358.1 million; a decade later, revenues were estimated at £E 1,092.2 and expenditures at £E 1,316.2. The most rapid increases in expenditure occurred in the late 1950s, when major purchases of armaments were undertaken, and in the early 1960s, when the government was incorporating nationalized industries into its fiscal statements (see Table 11).

The services budget, which is generally analogous to the central government budget in most Western countries, clearly reflects the regime's interest in both improved living standards and enhanced international prestige. As shown in Table 12, expenditures for education, health, the armed forces, and the Ministry of Foreign Affairs have increased very rapidly, although generally less than total expenditures under the services budget. (The individual items are not all strictly comparable, because the allocation of items among various budgets and sectors has changed.)

A separate production budget did not appear until 1962/63, but the government has recently published earlier budgets in a comparable form. Central government expenditures on agriculture, transportation, and other developmental activities in 1951/52 were included in what was then called the "ordinary budget." The data indicate that expenditure on such productive activities has risen markedly. Not all of the increase, however, is a real addition to total spending, inasmuch as a great deal of government spending now is substituted for private expenditures which were not included in the budgets of the pre-1961 era.

Even in the fields where government spending always has been important, however, expenditures have multiplied. Outlays on agriculture, irrigation, and drainage and those on transportation and communications almost tripled between 1960 and 1967. Spending for industry also has increased, although the major changes were recorded during 1958 and 1959, when the first industrialization program was undertaken. The Aswân High Dam and various electrification projects have come to absorb huge amounts of money.

The budget that was initially announced for 1968 looked little different from its predecessors. Total expenditure was slated to rise only slightly, to £E 1,340 million, and a deficit of £E 78 million was anticipated. Following the brief war with Israel, however, Egyptian fiscal authorities found themselves in a greatly changed position. For the duration of the closure of the Suez Canal, Egypt would have to forego revenues of about $20 million monthly. The country also lost control of oil fields on or near the Sinai Peninsula, and tourist revenues slowed to a trickle. Meanwhile, greatly increased costs for welfare programs and for rebuilding the armed forces were anticipated. In consequence, a revised "austerity" budget for the year was announced. Salaries were to be frozen or even cut, prices of various commodities were to be increased to reduce the cost of government subsidies, and a number of new or increased taxes were imposed. New investment, which already had been slashed from £E 393 million to £E 355 million in the course of the budget's formulation in the spring, was cut further to only £E 232 million. And even the latter figure included an unallocated fund of £E 25 million that would be spent only if available and only for projects of absolute necessity.

The final details of the revised budget for FY 1968 indicate that total expenditures have been set at £E 1,217 million—compared to a FY 1967 budget of £E 1,198 million and a prehostilities budget for FY 1968 of £E 1,316 million. The general categories of expenditure can be summarized as follows:

	1967 BUDGET (in million £E)	1968 BUDGET (postwar version) (in million £E)
Total net expenditures	1,316.2	1,217.0
Services budget	721.4	728.1
(current expenditure)	(670.0)	(694.2)
(capital expenditure)	(51.4)	(33.9)
Production budget	594.8	488.9
(current expenditure)	(278.0)	(315.3)
(capital expenditure)	(316.8)	(173.6)
Total revenues (including foreign loans)	1,157.6	1,176.0
Anticipated deficit	158.6	41.0

A number of new revenue-producing measures were adopted at the time the revised budget was announced. In addition to the "national security" taxes noted above, changes included higher deductions from salaries for pension funds, increased prices on consumer commodities handled by government agencies, and higher charges for such government services as railroad transportation.

The rapid rise of expenditures for the armed forces obviously has been a major factor in the increase of total current expenditure. Purchases of massive amounts of foreign armaments are responsible for a part of the increase, although it is generally believed that the Soviet Union has provided these arms on liberal credit terms which substantially reduce their current cost. But those arms also have a secondary impact on defense spending. It takes a great many men and a great deal of fuel, uniforms, and attendant costs to operate and maintain the equipment. With arms readily available, and with both Israel and various Arab countries looming as potential military opponents, the normal tendency of a military regime to build the size and status of the armed forces has been exacerbated. The armed forces recently have absorbed between 20 and 25 per cent of the services budget expenditure and some 6 to 8 per cent of

367

national income. The shares are not unusually large, but for Egypt, with all its needs, the burden is particularly heavy.

The cost of living subsidies that have recently absorbed another 5 per cent of the current budget reflect the leadership's desire to provide some "fruits of the revolution" to the current generation. Wages and incomes have risen more rapidly than productivity; under normal, unregulated conditions, prices would have risen to absorb some or all of the difference. To insure that living standards were kept on the rise, however, the government resorted to price controls for basic foodstuffs and other consumer commodities. In this, they were returning to a policy common under the Farouk regime, which they initially had rejected. Commodities, either imported or domestically produced, were purchased by the government and resold at a loss. (Other goods, principally sugar, were resold at a profit to the government, helping to cover some of the cost of this process.) Similarly, taxes were held down, leaving consumer incomes relatively high. The over-all result was to leave excess funds in the hands of the general public—money not needed to purchase basic consumer goods at prevailing controlled prices —money that inevitably was directed toward the purchase of imported goods.

To cover the excess of its domestic expenditures over its domestic revenues, the government increasingly turned to bank loans that were, in the final analysis, provided by adding to the currency in circulation. With both the government and the individual Egyptian spending in excess of real income, inflationary pressures began to build up in the early 1960s. The price control system kept this phenomenon from becoming apparent until about 1964. Until the autumn of 1964, Egypt had an official cost of living index that had remained almost unchanged for a decade. In the following two years, however, as the shortage of both foreign and domestic credit forced the relaxation of controls, prices rose more than 25 per cent.

Banking

European banking practices were not introduced into Egypt until after the middle of the nineteenth century. Both the Qur'anic proscription against the taking of interest and the subsistence character of Egypt's agriculture worked to delay the adoption of this innovation. The Napoleonic foray and the subsequent efforts of Muhammad Ali to modernize the country exposed Egypt to Western financial methods. The rapid growth of the cotton export market changed Egyptian economic life, and an expanding overseas trade gradually forced a compromise between the secularized business practices of Europe and the traditional commercial patterns of the Moslem East.

The growth of modern banking in Egypt, like that of domestic trade, may be traced to European and Levantine initiative. The Anglo-Egyptian Bank was founded in 1864, and the establishment of Egyptian branches of the Crédit Lyonnais (French), the Ottoman Bank (British), and the Crédit Foncier (French) followed within the next few years. Italian and Greek bankers entered the field shortly thereafter. The National Bank of Egypt, founded in 1898, and the Agricultural Bank of Egypt, founded in 1902, were organized with British capital. It was not until 1920 that the first purely Egyptian bank, the Banque Misr, opened its doors. The German, Italian, and Japanese banking firms that were closed or sequestered during World War II resumed business in the 1940s, some of them with different names. In 1954, the National City Bank of New York established an office in Cairo, the first American bank to do so.

Adequate banking controls were maintained through articles in the Central Bank Law, which came into force in May 1951. Under this law, the National Bank of Egypt assumed many of the normal functions of a central bank. All commercial banks operating in Egypt were required to maintain with the National Bank an account carrying no interest and representing a fixed portion (currently 20.0 per cent) of its deposits. The law also established liquidity requirements and provided for monthly statements of financial position to the National Bank.

Traditionally, the banks of Egypt were of four distinct types: the central bank, the clearing banks (which exchange checks and bills and foreign currency), the nonclearing banks, and those which are classified as noncommercial. Not including the National Bank of Egypt, which performed the functions of a central bank, there were 11 clearing banks in 1955; all were members of either Cairo or Alexandria clearinghouses. All clearing banks belonged to the Association of Egyptian Banks, which regulated charges and rates of interest. With the exception of the Import and Export Bank of Egypt, which was not founded until 1946, the clearing banks were old, established institutions. Of the 11, however, only the Import and Export Bank and Banque Misr were Egyptian owned. There were 16 nonclearing banks; half of them were foreign houses. Only 8 had existed before World War II. The noncommercial category included institutions for agricultural, mortgage, and industrial credit. Agricultural and urban mortgage credit was offered by four main concerns: the Crédit Agricole et Coopératif, the Crédit Foncier Egyptien, the Crédit Hypothecaire Agricole, and the Land Bank of Egypt. Industrial credit was handled by the Industrial Bank and by some commercial banks, notably the Banque Misr.

In 1957, under Law No. 22, all banks were "Egyptianized," i.e. they were required to become joint stock companies, with all shares owned by Egyptians. This law applied immediately to British and French banks and insurance companies, and other foreign-owned banks were required to change over to Egyptian ownership within five years. Several locally-owned banks bought up the assets and properties of the British and French banks. At this same time, there was a major change in the entire banking structure, as the Economic Development Organization bought up all foreign-owned shares in the National Bank of Egypt and the Egyptian Land Bank, and took over the Land Credit Bank, the Egyptian Land Bank, the Industrial Bank, the Agricultural Credit Bank, the Bank of Alexandria, the Banque de Caire, and the Gumhuriya Bank.

Law No. 163 of 1959, concerned with banks and credit facilities, served to define more precisely the central bank role of the National Bank of Egypt and its control over the other banks; some 32 banks registered with it. Laws No. 250 and 277 of 1960 split the National Bank of Egypt into the National Bank of Egypt and the Central Bank of Egypt, with the former to handle only commercial business. At this same time, the Banque Misr, the Bank of Alexandria, and the Banque de Port Said were nationalized. In another step, Law No. 117 of 1961 nationalized all banks. Compensation to shareholders was to be given through bonds bearing 4 per cent interest: in 1964 such compensation was limited to £E 15,000 for any one person. Presidential Decree No. 872 of 1965 converted the National Bank of Egypt, the Banque Misr, and the Banque de Port Said into public joint-stock companies under the supervision of the Central Bank.

In 1962 and 1963, all existing banks and branches were amalgamated into six nationwide institutions, and each of the six was assigned the responsibility for handling the financial affairs of specified segments of the economy. In 1964, the total was reduced to only five such institutions. The National Bank of Egypt handles

370

companies affiliated with the Ministries of Agriculture, Agrarian Reform, Land Reclamation, and Transport and Communications, as well as military factories and the Suez Canal Authority. The Banque Misr deals with spinning and weaving companies and with insurance companies. The Bank of Alexandria deals with companies that come under the Ministry of Industry, and the Banque de Caire services companies associated with the Ministries of Commerce, Housing, Information, and Tourism. The Banque de Port Said provides credits for companies operating under the Ministries of Health, Supply, and Home Trade. The financing of the cotton and rice crops is spread among all the commercial banks. As of the end of June 1966, the commercial banks had extended loans totaling £E 447.3 million, compared with £E 111.5 million at the end of 1952.

Specialized banks, all of which are under government control, include the Agricultural and Cooperative Credit Bank, the Mortgage Bank, and the Industrial Bank. They were established to take over the specialized functions of certain departments of the foreign and privately-owned institutions they displaced. Only the Agricultural Bank (now known as the Egyptian Public Organization for Agricultural and Cooperative Credit) engages in a significant volume of business.

The Currency System

Prior to 1860, Egypt operated on a bimetallic currency system, but the rapid fall of silver prices forced the adoption of a gold standard based on the Egyptian gold pound. Silver coins retained a token value only; the English gold sovereign, the gold Napoleon, and the Turkish pound were used along with the Egyptian pound in commercial transactions. The Egyptian pound was in short supply, and the English sovereign became for all practical purposes a standard unit of currency.

The gold shortage of World War I found Egypt without sufficient gold reserves to cover the note issue. Authorization was obtained to use British treasury bonds and bills as backing, and this drew Egypt more deeply into the British monetary orbit. Egypt was never formally integrated into the sterling area, but it enjoyed de facto membership from 1916 to 1947, when all special arrangements were terminated. In July 1948, new regulations concerning the coverage for the note issue were published, and at the same time the Egyptian government was authorized to issue £E 50 million in treasury bills. This amount was raised to £E 100 million the next year. These new issues were backed by gold, Egyptian treasury bills, government securities, and securities guaranteed by the Egyptian government.

For some years prior to 1962, the Egyptian pound (£E) of 100 piasters or 1,000 milliemes was equal at the standard rate of exchange to US $2.872. Since May 1962, most official transactions have been conducted at the rate of 1 £E = US $2.30, although the official par value has not changed. The lower rate was not applied to Suez Canal tolls or the valuation of official gold reserves until somewhat later. In July 1967, the £E could be bought or sold in New York City for US $1.35. The public rarely refers to piasters and milliemes, the vernacular terms for coins being: one half piaster = *tarifa;* 1 piaster = *qirsh sagh;* 2 piasters = *nussfrank;* 20 piasters = *riyal;* and 20 piasters (formerly used on the cotton exchange) *talari* (dollar).

Egypt has a wide variety of bronze and silver alloy coins, ranging from 1 millieme to 20 piasters, the latter, one-fifth of a pound. Silver coin is legal tender only up to £E 2, and bronze up to 10 piasters. In the cities, bank notes are freely offered and accepted in money transactions; but in the countryside, paper currency is still subject to a lingering suspicion which is by no means accounted for by its lack of durability. Coins are still used in feminine headdresses and necklaces as an evidence of wealth, and the large silver 20-piaster piece often finds its way into a pot buried beneath a tree. Since metal coins are no longer minted, they have virtually disappeared from circulation, and even paper bills in small denominations are extremely scarce.

Insurance and Stock Markets

Prior to the Egyptianization measures of 1957, at least a score of local and foreign insurance companies were active. This number shrank after the foreign firms ceased activity, and Presidential Decree No. 714 of 1965 amalgamated seven insurance companies into three: the Misr Insurance Company, the Al-Sharq Insurance Company, and the Egyptian National Insurance Company. Later in that same year, the Egyptian Public Organization for Insurance was established as a governing body.

Stock exchanges still exist in Cairo and Alexandria which deal in state bonds and notes, bank stocks, and industrial stocks in a desultory manner. The long-famed Cotton Exchange of Alexandria was liquidated in 1966, when the government took over all facets of the buying and selling of cotton.

Savings and Investment Laws

Foreign investment laws adopted in 1953 and 1954 were designed to encourage foreign investments that would contribute to the development of industry and agriculture. They made particularly liberal provisions for extractive (mining and petroleum) investments. The vagaries of international politics, the accelerating pace of the government's nationalization measures, and the cumbersome bureaucratic procedures involved in attempting to invest foreign capital in Egypt all have discouraged foreign investors from taking advantage of these laws. The major exceptions have been petroleum companies—since 1964, both Pan American Oil (a subsidiary of Standard Oil of Indiana) and Phillips Petroleum have invested large sums under the provisions of their petroleum concessions in Egypt.

Until the early 1960s, the government was able to finance the bulk of its planned investment from the foreign exchange reserves left over after Farouk's extravagances, the earnings of profitable enterprises, and the loans it had received from foreign governments. The first nest egg was exhausted in the aftermath of a crop failure in 1961, however, just as the goals of the development plan were demanding greater and greater amounts of investment. Faced by the need to curtail either current or capital expenditure, the government initially did neither. Instead, it resorted to short-term borrowing from foreign commercial banks—a very costly process. Such loans involve interest charges of 7 to 8 per cent annually, with capital repayment due within two years or so. When these loans began coming due, Egypt's financial difficulties rapidly became all too apparent.

The obvious need to mobilize domestic savings, both to finance investment and to drain excess purchasing power from the pockets of consumers, led to a series of savings-inducement measures on the home front. A Post Office Savings Bank had been organized at the beginning of the century to encourage small savings; it permits holdings of no more than £E 500. By early 1967, a total of some £E 75 million was on deposit. Larger savings accounts were encouraged by relatively generous rates of interest offered by the commercial banks. In early 1967, these banks held some £E 190 million in time and savings deposits. To supplement measures designed to encourage voluntary savings, the government increasingly has turned to regulated savings through pension funds and similar schemes. The deposits required of an individual or a corporate entity into such funds become available to the government for use as a noninflationary source of investment financing. Following the June 1967 war, the required rate of savings was raised to 2.5 per cent of monthly salary. Thus, along with 8 per cent for old age and survivors' insurance and 1 per cent for unemployment insurance, total deductions from wage payments had reached 11.5 per cent. An investment fund was established in 1966 that incorporates all available sources of revenue for investment and balances the total against investment requirements for the year. The anticipated sources of financing for FY 1968 investment, as formulated before the June 1967 war, and as revised after that war, are shown in Table 13.

Foreign Finance

Egypt's foreign payments deficit is by no means new; in fact, the foreign trade gap was larger under Farouk than in the early years of the revolutionary government. However, the large sterling reserves accumulated during World War II were sufficient to cover the imbalance until the early 1960s. A new element was introduced with the assumption of large foreign debts, starting in the late 1950s, that involved large foreign debt service payments (see Table 14). Add the ambitious development plans undertaken after 1958 and such expensive foreign initiatives as the Yemen war and the world's sixth-largest international broadcasting network, and all the basic elements are present for a balance of payments crisis. The balance of payments for 1964 and 1965 is outlined in detail in Table 15, and an historical summary is contained in Table 16.

In 1952, the spending policies of the Farouk regime combined with the disturbances of the revolution to create a deficit on current account (all current purchases and sales of goods and services) of £E 53.4 million. The new government adopted a conservative approach, cutting back drastically on imports and actually achieving a small surplus in 1954. Import restrictions subsequently were eased, but in spite of the loss of revenues occasioned by the 1957 Suez crisis, the over-all deficit remained around £E 30 million through 1960. The turning point was a crop failure in 1961, brought on by a combination of insect infestation of the cotton crop and a low Nile flood, which reduced planted acreage of other crops. Export proceeds dropped from £E 200.2 million in 1960 to £E 161.3 million in 1961 and £E 145.2 million in 1962. Imports, which had totaled £E 255.2 million in 1960 were held to only £E 237.8 million in 1961; when the magnitude of the prospective food shortage became apparent, however, imports were rapidly increased, and reached £E 294.2 million in 1962. The trade imbalance in the three years went from £E 55.0 million to £E 76.5 million to £E 149.0 million. Suez Canal revenues—the major source of current income aside from exports—grew steadily, but they could not begin to absorb the difference. In consequence, the current account deficit reached £E 53.3 million in 1961 and £E 117.6 million in 1962 ($380.6 million). Although the 1962 imbalance has not subsequently been equaled in hard currency terms, the imbalance remains large. (The changing exchange rate for the Egyptian pound means that the trends shown in local currency and in hard currency are not identical.) For the calendar year 1965, the current account deficit came to £E 113.7 million ($261.6 million).

Foreign loans became a sizable factor in the Egyptian balance of payments in 1959, and the size of this inflow accelerated rapidly (see Table 17). Loans from the United States repayable in local currency were the largest single source of capital inflow until 1962; in 1963 and 1964, U.S. loans remained relatively constant in size, while other loans, largely from the Communist countries, grew from their 1962 level of £E 31.8 million to £E 63.0 million in 1963 and £E 114.8 million in 1964. Even with this large inflow of funds, however, Egypt has faced deficits ranging from £E 9.2 million to £E 36.9 million annually during the 1960s. These shortfalls have been covered by drawdown of remaining foreign exchange reserves, by borrowing from the International Monetary Fund, by accumulating short-term debts to foreign commercial banks, by running up debits on trade agreement accounts with other countries, and finally—in late 1964 and again in late 1966—by selling gold formerly held as currency cover.

The current account deficit is entirely due to transactions with the hard currency countries of the dollar area and Western Europe; as such, it is almost wholly payable in hard currency. Egypt normally manages to register a small surplus on its transactions with the Communist countries and with such soft currency trading part-

375

ners as India, Ceylon, Spain, and Greece. The hard currency situation has become especially acute since the United States last sold food to Egypt for local currency in 1966. The loss of foreign income as the result of the June 1967 war with Israel (about $350 million annually while the stalemate persists) simply adds another straw to the already broken back of the camel.

By early 1967, Egypt was admittedly unable to meet current payments on its foreign debt. Teams of economists visited major Western capitals, seeking refinancing of the debts. In the first three months of the year, Egypt defaulted on payments of $40.5 million due to the International Monetary Fund, and when the war with Israel broke out, negotiations were underway with the Fund that would have entailed economic reform and a domestic austerity program, combined with increased drawing rights against the Fund.

The precise total of Egypt's foreign debt is conjectural, but the sum probably is not far short of $3 billion. Based on speeches by Nasser himself, budget and development plan data, and data provided in the reports of various international agencies, the situation as of January 1967 may be summarized roughly as follows:

	Million
Long-term debt accumulated before July 1960	$200
Foreign credit used to finance projects under the First Plan	943
Hard currency credits: $460 million	
Communist and other soft currency loans: $483 million	
Foreign credit used to finance investment during July 1965-December 1966	200
Debts to the U.S., payable in local currency, for food shipments	459
Drawings outstanding from International Monetary Fund	105
Short-term debts to Western commercial banks	250
Deficit balance under bilateral trade and payments agreements (primarily debts to Communist countries)	354
Total	$2,511

In addition to the known debts of over $2.5 billion incurred to finance investment and consumption, Egypt also has an obligation for arms received from the Communist countries. Payment conditions for over $1 billion worth of equipment received from the USSR and Czechoslovakia since 1955 are not known, but the debt in this regard must amount to several hundred million dollars. By the end of 1966, therefore, the debt could not have been far short of $3.0 billion. Debts incurred in early 1967 to finance food purchases and new obligations assumed in connection with emergency aid received in the wake of the Arab-Israeli war must have pushed the total foreign debt to over $3 billion by the end of 1967.

Egypt has been one of the world's most successful collectors of foreign aid. The economic credits and grants that have been made available under government programs throughout the world now total almost $4 billion—$1.7 billion from Communist countries and $2.3 billion from the rest of the world. Of loans totaling $3.5 billion, Egypt has used almost $2.5 billion and repaid about $425 million. The debt for investment and consumption thus stands at about $2.0-2.1 billion, and Egypt has another $1.1 billion to draw on as the need arises. It is notable that the credit still available is very preponderantly from the Communist countries; the atmosphere during 1965-67 has not encouraged Western nations to extend new largesse. These credits have been used for a wide variety of purposes. According to the Egyptian Ministry of Industry, the USSR had participated in 72 industrial projects in Egypt by 1966. Included are such divergent activities as the Aswân High Dam, textile factories, geological research, expansion projects at the Hilwân iron and steel plant, thermal power plants, a shipyard, a surgical instruments' plant, and land reclamation. The United States has built a power plant for the city of Cairo, provided technical assistance, and financed sales of railroad equipment from hard currency loans and grants. And the local currency loans generated by sales of surplus food have financed 65 per cent of all paved roads built since the revolution, 62 per cent of all land reclaimed, and nearly 30 per cent of all schools. Land reclamation projects have also drawn $21.0 million in Italian financing and $40.0 million in credits from Yugoslavia. French industrial credits extended in 1966 apparently have not been allocated, but discussions have centered around a steel plant at Aswân and an ammonium sulphate fertilizer complex. West German money has gone into fertilizer plants, a dry dock, ships, bridges, and irrigation; while the Japanese have been particularly active in textile manufacturing and such food-processing facilities as canneries and sugar mills. Money from Kuwait has gone directly to the Egyptian government or banks, without allocation to specific projects, except for a $28 million loan for improvements to the Suez Canal that presumably has not yet been used. Eastern European countries have almost all provided agricultural machinery and assistance in land reclamation. In addition, the Czechoslovakians have been heavily involved in oil refinery expansion and in sugar refineries, tanneries, and bicycle plants, among others. Rumania is providing equipment for the oil industry, river barges, and mining equipment; Bulgaria is concentrating on food processing; East Germany is involved in electrification, textile mills, etc.; Hungary is providing equipment for power plants, railways, and pumping stations; Poland is building dyestuffs factories and eventually an aluminum plant and a zinc plant; and so on. The Communist Chinese extended a credit of $80 million to Egypt in 1964 for machinery and equipment, but there is no evidence of any Chinese project underway in the country. Table 17 contains an admittedly incomplete tabulation of the status of medium- and long-term loans that have been made available for development and consumption purposes. To the extent possible, it outlines the situation as of January 1, 1967.

To service this foreign debt, Egypt probably has been spending about $200 million annually during the past few years. Balance of payments data indicate capital repayments of $94.7 million in 1965 and $113.2 million in 1966. These same data suggest that interest payments on foreign loans totaled between $30 million and $35 million in each of these years. Payments on both economic and military debts to the Communist countries presumably are subsumed in the trade figures or in the data on monetary movements. Budget figures released in August 1967 included about $115 million in payments due on foreign loans from the investment fund—apparently only the principal repayment due on long-term loans used to finance development projects in the public sector.

The debt service situation is likely to worsen by the early 1970s. By that time, installments will be due on the second stage of the Aswân High Dam ($18.75 million annually for 12 years, starting in 1972) and on a number of other major industrial projects that are not yet completed. Wheat purchases in both hard currency markets and in Communist countries have been made since 1966 on terms that require repayment within 18 months to three years. Recent defaults will have to be made up, and higher interest charges will be added to the amounts due.

The picture looked particularly bleak at the end of June 1967, with almost a third of foreign earnings apparently lost in the wake of the war. In the weeks just after the war, however, a number of countries offered emergency assistance in the form of either cash or food to help cushion the shock. Cash donations included $28 million from Kuwait, $31 million from Libya, $10 million from Communist China, $8 million from Poland, $3 million from Qatar, $10 million as a personal gift from ex-King Saud of Saudi Arabia, and various small amounts from other sources. The total of about $100 million, however, could cover Egypt's losses for only about three months. At a conference in Khartoum, Sudan, in late August and early September 1967, the Arab heads of state met in a summit meeting to formulate a joint policy toward Israel and the problems left by the short war. To compensate Egypt for continuing to keep the Suez Canal closed, three oil-rich states—Kuwait, Saudi Arabia, and Libya—agreed to contribute to Egypt a total of $66.5 million each quarter. For as long as the state of inter-Arab politics assures the continued transfer of these funds, Egypt will be able to meet its immediate needs for food and imported raw materials. Both its ambitious development plans and its attempt to maintain a reasonable credit rating will be endangered, however, unless normal revenue sources are regained.

CHAPTER 21

Domestic and Foreign Trade

THE DOMESTIC TRADE OF EGYPT is very largely bound up with foreign trade. The rural areas are nearly self-sufficient, but in order to obtain manufactured goods and pay their taxes, the people must sell their cash crops, especially cotton, rice, and onions. The rapid growth of new industries has meant that practically all the textiles and household equipment and supplies used in rural areas are produced domestically. Many of the consumption items and consumer durables common in the cities are, however, imported in whole or in part.

The highly organized and centralized nature of Egyptian life, stemming primarily from the country's unique geography, has long been apparent in domestic trade as well as other fields. With almost the entire population concentrated on the river banks and in the Delta, a relatively modern approach to the retail and wholesale trades is the rule rather than the exception. The Nile River, its branches, and its canals provide ready transportation and facilitate contact throughout the country. In consequence, goods are made available with relative ease to both villagers and city dwellers alike. Much trade in rural areas remains on an individual barter basis, but almost every citizen is in contact with the monetized economy.

Government control has permeated trade, as it has all other activities, although to a somewhat lesser extent. Domestic trade is a combination of public and private enterprise, under the general supervision of the Ministry of Supply and Internal Trade. The Ministry itself purchases basic commodities at home and abroad. Distribution by governorate and by major city is arranged through four subsidiary organizations—for grains, other commodities, consumer cooperative stores, and storage.

Traditional Patterns of Domestic Trade

The story of domestic trade in Egypt is different from that of many other Middle Eastern countries. At the turn of the century, the

Egyptians had long been considered the least commercially minded of the peoples of the area. The bazaars of Cairo were small and undiversified compared with those of Damascus, Aleppo, or Baghdad. When the land bridge between Africa and Asia declined in importance, relative to the rise of Western maritime enterprise, Egypt quickly lost any pretensions to commercial ascendancy over, or even equality with, the great trading centers of the region.

Egypt's native population in the early nineteenth century consisted mainly of landowners and peasants; "trade" was beneath the dignity of the former and beyond the dreams of the latter. There was some lively though comparatively small-scale commercial activity in the cities, and a large foreign population, sensing a potentially lucrative market, moved in, pushing the small Egyptian merchant aside. Many Egyptians remained as village and urban storekeepers and peddlers, but above this level, foreigners completely dominated Egypt's commercial and financial life, as well as what little industrial activity there was.

By the time Egypt achieved political independence in 1922, the realization that political freedom could only be consolidated by economic independence had become widespread in the more articulate Egyptian circles. After World War I, the Banque Misr began to found Egyptian companies in such fields as printing, cotton ginning, the cinema, transport, and navigation. The success of these enterprises—which later were augmented to include silk weaving and cotton textiles—showed the way to other enterprises.

Progress was nonetheless slow, especially in larger businesses. In 1951, a survey showed that in finance, commerce, and industry some 31 per cent of the enterprises were Moslem Egyptian by ownership, 4 per cent Copt, 17 per cent Jewish, 12 per cent Syrian or Lebanese, 9 per cent Greek or Armenian, and 31 per cent European, excluding Greek. The capital investment picture was similar, although a clear trend toward Egyptian ownership was developing. In 1933, the amount of share and bond capital originally subscribed by Egyptians was only 9 per cent of the total; by 1948 it had risen to 39 per cent. During the period 1946-48, Egyptians contributed 84 per cent of all new capital subscriptions and increases of capital of existing companies. Moreover, a substantial amount of share and bond capital originally subscribed by foreigners had changed hands and was held by Egyptians. But since the acquisition of land or buildings remained by far the preferred form of investment among Egyptians, the over-all rate of industrial capital expansion did not show any sharp upward trend. Such growth as took place was due mainly to the operations of a small number of family groups.

The revolution of July 1952 was followed, at first, by greater receptivity toward foreign investment and by measures to encourage increased investment of Egyptian private capital in "productive enterprise" rather than in real estate. The comparative failure of these measures, combined with the international political developments of 1956-57, worked to change the direction of government policy. A series of measures was developed and adopted in the period after nationalization of the Suez Canal Company that placed both business and commerce under the control and ownership of the state. During the 1960s, bursts of legislation to increase centralized control have been interspersed with regressions in favor of private ownership and initiative; the prevailing trend, however, has led to state domination of most commercial fields. Only the purchases and sales of the individual in the market or bazaar remain relatively unaffected by government intervention.

The weekly market day in an Egyptian town or village is an event of the greatest social importance. The markets (*halaka*), which draw great crowds, are usually held on waste land outside the town centers; sometimes they are enclosed, sometimes not. Customers of the country market are fellahin who need manufactured goods, which they cannot produce themselves. Provisions also have to be bought, according to need, opportunity, or means. As the fellah's wages or the income from his crops have increased somewhat, and as such incomes have increasingly come to be paid in currency, barter trading has begun to die out in Egypt. Banknotes are now the usual medium.

Egypt's city bazaars resemble those found elsewhere in the Middle East, but under the impact of heavier and longer-continued Western influence, they have undergone more change and are less the focus of urban trade than those in other countries in the area. The Egyptian bazaars, to an ever-increasing extent, are supplying goods and provisions for a "Westernized" population. The younger merchants, especially those who deal in commodities for which the manufacturers suggest retail prices, are beginning to mark goods with fixed prices in the manner of the Westernized stores in the main streets. Bazaar shopping also presents aspects which the Western mind finds it difficult to comprehend. The fact that hinges are bought in one store and screws to fit them in another is of no moment to the Middle Eastern merchant or his customer, and it is not unusual to buy a flashlight case in one store and its bulb in another. Such arrangements are only a facet of a larger pattern remarkable for its lack of attention to such complementary details as hinges and screws—and for its leisurely approach not only to business but to life in general. The situations arising from this lack of precision, however, dovetail with the Middle Eastern emphasis on sociability; since the purchaser is forced thus to circulate among the stores, social and business contacts on the personal level tend to multiply and be strengthened. This background also tends to explain the origin of many of modern Egypt's industrial problems; it is difficult to run a factory efficiently when the purchasing clerk who orders nuts or a government official who approves an import application for nuts can overlook the need or cancel the order for accompanying bolts.

Structure of Domestic Trade in the 1960s

Since 1952, and especially since the promulgation of the socialist laws of 1961, the government has moved to play an increasingly important role in domestic trade. Even in agriculture, where government direction and control has prevailed since early in the nineteenth century, the role of government has expanded. The individual farmer must sell minimum amounts of certain of his crops to organizations backed or controlled by the government at prices either fixed or supported by the regime. For example, each year decrees are published which detail the amounts of specific crops which must be turned over from the produce of a given area of land in a given geographical location. In 1967, farmers in all governorates except Qena and Aswân were required to sell between 150 and 375 kilograms of wheat for each feddan they cultivated to the Egyptian General Organization for the Cooperative and Agricultural Trust. In the same year, growers of black beans were required to sell between 200 and 300 kilograms per feddan cultivated. Rice is also subject to a quota system. The farmer is, however, free to sell any crop above the minimum quota for any price he can get. In practice, almost all staple crops in excess of the farmer's own needs are sold to the government agencies, because the government price for amounts above the quota usually exceeds the local market price. The government pays high prices for locally consumed items such as wheat and beans and resells them at a loss to keep the cost of living down. It pays high prices for such crops as rice to discourage local consumption and obtain increased amounts of rice for export.

Cotton formerly was sold at auction in local markets to brokers or merchants who then had it ginned, pressed, and sent to one of the several main cotton exchanges, where it was sold to the Egyptian Cotton Commission or to private exporters. Now cotton is bought directly by the Cotton Commission at a predetermined price, based on staple length and grade (with premiums for cleanliness, careful sorting, etc.). The government agency, in turn, sells to local yarn and textile mills or to government export agencies at prices nearly equivalent to prevailing world prices. The profits from cotton transactions are an important source of local financing for the development budget. Here again, however, the government is feeling the effects of its own policies; between 1961 and 1965, the price paid to growers increased 10 per cent, while the world market price for Egyptian cotton remained almost unchanged.

The government's newborn activities in the field of domestic trade are conducted principally through a variety of institutions called "cooperatives." Although these take many guises, only rural agricultural units are really member-owned and -operated cooperatives in the sense generally accepted in the West. Agricultural cooperatives exist in every village, and membership is compulsory for every farmer. The cooperative obtains and distributes seed, machinery, insecticides, credit, and all other farming necessities. It purchases the farmer's cash crop and markets it. The resulting authoritarian control can be criticized as unduly centralized, but Egyptian agriculture demands a high degree of control, and productivity has risen steadily as the cooperatives have become more experienced and more powerful.

Consumer cooperative stores exist in all urban areas and are accessible to much of the rural population. Most are simply government stores, although conversion to joint-membership societies is the long-range goal and has been accomplished in a few cases. These stores act as "safety valves" for particularly scarce consumer items, trying to provide equitable distribution at low (usually subsidized) prices. They currently handle only about 5 per cent of retail sales, but long-range plans call for distribution of about 25 per cent of all basic commodities through such outlets.

The government also has encouraged establishment of cooperatives for handicrafts and cottage industries. Privately formed groups can apply for assistance in training, marketing, and finance. A revolving loan fund equivalent to $5 million has been established, and marketing centers have been set up in each governorate to facilitate domestic sales and to act as agents for export transactions.

Wholesaling has remained primarily a private sector activity, particularly for agricultural produce. A greater degree of government control, however, appears to be one of the regime's medium-term goals. In 1964, about 400 cooperatives for wholesale distribution of consumer goods were established. They were designed to supply goods both to retail consumer cooperatives and to private shops and were made responsible for controlling supplies so that stores would have no large surpluses to be hoarded or diverted to the black market. In mid-1966, the government began establishing three public sector companies to handle wholesale trade between agricultural cooperatives and farmers on the one hand and factories and retail outlets on the other.

The two principal marketing areas are Cairo and Alexandria. Leading manufacturers, importers, exporters, and large distributors are located in or near these two cities. From these centers goods flow to individual retailers and small private wholesalers located throughout the country.

In 1964, some 500,000 retail establishments were in operation. In the cities and larger provincial towns, retail trade is handled by department stores, a number of which have been turned into state-owned cooperatives, and by small specialty shops and traditional bazaars. In addition to the department stores that have been turned into cooperatives, new retail cooperatives have been opened in Cairo and Alexandria. These stores sell principally foodstuffs, but some sell cotton and silk material and hosiery. These retail houses are supplied by the nationalized import companies and by wholesale distributors. Many of the wholesale and retail transactions in the towns are financed on a credit basis.

Foreign Trade

Egypt is predominantly an agricultural country which relies on foreign trade for the maintenance of its economic and political position. Cotton, the main crop, must be largely sold abroad, and the price and annual volume of sales on the world market are a primary determinant of the condition of the economy, for this is how the country acquires certain necessities of life, most of the raw materials for its industry, many of its manufactured goods, and the equipment for its armed forces. With the development of high-quality, low-cost, synthetic fibers for textiles, Egypt has been at an increasing disadvantage in world trade. Although no comprehensive measure of Egypt's terms of trade (price of export goods compared to price of import goods) is available, a reasonable indicator can be derived from the fact that world prices for Egyptian cotton moved downward during 1960-66, while the average export prices of the "industrial countries" from which Egypt procures most imports rose 6 per cent and the world price for wheat followed a similar trend. Thus, simply to keep its trade gap from growing, Egypt must increase the total quantity of exports relative to the quantity of imports.

Volume. As reflected in the growing foreign debt, exports have, in fact, increased steadily, but less rapidly than imports. As shown in Table 18, both foreign sales and purchases have continued upward since World War II—with two exceptions. World market prices for Egyptian cotton plummeted almost 50 per cent between 1951 and 1953. The 1952 revolutionary regime slashed imports to the bone, in a relatively successful attempt to return a favorable balance to foreign trade. But the uncertainties of the revolution, attended as they were by a general exodus of wealthy and skilled foreigners and Egyptians closely connected with Farouk, hampered attempts to inspire a resurgence of exports. Cotton prices had begun to recover, and other exports also were beginning to rise, when a new crisis occurred. The effect of the invasion by Israel, Britain, and France in 1956 was to slow the growth of foreign trade, instead of causing a decline in total value, and to spur a redirection of trade that already had been foreshadowed by Egypt's huge purchase of Communist weapons in 1955. In 1954, Britain and France had bought £E 30.3 million worth of Egyptian products; their combined purchases in 1957 totaled only £E 3.3 million—an example of the political responsiveness of foreign trade. Anglo-French sales to Egypt also fell—from £E 37.1 million in 1954 to only £E 4.8 million in 1957. Trade with these two countries has never returned to pre-Suez levels. Once the financial and political ramifications of the Suez crisis had subsided, exports resumed their upward trend, with another major downturn in 1961 and 1962 brought on by a crop failure. Imports, however, truly ballooned in the post-Suez era. The demands of industrial development, subsidized consumption, an enlarged military establishment, and an ill-advised attempt to manufacture sophisticated weapons all conspired to increase imports from £E 183 million in 1957 to a peak of £E 414 million in 1964. In late 1964, the realities of the foreign exchange situation finally intruded, and an austerity program was adopted that reduced imports slightly in 1965. However, import curtailment also brought a shortage of imported raw materials and components for industry and of consumer items to which the people of Cairo and Alexandria had grown accustomed. Faced with both an industrial slowdown and some popular discontent, the regime abandoned austerity and permitted imports to rise again, to £E 465 million ($1.07 billion) in 1966. By late 1966, however, Egypt's obvious inability to meet foreign debt commitments was limiting the availability of new foreign credit, and other facets of the lack of foreign exchange were becoming increasingly apparent. A new attempt was made to limit imports; it succeeded in reducing imports in the first three months of 1967 to £E 63 million—little more than half the figure for the same period of 1966. Import controls still were being honored in June 1967, and Egypt apparently had accepted the inevitability of the stabilization program proposed by the International Monetary Fund, which would have involved even more severe restrictions on foreign expenditure, when the Arab-Israeli war began. With the expected $240 million from Suez Canal revenues suddenly cut off, and with the Israelis pumping valuable oil from fields on the Sinai Peninsula, Egypt is faced with an import limitation program for the duration of the stalemate on the banks of the Canal. Attempts to increase exports to offset the loss are unlikely to be successful. The loss of oil to Israel probably will cost some $50 million in trade revenue each year, and exports of other commodities are hampered by the closure of the Canal. In particular, the 15 per cent of exports that normally go to Asian and East African markets will have to be shipped around Africa or carried across Egypt on inadequate overland transportation routes to Suez, where port facilities are scarcely adequate to handle such a volume of goods.

Commodity composition. Egypt in the nineteenth century was a self-sufficient country, producing a variety of food crops for home consumption and little in the way of export goods. With the introduction of cotton, the economy began to change and to be dominated by the value of annual cotton exports. For the past several years, exports have been equivalent to about one-fifth of national income, with imports standing a little higher. In broad economic terms, Egypt fits into the category of underdeveloped countries in the subtropical zone. Typically, per capita income and per capita exports are low in such countries. In Egypt, on the contrary, the proportion of exports to national income is high, ranging from 20 to 40 per cent.

Egypt's imports are made up in considerable part by durable manufactured goods, luxuries, and semiluxuries. Since such items are not staple necessities, their purchase may be postponed, and in consequence, their volume fluctuates somewhat with export earnings.

This flexibility is not, however, present in the case of food imports. Self-sufficiency in foodstuffs—at a very low standard of living—has wisely been relinquished in the interest of producing more profitable export crops, and Egypt now imports large quantities of wheat and other foodstuffs. This has required expenditures of foreign exchange, agreements under which wheat-exporting countries will accept payment in Egyptian pounds, and resort to foreign loans to purchase food. Basic food needs cannot be postponed, and accepted levels of food consumption cannot easily be reduced by a significant amount. Wheat requirements are somewhat harder to meet on a large scale than needs for many other foodstuffs, because only a few countries in the world are really major wheat exporters. During the period when the United States provided wheat on easy terms under a three-year agreement, so that Egyptian planners began to think of wheat as virtually costless, eating habits were developed that are hard to reverse. The problem became particularly apparent to Egyptian officialdom in 1966, when substantial purchases of wheat for hard currency were necessary. In 1967, the Communist countries pledged to sell over half the wheat Egypt needed for the year, somewhat lessening the immediate difficulty. Nevertheless, so long as Egypt requires large amounts of wheat and fails to allocate hard currency for its purchase, it remains at the mercy of fluctuating earnings and subject to economic and political pressures and sanctions from other states—a major economic vulnerability.

Egypt participates in world trade directly as a trader and indirectly as the route for a large volume of foreign trade between other countries. As seller, the country is an important source of certain raw materials and agricultural products. As consumer, it is a market for other agricultural products, agriculture-related goods such as fertilizers, insecticides, and farm machinery, large quantities of semifinished and finished industrial products, and, in the present political situation, large amounts of military equipment. The country's ability to buy abroad is closely linked to its success in selling its own products to others. Both a politically-motivated tendency toward overcentralization and leveling of incentives and a culturally-ingrained disregard for quality control and timely fulfillment of contract obligations seriously hamper export promotion efforts. Dependence on merchant shipping owned by other nations is a further weakness in the country's international economic position.

Cotton dominates all of the Egyptian export effort; rice, petroleum, and onions trail far behind (see Table 19). Raw cotton amounts to some 50 or 55 per cent of exports by value and brings in about a third of all current foreign earnings. Both the volume and the value of cotton exports fluctuate widely from year to year; thus far in the 1960s, the maximum volume of 374,000 metric tons was attained in 1960, the maximum value of £E 146 million in 1965, and the minimum on both counts (84,000 tons valued at £E 251 million) in 1962. Cotton yarn and textiles have become increasingly important exports in recent years. Heavy investments in spinning and weaving plants have been reflected in the growth of export value from £E 5.4 million in 1955 to £E 15.8 million in 1960 and £E 42.8 million in 1965. Such local manufacturing, of course, substantially increases the profit that a basic material-producing country receives for its products.

A similar policy has been pursued successfully in the case of petroleum. Although Egypt remained a net importer of petroleum in 1966, petroleum-refining capacity in excess of domestic consumption requirements has facilitated a rapid growth in export income. Egypt exports some locally-produced crude oil and imports a different quality, more suitable for local refineries; it also exports refined products (valued at over £E 10 million in 1965), while importing only small amounts of refined petroleum. By 1965, Egypt already was self-sufficient in volume terms, but remained a net importer in financial terms because of the poor quality (and price per ton) of oil from fields on the east side of the Gulf of Suez. Oil discovered by a U.S. company in the Al-Murjan field in the Gulf of Suez had been expected to make Egypt a net exporter in 1967, and oil income was expected to reach respectable proportions by 1970. That prospect has been postponed by the Israeli occupation of the Sinai Peninsula, which deprives Egypt of domestically-produced oil and also prevents the shipment of domestically-produced crude to the oil refinery in Alexandria via the normal Suez Canal route.

PETROLEUM: VALUE OF EXPORTS, IMPORTS, AND NET EXPENDITURES
(*in million £E*)

	1952	1959/60	1963/64	1964/65	1965/66
Import°	14.3	20.5	28.2	29.7	23.7
Export	......	4.5	22.4	22.2	15.8
Net expenditure	14.3	16.0	5.8	7.5	7.8

° Excluding imports of military forces

Rice has become an increasingly significant export item since water requirements have become assured by the Aswân High Dam. Rice exports were valued at £E 30.4 million in 1964. They fell to £E 19.8 million in 1965, when planted acreage was reduced to conform to water availability. With the High Dam storing water, however, planted acreage was increased over 25 per cent between 1966 and 1967, and export earnings totaled £E 26.9 million in the twelve months through June 1967.

Onions exceeded rice in export value until 1963, and they continue to earn £E 6 or £E 7 million annually. Vegetables, fruits, phosphates, manganese ores, skins and hides, and other agricultural goods also are exported in large but varying quantities. Such specialized items as cut flowers and perfume extracts are becoming increasingly important, and in the past several years, Egyptian factories have begun to produce exportable quantities of assorted manufactured items, including chemicals, bicycles, tires, and cement (see Table 20).

Imports are far more varied than exports, but food remains the most important single category (see Table 21). Food and other consumer goods make up about a third of the total imports; the balance is in the form of raw materials, components for domestically-assembled products, and capital goods. Imports of cereal grains and milled products in 1964 totaled about $172 million, including about $130 million purchased in Egyptian pounds from the U.S. Cereal imports were reduced somewhat, to $161.2 million by 1966, but the entire amount had to be paid for in hard currency or under short-term trade credits repayable in Egyptian goods that could be sold elsewhere for hard currency. Crude petroleum remains a major import ($56.3 million in 1966), because of the necessity to trade for crude types more suitable for local refineries. Some $74.1 million was spent on transportation equipment in 1965, and other machinery and electrical equipment accounted for $141.7 million. In 1966, both tobacco ($18.6 million) and sugar ($3.1 million) remained important items on the import list, and imports of fertilizers ($28.3 million), timber ($36.2 million), paper, pulp and cardboard ($18.9 million), insecticides ($15.4 million), and similar goods continued to underscore the dependence of both agriculture and industry on imports.

Geographical distribution. The distribution of Egyptian trade among geographical and political blocs has changed more rapidly than the commodity composition. Until the Suez crisis, the United Kingdom occupied first place in Egyptian world trade. The relationship declined during World War II, leaving a large decrease in trade with Europe as a whole, accompanied by a compensatory increase in trade with other areas—notably the rest of the Middle East, the United States, and India. Trade with Europe recovered after 1945, but the United Kingdom never regained its dominant position. With the trade cutoff that followed the Suez crisis in 1956, there was a decided shift of Egyptian foreign trade toward the Communist countries, accompanied by even closer trade relations with the United States, India, and the wheat-producing members of the British Commonwealth.

The shift occurred partly as a result of economic conditions, but primarily as a result of international politics. Both the decline of the British textile industry and the increased demand for cotton from other industrial countries such as Germany, Japan, and the United States played a part. Historically, Russia and the Eastern European states that came to be Communist countries had never been important in Egyptian foreign trade. In the years immediately following the revolution, they played no greatly increased role, accounting for only 10 to 15 per cent of Egyptian trade turnover. Following unsuccessful negotiations with the West, however, Egypt concluded an agreement with Czechoslovakia and the USSR in September 1955 for the purchase of several hundred million dollars worth of weapons. Under the agreement, Egypt apparently was to pay for these arms over some years, primarily by exporting cotton and other goods. And exports to Czechoslovakia, which totaled only £E 8.8 million in 1955, amounted to £E 20.8 million in 1956. The increase in exports to the USSR did not occur until 1957, when the total reached £E 31.3 million, compared to £E 5.6 million in 1956 and £E 7.0 million in 1955. A large proportion of the sudden increase was directly attributable to the arms purchase, but other international events reinforced the impetus toward greater trade with Communist countries. First and foremost, of course, was the Suez crisis and the subsequent freezing of Egyptian funds in European banks, the virtual cessation of trade with the United Kingdom and France, and the blockage of the Suez Canal. In 1957, when Egyptian relations with the industrial West were at their lowest, the Soviet Union provided $175 million in credits to finance Egyptian imports of Soviet factories and products for use in the new industrialization plan. And following the withdrawal of a Western offer to finance the Aswân High Dam, the USSR put up $100 million in credit for the first stage of the project. The Communist countries, at that time largely excluded from the trade of the Western world, also took advantage of their new relationship with Egypt to negotiate and sign trade and payments agreements that provided for increased levels of trade to be conducted on what was essentially a barter basis. Egyptian difficulties in disposing of large cotton crops on a shrinking world market were still another factor.

Within only two years, the Communist countries were accounting for 35 per cent of Egyptian foreign trade. The peak of this share was reached in 1958, when the Communists accounted for 39 per cent of total Egyptian trade. Between 1959 and 1964, the Communist share declined slightly, to some 34 per cent, as the Egyptians began to import more and more American wheat and as they found rising cotton prices and demands in hard currency markets. A small resumption of the trend toward Communist customers and markets began in late 1965, as mounting hard currency problems led Cairo to conduct as much of its foreign trade as possible in areas that did not necessitate settlement in hard currency. This development in trade with Communist countries paralleled an increased exchange of goods with other, non-Communist trade agreement countries such as Spain, India, and Ceylon. Agreements in 1967, under which the USSR and other Communist countries agreed to provide wheat on easy terms, as well as the strained relations with Western countries in the wake of the 1967 war with Israel, probably will insure that the Communist share of Egyptian trade in 1967 and 1968 is somewhat greater than the 1966 share. (For details on the geographical distribution of Egyptian trade, see Table 22). At least through 1966, however, the United States remained Egypt's largest single trading partner.

The dramatic decline of the British commercial position in Egypt and in the rest of the Middle East illustrates the intermeshing of trade and politics. The previously noted Suez imbroglio was one of the single major incidents; the disastrous British withdrawal from Palestine and the subsequent spread of Israeli dominance over Arab lands was at least as important. The British prestige that once helped to make British goods salable at relatively high prices is now gone in the Arab Middle East.

Foreign trade management. The increasing excess of imports over exports has created a mounting foreign currency problem, which can only be met by a sustained attempt to curtail imports and success in identifying and marketing exportable commodities. Oil fields recently discovered in the Gulf of Suez and in the Western Desert will provide Egypt with additional exports of up to $200 million annually by the early 1970s. Even this will not be enough, however, unless other exports also are increased and unless imports are held within reasonable limits. Egyptian industry soon will produce a number of manufactured items in excess of local demand. The question is whether Egypt can sell air conditioners, cold storage plants, auto batteries, and transistor radios in highly competitive markets. The cost structure of Egyptian industry, which emphasizes increased benefits for labor without regard for productivity, is a bar to competitive pricing abroad. An all-pervasive disregard for whether or not a given unit meets the specifications for the item similarly handicaps Egyptian exports of manufactured goods, and Egypt has little experience in the important skill of marketing. The exceptionally skillful handling by Egyptians of cotton exporting proves that none of these shortcomings are necessarily permanent. Only the years of concentrated effort that have been put into the job of learning to manage cotton, however, will bring Egypt similar results in learning to export manufactured goods.

The best opportunities for expanding Egyptian markets lie in those countries of Asia and Africa that share Egypt's foreign exchange problems and Egypt's general political views, but opportunities for a direct exchange of goods are limited. Trade with the underdeveloped world can become important for Egypt only when Egypt can afford to conduct such transactions on a hard currency basis. In anticipation of this day, Egypt has initiated a small-scale foreign aid program in Africa, tied to the purchase of Egyptian goods under long-term credit, which is very similar to trade promotion/foreign aid programs of the industrialized countries. Egypt has made such loans to Mali, Guinea, Nigeria, and Congo (Brazzaville), among others. To facilitate the exchange of goods outside the framework of hard currency transactions, Egypt has entered into trade and payments agreements with over 30 other countries. In addition, as the largest Arab exporter of manufactured goods, it has been the prime mover in the Arab Common Market, an arrangement promoted by the Arab League, which provides preferential tariff treatment for goods in inter-Arab trade.

Egyptian management of cotton trade has been remarkably astute over the years. The cotton experts in Alexandria and Cairo have managed to glean every possible dollar, pound, or deutsche mark from the annual cotton crop; helped by trade agreements with the Communist countries, they have also been able to dispose of every available bale. Contrary to the widely accepted notion, Egyptian trade agreements do not require delivery of a specified amount or value of cotton; rather they provide for export of anything *up to* a given quantity. In the years immediately after arms agreements were concluded with the Communists, the Egyptians found that Communist countries were buying cotton, holding it until the following season, and then dumping it on hard currency markets at cut rate prices, reducing Egyptian hard currency earnings. The Communists, for their part, were unhappy with the quality and price of the cotton they received. A truce apparently was reached in 1964. Egyptian officials announced that henceforth cotton would be sold for hard currency; for each bale sold, another bale of equal quality would be reserved for trade agreements countries at the identical price. The *quid pro quo* apparently was a Communist promise to forego re-exports of Egyptian cotton. Marketers in Alexandria evidently have calculated that Egypt can sell only a limited amount of cotton for hard currency in a given year; the price reduction necessary to sell a greater amount is so large that the total revenue derived from larger sales actually shrinks. The rule of thumb apparently is accurate; in most years Egypt sells just about that amount for hard currency. The Communists are not obligated to purchase the cotton remaining after hard currency sales and contracts with non-Communist trade agreement countries such as India and Ceylon have been met. In practice, however, Eastern European countries have proved willing to purchase the excess. In good cotton years, such as 1964/65, they receive as much as 669,000 bales. In poor years, such as 1963/64, they may get only 380,000 bales.

This cotton pricing policy is unique and most effective. It works because Egypt produces such a large share of the world's supply of long-staple and extra-long staple cotton. Prices are set shortly before the beginning of each export season, based on the estimated world demand and the known size of the Egyptian crop. They are fixed for only one week at a time, and they are *raised* as the export season progresses. The procedure is contrary to every commonly accepted concept of pricing. Most buyers of any commodity expect to be rewarded by lower prices if they delay their purchases until the seller is anxious to dispose of the unsold portion of his stock. Because this procedure has been rigidly followed, cotton purchasers know that they will save money by buying early in the season, and the major consumers place their orders without delay. Although the selling season does not start until August, this enables Cairo to make a good estimate of total revenue by September. And, if sales are going unusually well, it permits an increase in price that raises total income. To encourage rapid shipment, as well as early purchasing, a service charge of one-half of 1 per cent per month is added for holding the contracted amount in warehouses in Egypt after March. The latter charge insures that shipment will be made, and revenue accordingly received, as quickly as the customer can find storage space for the new stock. Only one serious miscalculation has been made in recent years. The opening price in the summer of 1964 evidently was set too low to take advantage of an unexpected increase in Western demand. Thus, the entire crop had been committed in the first week of sales, before there was an opportunity to increase prices to take advantage of the situation. In all other recent years, however, there has been an orderly upward progression of prices throughout the marketing year, and Egyptian cotton has maintained its reputation for quality, cleanliness, and efficient delivery. If other Egyptian export goods ever manage to attain a similar image, much of Egypt's foreign trade problem will be on the way to a solution.

395

Tables

Table 1. GROSS DOMESTIC PRODUCT BY SECTORS

(at constant FY 1960 prices—in million £E)

Sectors	Base Year						1964/65 (goal)	1964/65 (actual) as % of goal	1959/60-1964/65 (% increase)
	1959/60	1960/61	1961/62	1962/63	1963/64	1964/65			
Agriculture	405.0	402.7(a)	373.0(a)	426.4	452.9	477.0	512.0	93.5	17.8
Industry	256.3	285.6	309.9	329.2	369.6	385.0	516.4	74.6	50.2
Electricity	9.8	12.2	16.3	18.4	18.6	22.4	23.6	94.9	128.6
Construction	47.1	44.2	73.6	83.5	96.0	92.6	52.0	178.1	96.6
Transport and storage	92.9	102.2	116.9	127.1	144.0	157.6	117.0	134.7	25.9
Housing	73.0	73.8	76.2	77.6	78.7	80.1	84.0	95.2	15.1
Public utilities	6.4	6.8	7.0	7.4	7.6	7.0	9.0	77.8	40.6
Finance and commerce	129.2	145.1	151.6	154.0	148.3	151.9	162.1	93.7	25.5
Other services	265.5	290.9	286.6	308.3	332.1	391.6	329.0	119.0	23.9
Total	1,285.2	1,363.5	1,411.1	1,531.9	1,647.8	1,762.2	1,795.0	98.2	37.1
Annual increase (%)	6.1	3.5	8.6	7.6	6.9				

(Compound rate of increase: 6.5%)

(a) Depressed by 1961 crop failure

Table 2. INVESTMENTS DURING FY 1960-65, PLANNED AND ACTUAL

(at current prices—in million £E)

Sectors	Base Year 1959/60	1960/61	1961/62	1962/63	1963/64	1964/65	Total	Plan goals(a)	Actual as per cent of planned
Agriculture	16.7	16.6	17.8	20.6	30.9	32.5	118.4	117.1	101.1
Irrigation and drainage	8.6	14.8	19.7	29.2	36.4	37.9	138.0	183.0	75.4
High Dam	4.2	6.8	14.4	24.0	34.8	18.6	98.6	47.4	208.0
Industry	49.3	67.8	50.3	80.5	105.4	99.9	403.9	444.7	90.8
Electricity	6.2	5.6	6.3	11.9	35.6	53.2	112.6	144.2	78.1
Construction	...	...	...	3.5	4.5	5.2	13.2	15.0	88.0
Total, commodity sectors	85.0	111.6	108.5	169.7	247.6	247.3	884.7	951.4	93.0
Transportation, means of communication, and Suez Canal	35.8	68.9	66.5	48.6	40.9	45.9	270.8 ⎱	279.0	105.4
		5.9	4.7	5.2	4.2	3.4	23.4 ⎰		
Finance and trade	...	...	...	...					
Housing	31.1	19.1	37.8	37.6	37.4	29.6	161.5	199.0	81.2
Public utilities	7.5	7.7	10.2	13.5	8.2	10.9	50.5	50.4	100.2
Other services	12.0	12.4	23.4	25.0	34.1	27.2	122.1	97.2	125.6
Total, services sectors	86.4	114.0	142.6	129.9	124.8	117.0	628.3	625.6	100.4
Grand Total	171.4	225.6	251.1	299.6	372.4	364.3	1513.0	1577.0	95.9

(a) Plans were formulated in FY 1960 prices, but actual results have not been released on that basis. This figure does not include LE120 million planned for increases in inventories.

400

Table 3. NUMBERS OF EMPLOYEES IN AGRICULTURE AND INDUSTRY AND THEIR RELATIVE CHANGES DURING THE FIRST FIVE-YEAR PLAN[a]
(*in thousands*)

Sectors	Base year 1959/60		1st year 1960/61		2d year 1961/62	
	Number of workers	%	Number of workers	%	Number of workers	%
Agriculture	4325	54	3600	55.3	3600	54.1
Industry	601.8	10	625.6	9.6	679.0	10.2
Total number of workers in the Plan	6006.0	100	6511.9	100	6656.9	100

Sectors	3d year 1962/63		4th year 1963/64		5th year 1964/65	
	Number of workers	%	Number of workers	%	Number of workers	%
Agriculture	3632	52.9	3673	51.9	3780	51.5
Industry	725.9	10.5	789.7	11.1	825.0	11.2
Total number of workers in the Plan	6868.2	100	7085.0	100	7333.4	100

(a) Excludes seasonal workers in agriculture, most of whom are women and children. Coverage of the self-employed probably is incomplete. The armed forces apparently are excluded also.

Table 4. ACREAGE AND PRODUCTION OF VARIOUS FIELD CROPS IN 1963 COMPARED WITH 1952

Crop	1952 Acreage in 1,000 feddans	1952 Production in 1,000 tons	1963 Acreage in 1,000 feddans	1963 Production in 1,000 tons
Food Crops:				
Wheat	1,402	1,089	1,455[a]	1,593[a]
Rice	374	517	830[a]	204[a]
Corn	1,704	1,506	1,832[a]	2,004[a]
Barley	137	118	121	134
Millet	433	522	455[a]	659[a]
Onions	26	244	59	661
Sugar cane	92	3,265	121[a]	4,819[a]
Peanuts	26	20	53	45
Sesame	42	14	59	26
Beans (Vicia faba)	355	250	360	263
Lentils	58	32	78	47
Fenugreek	54	34	59	42
Lupins	11	6	19	13
Chickpeas	15	9	12	8
Clover (Berseem)	2,202	36[c]	2,434	27[c]
Fibre Crops:				
Cotton	1,967	446	1,627	442
Flax	13	{ 28[b] { 5[c]	26	{ 62[b] { 11[c]

(a) 1962 estimates
(b) Fibre
(c) Seeds

Source: Hassan Abdallah, *U.A.R. Agriculture*.

Table 5. AREA AND PRODUCTION OF IMPORTANT AGRICULTURAL CROPS IN 1952/64

1952

Crop	Unit	Area in feddans	Average crop yield per feddan	Total yield
Cotton	Kentar	1,966,955	4.53	8,910,172
Wheat	Ardab	1,402,005	5.18	7,260,407
Barley	Ardab	136,587	7.19	981,418
Fenugreek	Ardab	53,953	4.02	216,868
Maize—Indian Corn	Ardab	1,703,828	6.31	10,757,148
Egyptian Millet	Ardab	432,870	8.62	3,732,287
Rice	Dariba	373,609	1.46	546,829
Beans	Ardab	355,448	4.53	1,610,224
Lentils	Ardab	57,635	3.45	198,893
Egyptian Lupines	Ardab	11,064	3.85	42,598
Chick-Pea	Ardab	14,897	4.24	63,148
Pea Nut—Ground Nut	Ardab	26,481	10.13	268,266
Sesame seeds	Ardab	41,925	2.81	117,863
Winter Onions	Kentar	26,482	144.00	3,813,000
Flax (Straw)	Kentar	12,900	48.00	617,791
Linseed	Ardab	12,900	3.18	41,039
Sugar Canes	Kentar	92,405	785.00	72,561,000

1963

Crop	Unit	Area in feddans	Average crop yield per feddan	Total yield
Cotton	Kentar	1,627,269	5.43	8,833,461
Wheat	Ardab	1,345,101	7.40	9,953,448
Barley	Ardab	120,752	9.27	1,119,684
Fenugreek	Ardab	59,385	4.53	268,977
Maize—Indian Corn	Ardab	1,720,763	7.75	13,335,037
Egyptian Millet	Ardab	483,842	10.76	5,203,812
Rice	Dariba	959,477	2.45	2,348,628
Beans	Ardab	359,570	4.72	1,698,684
Lentils	Ardab	78,200	3.76	293,971
Egyptian Lupines	Ardab	18,514	4.63	85,710
Chick-Pea	Ardab	11,544	4.72	54,542
Pea Nut—Ground Nut	Ardab	53,416	11.29	603,067
Sesame seeds	Ardab	58,986	3.61	212,939
Winter Onions	Kentar	51,812	169.—	8,759,460
Flax (Straw)	Kentar	26,052	53.—	1,368,972
Linseed	Ardab	26,052	3.40	88,536
Sugar Canes	Kentar	133,282	861.—	114,755,802

continued on next page

Table 5. AREA AND PRODUCTION OF IMPORTANT AGRICULTURAL CROPS IN 1952/64—continued

Crop	Unit	Area in feddans	1964 Average crop yield per feddan	Total yield
Cotton	Kentar	1,610,863	5.66	10,081,420
Wheat	Ardab	—	—	—
Barley	Ardab	121,396	9.71	1,178,755
Fenugreek	Ardab	56,248	4.78	268,865
Maize—Indian Corn	Ardab	—	—	—
Egyptian Millet	Ardab	—	—	—
Rice	Dariba	—	—	—
Beans	Ardab	408,113	5.78	2,358,893
Lentils	Ardab	78,816	4.16	327,875
Egyptian Lupines	Ardab	18,624	4.78	89,023
Chick-Pea	Ardab	13,820	4.71	65,092
Pea Nut—Ground Nut	Ardab	50,204	12.24	614,497
Sesame seeds	Ardab	55,138	3.53	194,637
Winter Onions	Kentar	48,301	167.—	8,066,267
Flax (Straw)	Kentar	33,096	53.00	1,765,908
Linseed	Ardab	33,096	3.49	115,505
Sugar Canes	Kentar	—	—	—

Source: Ministry of Agriculture.

— Data not available

Table 6. CEREALS

Area in feddans 000's
Production in metric tons 000's
Yield in metric ton/feddan

Year	Wheat			Corn			Millet			Barley			Rice		
	Area	Production	Yield	Area	Production	Yield	Area	Production	Yield	Area	Production	Yield	Area	Production	Yield
Average 1935/39	1,410	1,248	0.89	1,540	1,606	1.04	358	456	1.27	266	233	0.88	446	685	1.53
1950	1,372	1,018	0.74	1,451	1,306	0.90	393	426	1.08	117	91	0.78	700	1,242	1.77
1951	1,497	1,209	0.81	1,655	1,421	0.86	423	517	1.22	118	100	0.85	488	620	1.27
1952	1,402	1,089	0.78	1,704	1,506	0.88	433	523	1.21	137	118	0.86	374	517	1.38
1953	1,790	1,547	0.86	2,015	1,853	0.92	486	582	1.20	116	103	0.89	423	652	1.54
1954	1,795	1,729	0.96	1,904	1,753	0.92	457	549	1.20	122	116	0.95	610	1,118	1.83
1955	1,523	1,451	0.95	1,834	1,714	0.93	437	537	1.23	136	127	0.93	600	1,244	2.07
1956	1,570	1,547	0.99	1,836	1,652	0.90	479	595	1.24	132	129	0.98	690	1,495	2.17
1957	1,514	1,467	0.97	1,769	1,495	0.85	449	566	1.26	133	131	0.98	731	1,624	2.22
1958	1,425	1,412	0.99	1,955	1,758	0.90	423	543	1.28	136	135	0.99	518	1,027	1.98
1959	1,475	1,443	0.98	1,859	1,500	0.81	467	630	1.35	141	141	1.00	729	1,536	2.11
1960	1,456	1,499	1.03	1,821	1,691	0.93	453	603	1.33	148	156	1.05	706	1,486	2.10
1961	1,384	1,436	1.04	1,603	1,617	1.01	457	631	1.38	121	133	1.10	537	1,142	2.13
1962	1,455	1,593	1.09	1,832	2,004	1.09	455	659	1.45	131	146	1.12	830	2,038	2.46
1963	1,345	1,493	1.11	1,721	1,867	1.08	484	729	1.51	121	134	1.11	952	2,213	2.32
1964	1,295	1,499	1.16	1,660	1,934	1.17	494	740	1.50	121	141	1.17	962	2,036	2.12
1965	n.a.	n.a.	n.a.	n.a.	n.a.	n.a.	n.a.	n.a.	n.a.	125	130	1.04	n.a.	n.a.	n.a.

Source: Ministry of Agriculture—*Monthly Bulletin of Agricultural Economy.*

Table 7. ACREAGE AND PRODUCTION OF MAJOR VEGETABLES IN 1963 AS COMPARED WITH 1952

Crops	1952 Acreage in 1,000 feddans	1952 Production in 1,000 tons	1963 Acreage in 1,000 feddans	1963 Production in 1,000 tons
Tomatoes	79	564	170	1,056
Potatoes	25	153	60	420
Marrows	16	146	32	230
Okra	4	20	13	70
Eggplants	5	45	18	161
Cabbage	13	134	22	229
Water melons	42	374	73	858
Sweet melons	9	56	18	209
Cucumbers	13	62	34	182
Garlic	9	24	20	119
Others	46	256	125	786
Total	261	1,834	585	4,320

Source: Hassan Abdallah, *U.A.R. Agriculture.*

Table 8. ACREAGE AND PRODUCTION OF MAJOR FRUITS IN 1952 AND 1963 COMPARED

Crop	1952 Acreage in 1,000 feddans	1952 Production in 1,000 tons	1963 Acreage in 1,000 feddans	1963 Production in 1,000 tons
Oranges	26	257	65	337
Mandarines	9	76	11	49
Limes	4	38	10	49
Sweet Lemons	1	4	1	1
Dates	—	248	—	440
Grapes	19	90	20	105
Mangoes	9	55	19	90
Bananas	6	47	7	56
Guavas	7	38	5	34
Olives	3	3	3	8
Figs	2	9	2	6
Apricots	1	7	2	8
Others	6	22	7	33
Total	93	894	152	1,216

Source: Hassan Abdallah, *U.A.R. Agriculture.*

Table 9. VALUE OF INDUSTRIAL OUTPUT: 1952, 1960, 1964, 1965
(in million current £E)

	Fiscal 1952		Fiscal 1960		Fiscal 1964		Fiscal 1965		Increase, 1952-65 (per cent)
	Value (million £E)	Share of total (per cent)	Value (million £E)	Share of total (per cent)	Value (million £E)	Share of total (per cent)	Value (million £E)	Share of total (per cent)	
Spinning and weaving	84.6	27.0	230.5	34.9	332.7	29.9	361.7	30.8	325.9
Foodstuffs	122.3	39.0	177.1	26.8	282.6	25.4	284.1	24.2	132.8
Engineering and electrical equipment	30.1	9.8	80.9	12.2	163.9	14.7	174.5	14.9	483.3
Chemicals and pharma- ceuticals	20.5	6.5	49.1	7.4	121.1	10.9	133.6	11.4	570.0
Petroleum	34.2	10.9	66.4	10.0	118.3	10.6	122.6	10.4	258.8
Electric power	10.1	3.2	29.4	4.4	54.4	4.9	54.7	4.7	450.0
Building materials and ceramics	8.4	2.7	20.0	3.0	29.0	2.6	31.0	2.6	244.4
Mining	3.6	1.1	7.5	1.1	11.3	1.0	11.2	1.0	175.0
Totals[a]	313.8	100.0	660.9	100.0	1,113.3	100.0	1,173.4	100.0	273.9

[a] Excludes government workshops, military production, cotton ginning and packing, bakeries, tea packing, printing, and publishing.

Table 10. THE UAR BUDGET
(Unit: £E 1)

	1952/53	1960/61	1961/62
Ordinary budget	206,000,000	301,010,900	335,000,000
Production budget	310,000	280,845,000	315,000,000
Appendixed budget	4,333,050	176,906,371	197,254,252
Total	210,643,050	763,762,271	847,254,252
The excluded, i.e. support and productive allocations to the independent budgets and appendixed budgets	2,756,550	73,697,221	73,378,737
Total public expenditures	207,886,500	700,065,050	773,875,515

	1962/63 (a)	1963/64	1964/65	1965/66
Services sectors				
Ordinary budget for services	471,767,000	490,103,500	449,221,000	471,913,400
Budget of the units of local administration	138,711,050	153,222,800	161,445,000	177,532,600
Services appendixed budget	31,363,600	(b)	(b)	(b)
Budget included into the works sectors	821,009,400	1,000,540,900	1,164,959,670	1,210,082,000
Total	1,462,851,050	1,643,867,200	1,775,625,670	1,859,258,000
Excluded to avoid repetition or because it does not correspond with the nature of expenditure	450,229,500	564,461,400 (c)	591,203,187	653,509,939
Total public expenditures	1,012,621,550	1,079,405,800	1,184,422,483	1,206,018,061

(a) The 1962/1963 budget is divided into two sectors: services and works. Comparison is made on the basis of total public expenditures.

(b) The appendixed budget is added to the services ordinary budget.

(c) 51 million pounds are excluded which represent the value of raw materials and petroleum products for operations in the petroleum foundation budget. In 1962/1963 the value amounting to 42.6 million pounds was included in the budget (fiscal years).

Source: Central Agency for Public Mobilisation and Statistics.

Table 11. GROWTH OF PUBLIC REVENUES AND EXPENDITURES[a]

(in million £E)

End of fiscal year	Revenue	Net expenditure	Surplus (+) or deficit (−)
1900	11.9	10.8	+ 1.1
1910	16.3	16.9	− 0.6
1920/21	46.6	62.2	− 15.6
1930/31	38.9	41.5	− 2.6
1940/41	44.4	43.3	+ 1.1
1950/51	185.1	190.6	− 5.5
1951/52	194.8	233.6	− 38.8
1952/53[b]	199.3	209.8	− 10.5
1953/54[b]	212.3	233.0	− 20.7
1954/55[b]	232.4	269.9	− 37.5
1955/56[b]	292.8	340.3	− 47.5
1956/57[b]	276.3	358.1	− 81.8
1957/58[b]	333.9	335.3	− 1.4
1958/59[b]	403.2	430.2	− 27.0
1959/60[b]	444.8	511.1	− 66.3
1960/61[b]	540.5	700.1	−159.6
1961/62[b]	550.3	779.7	−229.4
1962/63	727.5[c]	970.0	−242.5[d]
1963/64	774.3[c]	1079.4	−305.1[d]
1964/65	828.3[c]	1184.4	−356.1[d]
1965/66	957.1[c]	1206.0	−248.9[d]
1966/67	1092.2[c]	1316.2	−224.0[d]
1967/68[e]	970.7[c]	1217.0	−246.3[d]

(a) An aggregation of net revenues and expenditures of all budgets after deducting inter-budget subsidies and transfers. Figures as from 1957/58 are budgetary estimates, as final accounts are not available.

(b) Development budget revenue is not included, while its expenditure is. This revenue was not indicated in the annual budget reports and was composed mainly of foreign aid and loans, internal borrowings, and monetary expansion.

(c) A residual figure reached by deducting the sum of internal and foreign loans plus the deficit in the Services Budget from the budgets' total.

(d) This figure represents the total of internal loans, credit facilities, and foreign loans included in the revenue of both the Services and Business Budgets, plus the deficit in the Services Budget.

(e) Postwar revision.

Source: National Bank of Egypt, *Economic Bulletin*, Vol. *19*, No. 3, 1966.

Table 12. PUBLIC EXPENSES IN VARIOUS SECTORS, AC-CORDING TO STATE BUDGET 1951/52 COMPARED WITH 1966/67 .

(in million current £E)

	1951/52		1966/67		1966/67 as a multiple of 1951/52
	Amount	Per cent of total	Amount	Per cent of total	
Agriculture	7.9	3.4	118.2	9.0	15.0
Irrigation and drainage	14.4	6.1	36.6	2.8	2.5
Electricity	2.9	1.2	50.7	3.9	17.5
High Dam	—	—	69.1	5.3	—
Industry	4.9	2.1	138.7	10.5	28.3
Transport and communication	28.9	12.3	130.7	9.9	4.5
Suez Canal	—	—	18.4	1.4	—
Housing and utilities	5.9	2.5	88.8	6.7	15.1
Total "productive" sectors	64.9	27.5	651.2	49.5	10.0
Armed forces	45.9	19.6	171.4	16.4	3.7
Other defense, security, and justice	24.8	10.6	44.3	3.4	1.8
Education	40.1	17.1	111.9	8.5	2.8
Health	10.1	4.3	43.0	3.3	4.3
Tourism and culture	2.5	1.1	28.0	2.1	11.2
Social and religious services	5.9	2.5	22.5	1.7	3.8
Cost of living subsidies	18.0	7.7	36.0	2.7	2.0
Other supply and storage	0.8	0.3	17.7	1.3	22.1
Financial and commercial	16.0	6.3	139.6	10.6	8.7

continued on next page

Table 12. PUBLIC EXPENSES IN VARIOUS SECTORS, ACCORDING TO STATE BUDGET 1951/52 COMPARED WITH 1966/67—continued

(in million current £E)

	1951/52 Amount	1951/52 Per cent of total	1966/67 Amount	1966/67 Per cent of total	1966/67 as a multiple of 1951/52
Foreign affairs	1.4	0.6	14.4	1.5	10.3
Other administration	3.9	1.7	9.1	0.7	2.3
Scientific research	0.3	0.1	6.7	0.5	22.3
Other	—	—	14.4	1.1	—
Total services sector[a]	170.3	72.5	665.0	50.5	3.9
GRAND TOTAL	234.7	100.0	1316.2	100.0	5.6
Of which:					
Current expenditure	179.0	76.5	948.0	72.0	5.3
Investment	55.7	23.5	368.2	28.0	6.6

(a) Totals may not be exact, due to rounding.

Source: Federation of Industries, 1966.

Table 13. FY 1968: INVESTMENT FUND INCOME AND EXPENDITURE

(in million £E)

Sources of income	Prewar estimate	Postwar estimate
Surplus profits of enterprises	117	57.1
Reserve funds of enterprises	153.1	133.9
Surpluses of insurance and pension funds Borrowing from Postal Savings, etc.	137.3 }	240.3
Foreign loans		65.8
Other income		83.5
Total		581.0

Uses of funds		
Deficit in Services Budget		119.5
Deficit in Production Budget		39.5
New investment		232.2[a]
Loans to new companies		21.6

Payments on loans
   Foreign
   Domestic
		49.8
		72.4

Other		38.6
Total		622.0

Excess of requirements over resources,
  to be covered by borrowing from
  domestic banks if necessary
		41.0

(a) Including LE 24.7 million not allocated to projects

Table 14. PUBLIC DEBT
(in million £E)

End of fiscal year [a]	National and dev. loans [b]	T. bills	Loans for financing external debts	Nationalized [c] inst. bonds	Agrarian reform bonds	Loans from insurance and savings inst.	Others	Total	Government guaranteed bonds
1900	100.1	—	—	—	—	—	—	100.1	—
1910	92.6	—	—	—	—	—	—	92.6	—
1920/21	90.7	—	—	—	—	—	—	90.7	—
1930/31	87.4	—	—	—	—	—	—	87.4	—
1940/41	85.0	—	—	—	—	—	—	85.0	—
1950/51	108.0	67.0	—	—	—	—	—	175.0	—
1951/52	143.0	60.0	—	—	—	—	—	203.0	—
1952/53	123.0	135.0	—	—	—	—	—	258.0	—
1953/54	123.0	72.0	—	—	—	—	—	195.0	—
1954/55	148.0	55.0	—	—	14.5	—	—	217.5	—
1955/56	158.0	97.0	—	—	16.3	0.6	—	271.9	—
1956/57	158.0	135.0	—	—	17.6	0.6	2.7	313.9	20.0
1957/58	158.0	150.0	—	—	21.0	0.6	2.7	332.3	20.0
1958/59	198.0	165.0	—	—	32.5	0.6	2.7	398.8	20.0
1959/60	182.0	164.0	45.0	20.3	32.5	0.6	2.7	447.1	23.0
1960/61	232.0	185.0	53.0	22.2	37.1	7.0	1.6	537.9	28.0
1961/62	232.0	200.0	65.0	22.2	42.1	49.2	11.7	622.2	28.0
1962/63	232.0	235.0	100.0	296.5	42.5	107.5	11.7	1025.2	28.0
1963/64	232.0	335.0	100.0	33.4	—	183.5	43.5	927.4	28.0

(a) From 1st Jan. to 31st Dec. until 1914; from 1st April to 31st March until 1926/27; from 1st May to 30th April until 1946/47; from 1st March to 28th Feb. until 1950/51; and from 1st July to 30th June thereafter. Thereafter these debts were converted into National Loans.

(b) Until the fiscal year 1942/43, the total Public Debt consisted of the Guaranteed Debt 3%, the Privileged Debt 3½% and the Unified Debt 4%.

(c) Until 1961/62 includes bonds relating to nationalized banks only. As from 1962/63 bonds issued in conformity with the 1961 Nationalization Laws and subsequent legislation also included.

Source: Central Agency for Public Mobilisation and Statistics.

Table 15a. BALANCE OF PAYMENTS ESTIMATES: 1964-65
(*in million £E*)

A—Current Transactions	1964	1965[a]
Receipts:		
Proceeds of exports[b]	227.6	246.8
Insurance[c]	0.7	0.2
Shipping	8.8	12.6
Suez Canal dues	78.4	86.2
Interest, dividends, and other revenues	7.2	10.1
Travel and other receipts	51.0	46.7
Total	373.7	402.6
Disbursements:		
Payments for imports[b]	399.4	413.3
Films	0.8	0.6
Other commercial payments	5.2	5.1
Insurance[c]	0.6	0.3
Shipping	8.9	9.8
Interest, dividends, and other revenues	15.0	17.2
Travel and maintenance	12.3	13.3
Government expenditures	36.8	35.5
Other disbursements	17.8	17.5
Total	496.8	512.6
Balance of current transactions	−123.1	−110.0

(a) Provisional
(b) Including transit trade
(c) Other than on imports and exports
Source: Central Bank of Egypt, *Economic Review.*

Table 15b. BALANCE OF PAYMENTS ESTIMATES: 1964-65
(*in million £E*)

		1964	1965
B—Capital Transactions			
Inflow:			
U.S. counterpart funds and loans in £E		69.1	38.8
Foreign loans		114.8	69.9
Other inflow		1.3	24.2[a]
Total		185.2	132.9
Outflow:			
Repayment of loans and other liabilities		50.9	43.7
Other outflow[c]		23.2[b]	8.3
Total		74.1	52.0
Net capital transactions		+111.1	+ 80.9
C—Overall Surplus or Deficit		− 12.0	− 29.1
D—Accounted for as Follows:			
Net foreign exchange position	(decrease, −)	− 9.1	− 41.4
N/R banker's a/cs	(decrease, +)	+ 5.6	+ 17.7
Other N/R a/cs and other liabilities	(increase, −)	− 3.3	− 4.1
I.M.F. position	(increase, −)	− 1.9	+ 3.7
Errors and omissions		− 3.3	− 5.0
Total		− 12.0	− 29.1

(a) Including net utilisation of credit facilities
(b) Including net repayment of credit facilities
(c) Including loans granted by the U.A.R.

Source: Central Bank of Egypt, *Economic Review.*

Table 16. BALANCE OF PAYMENTS ESTIMATES: 1950-65
(in million £E)

Year	Merchandise transactions[a]		Other transactions		Balance of current transactions	Capital remittances (net)	Overall surplus (+) or deficit (−)
	Payments	Proceeds	Payments	Proceeds			
1950	221.7	188.5	57.2	80.0	− 10.4	− 3.6	−14.0
1951	241.9	201.9	65.5	90.3	− 15.2	− 4.6	−19.8
1952	210.5	145.6	61.6	73.1	− 53.4	− 2.0	−55.4
1953	165.2	135.3	57.8	79.8	− 7.9	− 0.4	− 8.3
1954	150.7	139.8	67.9	82.4	+ 3.6	− 0.3	+ 3.3
1955	190.3	133.1	71.0	94.2	− 34.0	+ 2.2	−31.8
1956	192.3	129.9	59.5	88.9	− 33.0	+ 2.0	−31.0
1957	217.5	166.0	50.9	71.2	− 31.2	− 0.1	−31.3
1958	214.0	161.0	56.3	89.2	− 20.1	− 3.8	−23.9
1959	235.3	164.3	65.6	100.6	− 36.0	+ 11.4	−24.6
1960	255.2	200.2	70.1	101.5	− 23.6	+ 11.1	−12.5
1961	237.8	161.3	71.6	94.8	− 53.3	+ 33.9	−19.4
1962	294.2	145.2	70.3	101.7	− 117.6	+ 80.7	−36.9
1963[b]	402.6	228.8	84.1	135.0	− 122.9	+ 93.7	−29.2
1964	399.4	227.6	97.4	146.1	− 123.1	+111.1	−12.0
Jan./June 1964	207.8	145.2	47.7	70.2	− 40.1	+ 43.7	+ 3.6
Jan./June 1965[c]	202.4	162.4	42.4	78.4	− 4.0	+ 7.6	+ 3.6

(a) As from 1962, merchandise transactions figures include transit trade, which was previously included among other transactions.
(b) Figures of 1963 are calculated on the basis of the new exchange rate of LE 1 = $2.3.
(c) Provisional

Source: Central Bank of Egypt, *Economic Review*.

Table 17. SUMMARY OF ESTIMATED FOREIGN AID TO EGYPT

(in million US $)

Donor	Total aid	Aid as credit	Credit used through 1966	Credit repaid through 1966	Debt as of Jan. 1967	Credit available Jan. 1967
USA	1,232	834	817	286	531	29
Food for Peace	(1,001)	(690)	(690)	(231)	(459)	(17)
Development loans	(96)	(96)	(79)	(23)	(56)	(12)
Export-Import Bank	(60)	(48)	(48)	(32)	(16)	(—)
Grants	(75)	(—)	(—)	(—)	(—)	
UK	10	10	10	1	9	—
West Germany	90	77	68	9	59	9
Italy	179	172	122	50	72	50
Belgium	12	12	n.a.	n.a.	n.a.	12
Spain	18	18	n.a.	n.a.	n.a.	18
Japan	30	30	30	12	18	—
France	100	100	60	n.a.	60	40
Switzerland	5	5	5	n.a.	n.a.	n.a.
Kuwait	256	256	228	—	228	28
IBRD	57	57	57	11	46	—
United Nations	30	—	—	—	—	
Total non-Communist	2,019	1,571	1,397	369	1,023	186

continued on next page

Table 17. SUMMARY OF ESTIMATED FOREIGN AID TO EGYPT—continued

(in million US $)

Donor	Total aid	Aid as credit	Credit used through 1966	Credit repaid through 1966	Debt as of Jan. 1967	Credit available Jan. 1967
USSR	1,011	1,011	500	50	450	511
Including:						
Aswan Dam	325					
First Plan	219					
Second Plan	280					
East Europe	600	600	300	50	250	300
Including:						
Bulgaria	12					
Czechoslovakia	140					
East Germany	135					
Hungary	75					
Poland	80					
Rumania	70					
Yugoslavia	55					
Communist China	80	80	n.a.	n.a.	n.a.	80
Total Communist	1,691	1,691	800	100	700	891
GRAND TOTAL	3,710	3,262	2,197	469	1,723	1,077

Note: For non-Communist countries, where figures on use and repayment are not available, the assumption has been made that new credits are unused and old credits are fully used. The breakdown between debt and repayment similarly is estimated on the basis of the age of the credit involved. For Communist countries, estimates are based on fragmentary news reports.

Symbols: n.a.: not available

—: zero or insignificant

Table 18. VOLUME OF FOREIGN TRADE
(in million £E)

Year	Exports	Imports	Trade balance
1952	150.2	227.7	− 77.5
1953	142.6	180.0	− 37.4
1954	143.9	164.5	− 20.7
1955	146.0	187.3	− 41.3
1956	142.3	186.1	− 43.8
1957	171.6	182.6	− 11.0
1958	166.3	240.2	− 73.9
1959	160.5	222.2	− 61.7
1960	197.8	232.5	− 34.7
1961	168.9	243.8	− 74.8
1962	158.3	300.9	−142.6
1963	226.8	398.4	−171.6
1964	234.4	414.4	−180.0
1965	263.1	405.9	−142.8
1966	263.1	465.4	−202.3

Source: Central Agency of General Mobilisation and Statistics.

Table 19. EXPORTS OF COTTON
(in metric cantars(a) 000's)

Country/ Cotton Season	1950/ 51	1954/ 55	1955/ 56	1956/ 57	1957/ 58	1958/ 59	1959/ 60	1960/ 61	1961/ 62	1962/ 63	1963/ 64	1964/ 65
Austria	69	96	116	95	139	97	94	131	63	22	38	38
Belgium	46	69	72	123	28	32	43	30	26	45	52	37
China	64	452	323	424	552	804	887	231	256	487	306	472
Czechoslovakia	251	247	1,029	406	573	689	770	1,346	464	701	614	733
France	451	601	614	216	180	147	275	198	268	206	255	230
Western Germany }	224	343	182	182	39	265	425	104	143	252	416	431
Eastern Germany {		39	99	257	261	318	312	222	198	186	165	196
Hungary	68	173	140	32	120	104	158	181	101	139	114	137
India	897	575	670	293	165	268	714	315	329	522	508	470
Italy	664	311	409	266	104	170	376	140	253	275	347	274
Japan	274	318	470	383	296	262	356	265	154	296	401	496
Poland	48	139	221	184	226	257	358	343	156	209	220	257
Rumania	118	69	198	105	126	107	153	277	234	224	184	257
Spain	208	127	31	30	184	209	57	160	290	3	18	99
Switzerland	151	214	259	130	129	96	129	93	39	97	130	61
United Kingdom	1,669	263	187	1	32	356	190	68	131	130	234	137
United States	286	296	212	212	273	38	421	462	266	171	143	116
U.S.S.R.	2	293	239	959	1,412	1,958	1,469	1,627	895	1,744	1,307	1,968
Yugoslavia	4	74	63	92	118	138	248	389	218	210	177	276
Other countries	289	251	324	235	142	242	212	168	104	142	136	158
Total	5,783	4,950	5,858	4,625	5,099	6,557	7,647	6,750	4,588	6,061	5,835	6,843

(a) One metric cantar = 50 kgs. = 110 lb.

Source: Central Agency for Public Mobilisation and Statistics.

Table 20. EXPORTS
(*Unit: £E 1,000*)

Kind of export	1960	1961	1962	1963	1964	1965
Living animals and animal products	599	753	1,212	1,394	1,210	930
Products of the plant realm	20,565	16,767	20,983	34,669	45,007	34,252
Fats, grease, oils, and products	257	121	192	261	181	178
Food products, drinks, and tobacco	3,327	4,432	4,058	3,584	5,958	4,067
Metal products	7,675	11,682	19,673	24,317	24,899	22,005
Chemical products	2,628	3,058	877	1,496	2,130	1,814
Plastics, sillilouse, and rubber	1,181	718	274	710	685	168
Skins, furs, and products	395	629	526	612	485	427
Coal, charcoal, mats, and baskets	278	291	132	165	166	165
Material for manufacturing paper, paper, and products	919	1,189	1,283	1,632	1,805	1,895
Textiles and products	156,120	125,196	106,484	153,854	148,438	193,167
Shoes, head covers, and artificial flowers	510	370	238	224	328	262
Nonmetal products and asbestos	506	703	148	640	195	321
Precious minerals, gems, jewels, and currency	84	137	206	203	202	191
Ordinary metals and products	1,683	1,812	524	780	718	494
Electric instruments and equipment and spare parts	701	428	147	198	193	471
Transportation means	80	82	48	242	136	685
Optical and cinema equipment	22	34	26	69	73	74
Weapons, ammunition, and parts	2	8	00	8	00	00
Various other goods and products	280	511	1,254	1,672	1,537	1,535
Masterpieces of art and historical relics for museums	6	15	25	38	32	31
Total	197,757	168,936	158,310	226,768	234,377	263,132

Source: Central Agency for Public Mobilisation and Statistics.

Table 21. IMPORTS

(Unit: £E 1,000)

Kind of import	1960	1961	1962	1963	1964	1965
Living animals and animal products	3,051	3,709	2,084	8,110	6,529	9,775
Products of the plant realm	39,923	42,394	64,422	84,956	91,455	84,210
Fats, grease, oils, and products	3,088	5,878	4,440	13,492	13,880	10,271
Food products, drinks, and tobacco	8,252	9,412	11,664	14,036	15,432	14,043
Metal products	25,577	26,363	33,595	40,388	42,727	36,425
Chemical products	26,868	20,930	28,822	45,998	39,569	49,112
Plastics, sililouse, and rubber	2,302	1,869	3,806	5,626	5,269	7,458
Skins, furs, and products	933	812	689	972	1,017	911
Charcoal, mats, and baskets	8,500	10,721	9,649	10,448	14,795	16,500
Material for manufacturing paper, paper, and products	10,579	12,139	12,728	11,689	10,202	11,555
Textiles and products	16,152	14,789	10,941	13,330	14,419	25,569
Shoes, head covers, umbrellas, and artificial flowers	26	20	6	5	11	2
Nonmetal products and asbestos	3,093	2,215	1,918	3,536	2,660	3,055
Precious metals, gems, jewels, and currency	197	180	862	1,325	1,244	883
Ordinary metals and products	22,535	23,420	35,532	37,962	41,671	38,013
Electric instruments and equipment and spare parts	42,323	46,321	42,386	65,816	73,882	61,624
Transportation means	13,221	17,719	33,424	33,434	34,542	32,210
Optical and cinema equipment	2,325	3,013	3,001	5,888	3,905	3,144
Weapons, ammunition, and parts	91	185	68	80	44	14
Various other goods and products	2,718	1,686	884	1,263	1,143	1,098
Masterpieces of art and historical relics for museums	2	3	2	2	19	3
Total	232,476	243,779	300,923	398,356	414,415	405,875

Source: Central Agency for Public Mobilisation and Statistics.

Table 22. GEOGRAPHICAL DISTRIBUTION OF FOREIGN TRADE 1964 AND 1965

(in million current US $)

	1964			1965		
	Exports	Imports	Balance	Exports	Imports	Balance
Major hard currency markets						
USA	18	284	−266	19	189	−170
West Europe	124	269	−145	129	303	−174
Japan	18	19	−1	21	15	6
Australia and New Zealand	(a)	4	−4	1	6	−5
Canada and Mexico	(a)	(a)	(a)	(a)	13	−12
Subtotal	160	576	−417	170	525	−355
Major free world bilateral partners						
India	31	29	2	26	55	−29
Spain	14	5	9	6	15	−8
Subtotal	44	33	10	32	69	−37
Other free world	69	149	−78	64	107	−43
Total free world	273	758	−485	265	701	−435
Communist bilateral partners						
USSR and East Europe(b)	235	168	67	284	200	84
China	17	18	−1	45	27	18
Cuba and other(c)	14	9	5	10	6	4
Subtotal	266	195	71	340	233	107
TOTAL WORLD	539	953	−414	605	934	−328

(a) Less than $500,000
(b) Including Yugoslavia
(c) Mongolia, North Korea, North Vietnam

A Selected Bibliography

A Selected Bibliography

In the selection of the titles that follow, three decisions, possibly rather arbitrary ones, were made: (1) The main emphasis has been placed on works published in recent years. (2) Only books and periodicals are included. (3) The government of the United Arab Republic puts out about 120 regular publications, which appear at intervals of from one day to one year. Most are in Arabic; a number have both Arabic and English or French editions; and a number appear in only one of these foreign languages. In the pages that follow, a selection has been made from the publications that are published in English or in French.

Section I. Sociological

AKRAWI, MATTA, "The Arab World: Nationalism and Education," in *The Year Book of Education*, London, Evans Brothers, 1949.

ALLEN, HAROLD B., *Rural Education and Welfare in the Middle East*, London, His Majesty's Stationery Office, 1946.

ALWAN, MUHAMMAD M., *Al-Tasawwuf al-Islami*, Cairo, 1958.

American University (Washington, D.C.), Foreign Area Studies Division, *Area Handbook for the United Arab Republic (Egypt)*, Washington, D.C., Superintendent of Documents, U.S. Government Printing Office, 1964.

'AMMAR, HAMID, *Growing Up in an Egyptian Village*, New York, Grove Press, 1954.

AYROUT, HENRY, *The Fellaheen*, Cairo, Schindler, 1945.

BADAOUI, ZAKI, *Les problèmes du travail et les organisations ouvrières en Égypte*, Alexandrie, Société des Publications Egyptiennes, 1948.

BAER, GABRIEL, *Egyptian Guilds in Modern Times*, Jerusalem, Israel Oriental Society, 1964.

––––––, *Population and Society in the Arab East*, New York, Praeger, 1964.

BERQUE, JACQUES, *Histoire sociale d'un village égyptien au XXème siècle*, Paris, Mouton, 1957.

BINDER, LEONARD, *The Ideological Revolution in the Middle East*, New York, Wiley, 1964.

BUTLER, HAROLD B., *Report on Labour Conditions*, Cairo, Ministry of Interior, 1932.

CHARNAY, JEAN-PAUL, ed., *Normes et valeurs dans l'Islam contemporain*, Paris, Payot, 1966.

CLELAND, WENDELL, *The Population Problem in Egypt*, Lancaster, Pennsylvania, Science Press Printing Co., 1936.

Columbia University, Bureau of Applied Social Research, *Climates of Opinion in Egypt,* New York, 1952.

————, *Communications Behavior of Selected Social Groups in Egypt,* New York, 1952.

CRAGG, KENNETH, *The Call of the Minaret,* New York, Oxford University Press, 1956.

CRARY, DOUGLAS D., "The Villager," in *Social Forces in the Middle East,* Sydney N. Fisher, ed., Ithaca, Cornell University Press, 1955.

DODGE, BAYARD, *Al-Azhar. A Millennium of Muslim Learning,* Washington, D.C., The Middle East Institute, 1961.

FISHER, SYDNEY N., ed., *Social Forces in the Middle East,* Ithaca, Cornell University Press, 1955.

FURFEY, PAUL H., *A History of Social Thought,* New York, Macmillan, 1942.

GADALLA, SAAD M., *Land Reform in Relation to Social Development, Egypt,* Columbia, University of Missouri Press, 1962.

GIBB, H. A. R., *Arabic Literature,* London, Oxford University Press, 1926.

————, *Modern Trends in Islam,* Chicago, University of Chicago Press, 1947.

————, *Mohammedanism,* 2d ed., London, Oxford University Press, 1954.

GLANVILLE, S. R. K., ed., *The Legacy of Egypt,* Oxford, Clarendon Press, 1942.

HAKIM, GEORGE, "Social and Economic Problems in the Middle East," in *Background of the Middle East,* Ernest Jackl, ed., Ithaca, Cornell University Press, 1952.

EL-HAKIM, TAWFIQ, *Maze of Justice* (A. S. Eban, trans.), London, Harvill Press, 1947.

EL-HAKIM, TEWFIK (sic), *La caverne des songes,* Cairo, Éditions de la Revue du Caire, 1940.

HARBI, M. K. and EL-SAYED M. EL-AZZAWI, *Education in Egypt (U.A.R.) in the 20th Century,* Cairo, Ministry of Education, 1960.

HARBISON, F. and I. A. IBRAHIM, *Human Resources for Egyptian Enterprise,* New York, McGraw-Hill, 1958.

HOURANI, A. H., *Minorities in the Arab World,* London, Oxford University Press, 1947.

HURST, H. E., *The Nile,* London, Constable, 1952.

HUSSEIN, DR. AHMED, *Rural Social Welfare Centres in Egypt,* Cairo, Egyptian Ministry of Social Affairs, 1951.

————, *Social Welfare in Egypt,* Cairo, Egyptian Ministry of Social Affairs, 1956.

HUSSEIN, TAHA, *The Future of Culture in Egypt* (S. Glazer, trans.), Washington, D.C., American Council of Learned Societies, 1954.

OMAR, ABDEL MONEIM, *The Sudan Question Based on British Documents*, 2d ed., Cairo, Misr Press, 1952.

Orient, Paris (monthly).

Revolution in . . . Years, The, Cairo (annual, with some issues entitled: . . . Years of Revolution).

Revue de la Presse Arabe, La, Damascus (biweekly).

RIAD, HASSAN, *L'Égypte nassérienne*, Paris, Éditions de Minuit, 1964.

RIFAAT, M., *The Awakening of Modern Egypt*, London, Longmans, Green, 1947.

ROBERTSON, TERENCE, *Crisis: The Inside Story of the Suez Conspiracy*, New York, Atheneum, 1965.

Royal Institute of International Affairs, *Great Britain and Egypt, 1914-1936*, London, 1936.

————, *Great Britain and Egypt, 1914-1954*, London, 1954.

AL-SADAT, ANWAR, *Revolt on the Nile*, London, A. Wingate, 1957.

SAFRAN, NADAV, *Egypt in Search of Political Community*, Cambridge, Harvard University Press, 1961.

SAYEGH, FAYEZ A., *Arab Unity: Hope and Fulfillment*, New York, Devin-Adair, 1958.

————, ed., *The Dynamics of Neutralism in the Arab World*, San Francisco, Chandler Publishing Co., 1964.

————, "The Theoretical Structure of Nasser's Arab Socialism," in *Middle Eastern Affairs: No. Four*, Albert Hourani, ed., London, Chatto and Windus, 1965.

SCHONFIELD, HUGH J., *The Suez Canal in World Affairs*, London, Constellation Books, 1952.

SEALE, PATRICK, *The Struggle for Syria: A Study of Post-War Arab Politics*, London, Oxford University Press, 1965.

SHARABI, H. R., *Nationalism and Revolution in the Arab World*, Princeton, Van Nostrand, 1966.

STEINDORFF, GEORG and K. G. SEELE, *When Egypt Ruled the East*, Chicago, University of Chicago Press, 1942.

STEVENS, GEORGIANA G., *Egypt, Yesterday and Today*, New York, Holt, Rinehart and Winston, 1963.

ST. JOHN, ROBERT, *The Boss; The Story of Gamal Abdel Nasser*, New York, McGraw-Hill, 1960.

THOMAS, HUGH, *Suez*, New York, Harper and Row, 1967.

TIGNOR, ROBERT L., *Modernization and British Colonial Rule in Egypt, 1882-1914*, Princeton, Princeton University Press, 1966.

TOMICHE, NADA, *L'Égypte moderne*, Paris, Presses Universitaires de France, 1966.

United Arab Republic, Information Department, *Statute of the Arab Socialist Union*, Cairo, n.d.

VATIKIOTIS, P. J., *The Egyptian Army in Politics*, Bloomington, Indiana University Press, 1961.

433

————, *A Modern History of Egypt*, New York, Praeger, 1966.

VAUCHER, GEORGES, *Gamal Abdel Nasser et son équipe*, 2 vols. Paris, R. Julliard, 1959/60.

VERNIER, BERNARD, *Armée et politique au Moyen-Orient*, Paris, Payot, 1966.

WAHBY, MOHAMMED, *Arab Socialism: Ferment and Commitment*, New Delhi, Afro-Asian Publications, 1966.

WATERFIELD, GORDON, *Egypt*, London, Thames and Hudson, 1967.

WHEELOCK, KEITH, *Nasser's New Egypt*, New York, Praeger, 1960.

WILSON, SIR ARNOLD T., *The Suez Canal: Its Past, Present, and Future*, 2d ed., London, Oxford University Press, 1939.

WYNN, WILTON, *Nasser of Egypt: The Search for Dignity*, Cambridge, Mass., Arlington Books, 1959.

Section III. Economic

ABDALLAH, HASSAN, *The Handbook of Egypt*, Cairo, National Publication and Printing House, 1966.

————, *U.A.R. Agriculture*, Cairo, Ministry of Agriculture, Foreign Relations Department, 1965.

African and Middle East Economist, The, Cairo (monthly).

Afro-Asian Economic Review, Cairo (monthly, mimeographed).

Agrarian Reform in the U.A.R. Texts and Documents, Cairo, Middle East Publications, n.d.

AMIN, GALAL, *Food Supply and Economic Development; with Special Reference to Egypt*, London, Cass, 1966.

Arab Petroleum, The, Cairo (monthly).

BAER, GABRIEL, *A History of Landownership in Modern Egypt*, London, Oxford University Press, 1962.

Bank Misr, *Economic Bulletin* (monthly).

Banque de Port Said, *Revue Economique Trimestrielle*.

Basic Statistics, Cairo (annual).

BONNE, ALFRED, *State and Economics in the Middle East: A Society in Transition*, London, Kegan Paul, Trench, Trubner, 1948.

Central Bank of Egypt, *Economic Review* (quarterly).

————, *Report of the Board of Directors for the Year . . .* (annual).

Commercial Directory of Egypt, Cairo, Modern Publishing House (annual, in English and Arabic).

Economic Review of the Arab World, Beirut, Bureau of Lebanese and Arab Documentation (monthly).

Economist Intelligence Unit, *EIU Quarterly Economic Review, Egypt (UAR), Libya, Sudan*, and its *Annual Supplement*, London.

Egypt-U.A.R. 1967 Year-Book, Cairo, Ptolemies Publications, n.d.

Egyptian Directory of the United Arab Republic, The, Cairo, Egyptian Directory (annual).

Egyptian Economic and Political Review, The, Cairo (monthly, in Arabic, English, and French).

Federation of Industries in the United Arab Republic, Year Book, Cairo, Société Orientale de Publicité (annual).

Foreign Trade of Egypt (Le Commerce Extérieur de l'Égypte), Cairo, Federation Égyptienne de l'Industrie, 1955.

GOLDMAN, MARSHALL I., *Soviet Foreign Aid,* New York, Praeger, 1967.

HANSEN, BENT and GIRGIS A. MARZOUK, *Development and Economic Policy in the U.A.R. (Egypt),* Amsterdam, North-Holland Publishing Company, 1965.

International Monetary Fund, *Balance of Payments Yearbook.*

————, *Annual Report on Exchange Restrictions.*

————, *International Financial Statistics* (monthly).

ISSAWI, CHARLES, *Egypt at Mid-Century: An Economic Survey,* New York, Oxford University Press, 1954.

————, "The Entrepreneur Class," in *Social Forces in the Middle East,* Sydney N. Fisher, ed., Ithaca, Cornell University Press, 1955.

————, *Egypt in Revolution, An Economic Analysis,* London, Oxford University Press, 1963.

KARDOUCHE, GEORGE K., *The U.A.R. in Development: A Study in Expansionary Finance,* New York, Praeger, 1966.

KHALIL, MAGDI S., *Le dirigisme économique et les contrats (étude de droit comparé: France, Égypte, U.R.S.S.),* Paris, 1967.

MEAD, DONALD C., *Growth and Structural Change in the Egyptian Economy,* Homewood, Illinois, Richard D. Irwin, 1967.

MEYER, ALBERT J., *Entrepreneurship: The Missing Link in the Arab States,* Beirut, Middle East Papers of the American University of Beirut, 1954.

Middle East Business Digest, London, Overseas Publishing (monthly).

Middle East Economic Digest, Monthly Statistical and Documentary Service, London, Economic Features.

————, *Weekly Report,* London, Economic Features.

Middle East Economic Survey, Beirut (weekly).

Middle East News: Weekly Research Review, Cairo.

Monthly Review of Economic and Social Events in the U.A.R., Cairo, Institute of National Planning, Documentation Centre.

EL-NAJJAR, SA'ID, *Foreign Aid to U.A.R.,* Cairo, Institute of National Planning, n.d.

————, *Foreign Aid and the Economic Development of the U.A.R.,* Princeton, Princeton University Press, 1965.

National Bank of Egypt, *Economic Bulletin* (monthly).

O'BRIEN, PATRICK K., *The Revolution in Egypt's Economic System: From Private Enterprise to Socialism, 1952-1965,* London, Oxford University Press, 1966.

435

Organization for Economic Co-operation and Development, *Geographical Distribution of Financial Flows to Less Developed Countries, 1960-64,* Paris, 1966.

——————, *Geographical Distribution of Financial Flows to Less Developed Countries, 1965,* Paris, 1967.

Overall Five Year Plan for Economic and Social Development, 1960-1965, Cairo, n.p., n.d.

POTTER, DALTON, "The Bazaar Merchant," in *Social Forces in the Middle East,* Sydney N. Fisher, ed., Ithaca, Cornell University Press, 1955.

PREST, ALAN R., *War Economics of Primary Producing Countries,* Cambridge, University Press, 1948.

RIFAAT, MOHAMMED ALI, *The Monetary System of Egypt,* London, Allen and Unwin, 1935.

Royal Institute of International Affairs, *The Middle East: A Political and Economic Survey,* London, 1954.

SAAB, GABRIEL S., *The Egyptian Agrarian Reform 1952-1962,* London, Oxford University Press, 1967.

SAWYER, CAROLE A., *Communist Trade with Developing Countries, 1955-1965,* New York, Praeger, 1966.

Suez Canal Report, Ismailia (monthly).

TANSKY, LEO, *U.S. and U.S.S.R. Aid to Developing Countries: A Comparative Study of India, Turkey, and the U.A.R.,* New York, Praeger, 1967.

United Arab Republic, *Organizations Directory, 1965-1966,* The Middle East Observer, Cairo (annual).

——————, Central Agency for Mobilisation and Statistics, *Foreign Trade of the U.A.R.,* Cairo (annual, in English and Arabic).

——————, Central Agency for Mobilisation and Statistics, *Statistical Handbook of the United Arab Republic, 1952-1965,* Cairo, 1966.

——————, Central Agency for Mobilisation and Statistics, *U.A.R. Basic Statistics,* Cairo, 1964.

——————, Federation of Industries, *Guide to Industries,* Cairo (in English and Arabic), 1966.

——————, General Organization for Industrialization, *U.A.R. Second Social and Economic Development Plan. Industry, 1965/66-1971/72, General Description of the Projects,* Cairo, 1966.

——————, Information Department, *Pocket Book,* Cairo (annual).

——————, Information Department, *Year Book,* Cairo (annual).

——————, Institute of National Planning, *U.A.R. News Review,* Cairo (monthly).

——————, Ministry of the Treasury, *Draft of the State Budget for the Fiscal Year 1966-67,* General Organization for Government Printing Offices, Cairo, 1966 (issued annually).

United Nations, Department of Economic and Social Affairs, *Economic Development in the Middle East, 1945 to 1954,* New York, 1955.

————, *Public Finance Information Papers: Egypt,* Lake Success, 1950.

————, *Review of Economic Conditions in the Middle East,* New York, 1955.

United States, Agency for International Development, *AID Programs in the Near East and South Asia,* Washington, D.C., 1966.

————, *U.S. Overseas Loans and Grants and Assistance from International Organizations,* Washington, D.C., Special Report Prepared for the House Foreign Affairs Committee, March 17, 1967.

————, Department of Agriculture, Economic Research Service, *The Africa and West Asia Agricultural Situation, Review of 1965 and Outlook for 1966,* Washington, D.C., 1966.

————, Department of Agriculture, *The Agricultural Economy of the United Arab Republic (Egypt),* Washington, D.C., Foreign Agriculture Economic Report No. 21.

————, Department of Agriculture, *Public Law 480 and Other Economic Assistance to the United Arab Republic (Egypt),* Washington, D.C., 1964.

————, Department of Commerce, *World Trade Information Series,* Washington, D.C. (monthly).

————, Department of State, *Communist Governments and Developing Nations: Economic Aid and Trade,* Washington, D.C., July 21, 1967 (annual, with slight variation in title).

WARRINER, DOREEN, *Land and Poverty in the Middle East,* London, Royal Institute of International Affairs, 1948.

————, *Land Reform and Development in the Middle East,* London, Royal Institute of International Affairs, 1962.

Index

Index

441

208-9, 214; scientists, 19; symbol-
ists, 123
French-British Debt Commission, 21
Front for the Liberation of Occupied
South Yemen (FLOSY), 232
Fruits, 311, 325, 327, 390
Fuad, King, 25, 90
Fuad, Ahmad, Prince, 22, 23
Fuad I University, 113
Fujaira, 233
Furnishings, 102-3

gadid (new), 97, 99
galabia, 47, 48, 104, 302
Gallicizing, 60-61
al-Gamahir (*Masses*), 208
Gandhi, 295
Gaza, 28, 287
Gaza Strip, 27, 28, 223, 225
GDP. *See* Gross Domestic Product
General Agency for Land Reform, 315
General Assembly (*al-jamiyyah al-
umumiyyah*), 137, 138
General Committee, 201, 202, 203
General Congress, 197
General Egyptian Establishment for
Cinema, Broadcasting, and Tele-
vision, 212-13
General Federation of Labor (GFL),
263-64
General National Congress, 201
General Organization for Social In-
surance, 257-58
Geography, 2-4, 11-12, 27-34, 45,
217-18, 380; influence of, 11-12;
and foreign policy, 217-18
German (language), 59, 214, 369
German Democratic Republic (East
Germany), 238, 378
German Federal Republic (West Ger-
many), 61, 114, 224, 241, 287, 355,
377
Germany, 174, 391
Ghab, 43
ghada (mid-morning meal), 268
ghaffirs (guards), 89
Ghanem, Fathy (editor), 126
Gharbiya, 41, 272
al-Ghazali (philosopher), 70

Girga, 306
Giza, 40, 43, 120, 306
Gnosticism, 16
Goats, 330-32
Gold standard, 371-72
Gorst, Sir Eldon, 21
Gourna (village), 132
Government, 1, 3, 5, 6-8, 24, 118-19,
132-35, 285-89, 352-54, 380, 382-
85; and the arts, 118-19, 132; con-
trol, 285-89, 352-54, 380, 382-85;
officials, 79, 89-90; parliamentary,
24; role of, 6-8, 192-93; service,
94, 97-98
Governorates, 40-41, 190, 199, 200-1,
328, 380; councils, 190, 191, 194,
204; frontier, 40-41
Grain, 325
Grand Imam of Egypt, 112
Grand Sheikh of al-Azhar University,
68
Great Britain, 25, 36-38, 114, 176,
217-22, 223, 225, 232, 236, 241-43,
284, 322, 386, 391-95; agreement
with, 25; and the Canal, 36-38;
1956 invasion by, 386. *See also*
British
Great Powers, 20
Great Pyramid, 12, 120
Greece, 376
Greek (language), 57, 59, 60-61, 120,
208, 209, 214, 369, 381
Greek Orthodox Church, 77
Greeks, 12, 14-15, 40, 51, 61, 95, 96,
118, 119, 120, 173, 179, 254, 320
Green Shirts, 142
Gross Domestic Product (GDP), 290-
92, 296, 334, 343
Guinea, 394
Gulf of Suez, 389
al-Gumhuriya (*Republic*), 125, 126,
208, 209, 210

al-Hadi, Abd, 169
Hadith, 63, 165
hadra, 70
al-Haggag, Abu (saint), 71
Haifa, 28
Hajj (pilgrimage), 66

448